A TEXT BOOK OF

EMBEDDED OPERATING SYSTEMS

FOR SEMESTER – II

THIRD YEAR DEGREE COURSE IN COMPUTER ENGINEERING
According to New Revised Syllabus of
Savitribai Phule, Pune University
[2012 Pattern]

SWATI D. SHIRKE
M.E. (Computer)
Assistant Professor,
Deptt. of Computer Engg.
STES, NBN Sinhgad School of Engineering,
Ambegoan (BK), Pune.

SHAILESH P. BENDALE
M.Tech. (Computer)
Assistant Professor,
Deptt. of Computer Engg.
STES, NBN Sinhgad School of Engineering,
Ambegoan (BK), Pune

NILAM K. KADALE
M.E. (Computer)
Assistant Professor,
Deptt. of Computer Engg.
STES, NBN Sinhgad School of Engineering,
Ambegoan (BK), Pune.

PRIYANKA D. PATIL
M.E. (Computer)
Assistant Professor,
Deptt. of Computer Engg.
STES, Sinhgad Academy of Engineering,
Kondhwa, Pune

N 3317

EMBEDDED OPERATING SYSTEMS (TE COMPUTER SEM. II - PU) ISBN : 978-93-5164-367-8
First Edition : January 2015
© : Authors

The text of this publication, or any part thereof, should not be reproduced or transmitted in any form or stored in any computer storage system or device for distribution including photocopy, recording, taping or information retrieval system or reproduced on any disc, tape, perforated media or other information storage device etc., without the written permission of Authors with whom the rights are reserved. Breach of this condition is liable for legal action. Every effort has been made to avoid errors or omissions in this publication. In spite of this, errors may have crept in. Any mistake, error or discrepancy so noted and shall be brought to our notice shall be taken care of in the next edition. It is notified that neither the publisher nor the authors or seller shall be responsible for any damage or loss of action to any one, of any kind, in any manner, therefrom.

Published By :
NIRALI PRAKASHAN
Abhyudaya Pragati, 1312, Shivaji Nagar,
Off J.M. Road, PUNE – 411005
Tel - (020) 25512336/37/39, Fax - (020) 25511379
Email : niralipune@pragationline.com

Printed By :
Repro India Ltd, Mumbai.

DISTRIBUTION CENTRES
PUNE

Nirali Prakashan
119, Budhwar Peth, Jogeshwari Mandir Lane
Pune 411002, Maharashtra
Tel : (020) 2445 2044, 66022708, Fax : (020) 2445 1538
Email : bookorder@pragationline.com

Nirali Prakashan
S. No. 28/25, Dhyari,
Near Pari Company, Pune 411041
Tel : (020) 24690204 Fax : (020) 24690316
Email : dhyari@pragationline.com
bookorder@pragationline.com

MUMBAI
Nirali Prakashan
385, S.V.P. Road, Rasdhara Co-op. Hsg. Society Ltd.,
Girgaum, Mumbai 400004, Maharashtra
Tel : (022) 2385 6339 / 2386 9976, Fax : (022) 2386 9976
Email : niralimumbai@pragationline.com

DISTRIBUTION BRANCHES

NAGPUR
Pratibha Book Distributors
Above Maratha Mandir, Shop No. 3, First Floor,
Rani Jhanshi Square, Sitabuldi, Nagpur 440012,
Maharashtra, Tel : (0712) 254 7129

BENGALURU
Pragati Book House
House No. 1, Sanjeevappa Lane, Avenue Road Cross,
Opp. Rice Church, Bengaluru – 560002.
Tel : (080) 64513344, 64513355,
Mob : 9880582331, 9845021552
Email: bharatsavla@yahoo.com

JALGAON
Nirali Prakashan
34, V. V. Golani Market, Navi Peth, Jalgaon 425001,
Maharashtra, Tel : (0257) 222 0395
Mob : 94234 91860

KOLHAPUR
Nirali Prakashan
New Mahadvar Road,
Kedar Plaza, 1st Floor Opp. IDBI Bank
Kolhapur 416 012, Maharashtra. Mob : 9855046155

CHENNAI
Pragati Books
9/1, Montieth Road, Behind Taas Mahal, Egmore,
Chennai 600008 Tamil Nadu, Tel : (044) 6518 3535,
Mob : 94440 01782 / 98450 21552 / 98805 82331, Email : bharatsavla@yahoo.com

RETAIL OUTLETS
PUNE

Pragati Book Centre
157, Budhwar Peth, Opp. Ratan Talkies,
Pune 411002, Maharashtra
Tel : (020) 2445 8887 / 6602 2707, Fax : (020) 2445 8887

Pragati Book Centre
Amber Chamber, 28/A, Budhwar Peth,
Appa Balwant Chowk, Pune : 411002, Maharashtra,
Tel : (020) 20240335 / 66281669
Email : pbcpune@pragationline.com

Pragati Book Centre
676/B, Budhwar Peth, Opp. Jogeshwari Mandir,
Pune 411002, Maharashtra
Tel : (020) 6601 7784 / 6602 0855

PBC Book Sellers & Stationers
152, Budhwar Peth, Pune 411002, Maharashtra
Tel : (020) 2445 2254 / 6609 2463

MUMBAI
Pragati Book Corner
Indira Niwas, 111 - A, Bhavani Shankar Road, Dadar (W), Mumbai 400028, Maharashtra
Tel : (022) 2422 3526 / 6662 5254, Email : pbcmumbai@pragationline.com

www.pragationline.com info@pragationline.com

PREFACE

It gives us immense pleasure to present this book **"Embedded Operating Systems"** to the Students of Third Year (TE) Degree Course in Computer Engineering of Savitribai Phule Pune University. The book is written strictly as per New Revised Syllabus (2012 Pattern) which has been implemented from Academic Year (2014-2015).

As per New Revised Examination Scheme which has been implemented from this academic year, **In-semester Examination carries 30 Marks**, over First Three units and **End Semester Examination carries 70 Marks** over entire syllabus of which First Three Units will carry 20 Marks and Units 4, 5, 6 will carry 50 Marks.

The objectives of this text are :

- **Unit I** : Operating Systems Concepts and Real-Time Operating Systems.
- **UNIT II** : Details of ARM Processors, Arm Programming, Assembly language.
- **Unit III** : Tool Chain, Linux Kernel, Anatomy of Embedded Systems, U-Boot.
- **Unit IV** : Bootloaders, Device Driver Basics, File Systems, Device Tree.
- **Unit V** : Kernel Debugging Techniques, Development Tools.
- **Unit VI** : Porting Linux, Linux and Real Time, Embedded Android.

We have included four In-Semester Model Question Paper (30 Marks) for University Examination.

We would like to extend our sincere thanks to Management of STES, Dr. S.D. Markande (Principal, NBN SSOE), Dr. R.S. Prasad (Head, Comp. Deptt, NBNSSOE) & Prof. A.V. Dhumane for their untiring support in our work.

We take this opportunity to express thanks to all members of Nirali Prakashan for their excellent co-operation. A special thanks to Publisher Mr. Dineshbhai Furia, Mr. Jignesh Furia and Mr. M. P. Munde and team namely Mrs. Deepali Lachake (Co-ordinator), Mrs. Shilpa Kale, Mrs. Neeta Kulkarni, Mrs. Ulka Chavan, Mrs. Pratibha Bele, Mrs. Roshan Khan, Miss Sarika Shinde, Miss Kalyani Rathod, Miss Neha Bhagat, Miss Rani Zinjade for taking great efforts to publish this book within very short time.

We are also thankful to Marketing Executives namely, Mr. Sachin Shinde, Mr. Ashok Bodke, Mr. Balasaheb Thorat, Mr. Nilesh Deshmukh, Mr. Mohsin Shaikh, Mr. Parag Ghamandi (Nashik) and Mr. Raju Shaikh (Ahmednagar) for their valuable help and efforts for promotion of our book.

Thanks to all those who directly and indirectly helped for this project.

Any suggestions for the improvement of this book are always welcome.

January 2015

Pune **Authors**

SYLLABUS

Unit I (4 Hours)

Operating Systems Concepts, Real-Time Tasks, Real-Time Systems, Types of Real-Time Tasks, Real-Time Operating Systems,

Unit II (8 Hours)

Processor Basics, Integrated Processors: Systems on Chip, ARM Processors history, Hardware Platforms, ARM Architecture, Interrupt Vector Table, Arm Programming, Assembly language, Instruction Set, Arithmetic, Logical and Conditional, load-store instructions,Constants, Readonly and Read-write memory, Multiple Register Load Store. ARM-9, ARM Cortex-M3, Case Study of Begal- Black-Bone: Architecture, Uboot, Interfacing and Programming

Unit III (8 Hours)

LSB, OSDL, OSDL Mobile Linux Initiative, Linux Background, Linux Kernel Construction, Tool Chain, Tools Overview, Kernel Build System, Kernel Initialization: BIOS verses Boot loader, U-Boot, Anatomy of Embedded Systems: POST and Boot Process, Kernel Initialization, *init*, Storage Considerations and memory management, BusyBox, Execution Context,Process Virtual Memory, Cross-Development Environment, Embedded Linux Distributions, Do-It-Yourself Linux Distributions, Initialization Flow of Control, Kernel Command Line Processing, Subsystem Initialization, The *init* Thread, System Initialization,

Unit IV (6 Hours)

Bootloaders, Device Driver Basics: Character Device, PCI Device Drivers, File Systems, Device Tree, MTD Subsystem, Embedded Development Environment

Unit V (6 Hours)

Development Tools, ssh, Kernel Debugging Techniques, Debugging Embedded Linux Applications, Stepper Motor Controller interfacing using Begal Black Bone Embedded System, Embedded Graphics and Multimedia Tools and Applications.

Unit VI (6 Hours)

Porting Linux, Linux and Real Time, Embedded Android: Bootloader, Kernel, Init, Zygote, System Server, Activity Manager, Launcher (Home), Embedded Android Applications: Calculator, Twitter Search App, Slide Show App.

CONTENTS

Unit I : Introduction to Embedded Operating System and Real Time Operating System
1.1-1.34

1.1	Operating Systems Concepts	1.1
	1.1.1 Network Operating System	1.2
	1.1.2 Operating System Layers	1.3
	1.1.3 The History of Operating Systems	1.4
	1.1.4 Functions of Operating System	1.6
	1.1.5 What Is Kernel?	1.9
	1.1.6 Task, Process and Threads	1.11
	1.1.7 Scheduling Algorithms	1.13
	1.1.8 Interprocess Communications	1.16
	1.1.9 Task Synchronization	1.22
	1.1.10 Priority Inversion	1.24
	1.1.11 What is a Semaphore?	1.27
	1.1.12 Device Driver Basics	1.27
1.2	Real Time Tasks	1.28
	1.2.1 Criteria for Real-Time Computing Task	1.29
	1.2.2 Real Time Systems	1.30
	1.2.3 Real-Time Operating System	1.32
•	Questions	1.34

Unit II : Embedded Arm Processes
2.1 – 2.52

2.1	Processor Basics	2.1
	2.1.1 Stand-Alone Processors	2.1
2.2	Integrated Processors : Systems on Chip	2.4
	2.2.1 Power Architecture	2.4
	2.2.2 Free Scale Power Architecture	2.4
	2.2.3 Free Scale Power QUICC I	2.5
	2.2.4 Free Scale Power QUICC II	2.6
	2.2.5 Power QUICC II Pro	2.7
	2.2.6 Free Scale Power QUICC III	2.7
	2.2.7 Free Scale QorIQ	2.8
	2.2.8 AMCC Power Architecture	2.9
2.3	ARM	2.11
	2.3.1 TI Arm	2.12
2.4	Hardware Platforms	2.12
	2.4.1 Compact PIC	2.13
	2.4.2 ATCA	2.13
2.5	ARM Processor History	2.13
	2.5.1 ARM Core	2.14
	2.5.2 ARM Microcontroller	2.14
	2.5.3 RISC Vs CISC	2.15

2.5.4	Advanced Features	2.15
2.5.5	Architecture Versions	2.16
2.5.6	ARM CORTEX	2.16

2.6 ARM Architecture … 2.17
    2.6.1 Instruction Set Architecture … 2.17
    2.6.2 Operating Modes … 2.17
    2.6.3 Register Set … 2.18
    2.6.4 Mode Switching … 2.19
    2.6.5 Conditional Flags … 2.21

2.7 Interrupt Vector Table … 2.21
2.8 Programming the Arm Processor … 2.22
    2.8.1 Programming Assembly Vs C … 2.23
2.9 ARM Assembly Language … 2.23
    2.9.1 Data Types … 2.24
    2.9.2 Data Alignment … 2.24
    2.9.3 Assembly Language Rules … 2.25

2.10 Instruction Set … 2.26
    2.10.1 Main Features of the ARM Instruction Set … 2.26
    2.10.2 Thumb Instruction Set … 2.26
    2.10.3 ARM Instruction Set Format … 2.27
    2.10.4 Conditional Execution … 2.27
    2.10.5 Using and Updating the Condition Field … 2.28
    2.10.6 Branch Instructions … 2.28
    2.10.7 Data Processing Instructions … 2.29
    2.10.8 Load/Store Instructions … 2.31
    2.10.9 Stack … 2.35
    2.10.10 Software Interrupt (SWI) … 2.38
    2.10.11 Read Only and Read Write Memory … 2.38
    2.10.12 Multiple Register Load Store … 2.40

2.11 ARM 9 … 2.41
    2.11.1 ARM 9 Family Technical Features … 2.41
    2.11.2 ARM 9 Family Processor Naming – ARM9xxE(J)–S … 2.42

2.12 ARM Cortex-M … 2.43
    2.12.1 Why Cortex-M3? … 2.43

2.13 Case Study of Beagal-Black-Bone … 2.44
    2.13.1 The Beagle Bone Black Features … 2.44
    2.13.2 Beagle Bone Black Key Component Locations … 2.45
    2.13.3 Beagle Bone Black Connector and Switch Locations … 2.45
    2.13.4 U-Boot … 2.46

- Questions … 2.52

Unit III : Embedded Linux Kernel   **3.1 – 3.72**

3.1 Linux Standard Base (LSB) … 3.1
3.2 OSDL (Open Source Development Lab) … 3.3
3.3 OSDLs Mobile Linux Initiative … 3.3

	3.3.1	OSDL MLI - Bridging Gaps	3.4
	3.3.2	Technical Challenges	3.4
	3.3.3	Security	3.5
	3.3.4	Storage	3.6
	3.3.5	Memory Management	3.6
	3.3.6	Multimedia	3.6
	3.3.7	Performance	3.6
	3.3.8	MLI Goals/ Mission	3.7
3.4	Linux Background		3.7
	3.4.1	Kernel Versions	3.7
	3.4.2	Kernel Source Repositories	3.9
	3.4.3	Using Git to Download a Kernel	3.9
3.5	Linux Kernel Constructions		3.10
	3.5.1	Top-Level Source Directory	3.10
	3.5.2	Compiling the Kernel	3.11
	3.5.3	The Kernel Proper: vmlinux	3.13
	3.5.4	Kernel Image Components	3.15
	3.5.5	Subdirectory Layout	3.17
	3.5.6	Why TOOL CHAIN?	3.19
3.6	Kernel Build System		3.23
	3.6.1	The Dot-Config	3.23
	3.6.2	Configuration Editor(s)	3.25
	3.6.3	Makefile Targets	3.27
	3.6.4	The Image Object	3.30
	3.6.5	Architecture Objects	3.30
	3.6.6	Bootstrap Loader	3.31
	3.6.7	Boot Messages	3.32
3.7	Kernal Initialization		3.35
	3.7.1	BIOS Versus Bootloader	3.35
	3.7.2	U-Boot	3.36
3.8	Anatomy of an Embedded System		3.39
	3.8.1	POST and Boot Process Linux Boot Process for Embedded Systems	3.40
	3.8.2	Kernel Initialization : Overview	3.43
	3.8.3	First User Space Process : init	3.44
3.9	Storage Considerations		3.45
	3.9.1	Flash Memory	3.45
	3.9.2	NAND Flash	3.46
	3.9.3	NAND Flash	3.47
	3.9.4	Flash Usage	3.47
	3.9.5	Flash File Systems	3.48
	3.9.6	Memory Space	3.49
	3.9.7	Execution Contexts	3.50
3.10	Busybox		3.52
	3.10.1	BusyBox Configuration	3.53
	3.10.2	BusyBox Operation	3.54
3.11	Process Virtual Memory		3.56

3.11.1	Cross-Development Environment	3.57
3.11.2	Embedded Linux Distributions	3.57
3.11.3	Do-It-Yourself Linux Distributions	3.59
3.12 Initialization Flow of Control		3.60
3.12.1	Kernel Entry Point : head.o	3.61
3.12.2	Kernel Startup: main.c	3.61
3.12.3	Architecture Setup	3.62
3.12.4	The Setup Macro	3.64
3.13 Subsystem Initialization		3.64
3.13.1	The *_initcall Macros	3.65
3.14 The init Thread		3.67
3.14.1	Initialization Via initcalls	3.68
3.14.2	Initcall_debug	3.69
3.14.3	Final Boot Steps	3.69
3.15 System Initialization		3.71
• Questions		3.71

Unit IV : Bootloaders and Device Drivers 4.1 – 4.94

4.1 Introduction to Bootloaders		4.1
4.1.1	Role of Bootloader	4.1
4.1.2	Bootloader Challenges	4.2
4.1.3	A Universal Bootloader (Das U-Boot)	4.4
4.1.4	Porting U-Boot	4.8
4.1.5	Device Tree Blob (Flat Device Tree)	4.12
4.1.6	Other Bootloaders	4.13
4.2 Device Driver Basics		4.15
4.2.1	Device Driver Concepts	4.15
4.2.2	Driver Methods	4.21
4.2.3	Device Drivers and the GPL	4.23
4.3 Character Device		4.23
4.3.1	Major and Minor Numbers	4.24
4.3.2	Allocating and Freeing Device Numbers	4.25
4.3.3	Dynamic Allocation of Major Numbers	4.26
4.3.4	Implementing a Character Driver	4.27
4.3.5	File Operations	4.28
4.3.6	Registering Device Numbers	4.30
4.3.7	Information of Registered Devices	4.31
4.3.8	Character Device Registration	4.31
4.3.9	Character Device Unregistration	4.32
4.4 PCI Devices Drivers		4.32
4.4.1	The PIC Interface	4.32
4.4.2	PCI Addressing	4.32
4.4.3	PCI-PCI Bridges	4.33
4.4.4	Linux PIC Initialization	4.34
4.4.5	PCI Device Driver	4.34
4.5 File Systems		4.35

	4.5.1	Linux File System Concepts	4.35
	4.5.2	ext2	4.37
	4.5.3	ext3	4.39
	4.5.4	ext4	4.40
	4.5.5	ReiserFS	4.41
	4.5.6	JFFS2 (Journaling Flash File System)	4.42
	4.5.7	cramfs	4.44
	4.5.8	Network File System	4.45
	4.5.9	Pseudo File Systems	4.46
	4.5.10	Other File Systems	4.47
	4.5.11	Building a Simple File System	4.47
4.6	Device Tree		4.48
	4.6.1	History of Device Tree	4.48
	4.6.2	High Level View	4.48
	4.6.3	Basic Concepts	4.50
	4.6.4	How Interrupts Work	4.59
	4.6.5	Device Specific Data	4.60
	4.6.6	Special Nodes	4.60
	4.6.7	Purpose of Device Tree	4.61
4.7	MTD Subsystem		4.62
	4.7.1	MTD Overview	4.63
	4.7.2	MTD Partitions	4.66
	4.7.3	MTD Utilities	4.68
	4.7.4	UBI File System	4.73
4.8	Embedded Development Environment		4.76
	4.8.1	Cross-Development Environment	4.76
	4.8.2	Host System Requirements	4.81
	4.8.3	Hosting Target Boards	4.82
•	Questions		4.91

Unit V : Debugging Techniques for Embedded Linux			**5.1 – 5.36**
5.1	GNU Debugger (GDB)		5.1
	5.1.1	Debugging a Core Dump	5.1
	5.1.2	Invoking GDB	5.2
	5.1.3	Debug Session in GDB	5.4
5.2	Data Display Debugger		5.6
5.3	C Brownser/C Scope		5.8
5.4	Tracking and Profiling Tools		5.9
	5.4.1	Strace	5.9
	5.4.2	Strace Variations	5.11
	5.4.3	ltrace	5.12
	5.4.4	ps	5.14
	5.4.5	top	5.15
	5.4.6	mtrace	5.17
	5.4.7	dmalloc	5.18
	5.4.8	Kernel Oops	5.18

5.5	Kernel Debugging Techniques	5.20
	5.5.1 Challenges to Kernel Debugging	5.20
	5.5.2 Kernel Debugging Techniques	5.21
5.6	Debugging Embedded Linux Applications	5.25
	5.6.1 Target Debugging	5.25
	5.6.2 Remote (Cross) Debugging	5.26
	5.6.3 Debugging with Shared Libraries	5.28
	5.6.4 Additional Remote Debug Options	5.30
5.7	Stepper Motor	5.31
	5.7.1 BeagleBone Black	5.31
5.8	Embedded Graphics and Multimedia	5.31
•	Questions	5.36

Unit VI : Embedded Android   6.1 – 6.34

6.1	Porting Linux	6.1
	6.1.1 Why Port Linux Anyway?	6.1
	6.1.2 Background Pre-Requisites	6.1
	6.1.3 Bootloader Bringup	6.2
	6.1.4 Porting the Linux Kernel	6.2
	6.1.5 Architecture, CPU and Machine	6.2
6.2	Linux and Real Time	6.3
	6.2.1 Real-Time System	6.3
	6.2.2 Real Time Linux	6.4
	6.2.3 Linux Scheduling	6.5
	6.2.4 Latency	6.5
	6.2.5 Kernel Preemption	6.6
6.3	Embedded Android	6.11
6.4	Embedded Android Applications	6.15
	6.4.1 Calculator	6.15
	6.4.2 Twitter Search App	6.23
	6.4.3 Slide Show App	6.24
•	Questions	6.34

• **Model Question Papers for In-Semester Exam. [30 Marks]**   **MQP.1 – MQP.2**

UNIT I

INTRODUCTION TO EMBEDDED OPERATING SYSTEM AND REAL TIME OPERATING SYSTEM

1.1 OPERATING SYSTEMS CONCEPTS

- An embedded operating system is an operating system for embedded computer systems.
- These operating systems are designed to be compact, efficient, and reliable.
- E-OS are frequently also real-time operating systems, and the term RTOS is often used as a synonym for embedded operating system.
- An important difference between most embedded operating systems and desktop operating systems is that the application, including the operating system, is usually statically linked together into a single executable image.
- Unlike a desktop operating system, the embedded operating system does not load and execute applications. This means that the system is only able to run a single application.
- An operating system is the most important software that runs on a computer. It manages the computer's memory, processes, and all of its software and hardware. It also allows you to communicate with the computer without knowing how to speak the computer's language. Without an operating system, a computer is useless.

The Operating System's Job

- Your computer's **operating system** (**OS**) manages all of the **software** and **hardware** on the computer. Most of the time, there are many different computer programs running at the same time, and they all need to access your computer's Central Processing Unit (CPU), memory, and storage. The operating system coordinates all of this to make sure each program gets what it needs.

Handheld Computer

- First, handheld computers provide unprecedented convenience. No matter where you are when you get that brilliant world-changing idea, you can jont it down immediately in your handy digital notebook.
- Second, handheld computers provide great help in staying organized. When an employer or an instructor gives you an assignment, you can add the assignment to your digital task list, including the assignment's due date and priority level. Then, you can check your task list frequently to be sure you are on track to complete the tasks that are due soon, or those you are identified as high priority. If you need to look up someone's phone number, you can check your digital contact book.

Android
- Google's Android is an open-source platform that's currently available on a wide variety of smart phones.
- Android is a software stack for mobile devices that includes an operating system, middleware and key applications.
- The Android SDK provides the tools and APIs necessary to begin developing applications on the Android platform using the Java programming language.
- Based on the Linux kernel.

1.1.1 Network Operating System

- **Network operating system** refers to software that implements an operating system of some kind that is oriented to computer networking. For example, one that runs on a server and enables the server to manage data, users, groups, security, applications, and other networking functions. The network operating system is designed to allow shared file and printer access among multiple computers in a network, typically a Local Area Network (LAN), a private network or to other networks.

Types of Network Operating System

1. Peer-to-Peer

- In a peer-to-peer network operating system users are allowed to share resources and files located on their computers and access shared resources from others. This system is not based with having a file server or centralized management source. A peer-to-peer network sets all connected computers equal; they all share the same abilities to use resources available on the network.
  - **Examples :**
    - AppleShare used for networking connecting Apple products.
    - Windows for Workgroups used for networking peer-to-peer windows computers.

Advantages
- Ease of setup
- Less hardware needed, no server needs to be purchased.

Disadvantages
- No central location for storage.
- Lack of security that a client/server type offers.

2. Client/Server

- Network operating systems can be based on a client/server architecture in which a server enables multiple clients to share resources. Client/server network operating systems allow the network to centralize functions and applications in one or more dedicated file servers. The server is the centre of the system, allowing access to resources and instituting security. The network operating system provides the mechanism to integrate all the components on a network to allow multiple users to simultaneously share the same resources regardless of physical location.

- **Examples :**
    - Novell NetWare
    - Windows Server
    - Banyan VINES

Advantages

- Centralized servers are more stable.
- Security is provided through the server.
- New technology and hardware can be easily integrated into the system.
- Servers are able to be accessed remotely from different locations and types of systems.

Disadvantages

- Cost of buying and running a server are high.
- Dependence on a central location for operation.
- Requires regular maintenance and updates.

1.1.2 Operating System Layers

- The operating system is generally the most complex item of software on a computer, as well as the most important. However, it can be broken down into a number of discrete layers, or functional elements, each of which is responsible for a specific task. A five layer model is often used :
    - User Interface
    - File Management System
    - Input / Output
    - Memory Management
    - Kernel

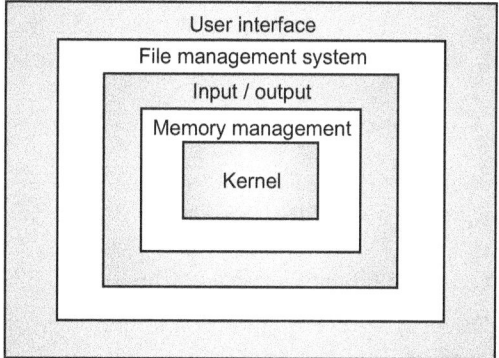

Fig. 1.1

1.1.3 The History of Operating Systems

- **1956, GM-NAA I/O :** Developed by Robert L. Patrick of General Motors for use on their IBM 704 mainframe. This early OS was primarily designed to automatically switch to the next job once its current job was completed. It was used on about fourty IBM 704 mainframes.

- **1961, MCP (Master Control Program) :** Developed by Burroughs Corporations for their B5000 mainframe. MCP is still in use today by the Unisys ClearPath/MCP machines.

- **1966, DOS/360 :** After years of being strictly in the hardware business, IBM ventured into the OS. IBM developed a few unsuccessful mainframe Operating Systems until it finally released DOS/360 and its successors, which put IBM in the driver seat for both the hardware and OS industries.

- **1969, Unix :** Developed by AT and T Bell Labs programmers Ken Thompson, Dennis Ritchie, Douglas McIlroy, and Joe Ossanna. It gained widespread acceptance first within the large AT and T company, and later by colleges and universities. It is written in C, which allows for easier modification, acceptance, and portability.

- **1973, CP/M (Control Program/Monitor (later re-purposed as "Control Program for Microcomputers") :** Developed by Greg Kildall as a side project for his company Digital Research. CP/M became a popular OS in the 1970's. It had many applications developed for it, including WordStar and dBASE. It was ported to a variety of hardware environments. In fact, IBM originally wanted CP/M for its new Personal Computers, but later selected MS-DOS when a deal could not be reached.

- **1977, BSD (Berkeley Software Distribution) :** Developed by the University of California, Berkeley. BSD is a Unix variant based on early versions of Unix from Bell Labs.

- **1981, MS-DOS :** Developed by Microsoft for the IBM PC's. It was the first widely available Operating Systems for home users. In 1985, Microsoft released Microsoft Windows, which popularized the Operating System even more. Microsoft Windows allowed users a Graphical User Interface (GUI), which rapidly spread Microsoft's product.

- **1982, SunOS :** Developed by Sun Microsystems, SunOS was based on BSD. It was a very popular Unix variant.

- **1984, Mac OS :** Developed by Apple Computer, Inc for their new product, the Macintosh home PC. The Macintosh was widely advertised (the famous 1984 commercial is available below). Mac OS was the first OS with a GUI built-in. This lead to a very stable OS, as well as wide acceptance due to its ease of use.

- **1987, OS/2 :** Developed by a joint venture of IBM and Microsoft. Though the OS was heavily marketed, it did not pick up in popularity.

- **1991, Linux :** Developed by Linus Torvalds as a free Unix variant. Linux today is a very largely contributed Open Source project that plays a very prominent role in today's server industry.
- **1992, Sun Solaris :** Developed by Sun Microsystems, Solaris is a widely used Unix variant, and partially developed based on Sun's SunOS.
- **1993, Windows NT :** Developed by Microsoft as a high-end server Operating System, the NT code became the basis for Operating Systems to this day. NT was primarily used on computers used as servers to counter the Unix dominance in the arena.
- **1995, Windows95 :** Developed by Microsoft, it was the first Microsoft Operating system to have a graphical user interface built into it. It was tremendously marketed (successfully) and quickly swept across the country and the globe. Below is one of Microsoft's popular commercials, featuring the Rolling Stones with "Start Me Up", drawing attention to Microsoft's "Start" button, which to this day is a dominant feature of their Operating Systems.
- **1997, JavaOS :** Developed by Sun Microsystems, JavaOS was developed primarily using the Java programming language. The OS was created to be installed on any device, including PC's.
- **1998, Windows98:** Developed by Microsoft, Windows 98 was the next iteration of the Microsoft Windows95 Operating System.
- **1999, MacOS X Server 1.0 :** Developed by Apple Computer, Inc., MacOS X Server 1.0 was a precursor to Apple's MacOS X desktop version, which replaced it in 2001. MacOS X Server 1.0 was developed for Apple's popular Macintosh PC.
- **2000, Windows 2000 :** Developed by Microsoft, Windows 2000 was a much improved Operating System over Windows 98. It was developed from a dramatically different code base. It was targetted for business oriented uses.
- **2000, Windows ME :** Developed by Microsoft, Windows ME (also called Windows Millenium) was a rather unsuccessful new version of Windows 98 and had a short shelf life. It was released just seven months after Windows 2000 and just a year before Windows XP.
- **2001, MacOS X Version 10.0 :** Developed by Apple Computer, Inc., MacOS X Version 10.0 dramatically changed the user interface for Apple's Macinstosh users.
- **2001, Windows XP :** Developed by Microsoft, Windows XP was an enhanced version of Windows 2000 code base. XP became widely popular and is used extensively today, despite the release of newer versions of Windows.
- **2003, Windows Server 2003 :** Developed by Microsoft as an improved version of their NT OS.
- **2007, Windows Vista:** Developed by Microsoft, Windows Vista had been slow in taking off.

- **2008, Windows Server 2008 :** Developed by Microsoft as an upgrade to Windows Server 2003.
- **2009, Windows 7 :** Developed by Microsoft to replace Vista, "Win7" is currently used by over 50% of internet users.
- **2012, Windows 8 :** Developed by Microsoft to replace Win7, "Win8" was just released October 26th, 2012

1.1.4 Functions of Operating System

- Operating systems perform the following important functions :

    (1) Processor Management : It means assigning processor to different tasks which has to be performed by the computer system.

    (2) Memory Management : It means allocation of main memory and secondary storage areas to the system programmes, as well as user programmes and data.

    (3) Input and Output Management : It means co-ordination and assignment of the different output and input devices while one or more programmes are being executed.

    (4) File System Management : Operating system is also responsible for maintenance of a file system, in which the users are allowed to create, delete and move files.

    (5) Establishment and Enforcement of a Priority System : It means the operating system determines and maintains the order in which jobs are to be executed in the computer system.

    (6) Assignment of system resources, both software and hardware to the various users of the system.

An operating system has three main responsibilities :

- Perform basic tasks, such as recognizing input from the keyboard, sending output to the display screen, keeping track of files and directories on the disk and controlling peripheral devices such as disk drives and printers.
- Ensure that different programs and users running at the same time do not interfere with each other.
- Provide a software platform on top of which other programs (i.e., application software) can run.
- The first two responsibilities address the need for managing the computer hardware and the application programs that use the hardware. The third responsibility focuses on providing an interface between application software and hardware so that application software can be efficiently developed. Since the operating system is already responsible for managing the hardware, it should provide a programming interface for application developers.

Process Management

- The operating system manages many kinds of activities ranging from user programs to system programs like printer spooler, name servers, file server etc. Each of these activities is encapsulated in a process. A process includes the complete execution context (code, data, PC, registers, OS resources in use etc.).
- It is important to note that a process is not a program. A process is only ONE instant of a program in execution. There are many processes can be running the same program.
- The five major activities of an operating system in regard to process management are
    - Creation and deletion of user and system processes.
    - Suspension and resumption of processes.
    - A mechanism for process synchronization.
    - A mechanism for process communication.
    - A mechanism for deadlock handling.

Main-Memory Management

- Primary-Memory or Main-Memory is a large array of words or bytes. Each word or byte has its own address. Main-memory provides storage that can be access directly by the CPU. That is to say for a program to be executed, it must in the main memory.
- The major activities of an operating in regard to memory management are :
    - Keep track of which part of memory are currently being used and by whom.
    - Decide which process are loaded into memory when memory space becomes available.
    - Allocate and deallocate memory space as needed.

File Management

- A file is a collection of related information defined by its creator. Computer can store files on the disk (secondary storage), which provide long term storage. Some examples of storage media are magnetic tape, magnetic disk and optical disk. Each of these media has its own properties like speed, capacity, data transfer rate and access methods.
- A file system normally organized into directories to ease their use. These directories may contain files and other directions.
- The five main major activities of an operating system in regard to file management are :
    1. The creation and deletion of files.

2. The creation and deletion of directions.
3. The support of primitives for manipulating files and directions.
4. The mapping of files onto secondary storage.
5. The back up of files on stable storage media.

I/O System Management

- I/O subsystem hides the peculiarities of specific hardware devices from the user. Only the device driver knows the peculiarities of the specific device to which it is assigned.

Secondary-Storage Management

- Generally speaking, systems have several levels of storage, including primary storage, secondary storage and cache storage. Instructions and data must be placed in primary storage or cache to be referenced by a running program. Because main memory is too small to accommodate all data and programs, and its data are lost when power is lost, the computer system must provide secondary storage to back up main memory. Secondary storage consists of tapes, disks, and other media designed to hold information that will eventually be accessed in primary storage (primary, secondary, cache) is ordinarily divided into bytes or words consisting of a fixed number of bytes. Each location in storage has an address; the set of all addresses available to a program is called an address space.

- The three major activities of an operating system in regard to secondary storage management are :
  1. Managing the free space available on the secondary-storage device.
  2. Allocation of storage space when new files have to be written.
  3. Scheduling the requests for memory access.

Networking

- A distributed system is a collection of processors that do not share memory, peripheral devices, or a clock. The processors communicate with one another through communication lines called network. The communication-network design must consider routing and connection strategies, and the problems of contention and security.

Protection System

- If a computer system has multiple users and allows the concurrent execution of multiple processes, then the various processes must be protected from one another's activities. Protection refers to mechanism for controlling the access of programs, processes, or users to the resources defined by a computer system.

Command Interpreter System

- A command interpreter is an interface of the operating system with the user. The user gives commands with are executed by operating system (usually by turning them into system calls). The main function of a command interpreter is to get and execute the next user specified command. Command-Interpreter is usually not part of the kernel, since multiple command interpreters (shell, in UNIX terminology) may be support by an operating system, and they do not really need to run in kernel mode. There are two main advantages to separating the command interpreter from the kernel.

    1. If we want to change the way the command interpreter looks, i.e., I want to change the interface of command interpreter, I am able to do that if the command interpreter is separate from the kernel. I cannot change the code of the kernel so I cannot modify the interface.

    2. If the command interpreter is a part of the kernel it is possible for a malicious process to gain access to certain part of the kernel that it showed not have to avoid this ugly scenario it is advantageous to have the command interpreter separate from kernel.

1.1.5 What Is Kernel?

- A kernel is a central component of an operating system. It acts as an interface between the user applications and the hardware. The sole aim of the kernel is to manage the communication between the software (user level applications) and the hardware (CPU, disk memory etc). The main tasks of the kernel are :

    - Process management
    - Device management
    - Memory management
    - Interrupt handling
    - I/O communication
    - File system ...etc.

2. Is LINUX A Kernel Or An Operating System?

- Well, there is a difference between kernel and OS. Kernel as described above is the heart of OS which manages the core features of an OS while if some useful applications and utilities are added over the kernel, then the complete package becomes an OS. So, it can easily be said that an operating system consists of a kernel space and a user space.

- So, we can say that Linux is a kernel as it does not include applications like file-system utilities, windowing systems and graphical desktops, system administrator commands, text editors, compilers etc. So, various companies add these kind of applications over linux kernel and provide their operating system like ubuntu, suse, centOS, redHat etc.
- The kernel is responsible for :
  - Process management for application execution
  - Memory management, allocation and I/O
  - Device management through the use of device drivers
  - System call control, which is essential for the execution of kernel services

There are five types of kernels :

1. **Monolithic Kernels :** All operating system services run along the main kernel thread in a monolithic kernel, which also resides in the same memory area, thereby providing powerful and rich hardware access.
2. **Microkernels :** Define a simple abstraction over hardware that use primitives or system calls to implement minimum OS services such as multitasking, memory management and interprocess communication.
3. **Hybrid Kernels :** Run a few services in the kernel space to reduce the performance overhead of traditional microkernels where the kernel code is still run as a server in the user space.
4. **Nano Kernels :** Simplify the memory requirement by delegating services, including the basic ones like interrupt controllers or timers to device drivers.
5. **Exo Kernels :** Allocate physical hardware resources such as processor time and disk block to other programs, which can link to library operating systems that use the kernel to simulate operating system abstractions.

1. Monolithic Kernels

Earlier in this type of kernel architecture, all the basic system services like process and memory management, interrupt handling etc were packaged into a single module in kernel space. This type of architecture led to some serious drawbacks like (1) Size of kernel, which was huge. (2) Poor maintainability, which means bug fixing or addition of new features resulted in recompilation of the whole kernel which could consume hours

- In a modern day approach to monolithic architecture, the kernel consists of different modules which can be dynamically loaded and un-loaded. This modular approach allows easy extension of OS's capabilities. With this approach, maintainability of kernel became very easy as only the concerned module needs to be loaded and unloaded every time there is a change or bug fix in a particular module. So, there is

no need to bring down and recompile the whole kernel for a smallest bit of change. Also, stripping of kernel for various platforms (say for embedded devices etc.) became very easy as we can easily unload the module that we do not want.
- Linux follows the monolithic modular approach

2. **Microkernels**
   - This architecture majorly caters to the problem of ever growing size of kernel code which we could not control in the monolithic approach. This architecture allows some basic services like device driver management, protocol stack, file system etc. to run in user space. This reduces the kernel code size and also increases the security and stability of OS as we have the bare minimum code running in kernel. So, if suppose a basic service like network service crashes due to buffer overflow, then only the networking service's memory would be corrupted, leaving the rest of the system still functional.
   - In this architecture, all the basic OS services which are made part of user space are made to run as servers which are used by other programs in the system through inter process communication (IPC). For example : we have servers for device drivers, network protocol stacks, file systems, graphics, etc. Microkernel servers are essentially daemon programs like any others, except that the kernel grants some of them privileges to interact with parts of physical memory that are otherwise off limits to most programs. This allows some servers, particularly device drivers, to interact directly with hardware. These servers are started at the system start-up.
   - So, what the bare minimum that microKernel architecture recommends in kernel space?
     - Managing memory protection
     - Process scheduling
     - Inter Process communication (IPC)
     - Apart from the above, all other basic services can be made part of user space and can be run in the form of servers.
     - QNX follows the Microkernel approach.

1.1.6 Task, Process and Threads

Task
- An application program can also be said to be a program consisting of the tasks and task behaviours in various states that are controlled by OS.
- A task is like a process or thread in an OS.

Process
- A program in execution.
- An instance of a program running on a computer.
- The entity that can be assigned to and executed on a processor.

- A unit of activity characterized by the execution of a sequence of instructions, a current state, and an associated set of system instructions.
- A process is comprised of :
  - Program code (possibly shared)
  - A set of data
  - A number of attributes describing the state of the process

Processes and Threads

We can think of a **thread** as basically a *lightweight* process. In order to understand this let us consider the two main characteristics of a process:

Unit of Resource Ownership

A process is allocated :

- A virtual address space to hold the process image
- Control of some resources (files, I/O devices...)

Unit of Dispatching

A process is an execution path through one or more programs:

- Execution may be interleaved with other processes
- The process has an execution state and a dispatching priority

If we treat these two characteristics as being independent (as does modern OS theory):

- The unit of resource ownership is usually referred to as a **process** or task. This Processes have :
  - A virtual address space which holds the process image.
  - Protected access to processors, other processes, files, and I/O resources.
- The unit of dispatching is usually referred to a **thread** or a lightweight process. Thus a thread :
  - Has an execution state (running, ready, etc.)
  - Saves thread context when not running
  - Has an execution stack and some per-thread static storage for local variables
  - Has access to the memory address space and resources of its process
- All threads of a process share this when one thread alters a (non-private) memory item, all other threads (of the process) sees that a file open with one thread, is available to others

Benefits of Threads vs Processes

If implemented correctly then threads have some advantages over (multi) processes, they take :

- Less time to create a new thread than a process, because the newly created thread uses the current process address space.
- Less time to terminate a thread than a process.
- Less time to switch between two threads within the same process, partly because the newly created thread uses the current process address space.
- Less communication overheads communicating between the threads of one process is simple because the threads share everything: address space, in particular. So, data produced by one thread is immediately available to all the other threads.

Multithreading vs. Single Threading

Just we can multiple processes running on some systems we can have multiple threads running :

Single Threading

When the OS does not recognize the concept of thread.

Multithreading

When the OS supports multiple threads of execution within a single process

- First Come First Serve (FCFS) Scheduling
- Shortest-Job-First (SJF) Scheduling
- Priority Scheduling
- Round Robin(RR) Scheduling
- Multilevel Queue Scheduling

1.1.7 Scheduling Algorithms

First Come First Serve (FCFS)

- Jobs are executed on first come, first serve basis.
- Easy to understand and implement.
- Poor in performance as average wait time is high.

Table 1.1

Process	Arrival Time	Execute Time	Service Time
P0	0	5	0
P1	1	3	5
P2	2	8	8
P3	3	6	16

```
|  PO  | P1 |  P2  |  P3  |
0      5    8      16     22
```

Wait time of each process is following

Process	Wait Time : Service Time - Arrival Time
P0	0 – 0 = 0
P1	5 – 1 = 4
P2	8 – 2 = 6
P3	16 – 3 = 13

Average Wait Time : (0+4+6+13) / 4 = 5.55

Shortest Job First (SJF)

- Best approach to minimize waiting time.
- Impossible to implement
- Processer should know in advance how much time process will take.

Table 1.2

Process	Arrival Time	Execute Time	Service Time
P0	0	5	0
p1	1	3	3
p2	2	8	8
p3	3	6	16

```
| P1 |  PO  |  P3  |  P2  |
0    3     8      16      22
```

Wait time of each process is following

Process	Wait Time : Service Time - Arrival Time
P0	3 – 0 = 3
P1	0 – 0 = 0
P2	16 – 2 = 14
P3	8 – 3 = 5

Average Wait Time : (3 + 0 + 14 + 5) / 4 = 5.50

Priority Based Scheduling

- Each process is assigned a priority. Process with highest priority is to be executed first and so on.
- Processes with same priority are executed on first come first serve basis.
- Priority can be decided based on memory requirements, time requirements or any other resource requirement.

Table 1.3

Process	Arrival Time	Execute Time	Priority	Service Time
P0	0	5	1	0
P1	1	3	2	3
P2	2	8	1	8
P3	3	6	3	16

P3	P1	P0	P2
0	6	9	14 22

Wait time of each process is following

Process	Wait Time : Service Time - Arrival Time
P0	9 – 0 = 9
P1	6 – 1 = 5
P2	14 – 2 = 12
P3	0 – 0 = 0

Average Wait Time : (9 + 5 + 12 + 0) / 4 = 6.5

Round Robin Scheduling

- Each process is provided a fix time to execute called quantum.
- Once a process is executed for given time period. Process is pre-empted and other process executes for given time period.
- Context switching is used to save states of pre-empted processes.

Quantum = 3

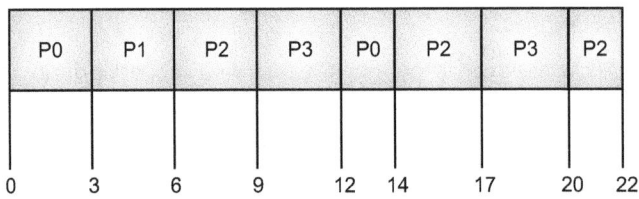

Wait time of each process is following

Process	Wait Time : Service Time - Arrival Time
P0	(0 - 0) + (12 - 3) = 9
P1	(3 - 1) = 2
P2	(6 - 2) + (14 - 9) + (20 - 17) = 12
P3	(9 - 3) + (17 - 12) = 11

Average Wait Time : (9 + 2 + 12 + 11) / 4 = 8.5

Multi Queue Scheduling
- Multiple queues are maintained for processes.
- Each queue can have its own scheduling algorithms.
- Priorities are assigned to each queue.

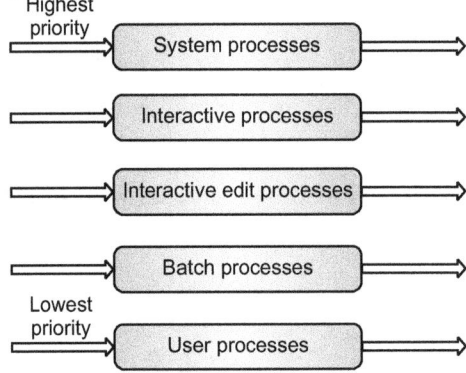

Fig. 1.2

1.1.8 Interprocess Communications

- **Exchange of data** between two or more separate, independent **processes/threads**.
- Operating systems provide facilities/resources for Inter-Process Communications (**IPC**), such as message queues, semaphores, and shared memory.
- Distributed computing systems make use of these facilities/resources to provide **Application Programming Interface** (API) which allows IPC to be programmed at a higher level of abstraction. (For example, send and receive)

- Distributed computing requires information to be exchanged among independent processes.
- In distributed computing, two or more processes engage in IPC using a protocol agreed upon by the processes. A process may be a sender at some points during a protocol, a receiver at other points.
- When communication is from one process to a single other process, the IPC is said to be a *unicast*, For example, Socket communication. When communication is from one process to a group of processes, the IPC is said to be a *multicast*, e.g., Publish/Subscribe Message model, a topic that we will explore in a later chapter.
- **Unicast vs. Multicast**

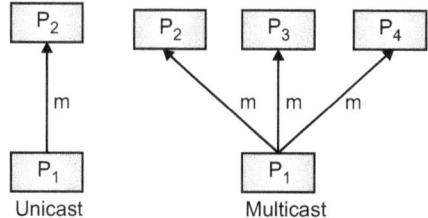

Fig. 1.3

Operations Provided in an Archetypal Interprocess Communications API

- **Receive** ([sender], message storage object)
- **Connect** (sender address, receiver address), for connection-oriented communication.
- **Send** ([receiver], message)
- **Disconnect** (connection identifier), for connection-oriented communication.

Event Synchronization

- Interprocess communication may require that the two processes synchronize their operations: one side sends, and then the other receives until all data has been sent and received.
- Ideally, the send operation starts before the receive operation commences.
- In practice, the synchronization requires system support.

Synchronous vs. Asynchronous Communication

- The IPC operations may provide the synchronization necessary using *blocking*. A blocking operation issued by a process will block further processing of the process until the operation is fulfilled.
- Alternatively, IPC operations may be asynchronous or non blocking. An asynchronous operation issued by a process will not block further processing of the process. Instead, the process is free to proceed with its processing, and may optionally be notified by the system when the operation is fulfilled.

Synchronous Send and Receive

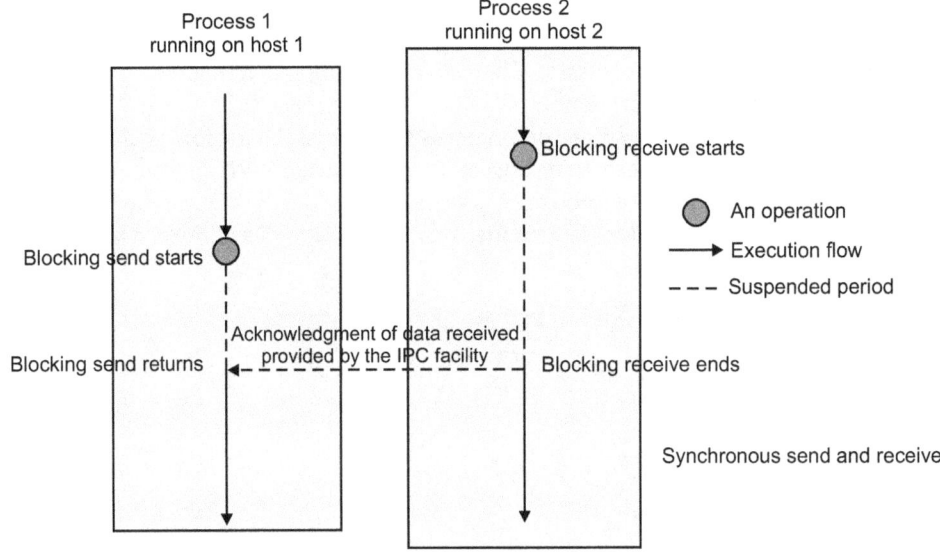

Fig. 1.4 : Synchronous send and receive

Asynchronous Send and Synchronous Receive

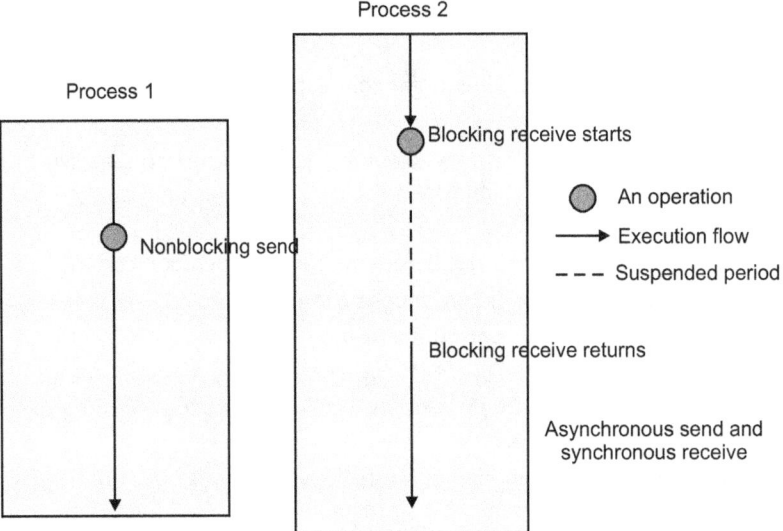

Fig. 1.5 : Asynchronous send and synchronous receive

Synchronous Send and Asynchronous Receive

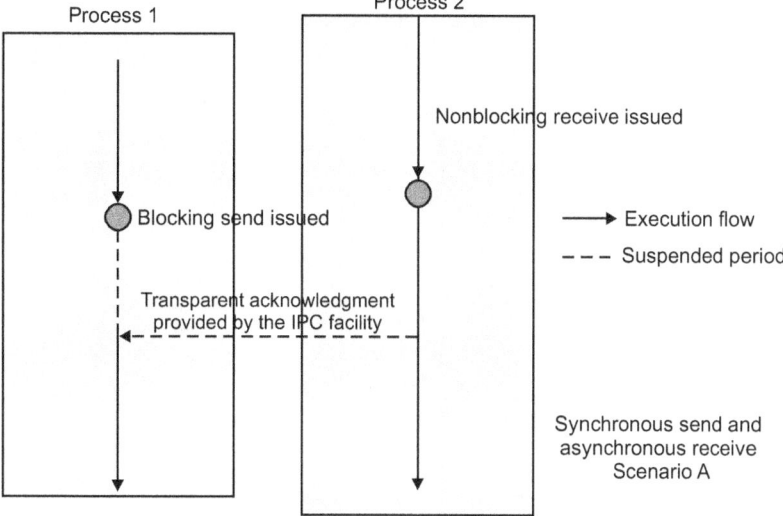

Fig. 1.6 : Synchronous send and async. receive

Data from P1 was received by P2

Before issuing a non-blocking receive op in P2

Event Diagram

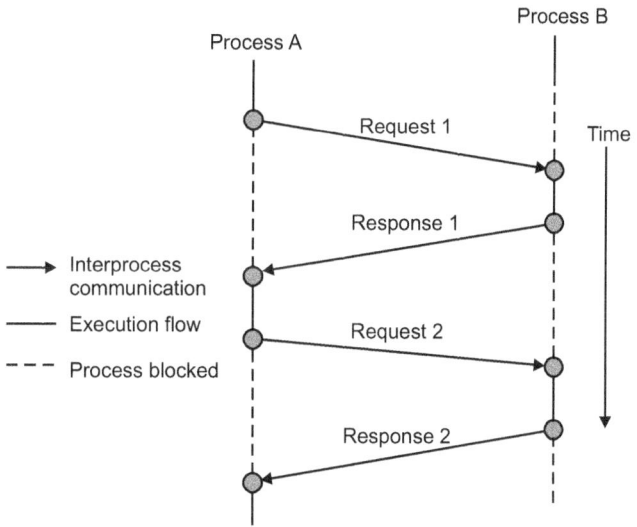

Fig. 1.7 : Event diagram

Blocking, Deadlock, and Timeouts

- Blocking operations issued in the wrong sequence can cause *deadlocks*.
- Deadlocks should be avoided. Alternatively, *timeout* can be used to detect deadlocks.

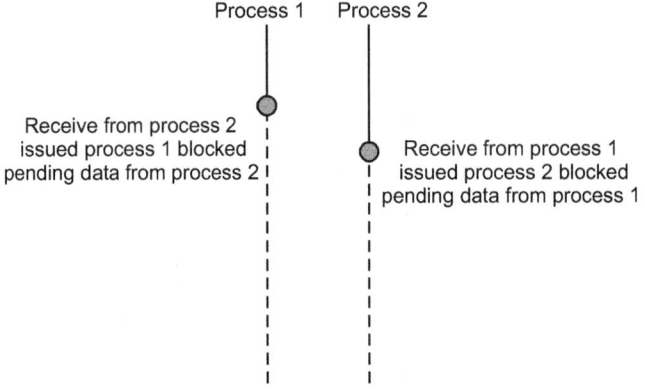

Fig. 1.8 : Blocking deadlock and timeouts

P1 is waiting for P2's data; P2 is waiting for P1's data.

Using Threads for Asynchronous IPC

- When using an IPC programming interface, it is important to note whether the operations are synchronous or asynchronous.
- If only blocking operation is provided for send and/or receive, then it is the programmer's responsibility to use child processes or threads if asynchronous operations are desired.
- Connect and receive operations can result in indefinite blocking.
- For example, a blocking connect request can result in the requesting process to be suspended indefinitely if the connection is unfulfilled or cannot be fulfilled, perhaps as a result of a breakdown in the network.
- It is generally unacceptable for a requesting process to "hang" indefinitely. Indefinite blocking can be avoided by using timeout.
- Indefinite blocking may also be caused by a *deadlock*.

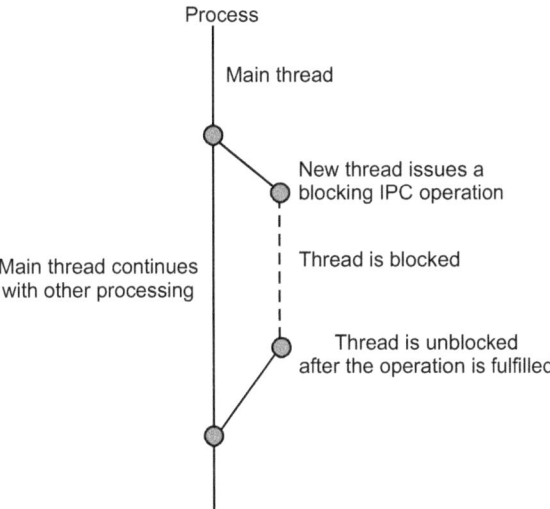

Fig. 1.9 (a) : Blocking IPC operation

Indefinite Blocking Due to a Deadlock

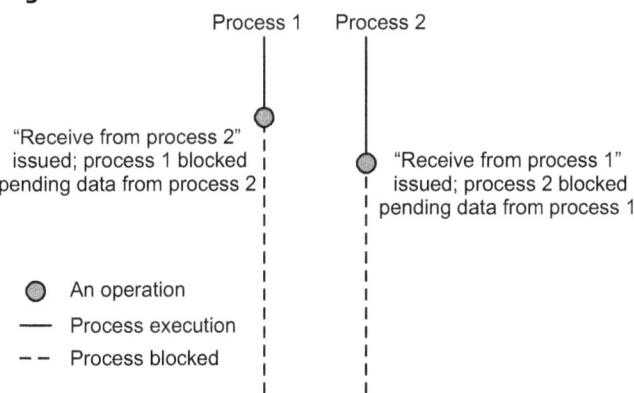

Fig. 1.9 (b) : Indefinite blocking due to deadlock

P1 is waiting for P2's data; P2 is waiting for P1's data.

How RPC Works ?

An RPC is analogous to a function call. Like a function call, when an RPC is made, the calling arguments are passed to the remote procedure and the caller waits for a response to be returned from the remote procedure. Fig. 1.10 the flow of activity that takes place during an RPC call between two networked systems. The client makes a procedure call that sends a request to the server and waits. The thread is blocked from processing until either a reply is received, or it times out. When the request arrives, the server calls a dispatch routine that performs the requested service, and sends the reply to the client. After the RPC call is completed, the client program continues. RPC specifically supports network applications.

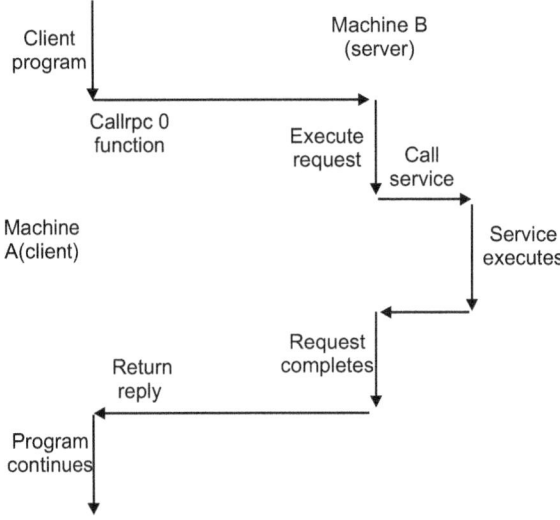

Fig. 1.10 : Remote Procedure Calling Mechanism

A remote procedure is uniquely identified by the triple: (program number, version number, procedure number) The program number identifies a group of related remote procedures, each of which has a unique procedure number. A program may consist of one or more versions. Each version consists of a collection of procedures which are available to be called remotely. Version numbers enable multiple versions of an RPC protocol to be available simultaneously. Each version contains a number of procedures that can be called remotely. Each procedure has a procedure number.

1.1.9 Task Synchronization

Race Conditions and Critical Sections

- The situation where two threads compete for the same resource, where the sequence in which the resource is accessed is significant, is called race conditions.
- A code section that leads to race conditions is called a critical section. In the previous example the method add() is a critical section, leading to race conditions. Race conditions can be avoided by proper thread synchronization in critical sections.

Deadlock

A **deadlock** is a situation in which two or more competing actions are each waiting for the other to finish, and thus neither ever does.

A condition that occurs when two processes are each waiting for the other to complete before proceeding. The result is that both processes hang. Deadlocks occur most commonly in multitasking and client/server environments. Ideally, the programs that are deadlocked, or the operating system, should resolve the deadlock, but this doesn't always happen.

Traffic gridlock is an everyday example of a deadlock situation.

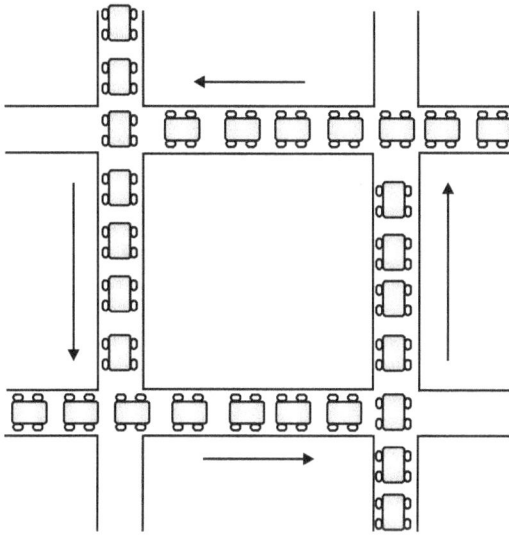

Fig. 1.11

In order for deadlock to occur, four conditions must be true.

- **Mutual Exclusion :** Each resource is either currently allocated to exactly one process or it is available. (Two processes cannot simultaneously control the same resource or be in their critical section).
- **Hold and Wait :** processes currently holding resources can request new resources.
- **No Pre-emption :** Once a process holds a resource, it cannot be taken away by another process or the kernel.
- **Circular Wait :** Each process is waiting to obtain a resource which is held by another process.

The dining philosophers problem discussed in an earlier section is a classic example of deadlock. Each philosopher picks up his or her left fork and waits for the right fork to become available, but it never does.

Deadlock can be modeled with a directed graph. In a deadlock graph, vertices represent either processes (circles) or resources (squares). A process which has acquired a resource is shown with an arrow (edge) from the resource to the process. A process which has requested a resource which has not yet been assigned to it is modeled with an arrow from the process to the resource. If these create a cycle, there is deadlock.

The deadlock situation in the above code can be modeled like this.

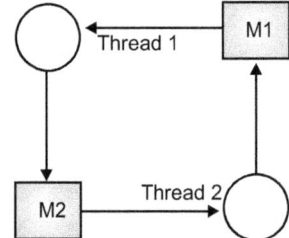

Fig. 1.12

This graph shows an extremely simple deadlock situation, but it is also possible for a more complex situation to create deadlock. Here is an example of deadlock with four processes and four resources.

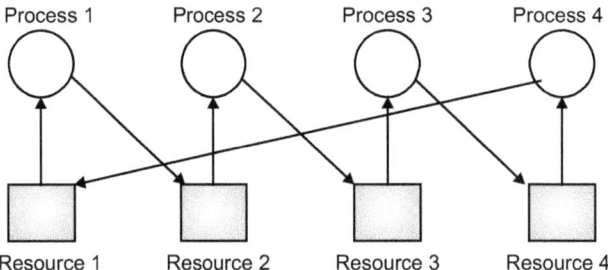

Fig. 1.13

There are a number of ways that deadlock can occur in an operating situation. We have seen some examples, here are two more.

- Two processes need to lock two files, the first process locks one file the second process locks the other, and each waits for the other to free up the locked file.
- Two processes want to write a file to a print spool area at the same time and both start writing. However, the print spool area is of fixed size, and it fills up before either process finishes writing its file, so both wait for more space to become available.

1.1.10 Priority Inversion

- In real-time system execution, priority inversion is something that needs to be avoided, as it can lead to a great deal of unpredictable behaviour and unbounded latency. How? I'll explain.

- The priority-based model of execution states that a task can only be pre-empted by another task of higher priority. However, scenarios can arise where a lower priority task may *indirectly* preempt a higher priority task, in a sense inverting the priorities of the associated tasks, and violating the priority-based ordering of execution. This is called "priority inversion", and usually occurs when resource sharing is involved.
- The classic example to explain priority inversion is to imagine a system with three active threads, each at three different thread priorities (see Fig. 1.14). Assuming there are no other threads of higher priority in the system, thread T3, which has the highest priority, is meant to run as soon as it's released. No other thread should pre-empt it, nor should any other thread interfere with it since the others (T1 and T2) are all of lower priority.

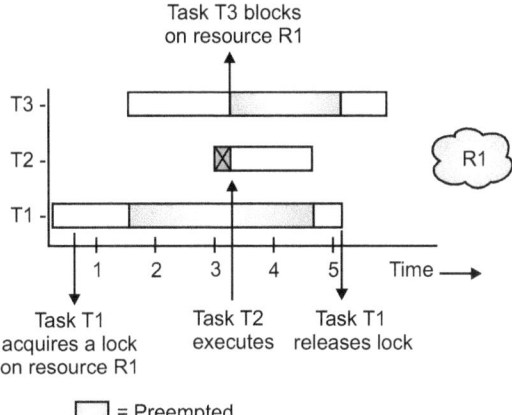

Fig. 1.14

- When the system begins execution, thread T1 is released and executes immediately since there are no other higher priority threads executing. Shortly after it starts, it acquires a lock on resource R1. At time t = 1.5, thread T3 is released and preempts thread T1 since it's of higher priority. At time t = 3, thread T2, a medium priority thread, is released but doesn't execute because higher priority thread T3 is still executing. Shortly afterward, however, thread T3 attempts to acquire a lock on resource R1, but cannot since thread T1 (a lower priority thread) still owns it. This allows thread T2 to execute in its place, which effectively violates the priority-order execution of the system, resulting in what we call priority inversion.
- In this situation, thread T3 will continue to block on resource R1, for an unbounded and unknown amount of time, until thread T2 blocks (or terminates). For a real-time system, where thread T3 controls something time-critical (i.e. the ailerons on an airplane to maintain level flight), the result can be disastrous. When T2 finally does

block, thread T1 will continue execution and release its lock on R1. At that point, thread T3 will preempt it, acquire its lock on R1, and continue. But it may be too late, and execution deadlines may have been missed.

- Think this scenario is farfetched and unlikely to cause issues in the real world? Think again. If you do a quick search on the Mars Pathfinder, you'll discover how priority inversion nearly doomed the mission.

Priority Inheritance - A Practical Solution

- There are a few solutions to the priority-inversion problem in real-time systems. One is to turn off all system interrupts, effectively halting thread preemption in the system, while critical tasks execute. However, to make this work, you cannot implement more than two thread priorities, and critical sections where resources are locked need to be very brief and tightly controlled.

- Another solution is to implement priority ceilings, or priority boosting, where a lower priority thread that acquires a lock has its priority temporarily increased to help ensure that it will complete its execution, and release its lock, as quickly as possible. However, a more practical and less-invasive solution is to implement the priority inheritance protocol.

- With priority inheritance, the system code that implements resource locking checks to see if a lower priority thread already owns a lock on the associated resource when a thread attempts to lock it. If one does, that owning thread's priority is temporarily increased to match that of the higher priority thread attempting to acquire the lock. As a result, the lock owner (once blocked at lower priority) will execute, release the lock, and then be restored to its original priority level.

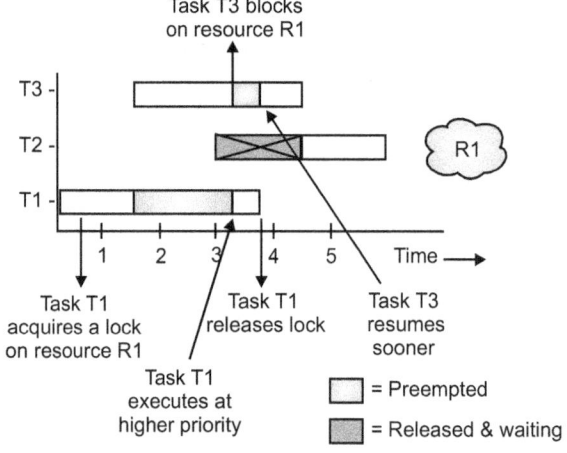

Fig. 1.15

- Going back to our original example, priority inheritance would effectively boost thread T1's priority to equal that of thread T3, where thread T2 would continue to block, allowing T1 to release its lock sooner. In Fig. 1.15, you can see how this allows thread T3 to resume sooner, without the unbounded latency caused by thread T2's unknown execution time. Once the lock on R1 is released by thread T1, its priority is restored to its original value and the system executes according to normal priority-based rules.

1.1.11 What is a Semaphore?

- A semaphore is hardware or a software tag variable whose value indicates the status of a common resource. Its purpose is to lock the resource being used. A process which needs the resource will check the semaphore for determining the status of the resource followed by the decision for proceeding. In multitasking operating systems, the activities are synchronized by using the semaphore techniques.
- A semaphore is a variable. There are two types of semaphores:
    - Binary semaphores
    - Counting semaphores
- Binary semaphores have two methods associated with it. (up, down / lock, unlock) Binary semaphores can take only two values (0/1). They are used to acquire locks. When a resource is available, the process in charge set the semaphore to 1 else 0.
- Counting Semaphore may have value to be greater than one, typically used to allocate resources from a pool of identical resources.

1.1.12 Device Driver Basics

- One of the more challenging aspects of system design is partitioning functionality in a rational manner. The familiar device driver model found in UNIX and Linux provides a natural partitioning of functionality between your application code and hardware or kernel devices.
- A device driver is a hide the details of a particular peripheral and provides a slightly high-level programming interface to it. A device driver is typically specific to a given operating system.
- Device drivers allow application software to attach to, read and write data from, and change the behavior of the peripheral device. This section helps you understand this model and the basics of Linux device driver architecture.

Device Driver Concepts

- A device driver or software driver is a computer program allowing higher-level computer programs to interact with a hardware device.

- Device drivers are integral components of operating systems.
- One of the fundamental purposes of a device driver is to isolate the user programs from ready access to critical kernel data structures and hardware devices. Furthermore, a well-written device driver hides from the user the complexity and variability of the hardware device.
- For example, a program that wants to write data to the hard disk doesn't need to know if the disk drive uses 512-byte or 1024-byte sectors. The user simply opens a file and issues a write command. The device driver handles the details and isolates the user from the complexities and perils of hardware device programming.
- The device driver provides a consistent user interface to a large variety of hardware devices. It provides the basis for the familiar UNIX/Linux convention that everything must be represented as a file.

1.2 REAL TIME TASKS

The term *real-time* derives from its use in early simulation, in which a real-world process is simulated at a rate that matched that of the real process (now called real-time simulation to avoid ambiguity). Analog computers, most often, were capable of simulating at a much faster pace than real-time, a situation that could be just as dangerous as a slow simulation if it were not also recognized and accounted for.

It is task in which the performance is judged on the basis of time; this means that the result of a computation is 'Correct' only if has produced its correct output within the specified time constrains is designed either 'system failure or reduce value for a quality of service.

Here we define some examples of real time tasks:
- Telecommunication
- Robotics
- Real time database
- Automobile engine control systems
- Process control in industrial plants

Real Time Speech /Video Processing

A speech or moving picture sample of 1 second, if processed in 1 second or less makes it real-time processing. If the processing takes more than 1 second, it is no longer real time processing.

Is Embedded system and real time systems are same?

No, all embedded systems are not real-time systems, a printer is not a real-time system, though it belongs to the Class of embedded system, but a robot which counts objects passing through a conveyor belt is realtime system.

Embedded systems are systems designed for a specific set of application. when such a system requires' time constrained operation, it becomes a real-time embedded system.

1.2.1 Criteria for Real-Time Computing Task

A system is said to be *real-time* if the total correctness of an operation depends not only upon its logical correctness, but also upon the time in which it is performed. Real-time systems, as well as their deadlines, are classified by the consequence of missing a deadline:

- **Hard** : Missing a deadline is a total system failure.
- **Firm** : Infrequent deadline misses are tolerable, but may degrade the system's quality of service. The usefulness of a result is zero after its deadline.
- **Soft** : The usefulness of a result degrades after its deadline, thereby degrading the system's quality of service.

Hard Real-Time System

Thus, the goal of a *hard real-time system* is to ensure that all deadlines are met, Hard real-time systems are used when it is imperative that an event be reacted to within a strict deadline. Such strong guarantees are required of systems for which not reacting in a certain interval of time would cause great loss in some manner, especially damaging the surroundings physically or threatening human lives (although the strict definition is simply that missing the deadline constitutes failure of the system). For example, a *car engine* control system is a hard real-time system because a delayed signal may cause engine failure or damage. Other examples of hard real-time embedded systems include medical systems such as heart *pacemakers* and industrial process controllers. Hard real-time systems are typically found interacting at a low level with physical hardware, in embedded systems. Early *video game* systems such as the Atari 2600 and *Cinematronics* vector graphics had hard real-time requirements because of the nature of the graphics and timing hardware.

Firm Real-Time Systems

The Firm real time system infrequent deadline misses are tolerable, but may degrade the system's quality of service. The usefulness of a result is zero after its deadline. This means that output of the task is discarded if the deadline is not meet. This is somewhat slightly different from a 'hard' real-time task, in the sense here missing the deadline is not catastrophic, it is nothing but the output of delayed execution is dropped. For such a system to be useful, the point is that deadlines are allowed to be missed once in a while, but not too frequently.

For example handheld device which send/receives video frames. The process of decoding a video frames. The process of decoding a video frame may occasionally get delayed by reasons like unexpected interrupts. When such video frame delived late, the playback does not look good. Skipping such frames and making sure that not too many such frames are delayed will be better, because the effect might be less noticeable to the user than playing back the delayed frames.

Soft Real-Time Systems

Soft real-time systems the goal becomes meeting a certain subset of deadlines in order to optimize some application-specific criteria. The particular criteria optimized depend on the application, but some typical examples, include maximizing the number of deadlines met, minimizing the lateness of tasks and maximizing the number of high priority tasks meeting their deadlines. Soft real-time systems are typically used where there is some issue of concurrent access and the need to keep a number of connected systems up to date with changing situations; for example software that maintains and updates the flight plans for commercial *airliners*. The flight plans must be kept reasonably current but can operate to a latency of seconds. Live audio-video systems are also usually soft real-time; violation of constraints results in degraded quality, but the system can continue to operate.

1.2.2 Real Time Systems

Introduction

Definition : A real-time system is one in which the correctness of the computations not only depends on their logical correctness, but also on the time at which the result is produced. That is, a late answer is a wrong answer. For example, many embedded systems are referred to as real-time systems. Cruise control, telecommunications, flight control and electronic engines are some of the popular real-time system applications where as computer simulation, user interface and Internet video are categorized as non-real time application Below we discuss a couple of known real-time systems.

Electronic Engine : Here comes a real-time system example. Consider a computer-controlled machine on the production line at a bottling plant. The machine's function is simply to cap each bottle as it passes within the machine's field of motion on a continuously moving conveyor belt. If the machine operates too quickly, the bottle won't be there yet. If the machine operates too slowly, the bottle will be too far along for the machine to reach it. Stopping the conveyor belt is a costly operation as the entire production will come to halt.

Thus the range of motion of the machine coupled with the speed of the conveyor belt establishes a window of opportunity for the machine to put the cap on the bottle. This window of opportunity imposes timing constraints on the operation of the machine. Software applications with these kinds of timing constraints are termed as real-time applications. Here, the timing constraints are in the form of a period and deadline.

A real-time system is one which controls an environment by receiving data, processing them, and returning the results sufficiently quickly to affect the environment at that time. This usage of "real-time" should not be confused with the two other legitimate uses of the term: in simulation the term means that the simulation's clock runs as fast as a real clock, while in processing and enterprise systems the term is used to mean "without perceivable delay".

A real-time system may be one where its application can be considered (within context) to be mission critical. The anti-lock brakes on a car are a simple example of a real-time computing system – the real-time constraint in this system is the time in which the brakes must be released to prevent the wheel from locking. Real-time computations can be said to have *failed* if they are not completed before their deadline, where their deadline is relative to an event. A real-time deadline must be met, regardless of system load.

1.2.2.1 Types of Real Time Tasks

1. Periodic and Deadline-Oriented Tasks

The period is the amount of time between each iteration of a regularly repeated task. Such repeated tasks are called **periodic tasks.**

In the above example, suppose bottles pass under the machine at a rate of five per second. This means a new bottle has to show up every 200 millisecond. Thus the period of the task is 200 millisecond. This is the timing constraints within which the system has to perform the assigned task successfully. That is, real-time system is one that has to meet the timing constraints to avoid any possible failure. Thus every periodic task has to be finished within the defined period. It does not mean that a real-time system has to act fast.

Every task has to be **deadline-oriented**. That is, every task has to be accomplished within the set deadline. The deadline is a constraint on the latest time at which the operation has to come the end. Suppose the window of opportunity in the above example is 150 millisecond. The deadline is then 150 millisecond after the start time of the operation. Here the start time is the moment at which the bottle enters the working range of the machine.

Cruise Control : Consider a cruise control mechanism on an automobile. The basic operation of cruise control is to keep the speed of the vehicle constant. Suppose the driver has selected 60mph as the desired speed. If the vehicle is going slower or faster than the selected speed, then the embedded computer sends a signal to the engine controller to set the speed right. The frequency in which the computer checks whether the current speed of the vehicle is as per the set speed is called control rate and it is fixed by the control system designer. The checking frequency, on one side, should meet specifications but on the other side, it should not be obstructive to system functioning.

2. Aperiodic Tasks

All real-time tasks need not to be periodic. Aperiodic tasks respond to randomly arriving events. Consider anti-lock braking. If the driver presses the brake pedal, the car must respond very quickly. The response time is the time between the moment the brake pedal is pressed, and the moment the anti-lock braking software actuates the brakes. If the response time was one second, an accident might occur. So, the Fastest possible response is desired.

But, like the cruise control algorithm, fastest is not necessarily best, because it is also desirable to keep the cost of parts down by using small microcontrollers. The point here is the application has to specify a worst-case response time and both the hardware and software has to be designed to meet the specifications.

3. Sporadic Task

A sporadic task is an. Aperiodic tasks with a hard deadline and a minimum inter-arrival time(between two such tasks). Without a minimum inter-arrival time restriction, it is impossible to guarantee that deadline of Sporadic task would always be met. for example emergency condition like fire, over speed of critical machinery in a plant.

4. Preemptible/Non Preemptible Tasks

A task can be preempted if another task of higher priority becomes ready. In contrast, the execution of a non-preemptive task should be without interruption, once started.

1.2.3 Real-Time Operating System

A **Real-Time Operating System** (**RTOS**) is an operating system (OS) intended to serve real-time application process data as it comes in, typically without buffering delays. Processing time requirements (including any OS delay) are measured in tenths of seconds or shorter.

A key Characteristic of an RTOS:
- The level of its consistency concerning the amount of time it takes to accept and complete an application's task;
- The variability is *jitter* A *hard* real-time operating system has less jitter than a *soft* real-time operating system.
- The chief design goal is not high throughput, but rather a guarantee of a soft or hard performance category.
- An RTOS that can usually or *generally* meet a *deadline* is a soft real-time OS, but if it can meet a deadline deterministically it is a hard real-time OS.
- An RTOS has an advanced algorithm for scheduling.
- Scheduler flexibility enables a wider, computer-system orchestration of process priorities, but a real-time OS is more frequently dedicated to a narrow set of applications.
- Key factors in a real-time OS are minimal interrupt latency and minimal thread switching latency;
- A real-time OS is valued more for how quickly or how predictably it can respond than for the amount of work it can perform in a given period of time.

What does an RTOS do?

- An RTOS also provides an abstract layer between the embedded hardware and application software.
- The RTOS manages the interaction between applications and the hardware.
- The RTOS ensures that the multiple task that comes in ,are managed and done on time.
- RTOS are necessity in complex complex embedded real time systems.
- An RTOS has a kernel, which forms the one core of the os, besides that there are other components in it.

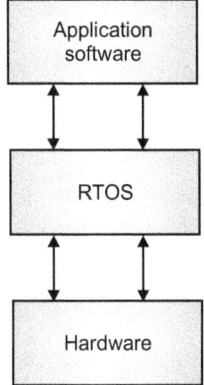

Fig. 1.16 : Hardware –software hierarchy in a complex embedded eystem

Fig. 1.17 shows the basic services that must be provided by an RTOS kernel.task managing is core is RTOS.

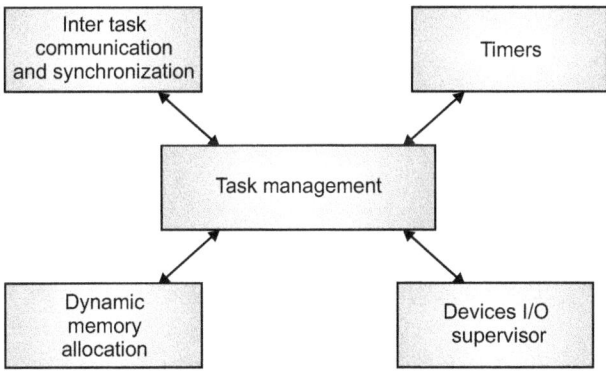

Fig 1.17 : Kernel services of an RTOS

QUESTIONS

1. Operating Systems Concepts
2. What exactly is operating system and what does it do?
3. Why would you want a handheld computer?
4. What do you mean by network operating system?
5. What are the different types of Network operating system?
6. What are the different types f layers in operating system?
7. Explain the history of operating systems ?
8. Explain the various functions of operating system?
9. What Is Kernel? What are the types of kernel?
10. Explain in details: task, process and threads
11. Explain the various scheduling algorithm FCFS, SJF, priority, RR
12. Write a short note on priority inversion?
13. Explain Device drivers in details?
14. What is Real Time Task?
15. How to define real time task?
16. How to differentiate between soft, hard and firm real-time tasks?
17. Explain in detail Real Time Systems?
18. What are the different types of real time tasks?
19. Explain in detail the Concept of Real time operating Systems and their necessity?

UNIT II

EMBEDDED ARM PROCESSOR

2.1 PROCESSOR BASICS

2.1.1 Stand-Alone Processors

- Stand-alone processors are processor chips that are dedicated exclusively to the processing function. As opposed to integrated processors, stand-alone processors require additional support circuitry for their basic operation. In many cases, this means a chipset or custom logic surrounding the processor to handle functions such as DRAM controller, system bus addressing configuration, and external peripheral devices such as keyboard controllers and serial ports. Stand-alone processors often offer the highest overall CPU performance.
- Numerous processors exist in both 32-bit and 64-bit implementations that have seen wide spread use in embedded systems. These include the IBM Power Architecture 970/970FX, the Intel Pentium M, and the Free scale MPC74xx Host Processors, among others. The Intel Atom family of processors has found a niche in embedded applications.
- The following processors are well supported under Linux and have been used in many embedded Linux designs.

2.1.1.1 IBM 970FX

- The IBM 970FX processor core is a high-performance 64-bit-capable stand-alone processor.
- The 970FX is a super scalar architecture. This means that the core can fetch, issue, and obtain results from more than one instruction at a time. This is done through a pipelining architecture, which provides the effect of multiple streams of instruction simultaneously under ideal circumstances. The IBM 970FX contains up to 25 stages of pipelining, depending on the instruction stream and operations contained there in.
- Some of the key features of the 970FX are as follows :
  - A 64-bit implementation of the popular Power Architecture.
  - Deeply pipelined design, for very-high-performance computing applications.
  - Static and dynamic power-management features.
  - Multiple sleep modes, to minimize power requirements and maximize battery life.
  - Dynamically adjustable clock rates, supporting lower-power modes.
  - Optimized for high-performance, low-latency storage management.
- The IBM 970FX has been incorporated into a number of high-end server blades and computing platforms, including IBM's own Blade Server platform.

2.1.1.2 Intel Pentium M

- The Intel Pentium M has been used in a wide variety of laptop computers and has found a niche in embedded products. Like the IBM 970FX processor, the Pentium M is a super scalar architecture. These characteristics make it attractive in embedded applications :
  - The Pentium M is based on the popular x86 architecture and thus is widely supported by a large ecosystem of hardware and software vendors.
  - It consumes less power than other x86 processors.
  - Advanced power-management features enable low-power operating modes and multiple sleep modes.
  - Dynamic clock speed capability enhances battery-powered operations such as standby.
  - On-chip thermal monitoring enables automatic transition to lower power modes to reduce power consumption in over temperature conditions.
  - Multiple frequency and voltage operating points (dynamically selectable) are designed to maximize battery life in portable equipment.
- Many of these features are especially useful for embedded applications. It is not uncommon for embedded products to require portable or battery-powered configurations. The Pentium M has enjoyed popularity in this application space because of its power- and thermal-management features.

2.1.1.3 Intel Atom

- The *Intel Atom* has enjoyed success in Netbooks and a range of embedded systems. The *Intel Atom* family of processors features low power consumption and binary compatibility with older 32-bit Intel processors, enabling a wide range of off-the-shelf software solutions. Like the other stand-alone processors described in this section, the Atom is paired with companion chipset(s) to build a complete solution. The N270 and Z5xx series of processors have been widely used in low-power products.

2.1.1.4 Free Scale MPC7448

- The Free scale MPC7448 contains what is referred to as a fourth-generation Power Architecture core, commonly called G4.3. This high-performance 32-bit processor is commonly found in networking and telecommunications applications. Several companies manufacture blades that conform to ATCA, an industry-standard platform specification, including this and other similar stand-alone Free scale processors.
- The MPC7448 has enjoyed popularity in a wide variety of signal-processing and networking applications because of its advanced feature set :
  - Operating clock rates in excess of 1.5 GHz.

- 1 MB onboard L2 cache.
- Advanced power-management capabilities, including multiple sleep modes.
- Advanced AltiVec vector-execution unit.
- Voltage scaling for reduced-power configurations.

- The MPC7448 contains a Free scale technology called AltiVec to enable very fast algorithmic computations and other data-crunching applications. The AltiVec unit consists of a register file containing 32 very wide (128-bit) registers. Each value within one of these AltiVec registers can be considered a vector of multiple elements. AltiVec defines a set of instructions to manipulate this vector data effectively in parallel with core CPU instruction processing. AltiVec operations include such computations as sum-across, multiply-sum, simultaneous data distribute (store), and data gather (load) instructions.
- Programmers have used the AltiVec hardware to enable very fast software computations commonly found in signal-processing and network elements. Examples include fast Fourier Transform, digital signal processing such as filtering, MPEG video encoding and decoding, and fast generation of encryption protocols such as DES, MD5, and SHA1.
- Other chips in the Free scale lineup of stand-alone processors include the MPC7410, MPC7445, MPC7447, MPC745x, and MPC7xx family.

2.1.1.5 Companion Chipsets

- Stand-alone processors such as those just described require support logic to connect to and enable external peripheral devices such as main system memory (DRAM), ROM or Flash memory, system buses such as PCI, and other peripherals, such as keyboard controllers, serial ports, IDE interfaces, and the like. This support logic often is accomplished by companion *chipsets*, which may even be purpose-designed specifically for a family of processors.
- For example, the Pentium M is supported by one such chipset, called the 855GM. The 855 GM chipset is the primary interface to graphics and memory, thus the suffix GM. The 855 GM has been optimized as a companion to the Pentium M. Fig. 2.1 illustrates the relationship between the processor and chipsets in this type of hardware design.
- The Intel 855 GM is an example of what is commonly referred to as a *northbridge* chip because it is directly connected to the processor's high-speed front-side bus (FSB). Another companion chip that provides I/O and PCI bus connectivity is similarly referred to as the *southbridge* chip because of its position in the architecture. The southbridge chip (actually, an I/O controller) in these hardware architectures is responsible for providing interfaces such as those shown in Fig. 2.1, including Ethernet, USB, IDE, audio, keyboard, and mouse controllers.

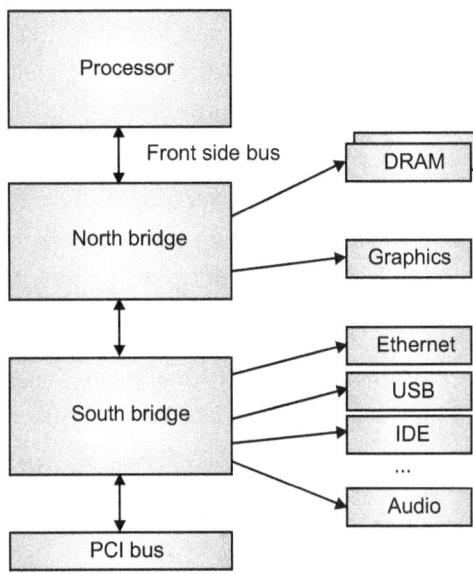

Fig. 2.1 : Processor/chipset relationship

2.2 INTEGRATED PROCESSORS : SYSTEMS ON CHIP

2.2.1 Power Architecture

- Power Architecture is the modern term that refers to the family of technology and products conforming to the various versions of the Power Architecture Instruction Set Architecture. Many good documents describe Power Architecture in great detail.
- Power Architecture processors have found their way into embedded products of every description. From automotive, consumer and networking applications to the largest data and telecommunications switches, Power Architecture is one of the most popular and successful architectures for embedded applications. Because of this popularity, there exists a large array of hardware and software solutions from numerous manufacturers targeted at Power Architecture.

2.2.2 Free Scale Power Architecture

- Free scale Semiconductor has a large range of Power Architecture processors with integrated peripherals. Free scale Power Architecture processors have enjoyed enormous success in the networking market segment. This lineup of processors has wide appeal in a large variety of network equipment, from the low end to the high end of the product space.
- More recently, Free scale has enjoyed success with its Power QUICC product line. The Power QUICC architecture has been shipping for more than a decade. It is based on a

Power Architecture core of a particular version integrated with a QUICC engine (also called a communications processor module or CPM in the Free scale literature). The QUICC engine is an independent RISC processor designed to offload the communications processing from the main Power Architecture core, thus freeing the Power Architecture core to focus on control and management applications. The QUICC engine is a complex but highly flexible communications peripheral controller.
- In its current incarnation, Power QUICC encompasses five general groups. Although somewhat dated, the Power QUICC I family (8xx) lives on. Power QUICC II (82xx) is still quite popular, as is Power QUICC II Pro (83xx). Power QUICC III (85xx) is hugely popular in networking and other gear.
- Power QUICC III gave rise to the new QorIQ family of processors, which employ the high-performance e500 core in single-core and multicore implementations. QorIQ processors promise to be market-leading multicore processing engines with powerful features that make them suitable for high-speed networking and other commercial and industrial applications.

2.2.3 Free Scale Power QUICC I

- The Power QUICC I family includes the original Power Architecture based Power QUICC implementations and consists of the MPC8xx family of processors. These integrated communications processors operate at 50 to 133 MHz and feature the embedded Power Architecture 8xx core. The Power QUICC I family has been used for ATM and Ethernet edge devices, such as routers for the Small Office/Home Office (SOHO) market, residential gateways, ADSL and cable modems, and similar applications.
- The CPM or QUICC engine incorporates two unique and powerful communications controllers. The Serial Communication Controller (SCC) is a flexible serial interface that can implement many serial-based communications protocols, including Ethernet, HDLC/SDLC, AppleTalk, synchronous and asynchronous UARTs, IrDA, and other bit stream data.
- The Serial Management Controller (SMC) is a module capable of similar serial communications protocols. It includes support for ISDN, serial UART and SPI protocols.
- Using a combination of these SCCs and SMCs, you can create flexible I/O combinations.
- An internal Time Division Multiplexer even allows these interfaces to implement channelized communications such as T1 and E1 I/O.

Table 2.1 summarizes a small sampling of the Power QUICC I product line.

Table 2.1 : Free Scale Power QUICC I Highlights

Feature	MPC850	MPC860	MPC875	MPC885
Core	PPC 8xx	PPC 8xx	PPC 8xx	PPC 8xx
Clock rates	Up to 80 MHz	Up to 80 MHz	Up to 133 MHz	Up to 133 MHz

...Contd.

DRAM controllers	Yes	Yes	Yes	Yes
USB	Yes	No	Yes	Yes
SPI controllers	Yes	Yes	Yes	Yes
I2C controllers	Yes	Yes	Yes	Yes
SCC controllers	2	4	1	3
SMC controllers	2	2	1	1
Security engine	No	No	Yes	Yes
DFE controllers	No	2	2	

2.2.4 Free Scale Power QUICC II

- The next step up in the Free scale Power Architecture product line is Power QUICC II. Power QUICC II incorporates the company's G2 Power Architecture core derived from the 603e embedded Power Architecture core. These integrated communications processors operate at 133 to 450 MHz and feature multiple 10/100 Mbps Ethernet interfaces, security engines, ATM and PCI support, and more. The Power QUICC II encompasses the MPC82xx products.
- Power QUICC II adds two new types of controllers to the QUICC engine. The FCC is a full-duplex fast serial communications controller. The FCC supports high speed communications such as 100 Mbps Ethernet and T3/E3 up to 45 Mbps. The MCC is a multichannel controller capable of 128 kB, 64 kB channelized data.

Table 2.2 summarizes the highlights of selected Power QUICC II processors.

Table 2.2 : Free Scale Power QUICC II Highlights

Feature	MPC8250	MPC8260	MPC8272	MPC8280
Core	G2/603e	G2/603e	G2/603e	G2/603e
Clock rates	150 to 200 MHz	100 to 300 MHz	266 to 400 MHz	266 to 400 MHz
DRAM controller	Yes	Yes	Yes	Yes
USB	No	No	Yes	Via SCC4
SPI controllers	Yes	Yes	Yes	Yes
I2C controllers	Yes	Yes	Yes	Yes
SCC controllers	4	4	3	4
Feature	MPC8250	MPC8260	MPC8272	MPC8280
SMC controllers	2	2	2	2
FCC controllers	3	3	2	3
MCC controllers	1	2	0	2

2.2.5 Power QUICC II Pro

- Based on the Free scale Power Architecture e300 core (evolved from the G2/603e), the Power QUICC II Pro family operates at 266 to 667 MHz and features support for Gigabit Ethernet, DDR SDRAM controllers, PCI, high-speed USB, security acceleration, and more. These are the MPC83xx family of processors. The Power QUICC II and Power QUICC II Pro families of processors have been designed into a wide variety of equipment, such as LAN and WAN switches, hubs and gateways, PBX systems, and many other systems with similar complexity and performance requirements.
- The Power QUICC II Pro contains three family members without the QUICC engine and two that are based on an updated version of the QUICC engine. The MPC8358E and MPC8360E both add a new Universal Communications Controller, which supports a variety of protocols.

Table 2.3 summarizes the highlights of selected members of the Power QUICC II Pro family.

Table 2.3 : Free Scale Power QUICC II Pro Highlights

Feature	MPC8343E	MPC8347E	MPC8349E	MPC8360E
Core	e300	e300	e300	e300
Clock rates	266 to 400 MHz	266 to 667 MHz	400 to 667 MHz	266 to 667 MHz
DRAM controller	Y-DDR	Y-DDR	Y-DDR	Y-DDR
USB	Yes	2	2	Yes
SPI controller	Yes	Yes	Yes	Yes
I2C controller	2	2	2	2
Ethernet 10/100/1000	2	2	2	Via UCC
UART	2	2	2	2
PCI controller	Yes	Yes	Yes	Yes
Security engine	Yes	Yes	Yes	Yes
MCC	0	0	0	1
UCC	0	0	0	8

2.2.6 Free Scale Power QUICC III

- At the top of the Power QUICC family are the Power QUICC III processors. These operate between 600 MHz and 1.5 GHz. They are based on the e500 core and support Gigabit Ethernet, DDR SDRAM, RapidIO, PCI and PCI/X, ATM, HDLC, and more. This family incorporates the MPC85xx product line. These processors have found their way into high-end products such as wireless base station controllers, optical edge switches, central office switches, and similar equipment.

Table 2.4 highlights some of the Power QUICC III family members.

Table 2.4 Free Scale Power QUICC III Highlights

Feature	MPC8540	MPC8548E	MPC8555E	MPC8560
Core	e500	e500	e500	e500
Clock rates	Up to 1.0 GHz	Up to 1.5 GHz	Up to 1.0 GHz	Up to 1.0 GHz
DRAM controllers	Y-DDR	Y-DDR	Y-DDR	Y-DDR
USB	No	No	Via SCC	No
SPI controllers	No	No	Yes	Yes
I2C controllers	Yes	Yes	Yes	Yes
Ethernet 10/100	1	Via Gigabit Ethernet	Via SCC	Via SCC
Gigabit Ethernet	2	4	2	2
UART	2	2	2	Via SCC
PCI controllers	PCI/PCI-X	PCI/PCI-X	PCI	PCI/PCI-X
RapidIO	Yes	Yes	No	Yes
Security engine	No	Yes		Yes
SCC	—	—	3	4
FCC	—	—	2	3
SMC	—	—	2	0
MCC	—	—	0	2

2.2.7 Free Scale QorIQ™

- Pronounced "core eye queue", QorIQ is Free scale's newest technology based on Power Architecture. Many chips in the QorIQ family are multicore processors based on the e500 and e500mc cores.
- The P1 series includes the *P1011/P1020* and the *P1013/P1022*. These processors contain the e500 Power Architecture core and each has a specialized set of peripherals aimed at the networking, communications and control plane applications. They have one or two cores, and they have a remarkably low power profile capable of roughly 3.5 watts. Table 2.5 summarizes the major highlights of the P1 series.

Table 2.5 : Free Scale QorIQ P1 Series Highlights

Feature	P1011	P1020	P1013	P1022
Core	e500	e500	e500	e500
Clock rates	Up to 800 MHz	Up to 800 MHz	Up to 1055 MHz	Up to 1055 MHz
Number of cores	1	2	1	2
USB	2.0	2.0	2.0	2.0

...Contd.

SPI controller	Yes	Yes	Yes	Yes
I2C controller	Yes	Yes	Yes	Yes
Ethernet	3 × Gigabit Ethernet	3 × Gigabit Ethernet	2 × Gigabit Ethernet	2 × Gigabit Ethernet
DUART	2	2	2	2
PCI	2 × PCI Express	2 × PCI Express	3 × PCI Express	3 × PCI Express
SATA	—	—	2 × SATA	2 × SATA
Security engine	Yes	Yes	Yes	Yes
SD/MMC	Yes	Yes	Yes	Yes

- The P2 series consists of the P2010 and P2020. This series also contains one or two cores. They offer a higher level of performance than the P1 series, with core speeds up to 1.2 GHz, and they have larger cache arrays. They have typical power requirements in the 6-watt range.

2.2.8 AMCC Power Architecture

- The 440EP is a popular integrated processor found in many networking and communications products. The following list highlights some of the features of the 440EP :
    - On-chip dual data rate (DDR) SDRAM controller.
    - Integrated NAND Flash controller.
    - PCI bus interface.
    - Dual 10/100Mbps Ethernet ports.
    - On-chip USB 2.0 interface.
    - Up to four user-configurable serial ports.
    - Dual I2C controllers.
    - Programmable Interrupt Controller.
    - Serial Peripheral Interface (SPI) controller.
    - Programmable timers.
    - JTAG interface for debugging.

- This is indeed a complete SOC. Fig. 2.2 is a block diagram of the AMCC Power Architecture 440EP Embedded Processor. With the addition of memory chips and physical I/O hardware, a complete high-end embedded system can be built around this integrated microprocessor with minimal interface circuitry.

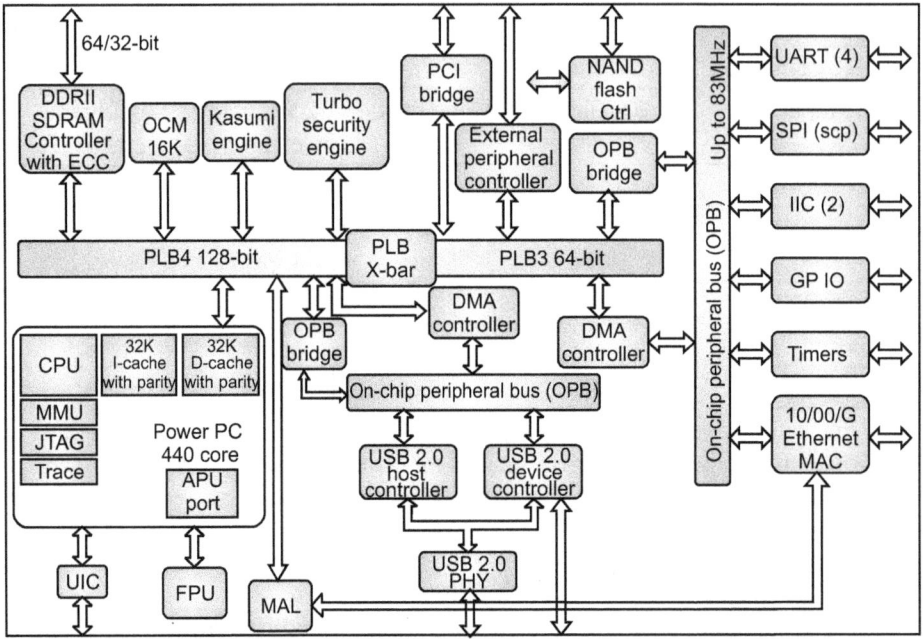

Fig. 2.2 : Block diagram of the AMCC power architecture

- Many manufacturers offer reference hardware platforms to enable a developer to explore the capabilities of the processor or other hardware.
- Numerous product configurations are available with Power Architecture processors. As shown in Fig. 2.2, the AMCC 440EP contains sufficient I/O interfaces for many common products, with very little additional circuitry. Because this processor contains an integrated Floating-Point Unit (FPU), it is ideally suited for products such as network-attached imaging systems, general industrial control and networking equipment.
- The AMCC 440-based core products raise the performance level and add peripherals. The 440EP featured in some of our examples includes a hardware FPU. The 440GX adds two triple-speed 10/100/1000 Mbps Ethernet interfaces (in addition to the two 10/100 Mbps Ethernet ports) and TCP/IP hardware acceleration for high performance networking applications. The 440SP adds hardware acceleration for RAID 5/6 applications. All these processors have mature Linux support. Table 2.6 summarizes the highlights of the AMCC 405xx family.

Table 2.6 : AMCC Power Architecture 405xx Highlights

Feature	405CR	405EP	405GP	405GPr
Core	PPC 405	PPC 405	PPC 405	PPC 405
Core speeds	133 to 266 MHz	133 to 333 MHz	133 to 266 MHz	266 to 400 MHz

...Contd.

DRAM controllers	SDRAM/133	SDRAM/133	SDRAM/133	SDRAM/133
Ethernet	10/100	No 2	1	1
GPIO lines	23	32	24	24
UARTs	2	2	2	2
DMA controllers	4 channel	4 channel	4 channel	4 channel
I2C controllers	Yes	Yes	Yes	Yes
PCI host controllers	No	Yes	Yes	Yes
Interrupt controllers	Yes	Yes	Yes	Yes

Table 2.7 summarizes the features of the AMCC 440xx family of processors.

Table 2.7 : AMCC Power Architecture 440xx Highlights

Feature	440EP	440GP	440GX	440SP
Core	PPC 440	PPC 440	PPC 440	PPC 440
Core speeds	333 to 667 MHz	400 to 500 MHz	533 to 800 MHz	533 to 667 MHz
DRAM controllers	DDR	DDR	DDR	DDR
Ethernet 10/100	2	2	2	Via Gigabit Ethernet
Gigabit Ethernet	No	No	2	1
GPIO lines	64	32	32	32
UARTs	4	2	2	3
DMA controllers	4 channel	4 channel	4 channel	3 channel
I2C controllers	2	2	2	2
PCI host controllers	Yes	PCI-X	PCI-X 3	PCI-X
SPI controllers	Yes	No	No	No
Interrupt controller	Yes	Yes	Yes	Yes

2.3 ARM

- The ARM architecture has achieved a very large market share in the consumer electronics market place. Many popular and now ubiquitous products contain ARM cores. Some well-known examples include the Sony PlayStation Portable (PSP), Apple iPhone, Blackberry Storm, TomTom GO 300 GPS, and the Motorola Droid mobile phone. The ARM architecture was developed by ARM Holdings, plc and is licensed to semiconductor manufacturers around the globe. Many of the world's leading semiconductor companies have licensed ARM technology and currently are shipping integrated processors based on one of several ARM cores.

2.3.1 TI ARM

- Texas Instruments uses ARM cores in the DaVinci, OMAP and other families of integrated processors. These processors contain many integrated peripherals intended to be used as single-chip solutions for various consumer products, such as cellular handsets, PDAs, and similar multimedia platforms. In addition to the interfaces commonly found on integrated processors, such as UARTs and I2C, the OMAP devices contain a wide range of special-purpose interfaces, including the following :
    - LCD screen and backlight controllers.
    - Buzzer driver.
    - Camera interface.
    - MMC/SD card controller.
    - Battery-management hardware.
    - USB client/host interfaces.
    - Radio modem interface logic.
    - Integrated 2D or 3D graphics accelerators.
    - Integrated security accelerator.
    - S-Video outputs.
    - IrDA controller.
    - DACs for direct TV (PAL/NTSC) video output.
    - Integrated DSPs for video and audio processing.
- Many popular cellular handsets and PDA devices have been marketed based on the TI OMAP platform. Because they are based on an ARM core, these processors are supported by Linux today.

2.3.1.1 Beagle Board

- The Beagle Board is a great platform for experimentation and learning, as well as a perfect development platform for various OMAP related development projects. The only drawback of the Beagle Board was the lack of an Ethernet port. Fortunately, this problem was remedied by a company called Tin Can Tools. It developed a companion board called the Beagle Buddy Zippy Ethernet Combo Board. In addition to adding an Ethernet port, it adds another SD/MMC interface, a battery-backed real-time clock, an I2C expansion interface, and another serial port.

2.4 HARDWARE PLATFORMS

- The idea of a common hardware reference platform is not new. The venerable PC/104 and VMEbus are two examples of hardware platforms that have withstood the test of time in the embedded market. More recent successful platforms include Compact PCI and its derivatives.

2.4.1 Compact PCI

- The Compact PCI (cPCI) hardware platform is based on PCI electrical standards and Eurocard physical specifications. cPCI has the following general features :
  - Vertical cards of 3U or 6U heights.
  - A latch system for securing and ejecting cards.
  - Front- or rear-panel I/O connections are supported.
  - High-density backplane connector.
  - Staggered power pins for hot-swap support.
  - Support by many vendors.
  - Compatibility with standard PCI chipsets.

2.4.2 ATCA

- ATCA platforms are leading the industry trend away from in-house proprietary hardware and software platforms. Many of the largest equipment manufacturers in the telecommunications and networking markets have been slowly moving away from custom, in-house-designed hardware platforms. This trend is also evident in the software platforms, from operating systems to so-called middleware such as high-availability and protocol stack solutions. Down sizing and time-to-market pressures are two key factors driving this trend.

2.5 ARM PROCESSOR HISTORY

- In 1985, Acorn Computers Ltd. was in search of a new processor to put up in the desktop market. While the technocrats were contemplating various design options, they came across a few papers published by a set of students in the University of Berkley (USA) outlining a very simple processor design based on RISC principles. The computer architects of Acorn Computers found the design very attractive and decided to build a new processor using sonic of these principles. "Ibis led to the development Of ARM1, which had less than 25,000 transistors, and operated at 6 MHz.
- This was followed by ARM2 (in 1987) with 30,000 transistors. Comparing this to an Intel Motorola's processor of that time having 70,000 transistors, this was a beauty in terms of a smaller die size and lower power dissipation. This was thus, the first ARM processor which was produced in bulk. It had a 32 bit data bus, a 26 bit address space and sixteen 32-bit registers and was clocked at 8 to 12 MHz. It dissipated much less power, and performed much better than Intel's 80286 which came up around the same time (but focused on the desktop market).
- ARM3, ARM4 and ARM5 were also designed, but never produced, because around this time, in 1990, Acorn Computers teamed up with Apple Computers and VLSI

Technology group to form a company named Advanced RISC Machines Ltd. This company continued with ARM6, ARM7, etc. The latter was the processor which became very popular and led to ARM being used in exotic products such as mobile phones, PDAs, IPods, computer hard disks, etc. After this, ARINI made rapid strides in the 32-bit embedded market, accounting for a very high percentage of applications in the high-end embedded systems market.

2.5.1 ARM Core

- What is meant by the 'core'? The core is the 'processing unit' or the 'computing engine' which has all the computing power, and this aspect is decided by the architecture, which represents the basic design of the processor.
- One special and unique feature of ARM as a company is that it designs the core and licenses this IP (Intellectual Property) to others. This simply means that the company does not fabricate the chip, but sells only the design. This design is taken by the licensee, who may or may not add more features (usually peripherals) to the design. Sometimes the buyer can also modify the basic design to a minor extent. The buyer company fabricates the design and sells it/uses it for its products.
- There are various ways in which ARM sells its IP. It could be in the form of a soft IP. In this case, the design is sold as RTL (VHDL/Verilog code), and this allows the buyer to modify the design to a certain extent. If the design is sold as a hard IP, it means the buyer gets only the layout or the net list (connection of nets or electronic wires). Thus, the buyer can add only peripherals to the black box design he has purchased.
- We can thus understand that ARM the company does not 'fabricate' ARM chips. It is because of this, that we have ARM chips and boards of various companies-Samsung, Philips, Atmel, Texas Instruments, ST Microelectronics and so on-the list is very long.

2.5.2 ARM Microcontroller

- ARM has been designated as a 'microprocessor' and indeed it is a processor which has very high computing capabilities. It has a rich set of features for handling complex computations.
- However, for using it as a embedded processor, it needs many more capabilities and these come in the forms of on-chip peripherals. To the ARM core, peripherals are added and thus it becomes a microcontroller or an MCU (Microcontroller Unit), rather than an MPU (Micro Processor Unit). Fig. 2.3 shows the ARM MCU. The number and kind of peripherals added, depends on the requirements of the buyer of the IP. It is because of this that we have varying number of peripherals for ARM processors supplied by different companies. It could be obvious that to support more peripherals, the core has to be more powerful. That is why we generally find more peripherals around an ARM9 core rather than around an ARM7 core. But as a rule, users have to spell out their requirements for the peripherals of an MCU.

- When a chip has the core and the necessary peripherals to perform as a system, it is called a System on Chip (SoC) and the term 'ARM SoC' is a very commonly used understandably it has some version of the ARM core and a large set of peripherals.

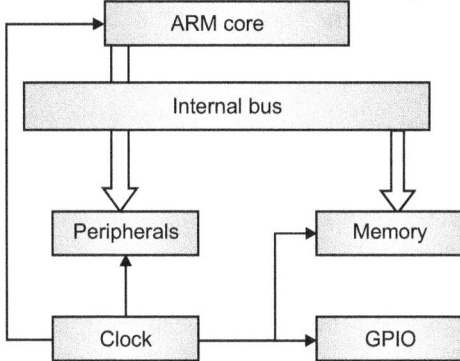

Fig. 2.3 : ARM SoC – core with peripherals

2.5.3 RISC Vs CISC

- Features of RISC are listed here in. These apply to most of the instructions of ARM, but not necessarily to all.
    1. Instructions arc of the same size, that is, 32 bits.
    2. Instructions are executed in one cycle.
    3. Only the load and store instructions access memory.
- Due to these simple guidelines in the design of the ISA (Instruction Set Architecture), the outstanding features of this RISC processor arc as follows :
- The number of transistors needed is much less than that of a CISC processor of comparable computational power.
- The die size is less because of the reduced hardware involved.
- Due to these aspects (and a few others, which will soon be elaborated), power dissipation is very low.

2.5.4 Advanced Features

Once the basic ARM core was designed, later numbers of the family kept on having more and more features added. Over the years, some of these became standard' and some are still optional. To specify what futures are available with a particular ARM core, naming conventions were adopted, but which have had to be changed over the years. Let us take a look into some of these features.

- **THUMB :** A new 16-bit instruction set called THUMB was made available. The logic of having this less powerful instruction set is that all applications do not need the full power of 32 bit ARM instructions. For such cases, the 16 bit Thumb set (which is a compressed form of the ARM instruction set) will be enough and the advantage obtained is that of high 'Code density'.

- **MMU and MPU :** These are two aspects related to memory. One is the 'Memory Management Unit' and the other is the 'Memory Protection Unit'. Such units arc mandatorily available in all advanced desktop processors (like Pentium), but for embedded systems, the necessity of such units is dictated by the product for which the processor is to be used. Thus, we have some ARM processors with both MPU and MMU, and others with one or neither of them.
- **Cache :** The first ARM1 processor with a cache was ARM3. It had an on chip cache of 4 KB. ARM 7 had a cache of 8 KB which was improved in ways other than just the size. Current ARM processors have cache as a standard component.
- **Debug Interface :** There is an on chip unit for testing called the JTAG interface. JTAG stands for Joint Test Action Group' and defines a set of standards for testing the functionality of hardware. For any chip/system there is a set of scan cells located at the boundaries and there are specific signals designed to enable testing' of the device. Such a unit is called the JTAG debug interface, and some ARM chips have this facility.
- **Embedded ICE Macrocell :** The current hardware trend is to design a system as 'macrocells', which is a hardware unit. The ARM core could be considered as a macrocell, while other units (peripheral units as well) may also be added as 'macrocells'. Some processors have an embedded ICE (In Circuit Emulator) macrocell to enable testing. "This unit is powered by break point and watch point registers and control and status registers. All this together can work to halt the ARXI core to read status and thus do active debugging.

2.5.5 Architecture Versions

Over the years, the architectural features have also been enhanced. Thus, later versions of the architecture are more powerful Versions v4 and v4T are the early versions, later versions are v5, v5E, v6 and v7. Table 2.8 lists various architecture variants of ARM.

2.5.6 ARM CORTEX

ARM has come a long way from ARM2, which was the first one to be commercially produced. ARM7 was a resounding success which made ARM the dominant player in the 32-bit embedded processor market. ARM7 was followed by all of which boasted of more and more computing powers. The latest in the sequence is the CORTEX series which has the architecture v7 version. To make this series cater to well defined application sets, the following three profiles have been defined :

- **The A Profile :** This profile which has the ARMv7-A architecture is meant for high end applications. It is meant to handle complex applications with high-end embedded operating systems, and typical applications requiring such a profile are mobile phones and video systems.

Table 2.8

Architecture Versions	Features
v4	ARM instructions only.
v4T	THUMB instructions also added.
v5	More advanced ARM and THUMB instructions.
v5E	Advanced ARM instructions and enhanced DSP instructions.
v6	Advanced ARM and THUMB. SIMD and memory support instructions added.
v7	THUMB-2 technology, in which both 16-bit and 32-bit instructions are supported, and there is no need to switching between ARM and THUMB instruction sets.

- **The R Profile :** This profile which has the ARMv7-R architecture has been designed for high-end applications which require real-time capabilities. Typical applications are automatic braking systems and other safety critical applications.
- **The M Profile :** This profile which has the ARMv7 M architecture has been designed for deeply embedded microcontroller type systems. This is to be used in industrial control applications where a large number of peripherals may have to be handled and controlled.

2.6 ARM ARCHITECTURE

With this background, let us get started on the more intricate details of the processor.

2.6.1 Instruction Set Architecture

- It is likely that you have heard the term 'Instruction Set Architecture' (ISA) mentioned in some context or the other. The term implies the user's i.e the programmer's view of the processor, which constitute the instruction set, addressing modes, registers, etc. ISA is the assembly programmer's or compiler designer's view of the processor. We will base most of our discussions on ARM7 which was the first and still the most popular of the ARM processors. Advanced versions may have more enhancements, but the basic architecture is more or less the same.

2.6.2 Operating Modes

- ARM has seven operating modes which arc listed here. It is not important to understand the exact functions of each mode right now but keep in mind that the user mode corresponds to the simplest mode, with least privileges, but is the mode under which most application programs run. 'The system mode is a highly privileged mode. 'This mode is used by operating systems to manipulate and control the activities of the processor. The other modes are entered on the occurrence of exceptions or rather, they arc interrupt modes. Sec the list of the operating modes of ARM.

- **User :** Unprivileged mode under which most tasks run.
- **FIQ (Fast Interrupt Request) :** Entered on a high priority (fast) interrupt request.
- **I RQ (Interrupt Request) :** Entered on a low priority interrupt request.
- **Supervisor :** Entered on reset and when a software interrupt instruction (SVVI) is executed.
- **Abort :** Used to handle memory access violations.
- **Undef :** Used to handle undefined instructions.
- **System :** Privileged mode using the same registers as user mode.

2.6.3 Register Set

- ARM has 37 registers each of which is 32 bits long. They are listed as follows :
- I dedicated program counter (PCJ).
- I dedicated current program status register (CPSR).
- 5 dedicated saved program status registers (SPSR).
- 30 general purpose registers.

Now, let's go into the details of the listed registers.

2.6.3.1 General Purpose Registers

- There are 30 of them, but they arc distributed among different modes. To understand this feature, see the case of one particular mode, say the user mode. In this mode, the registers act as shown in Table 2.9.

Table 2.9 Registers In The User Mode

Register Numbers	Designations
RO-R12	General urpose registers
R13	Stack pointer (SP)
R14	Link register (LR)
R15	Program counter (PC)

Table 2.10 shows the whole set of registers available for the processor. Look at the set of registers titled as user and system. Let's discuss the specific functions of each of them.

RO-R12 are general purpose registers, or what may be designated as scratch pad registers. These are the registers into which data and address arc loaded. They are also 'the' registers used in computations.

R13 is the pointer to the stack, and is the stack pointer (SP).

R15 acts as the program counter (PC), which, like in any other processor, is the register which sequences instructions as they arc fetched from memory.

R14 is the link register (LIZ), a special register. It is used whether there is a procedure call or an interrupt that is, branching to a location. When branching becomes necessary, the value of PC is saved in the link register, and PC takes on the new branch address. When returning to the original sequence, the PC value can be retrieved from the link register. This is a very convenient option, because the necessity to push the PC value to the stack is avoided. The stack is a memory area, saving and retriving from stack is time consuming. Having such a register, that is, the LR, to store return addresses helps to reduce the delay associated with procedure calls and interrupts.

Table 2.10 : Register set of ARM

User and System	Fast Interrupt Request	Interrupt Request	Supervisor	Undefined	Abort
R0					
R1					
R2					
R3					
R4					
R5					
R6					
R7					
R8	R8_FIQ				
R9	R9_FIQ				
R10	R10_FIQ				
R11	R11_FIQ				
R12	R12_FIQ				
R13SP	R13_FIQ	R13_RIQ	R13_SVC	R13_undef	R13_ABT
R14LR	R14_FIQ	R14_RIQ	R14_SVC	R14_undef	R14_ABT
R15PC					
CPSR					
------	SPSR_FIQ	SPSR_IRQ	SPSRSVC	SPSR_undef	SPSR_ABT

2.6.4 Mode Switching

We know that there are seven modes for the processor, which implies that it can be switched to different modes, as decided by the requirement. When the processor switches, say, from the user to another mode, some of the user mode registers are replaced by another set of registers. Sec the FIQ mode, for example, in this mode, R8 to R14 are replaced by another set of registers, and the names of these registers arc suffixed by FIQ, like R14_ FIQ, R12_FIQ and so on.

Note that this mode is entered on a 'fast interrupt' which means it requires fast action. One action during interrupts would be to save the contents of the currently used registers.

This saving takes some time. To ensure fast operation, in the case of being switched to the FIQ mode, new registers are used. No time is spent on saving the contents of register R8 to R14 of the user mode. Once the FIQ mode is entered, those registers are just swapped out, and replaced by a set of new registers. Note also, that all registers are not swapped out, however.

Now look at Table 2.10 once again to note the IRQ mode. Here only R13 and R14 are replaced by new registers. In the IRQ mode, the response is not expected to be, as fast is in the FIQ mode. Thus, there is sufficient time to allow the contents of most of the registers to be saved, before mode switching is done. This also applies to the modes 'undef, supervisor and abort'. In these modes too, only two registers are swapped out and replaced with new ones.

CPSR (Current Program Status Register)

The CPSR is a very important register, and there is only one such register for the processor. Fig. 2.4 and Table 2.11 gives its details. The CPSR contains the information about the current state of the processor. It has bits which specify the mode, control bits to enable/disable interrupts and also specifies whether the Thumb or ARM mode is currently in use.

Bits 0 to 4 specify the current mode of operation. Since there are only 7 modes of operation, only seven mode numbers are valid.

The J bit is for indicating whether the Jazelle state is valid or not. The T bit specifics whether the current operation is in the ARM or Thumb mode.

The contents of this register can be modified only in the highly privileged system mode. It also contains the condition flag bits. Most of you are likely to know the relevance of the conditional flag hits. But for those who might be new to the concept of flags, here is a concise description.

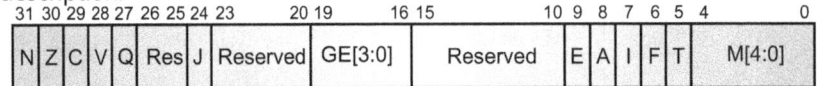

Fig. 2.4 : Current program status register (CPRS) and SPRS bit configuration

Table 2.11 CPRS Bits

Bit no.	Notation	Interpretation
0 to 4	Mode	Specifies the current mode of operation.
5	T	Specifies whether in ARM(T =1) or Thumb (T = 0) state.
6	F	Disables(F=1)FIQ.
7	I	Disables (I = 1)IRQ.
8 to 23, 25 to 26	Undefined	
24	J	In Jazelle state (J = 1).
27	Q	Sticky overflow flag.
28 to 31	V,C,Z,N	Conditional flags.

2.6.5 Conditional Flags

N (Negative Flag) : This flag indicates the status of the M'ISB of the result of an operation. If we are dealing with signed number N = 1 means that the sign bit = 1, which is a negative result.

C (Carry Flag) : This bit is set if there is an overflow from the FISH of the data being manipulated; this can happen in additions, shifts, rotates etc. It is also set when the result of subtraction is positive. If R1-R2 gives a positive result, C = 1, indicates that R1 is greater than R2. To be precise, let's say that 'A carry occurs if the result of an add, subtract or compare is greater than or equal to 232, or as the result of an inlinc barrel shifter operation in a move or logical instruction.

Z (Zero Flag) : If the result of an arithmetic or logical operation is zero, then Z = 1.

V (Overflow Flag) : This is the overflow flag, which is relevant only for signed operations. It indicates that the sign bit has possibly been corrupted because the result has gone out of the range.

When signed numbers are used, only 31 bits are available for the magnitude of the numbers. With 32 bits, overflow occurs if the result of an add, subtract or compare is greater than or equal to (231-1) or less than -231, which is the maximum range available for signed numbers.

To cite an example, say two positive numbers are added, and the magnitude. of the sum becomes greater than 31 bits. There will be an overflow into the sign bit, which will change the MSB to '1' and get wrongly interpreted as a negative number. This overflow into the sign bit (MSB) with no overflow out of the MSB causes the overflow (V) bit to be set.

Q (Sticky Overflow Flag) : This flag indicates overflow itself, but it is 'sticky' in the sense that it remains set until explicitly cleared.

Saved Program Status Registers (SPSR) : There is five 'Saved Program Status Registers', that is, one for each of the 'exception' modes of operation. When an exception, that is, an interrupt occurs, the corresponding SPSR saves the current CPSR value into it (so as to be able to retrieve it on returning to the previous node). The system mode and user modes do not have SPSRs because they are not entered through the mechanism of interrupts.

2.7 INTERRUPT VECTOR TABLE

We have seen that ARM has a number of exception moles. Exceptions are a class of interrupts which are internally generated due to the occurrence of some specific conditions. For example, when an undefined instruction is detected, the processor can't process it. The solution for such an undesired situation is to make the processor switch to another mode and generate an interrupt. This interrupt takes control to an interrupt service routine (ISR i.e. interrupt handler) residing in a specific location in memory. This specific location is termed the Interrupt Vector' corresponding to this exception.

Besides 'exceptions', the processor can be interrupted by instructions and this is called a software interrupt (S\VI). There are hardware interrupts as well, which are activated by FIQ or IRQ.

The aforesaid discussion is just to clarify the fact that associated with all exceptions, hardware and software interrupts; there is a fixed interrupt vector which leads to the ISR or the interrupt handler.

Sec Table 2.12 which shows the predefined interrupt vectors.

Table 2.12 : List of Interrupt Vector

Exception	Shorthand	Vector Address
Reset	RESET	0×00000000
Undefined instruction	UNDEF	0×00000004
Software interrupt	SWI	0×00000008
Prefetch abort	PABT	$0 \times 0000000c$
Data abort	DABT	0×00000010
Reserved	-	0×00000014
Interrupt request	IRQ	0×00000018
Fast interrupt request	FIQ	$0 \times 0000001C$

Note that the first entry in the table is 'Reset'. All processors have a address, termed 'reset vector which is the location to which control branches to, when it is first powered on, or when reset in the midst of processor activity. For ARM, this is 0×00000000. Since this location is always fixed, RESET is usually included in the class of vectored interrupts.

2.8 PROGRAMMING THE ARM PROCESSOR

Now that we have had a look at the concepts regarding the instruction set architecture (ISA) of ARN'I, we are in a position to understand it better by programming. Writing, running and testing programs is the key to understanding any processor. By doing programming, we become capable of understanding almost everything about how registers, memory and flags act on data. In short, we get a total feel about the processing activity done inside the processor.

- To get to this, we need a programming environment, that is, an Integrated Development Environment (IDE). There are many IDEs available for ARM, some of which are free of cost (and freely downloadable) and some of which arc proprietary and thus have to be paid for. However for students, an evaluation version is available which is freely clown loadable and available from the website www.keil.com. We will use the Keil IDE also called the RVDK (Real View Development Kit), which is very popular and easy to use. This version can be used for testing programs and for simulation also.

2.8.1 Programming Assembly Vs C

Programming can be done in assembly as well in high level languages. In the embedded design world, high level languages arc used in product design and C is a very popular language. As such we will also do C programming (in the next chapter). But before that, let's have a stint in assembly programming. Our approach will be such that to understand the ARM core, that is, to use its registers, do memory access and so on, we will do assembly programming. This ensures that we get a good grip on the ARM core architecture. In this context, it will turn out that we focus on the computational capabilities of the core. And when we start using ARM as a microcontroller, i.e. the core with a number of peripherals, we use C programming. "Ibis will allow us to use the processor in various practical applications involving peripherals and interaction with the external world.

2.9 ARM ASSEMBLY LANGUAGE

As mentioned earlier, the ARM instruction set has been cleverly designed to get more than one operation to be done in a single instruction. Let's list out some features of the ARM instruction set.

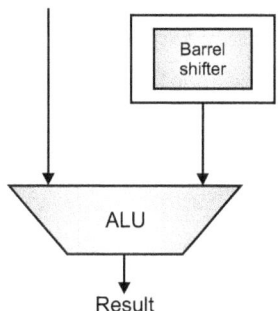

Fig. 2.5 : Data processing unit

- ARM is a RISC processor, in which every instruction has a maximum size of 32 bits. Instructions are expected to be executed in one cycle. "This is true for most instructions, but not for all. Therefore it is better to say that ARM is a RISC processor with a few CISC type instructions as well.
- Another feature of RISC and therefore of ARM, is that it is a load-store architecture. This means that all computations arc register based, that is, the operands arc to the brought to registers from memory, using a load instruction. After computation, the result is to be stored in memory. For the user, this means that there is no data processing instructions in which one of the operands is in memory. All operands are to be available in registers before computation can be done.
- A third feature of ARM is that its ALU has a barrel shifter (Fig. 2.5) associated with one of its operands. A barrel shifter is a unit that can perform more than one hit of

shift/rotation, to the right or to the left on an operand. As we will soon see, the barrel shifter adds some clever processing techniques to data processing and allows shifting and an arithmetic operation to be combined in the same instruction.
- 'Conditions' can be appended to instructions : this implies that we can choose to 'do or not do' a particular operation based on a status of a condition flag, For most other processors, only branching operations depend on flag status. We will see that data movement and data processing instructions can be made 'conditional'.

2.9.1 Data Types

ARM can operate on 32-bit data, which is termed a word, 16-bit data called a half word and also on byte operands. The processing tools offer the option of storing data as 'little endian' or 'big endian'. To clarify this concept, follow the forthcoming discussion, and observe.

The little endian format

Address	Data
0×00001200	A3
0×00001201	90
0×00001202	47
0×00001203	OE

The little endian format

Address	Data
0×00001200	OE
0×00001201	47
0×00001202	90
0×00001203	A3

A 32-bit data stored in memory needs 4 bytes of space which means 4 consecutive addresses are required, as one address can store only one byte. When the lowest byte of the 32-bit word is stored in the lowest of these four addresses, it is called the 'little endian' format. Otherwise, it is the 'big Indian' format. The 32-bit data word is $0 \times E4790A3$. The storage addresses are from 0×00001200 onwards.

In the processor industry, both formats are used. Intel prefers the little endian format, while Motorola uses the big endian format. ARM allows both formats (can be fixed up by software, in the initialization stage). In this ok, we assume the little endian format.

2.9.2 Data Alignment

Storing (and loading also) of 4 bytes in memory can be done in one cycle, because the processor has a 32-bit data bus. When 32-bit data is stored in memory, four addresses are needed. But we need to specify only one address in our instruction; but there is an aspect called 'alignment'. For 32-bit data alignment implies that the last two bits of this address arc zero. For example, the address 0 × 00001200 is an aligned address. When this address is used to store 32-bit data, this address and the next three addresses arc automatically accessed. "This is because of the way memory is organized, as four banks (see Fig. 2.6).

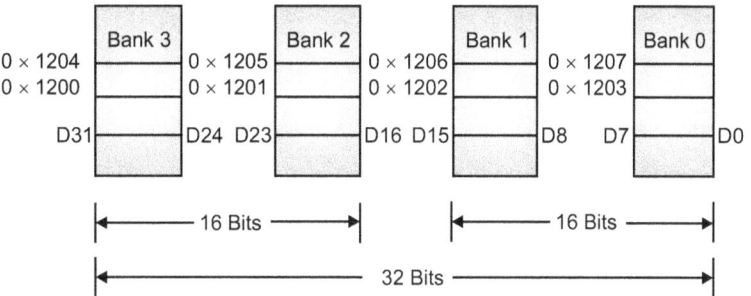

Fig. 2.6 : Memory banks

It the address of a 32-bit number is given as 0 × 1200, the accessed addresses are 0 × 1200 0 × 1201, 0 × 1202 and 0 × 1203. The 4 bytes in these addresses arc considered to be in the same row, that is, aligned. In this case, one byte each from each bank is accessed and only one memory cycle is needed to access an aligned word.

For unaligned data, one more cycle is necessary. Think of the address 0 × 1201. The locations to be accessed will be 0 × 1201, 0 × 1202, 0 × 1203 and 0 × 1204. Note that the first three bytes will be in the same row, while the last will be in a different row (bank), and so one more cycle of access will be required.

We summarize the conditions for aligned data as follows :

- For word (32-bit) data, the specified address should have its least significant two bits.
- For half word (16-bit) accesses, the specified address should have the LSB equal to 0.

Most of the tools for ARM ensure that data is stored in aligned locations, so as to avoid unnecessary extra cycles of operation.

2.9.3 Assembly Language Rules

An assembly language line has tour fields, namely, label, opcode, operand and comment. A label is positioned at the left of a line and is the symbol for the memory address which stores that line of information. There are certain rules regarding labels that arc allowed under the type of assembler being used. The manual of the specific assembler should be referred, to get this clear. The second field is the opcode instruction field. The third is the operand field, and the last is the comment field which starts with a semicolon. The use of comments is advised for making programs more readable.

A typical assembly language statement is :
BOSE   ADD   R1, R2, R3 ; add R2, R3 and copy the sum to R1.
The label is BOSE, the opcode is ADD, the operands arc R1, R2 and R3 and the line after the semicolon is the comment. While writing programs, make sure you don't write instructions at the extreme left of the page-that part is the 'label' field in this book. We will use the assembler which is part of the RVDK supplied by Keil.

2.10 INSTRUCTION SET

- Two instruction sets :

ARM
- Standard 32-bit instruction set.

THUMB
- 16-bit compressed form.
- Code density better than most CISC.
- Dynamic decompression in pipeline.

2.10.1 Main Features of the ARM Instruction Set

- All instructions are 32 bits long.
- Most instructions execute in a single cycle.
- Every instruction can be conditionally executed.
- A load/store architecture.

(a) Data processing instructions act only on registers.
- Three operand format.
- Combined ALU and shifter for high speed bit manipulation.

(b) Specific memory access instructions with powerful auto-indexing addressing modes.
- 32 bit and 8 bit data types and also 16 bit data types on ARM Architecture v4.
- Flexible multiple register load and store instructions.
- Uniform 16 × 32-bit register file (including the Program Counter, Stack Pointer and the Link Register).
- Fixed instruction width of 32-bits to ease decoding and pipelining, at the cost of decreased code density. Later, the Thumb instruction set added 16-bit instructions and increased code density.
- Instruction set extension via coprocessors.

2.10.2 Thumb Instruction Set

- Thumb is a 16-bit instruction set.
- Optimized for code density from C code (~65% of ARM code size).
- Improved performance from narrow memory.
- Subset of the functionality of the ARM instruction set.

Thumb is not a "regular" instruction set!
- Constraints are not generally consistent.
- Targeted at compiler generation, not hand coding.

2.10.3 ARM Instruction Set Format

31 28	27					16 15		8	7		0	Instruction type
Cond	0 0	I	Opcode	S	Rn	Rd		Operand 1				Data processing / PSR transfer
Cond	0 0 0 0 0 0		A	S	Rd	Rn	Rs	1 0 0 1		Rm		Multiply
Cond	0 0 0 0 1	U	A	S	RdHi	RdLo	Rs	1 0 0 1		Rm		Long multiply (v3M/v4 only)
Cond	0 0 0 1 0	B	0 0		Rn	Rd	0 0 0 0	1 0 0 1		Rm		Swap
Cond	0 1	I	P U	0 W L	Rn	Rd		Offset				Load/store byte/word
Cond	1 0 0	P	U 0 W L		Rn			Register list				Load/store multiple
Cond	0 0 0	P	U 0 W L		Rn	Rd	Offset 1	1 S H 1		Offset 2		Halfword transfer : Immediate offset
Cond	0 0 0	P	U 0 W L		Rn	Rd	0 0 0 0	1 S H 1		Rm		Halfword transfer : Register offset
Cond	1 0 1	L					Offset					Branch
Cond	0 0 0 1		0 0 1 0		1 1 1 1	1 1 1 1	1 1 1 1	0 0 0 1		Rn		Branch exchange (v4T only)
Cond	1 1 0	P	U N W L		Rn	CRd	CPNum	Offset				Coprocessor data transfer
Cond	1 1 1 0		Op1		CRn	CRd	CPNum	Op2		CRm		Coprocessor data operation
Cond	1 1 1 0		Op1	L	CRn	Rd	CPNum	Op2		CRm		Coprocessor register transfer
Cond	1 1 1 1						SWI Number					Software interrupt

Fig. 2.7 : ARM instruction set format

2.10.4 Conditional Execution

- Most instruction sets only allow branches to be executed conditionally.
- However by reusing the condition evaluation hardware, ARM effectively increases number of instructions.
  (a) All instructions contain a condition field which determines whether the CPU will execute them.
  (b) Non-executed instructions soak up 1 cycle.
- Still have to complete cycle so as to allow fetching and decoding of following instructions.
- This removes the need for many branches, which stall the pipeline (3 cycles to refill).
- Allows very dense in-line code, without branches.
- The Time penalty of not executing several conditional instructions is frequently less than overhead of the branch or subroutine call that would otherwise be needed.

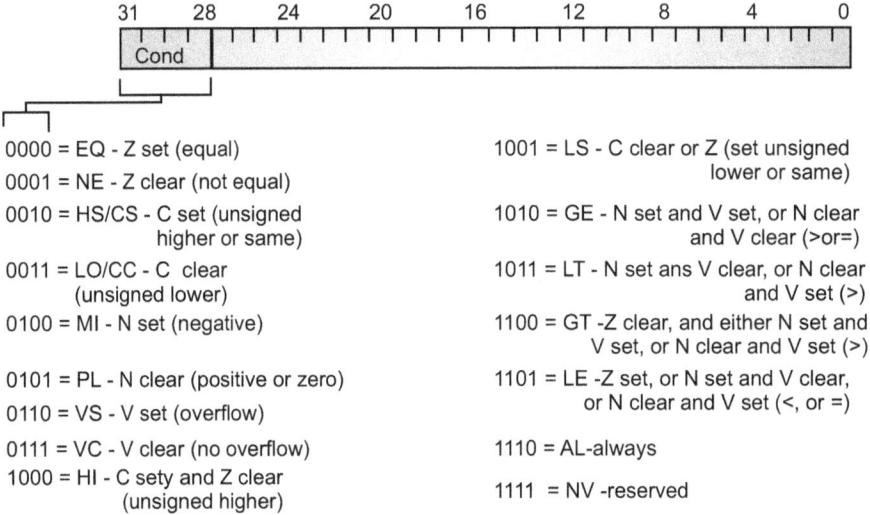

Fig. 2.8 : The condition field

2.10.5 Using and Updating the Condition Field

(a) To execute an instruction conditionally, simply postfix it with the appropriate condition :

For example an add instruction takes the form :

- ADD r0,r1,r2 ; r0 = r1 + r2 (ADDAL).
- To execute this only if the zero flag is set :
- ADDEQ r0,r1,r2 ; If zero flag set then...

    ; ... r0 = r1 + r2

(b) By default, data processing operations do not affect the condition flags (a part from the comparisons where this is the only effect). To cause the condition flags to be updated, the S bit of the instruction needs to be set by postfixing the instruction (and any condition code) with an "S".

(b) For example to add two numbers and set the condition flags :

- ADDS r0,r1,r2 ; r0 = r1 + r2 ; ... and set flags.

2.10.6 Branch Instructions

- **Branch :** B{<cond>} label.
- **Branch with Link :** BL{<cond>} sub_routine_label.
- **The offset for branch instructions is calculated by the assembler**
- By taking the difference between the branch instruction and the target address minus 8 (to allow for the pipeline).

- This gives a 26 bit offset which is right shifted 2 bits (as the bottom two bits are always zero as instructions are word – aligned) and stored into the instruction encoding.
- This gives a range of ± 32 Mbytes.
- When executing the instruction, the processor :
  shifts the offset left 2 bits, sign extends it to 32 bits and adds it to PC.
- Execution then continues from the new PC, once the pipeline has been refilled.
- The "Branch with link" instruction implements a subroutine call by writing PC-4 into the LR of the current bank. i.e. the address of the next instruction following the branch with link (allowing for the pipeline).
- To return from subroutine, simply need to restore the PC from the LR :
  - MOV pc, lr.
  - Again, pipeline has to refill before execution continues.
- The "Branch" instruction does not affect LR.
- Note : Architecture 4T offers a further ARM branch instruction, BX
  - See Thumb Instruction Set Module for details.

2.10.7 Data Processing Instructions

- Largest family of ARM instructions, all sharing the same instruction format.
- Contains :
  - Arithmetic operations.
  - Comparisons (no results - just set condition codes).
  - Logical operations.
  - Data movement between registers.
- Remember, this is a load / store architecture.
  - These instruction only work on registers, NOT memory.
- They each perform a specific operation on one or two operands.
  - First operand always a register – Rn.
  - Second operand sent to the ALU via barrel shifter.
- We will examine the barrel shifter shortly.

2.10.7.1 Arithmetic Operations

- **Operations are**
  - ADD   operand1 + operand2.
  - ADC   operand1 + operand2 + carry.
  - SUB   operand1 – operand2.

- SBC   operand1 – operand2 + carry –1.
- RSB   operand2 – operand1.
- RSC   operand2 – operand1 + carry – 1.
- **Syntax :**
  - <Operation>{<cond>}{S} Rd, Rn, Operand 2.
- **Examples**
  - ADD r0, r1, r2.
  - SUBGT r3, r3, #1.
  - RSBLES r4, r5, #5.

2.10.7.2 Comparisons
- The only effect of the comparisons is to :
  - Update the condition flags. Thus no need to set S bit.
- **Operations are**
  - CMP   operand1 – operand2, but result not written.
  - CMN   operand1 + operand2, but result not written.
  - TST   operand1 AND operand2, but result not written.
  - TEQ   operand1 EOR operand2, but result not written.
- **Syntax**
  - <Operation>{<cond>} Rn, Operand2.
- **Examples**
  - CMP r0, r1.
  - TSTEQ r2, #5.

2.10.7.3 Logical Operations
- **Operations are**
  - AND   operand1 AND operand2.
  - EOR   operand1 EOR operand2.
  - ORR   operand1 OR operand2.
  - BIC operand1 AND NOT operand2 [i.e. bit clear].
- **Syntax**
  - <Operation>{<cond>}{S} Rd, Rn, Operand2.
- **Examples**
  - AND   r0, r1, r2.
  - BICEQ r2, r3, #7.
  - EORS   r1, r3, r0.

2.10.7.4 Data Movement

- **Operations are**
  - MOV   operand2.
  - MVN   NOT operand2.

Note : These make no use of operand1.

- **Syntax**
  - <Operation>{<cond>}{S} Rd, Operand2.
- **Examples**
  - MOV   r0, r1.
  - MOVS   r2, #10.
  - MVNEQ   r1,#0.

2.10.8 Load / Store Instructions

- **The ARM is a Load / Store Architecture**
  - Does not support memory to memory data processing operations.
  - Must move data values into registers before using them.
- **This might sound inefficient, but in practice isn't**
  - Load data values from memory into registers.
  - Process data in registers using a number of data processing instructions which are not slowed down by memory access.
  - Store results from registers out to memory.
- **The ARM has three sets of instructions which interact with main memory. These are**
  - Single register data transfer (LDR / STR).
  - Block data transfer (LDM/STM).
  - Single Data Swap (SWP).

2.10.8.1 Single Register Data Transfer

- **The basic load and store instructions are :**
  - Load and Store Word or Byte.
  - LDR / STR / LDRB / STRB.

- **ARM Architecture Version 4 also adds support for halfwords and signed data.**
    - Load and Store Halfword.
    - LDRH / STRH.
    - Load Signed Byte or Halfword - load value and sign extend it to 32 bits.
    - LDRSB / LDRSH.
- **All of these instructions can be conditionally executed by inserting the appropriate condition code after STR / LDR.**
    - Example : LDREQB.
- **Syntax**
    - <LDR|STR>{<cond>}{<size>} Rd, <address>.

2.10.8.2 Load and Store Word or Byte : Base Register

- **The memory location to be accessed is held in a base register**
    - STR r0, [r1]   ; Store contents of r0 to location pointed to
                      ; by contents of r1.
    - LDR r2, [r1]   ; Load r2 with contents of memory location
                      ; pointed to by contents of r1.

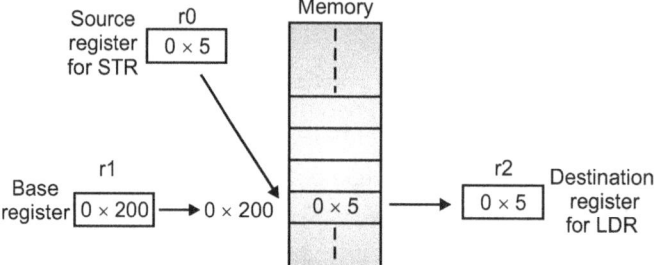

Fig. 2.9 : Example of load and store word or byte : base register

2.10.8.3 Load and Store Word or Byte : Offsets from the Base Register

- **As well as accessing the actual location contained in the base register, these instructions can access a location offset from the base register pointer.**
- **This offset can be**
    - An unsigned 12-bit immediate value (i.e. 0 - 4095 bytes).
    - A register, optionally shifted by an immediate value.
- **This can be either added or subtracted from the base register.**
    - Prefix the offset value or register with '+' (default) or '–'.

- **This offset can be applied**
  - Before the transfer is made: Pre-indexed addressing.
  - Optionally auto-incrementing the base register, by postfixing the instruction with an '!'.
  - After the transfer is **made** : Post-indexed addressing.
  - Causing the base register to be auto-incremented.

2.10.8.4 Load and Store Word or Byte : Pre-Indexed Addressing
- **Example :** STR r0, [r1,#12]

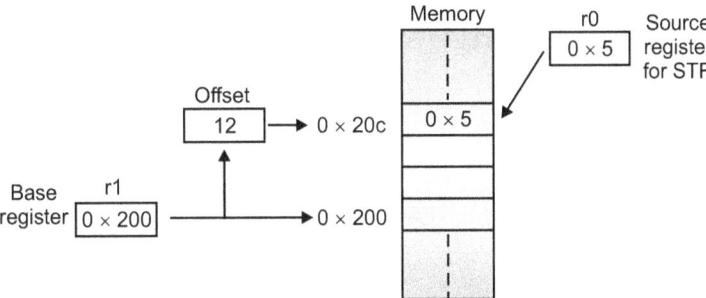

Fig. 2.10 : Load and store word or byte : pre-indexed addressing

- **To Store to Location $0 \times 1f4$ Instead Use :** STR r0, [r1, #-12].
- **To Auto-Increment Base Pointer to $0 \times 20c$ use :** STR r0, [r1, #12]!
- **If r2 Contains 3, Access $0 \times 20c$ by Multiplying this by 4 :** STR r0, [r1, r2, LSL, #2].

2.10.8.5 Load and Store Word or Byte : Post-Indexed Addressing
- **Example :** STR r0, [r1], #12.

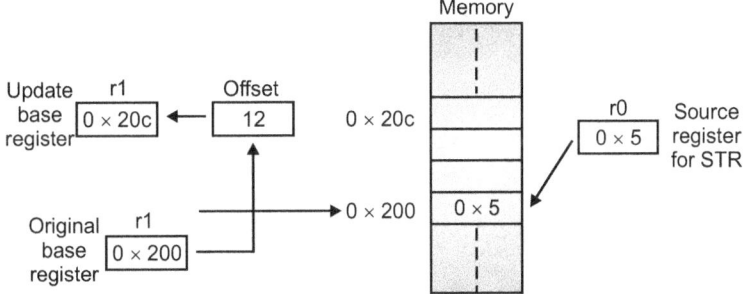

Fig. 2.11 : Example of load and store word or byte : post-indexed addressing

- To auto-increment the base register to location 0x1f4 instead use : STR r0, [r1], # –12.
- If r2 contains 3, auto-incremenet base register to 0x20c by multiplying this by 4: STR r0, [r1], r2, LSL #2.

2.10.8.6 Load and Stores with User Mode Privilege
- When using post-indexed addressing, there is a further form of Load/Store Word/Byte :
  - <LDR|STR>{<cond>}{B}T Rd, <post_indexed_address>.
- When used in a privileged mode, this does the load/store with user mode privilege.
  - Normally used by an exception handler that is emulating a memory access instruction that would normally execute in user mode.

2.10.8.7 Offsets for Halfword and Signed Halfword / Byte Access
- The Load and Store Halfword and Load Signed Byte or Halfword instructions can make use of pre- and post-indexed addressing in much the same way as the basic load and store instructions.
- However the actual offset formats are more constrained :
  - The immediate value is limited to 8 bits (rather than 12 bits) giving an offset of 0-255 bytes.
  - The register form cannot have a shift applied to it.

2.10.8.8 Effect of Endianess
- The ARM can be set up to access its data in either little or big endian format.
- Little Endian :
  - Least significant byte of a word is stored in bits 0-7 of an addressed word.
- Big Endian :
  - Least significant byte of a word is stored in bits 24-31 of an addressed word.
- This has no real relevance unless data is stored as words and then accessed in smaller sized quantities (halfwords or bytes).
  - Which byte/halfword is accessed will depend on the endianess of the system involved.

2.10.8.8.1 Endianess Example

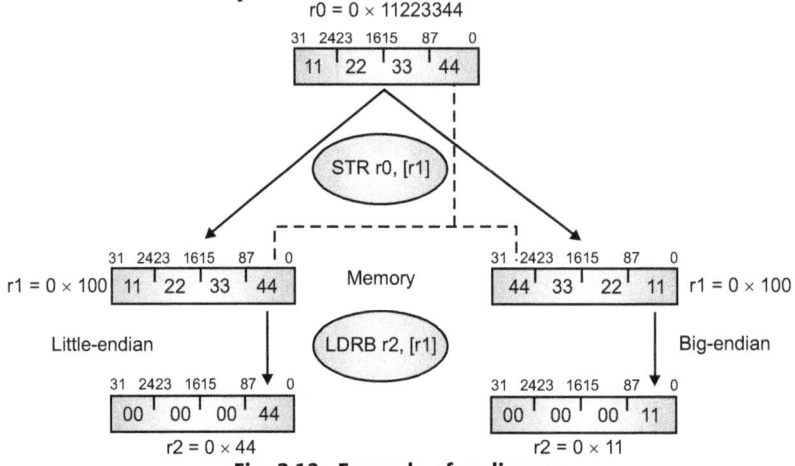

Fig. 2.12 : Example of endianess

2.10.8.9 Block Data Transfer

- The Load and Store Multiple instructions (LDM / STM) allow between 1 and 16 registers to be transferred to or from memory.
- The transferred registers can be either :
  - Any subset of the current bank of registers (default).
  - Any subset of the user mode bank of registers when in a priviledged mode (postfix instruction with a '^').

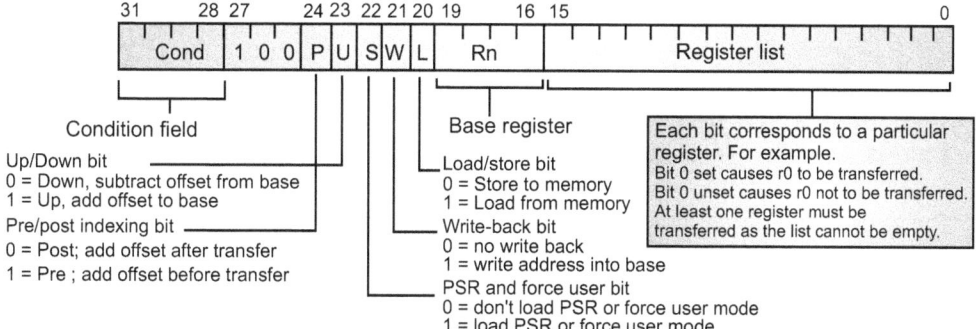

Fig. 2.13 : Format of data processing instruction

- **Base Register used to determine where Memory Access should occur.**
  - There are 4 different addressing modes allow increment and decrement inclusive or exclusive of the base register location.
  - Base register can be optionally updated following the transfer (by appending it with an '!'.
  - Lowest register number is always transferred to/from lowest memory location accessed.
- **These instructions are very efficient for**
  - Saving and restoring context.
    - For this useful to view memory as a stack.
  - Moving large blocks of data around memory
    - For this useful to directly represent functionality of the instructions.

2.10.9 Stack

- A stack is an area of memory which grows as new data is "pushed" onto the "top" of it, and shrinks as data is "popped" off the top.
- Two pointers define the current limits of the stack.
  - A base pointer.
    - Used to point to the "bottom" of the stack (the first location).

- A stack pointer.
  - Used to point the current "top" of the stack.

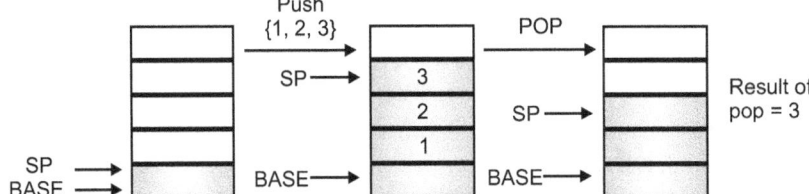

Fig. 2.14 : Stack example

2.10.9.1 Stack Operation

- Traditionally, a stack grows down in memory, with the last "pushed" value at the lowest address. The ARM also supports ascending stacks, where the stack structure grows up through memory.
- The value of the stack pointer can either :
  - Point to the last occupied address (Full stack) and so needs pre-decrementing (i.e. before the push).
  - Point to the next occupied address (Empty stack) and so needs post-decrementing (i.e. after the push).
- **The stack type to be used is given by the postfix to the instruction :**
  - STMFD / LDMFD : Full Descending stack.
  - STMFA / LDMFA : Full Ascending stack.
  - STMED / LDMED : Empty Descending stack.
  - STMEA / LDMEA : Empty Ascending stack.

Note : ARM Compiler will always use a Full descending stack.

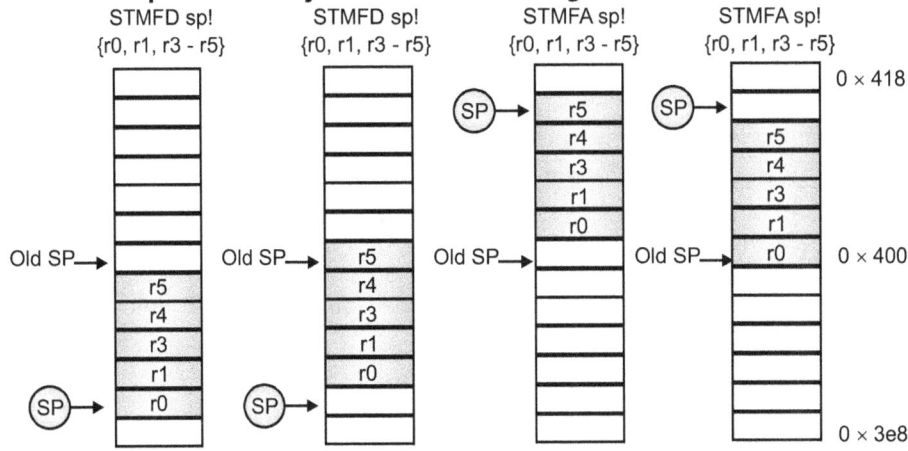

Fig. 2.15 : Stack example of postfix instruction

2.10.9.2 Stacks and Subroutines

- One use of stacks is to create temporary register workspace for subroutines. Any registers that are needed can be pushed onto the stack at the start of the subroutine and popped off again at the end so as to restore them before return to the caller :

  STMFD sp!,{r0-r12, lr}   ; stack all registers.
  ....   ; and the return address.
  ....
  LDMFD sp!,{r0-r12, pc}   ; load all the registers.
                            ; and return automatically.

- See the chapter on the ARM Procedure Call Standard in the SDT Reference Manual for further details of register usage within subroutines.
- If the pop instruction also had the 'S' bit set (using '^') then the transfer of the PC when in a priviledged mode would also cause the SPSR to be copied into the CPSR (see exception handling module).

2.10.9.3 Direct Functionality of Block Data Transfer

- When LDM / STM are not being used to implement stacks, it is clearer to specify exactly what functionality of the instruction is : i.e. specify whether to increment / decrement the base pointer, before or after the memory access.
- In order to do this, LDM / STM support a further syntax in addition to the stack one :
  - STMIA / LDMIA : Increment After
  - STMIB / LDMIB : Increment Before
  - STMDA / LDMDA : Decrement After
  - STMDB / LDMDB : Decrement Before

2.10.9.4 Swap and Swap Byte Instructions

- Atomic operation of a memory read followed by a memory write which moves byte or word quantities between registers and memory.
- Syntax :
  - SWP{<cond>}{B} Rd, Rm, [Rn].

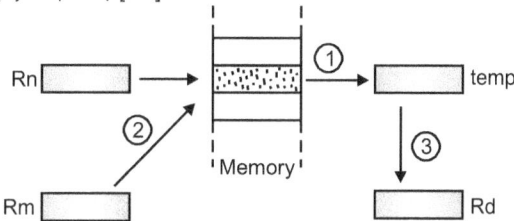

Fig. 2.16 : Example of swap instruction

- Thus to implement an actual swap of contents make Rd = Rm.
- The compiler cannot produce this instruction.

2.10.10 Software Interrupt (SWI)

- In effect, a SWI is a user-defined instruction.
- It causes an exception trap to the SWI hardware vector (thus causing a change to supervisor mode, plus the associated state saving), thus causing the SWI exception handler to be called.
- The handler can then examine the comment field of the instruction to decide what operation has been requested.
- By making use of the SWI mechanism, an operating system can implement a set of privileged operations which applications running in user mode can request.

2.10.11 Read Only and Read Write Memory

The two memory areas defined by the compiler are 'Readonly' for code and 'Read/ write' for data. Usually this corresponds to ROM and RAM phyrsical system. RAM is used for intermediate result, for temporary storage, etc., as this is volatile memory. We can store data permanently in the readonly memory, process it and copy it in RAM. In the readonly memory, data is written using directives like DCD, DCW etc. From there, it is copied to read-write memory using load and store instructions.

Example 2.1 :

```
    AREA FIRST, CODE,
    ENTRY
    LDR R7, = NUMS      ;load the address of NUMS in R7
    LDR R8, = NUMS1     ;load the address of NUMS1 in R8
    LDR R9, = NUMS2     ;load the address of NUMS2 in R9
    LDR R1,[R7]         ;load the word to R1.
    STR RI, [R9]        ;store the word in R1 in NUMS2
    STR Ri , [R8]       ;store the word in R1 in NUMS1
STOP   B STOP
NUMS DCD 653451134
       AREA SECOND, DATA,
NUMS2    SPACE 60
NUMS1DCD 0
END
```

READ WRITE to the address ;1,d the rens ;1---ad the load the art :..rd ?1 ;storethE.- *crd ;store the 10-15, three memory areas have been defined : in read only and two in read write memory. What is accomplished is just the transfer of a word from read only memory to read write memory. In read write memory, one part is a space of 60 bytes, The next is a word space which is initialized to O. After the execution of the program, the number 653451134 is copied to both these spaces.

Example 2.2 :

```
        AREA STRIN1 , CODE, READONLY
        ENTRY
STRT    LDR R1 = SOURCE         ;pointer to source string
        LDR R0, = DESTIN        ;pointer to destination string
        BL COPY                 ;call procedure for copying
STOP    B STOP                  ;last line of execution
COPY    LDR13 R2, [R1] ,#1      ;Load byte and update address.
        STRES P2, [R0] ,#1      ;Store byte and update address.
        CMP R2, #0              ;Check for 0
        BNE COPY                ;repeat until the string is over
        MOV PC,LR               ;return to calling program
        SOURCE DCB "I am sam",0
        AREA STRIN2,DATA,READWRITE
DESTIN  DCB 0
        END
```

Example 2.3 : uses many of the programming aspects that we have been discussing so far. Let's have a look at the important features of this program we have been discussing;

- There is an ASCII string written in readonly memory using the DCB directives. Such a string is enclosed in double quotes and each character is a byte.
- One readonly and one read/write memory areas have been defined.
- After the ASCII string, a 0 is used as a terminating character. The arrival of this 0 to R2 is used to check whether the required transfer of the string is done.
- The instructions for loading and storing are suffixed by 'B' which indicates that only a byte is transferred.
- Post-indexed mode of addressing is used for load and store. The address need to be incremented only by 1, as only a byte is transferred.
- The instructions for loading and storing are in a procedure named COPY. The procedure is 'called' by the BL instruction which does branching and also copies the current PC to the link register. The last line of the procedure is copying the LR back to PC. This constitutes the 'return' to the main program.

2.10.12 Multiple Register Load Store

- Transfer a block of data more efficiently.
- Used for procedure entry and exit for saving and restoring workspace registers and the return address.

Multiple Load/Store Register

    LDM   ; load multiple registers.

    STM   ; store multiple registers.

- The LDM Instruction : it has the syntax :

    LDM{cond}address-mode Rn{!},reg-listt{^}.

- Rn is the base register for the load operation.
- The address stored in this register is the starting address for the load operation.
- There can be a number of modes for specifying the address.
- register-list is a comma-delimited list of symbolic register names and register ranges enclosed in braces.
- There must be at least one register in the list. Register ranges are specified with a dash. For example, {RO-R5, R9} is a list. the ^ option is relevant for interrupts.
- Write back is not to be specified if the base register Rn is in register-list. Multiple register load means that multiple memory locations are to be accessed, and loaded into multiple registers.
- There is 'Base register' acting as a pointer for the first memory location to be accessed. This register is then incremented or decremented to point to the next memory addresses.
- There are four options for handling this. The base register can be incremented or decremented by 4 (one word needs four addresses) for each register in the operations, and decrement can occur before or after the operation.
- The suffixes for these option are as follows :

Suffix	Meaning
IA	; increase after.
IB	; increase before.
DA	; decrease after.
DB	; decrease before.

2.10.12.1 The STM Instruction

- This has the same format as the LDNI instruction.
- Consider the instruction STMIA R1, tR2-R41.

- This will be equivalent to the instructions STR R2, [R1] After the sequences of four stores are over, the base content does not vary, however, If you need it to be changed to that of the final address, the writeback operator "!" is to be used.
- So write the instruction as STMIA R1!,{R2-R4} Now let's use the LDM and STM instructions to simply Example 2.2 transfers bytes from one portion of memory (Readonly) to another portion (Read/write). But the multiple load/store instructions can be used only for words (32-bits).

2.11 ARM-9

- ARM9 is an ARM architecture 32-bit RISC CPU family.
- The ARM9 processor family enables single processor solutions for microcontroller, DSP and Java applications, offering savings in chip area and complexity, power consumption, and time-to-market.
- The ARM9 DSP-enhanced processors are well suited for applications requiring a mix of DSP and microcontroller performance.
- The ARM9 family is the most popular ARM processor family ever 250+ silicon licensees 100+ licensees of the ARM926EJ-S processor.
- ARM9 processors continue to be successfully deployed across a wide range of products and applications.
- The ARM9 family offers proven, low risk and easy to use designs which reduce costs and enable rapid time to market.
- The ARM9 processor family includes ARM926EJ-S™, ARM946E-S™ and ARM968E-S™ processors.
- ARM9 processors are at the heart of advanced digital products across multiple applications.

ARM9 family processors deliver deterministic high performance and flexibility for demanding and cost-sensitive embedded applications. The rich DSP extensions available remove the need for a separate DSP in the SoC design. In addition, the PPA is ideally suited to a wide range of applications.

2.11.1 ARM9 Family Technical Features

- Based on ARMv5TE architecture.
- Efficient 5-stage pipeline for faster throughput and system performance.
- Fetch/Decode/Execute/Memory/Writeback.
- Supports both ARM and Thumb instruction sets.
- Efficient ARM-Thumb interworking allows optimal mix of performance and code density.
- Harvard architecture - Separate Instruction and Data memory interfaces.

- Increased available memory bandwidth.
- Simultaneous access to I and D memory.
- Improved performance.
- 31 × 32-bit registers.
- 32-bit ALU and barrel shifter.
- Enhanced 32-bit MAC block.

The ARM9 family includes the ARM968E-S, the ARM946E-S and the ARM26EJ-S processors.

1. ARM968E-S

Smallest footprint ARM9 processor with DSP enhancements, for low power, data intensive, embedded real-time applications.

The smallest and lowest power ARM9 processor is ideal for many real time type applications. The processor operates efficiently from the Tightly Coupled Memory that can easily be integrated through standard interfaces.

2. ARM946E-S

DSP enhanced cached processor with an MPU for real-time applications running an RTOS.

A real time oriented processor with optional caches interfaces plus a full Memory Protection Unit. This processor is useful in applications where the majority of code exists in main memory and is loaded into cache on demand, while key exception handing code and data can be maintained locally in Tightly Coupled Memory.

3. ARM926EJ-S

Application processor with Java acceleration, DSP extensions and an MMU, for OS based applications.

The ARM926EJ-S is the entry point processor capable of supporting full Operating System including Linux, WindowsCE, and Symbian. As such this processor is ideal for many applications requiring a full Graphical User Interface.

2.11.2 ARM9 Family Processor Naming - ARM9xxE(J)-S

- **E** - DSP extensions.
  - Enhanced instructions for efficient fractional saturating arithmetic.
  - Single cycle 32 × 16 multiplier implementation.
  - 32 × 16 and 16 × 16 multiply instructions.
  - Count leading zeros instruction.

- **J** - Java acceleration through Jazelle.
  - Embedded Jazelle hardware acceleration Java performance of ~1300CM @ 220MHz.
  - Reduced complexity and power consumption over a typical Java hardware coprocessor solution.
  - Available on the ARM926EJ-S processor only.
- **S** - Fully synthesizable.

2.12 ARM CORTEX-M

The ARM Cortex - M3 processor is the industry-leading 32-bit processor for highly deterministic real-time applications, specifically developed to enable partners to develop high-performance low-cost platforms for a broad range of devices including microcontrollers, automotive body systems, industrial control systems and wireless networking and sensors. The processor delivers outstanding computational performance and exceptional system response to events while meeting the challenges of low dynamic and static power constraints. The processor is highly configurable enabling a wide range of implementations from those requiring memory protection and powerful trace technology to cost sensitive devices requiring minimal area.

2.12.1 Why Cortex-M3?

Delivering Higher Performance and Richer Features

Introduced in 2004 and recently updated with new technologies and configurability, the Cortex-M3 is the mainstream ARM processor developed specifically with microcontroller applications in mind.

Performance and Energy Efficiency

With high performance and low dynamic power consumption the Cortex-M3 processor delivers leading power efficiency. Coupled with integrated sleep modes and optional state retention capabilities the Cortex-M3 processor ensures there is no compromise for applications requiring low power and excellent performance.

Full Featured

The processor executes Thumb-2 instruction set for optimal performance and code size, including hardware division, single cycle multiply and bit-field manipulation. The Cortex-M3 NVIC is highly configurable at design time to deliver up to 240 system interrupts with individual priorities, dynamic reprioritization and integrated system clock.

Rich Connectivity

The combination of features and performance enables Cortex-M3 based devices efficiently to handle multiple I/O channels and protocol standards such as USB OTG (On-The-Go).

Table 2.13 : ARM Cortex-M3 Features

ARM Cortex-M3 Features	
ISA Support	Thumb / Thumb-2.
Pipeline	3-stage.
Performance Efficiency	3.32 CoreMark/MHz*.
Performance Efficiency	1.25 / 1.50 / 1.89 DMIPS/MHz**.
Memory Protection	Optional 8 region MPU with sub regions and background region.
Interrupts	Non-maskable Interrupt (NMI) + 1 to 240 physical interrupts.
Interrupt Priority Levels	8 to 256 priority levels.
Wake-up Interrupt Controller	Up to 240 Wake-up Interrupts.
Sleep Modes	Integrated WFI and WFE Instructions and Sleep On Exit capability. Sleep and Deep Sleep Signals. Optional Retention Mode with ARM Power Management Kit.
Bit Manipulation	Integrated Instructions and Bit Banding
Enhanced Instructions	Hardware Divide (2-12 Cycles), Single-Cycle (32x32) Multiply, Saturated Math Support.
Debug	Optional JTAG and Serial-Wire Debug Ports. Up to 8 Breakpoints and 4 Watchpoints.
Trace	Optional Instruction Trace (ETM), Data Trace (DWT), and Instrumentation Trace (ITM).

2.13 CASE STUDY OF BEAGAL-BONE BLACK

Beagle Bone Black is a $45 community-supported development platform for developers and hobbyists. This version contains many improvements over the previous Beagle Bone, including more and faster RAM, 2 GB of eMMC flash on-board, processor speed increase to 1 GHz, and a micro-HDMI port for video out. Power consumption is also lower, with the board only requiring 210-460mA @5V depending on activity and processor speed. The board comes with a USB-A to mini-B cable to power the board and get started right away.

2.13.1 The Beagle Bone Black Features

- TI Sitara AM3359 1-GHz superscalar ARM Cortex-A8.
- 2 × 200 MHz ARM7 programmable real-time coprocessors.

- 512-MB DDR3L RAM.
- 2 GB eMMC.
- PowerVR SGX 530 GPU, LCD expansion header, micro HDMI.
- Stereo audio-out via HDMI.
- 1x USB 2.0 host port.
- 1x USB 2.0 device port.
- On-chip 10/100 Ethernet, not off of USB.
- MicroSD slot.
- Add-on "capes" for expansion, compatible with original Bone capes.
- 1 power LED and 4 user controllable LEDs via GPIO.
- Industry standard 3.3V I/Os on the expansion headers with easy-to-use 0.1" spacing
- Multiple I/O bus : GPMC (nand), MMC, SPI, I2C, CAN, McASP, MMC, 4 Timers, XDMA interrupt.
- 5 serial ports (1 via debug header, 4 more on side headers).
- 65 GPIO pins.
- 8 PWM outputs
- 7 12-bit A/D converters (1.8V max)
- Board size : 3.4" × 2.1"

2.13.2 Beagle Bone Black Key Component Locations

Here are the locations of the key components on the Rev A5A.

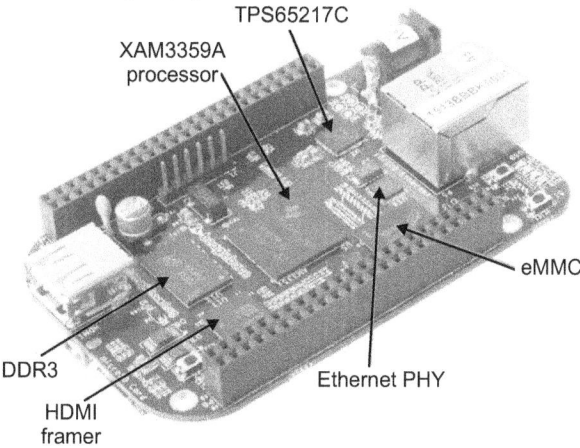

Fig. 2.17 : Beagle bone black key component locations

2.13.3 Beagle Bone Black Connector and Switch Locations

Below is the location of the connectors and switches on the Rev A5A board. The Power Button and Battery Connections are new additions to the Rev A5A.

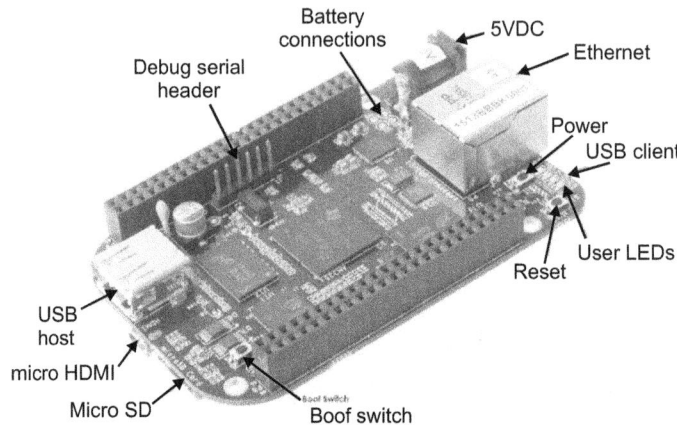

Fig. 2.18 : Beagle bone black connector and switch locations

2.13.4 U-BOOT

- Understanding the boot up mechanism of the Beagle Black Bone is important to be able to modify it. As we later want to change the Linux Kernel itself we need to know how it is started by the Beagle Bone.
- The AM335x processor on the Beagle Bone Black has many configurable options of the AM335x ARM Cortex-A8 Microprocessors Technical Reference Manual. The Beagle Black Bone provides by alternative boot sequences which are selectable by the boot switch (S2). In default mode (S2 not pressed) it tries to boot from :
  1. MMC1 (onboard eMMC),
  2. MMC0 (microSD),
  3. UART0,
  4. USB0.
- Usually it will find something in the on board eMMC and boot from there. If S2 is pressed during power-up the boot sequence is changed to,
  1. SPI0,
  2. MMC0 (microSD),
  3. UART0,
  4. USB0.
- As there is usually nothing bootable found on SPI0 it will boot from the microSD card. The onboard eMMC or an external microSD card have to be formatted in a special way for the AM335x processor to find its boot file, which is described very good on the MMC boot format wiki page at TI. If the AM335x processor finds a valid formatted MMC it searchings for a file named MLO on the first partition and if it is found it boots from that file.

- This is very U-Boot kicks in. U-Boot is a very versatile boot loader which can be used on the Beagle Bone Black. U-Boot provides this MLO file as a second-stage boot-loader which then loads the actual U-Boot which has to be provided as a file named U-Boot.bin in the same directory. U-Boot itself will then look for a file named uEnv.txt for further configuration and then act upon it.

2.13.4.1 Formatting a microSD card

Now as we have the theoretical background, let's try it our self. The following steps were all done on a (virtual) Ubuntu Linux system. Our microSD card is connected to /dev/sdb as has a size of 16 GB. The content of the SD card fill be deleted during this procedure. Instead of calculating the exact partitions sizes needed as explained by the MMC boot format wiki page we use a script which does everything for use. Download, make it executable and run it by

wget http://dev.gentoo.org/~armin76/arm/beaglebone/mkcard.sh

chmod +x mkcard.sh

sudo ./mkcard.sh /dev/sdb

Be sure to have /dev/sdb pointing to your microSD card and not anything else! In the output of the script you can see the partition table it created and in our case it was a primary FAT23 partition of 72261 blocks in size and a Linux ext4 partition of 15478627 blocks in size :

1024+0 records in

1024+0 records out

1048576 bytes (1.0 MB) copied, 0.447124 s, 2.3 MB/s

Disk /dev/sdb doesn't contain a valid partition table

DISK SIZE - 15931539456 bytes

CYLINDERS - 1936

Checking that no-one is using this disk right now ...

OK

Disk /dev/sdb: 1936 cylinders, 255 heads, 63 sectors/track

sfdisk: ERROR: sector 0 does not have an msdos signature

 /dev/sdb: unrecognized partition table type

Old situation:

No partitions found

New situation:

Units = cylinders of 8225280 bytes, blocks of 1024 bytes, counting from 0

Device Boot	Start	End	#cyls	#blocks	Id	System
/dev/sdb1 *	0+	8	9-	72261	c	W95 FAT32 (LBA)
/dev/sdb2	9	1935	1927	15478627+	83	Linux
/dev/sdb3	0	-	0	0	0	Empty
/dev/sdb4	0	-	0	0	0	Empty

Successfully wrote the new partition table

Re-reading the partition table ...

If you created or changed a DOS partition, /dev/foo7, say, then use dd(1) to zero the first 512 bytes: dd if=/dev/zero of=/dev/foo7 bs=512 count=1 (See fdisk(8).)

umount: /dev/sdb1: not mounted

mkfs.fat 3.0.26 (2014-03-07)

mkfs.fat: warning - lowercase labels might not work properly with DOS or Windows

umount: /dev/sdb2: not mounted

mke2fs 1.42.9 (4-Feb-2014)

Filesystem label=rootfs

OS type: Linux

Block size=4096 (log=2)

Fragment size=4096 (log=2)

Stride=0 blocks, Stripe width=0 blocks

969136 inodes, 3869656 blocks

193482 blocks (5.00%) reserved for the super user

First data block=0

Maximum filesystem blocks=3963617280

119 block groups

32768 blocks per group, 32768 fragments per group

8144 inodes per group

Superblock backups stored on blocks:
    32768, 98304, 163840, 229376, 294912, 819200, 884736, 1605632, 2654208

Allocating group tables : done.

Writing inode tables : done.

Creating journal (32768 blocks): done.

Writing superblocks and filesystem accounting information: done .

Now you can mount the boot partition manually or replug the microSD card as most systems will mount it then automatically.

2.13.4.2 Compiling U-Boot

- The next step is to compile U-Boot. As we need to cross compile this for the Beagle Bone Black we need a suitable compiler. On Ubuntu this can be installed relatively easy by sudo apt-get install gcc-arm-linux-gnueabihf.
- Now we clone the git repository, create a default configuration and cross compile it for the Beagle Bone Black by,

    git clone git://git.denx.de/u-boot.git && cd u-boot

    make am335x_boneblack_defconfig

    ARCH=arm CROSS_COMPILE=arm-linux-gnueabi- make

- We should get a MLO and u-boot.bin file in the current directory and can copy those onto the boot partition of microSD card.

2.13.4.3 Configuring U-Boot

To configure U-Boot we create a file uEnv.txt on the boot partition and fill it, e.g. with

console=ttyO0,115200n8

ipaddr=192.168.23.2

serverip=192.168.23.1

rootpath=/exports/rootfs

netargs=setenv bootargs console=${console} ${optargs} root=/dev/nfs

nfsroot=${serverip}:${rootpath},${nfsopts} rw

ip=${ipaddr}:${serverip}:192.168.23.1:255.255.255.0:beaglebone:eth0:none:192.168.23.1

netboot=echo Booting from network ...; tftp ${loadaddr} ${bootfile}; tftp ${fdtaddr} ${fdtfile}; run netargs; bootz ${loadaddr} - ${fdtaddr}

uenvcmd=run netboot

to instruct U-Boot to get the Linux Kernel and device tree via TFTP. The details are depending on your configuration :).

2.13.4.4 Booting

Finally we can now boot from our microSD card. To see the actual boot process a RS232 cable like the TTL-232R-3V3 from FTDI is very handy. Just plug it to the J1 connector and open a serial terminal of your choice. Plug in the microSD card and hold down the S2 boot switch to force booting from the microSD card. You will see hopefully something like

U-Boot SPL 2014.10-rc1 (Aug 22 2014 - 19:20:25)

reading u-boot.img

reading u-boot.img

```
U-Boot 2014.10-rc1 (Aug 22 2014 - 19:20:25)
I2C:   ready
DRAM:  512 MiB
MMC:   OMAP SD/MMC: 0, OMAP SD/MMC: 1
Using default environment
Net:   not set. Validating first E-fuse MAC
cpsw, usb_ether
Hit any key to stop autoboot:  0
switch to partitions #0, OK
mmc0 is current device
SD/MMC found on device 0
reading uEnv.txt
454 bytes read in 4 ms (110.4 KiB/s)
Loaded environment from uEnv.txt
Importing environment from mmc ...
Running uenvcmd ...
Booting from network ...
cpsw Waiting for PHY auto negotiation to complete. done
link up on port 0, speed 100, full duplex
Using cpsw device
TFTP from server 192.168.23.36; our IP address is 192.168.23.30
Filename 'zImage'.
Load address : 0x82000000
Loading : #################################################################
         #################################################################
         #################################################################
         #################################################################
         #################################################################
         #################################################################
         #################################################################
         #################################################################
```

done

Bytes transferred = 6342632 (60c7e8 hex)

link up on port 0, speed 100, full duplex

Using cpsw device

TFTP from server 192.168.23.36; our IP address is 192.168.23.30

Filename 'am335x-boneblack.dtb'.

Load address : 0x88000000

Loading : #######

    1.2 MiB/s

done

Bytes transferred = 31882 (7c8a hex)

Kernel image @ 0x82000000 [0x000000 - 0x60c7e8]

Flattened Device Tree blob at 88000000

  Booting using the fdt blob at 0x88000000

  Loading Device Tree to 8fff5000, end 8ffffc89 ... OK

Starting kernel ...

where we first can see of the U-Boot SPL (MLO file) and then afterwards U-Boot itself. Then it reads the uEnv.txt configuration file and acts upon it.

2.13.4.5 Always Boot From MicroSD

If you always want to boot from your microSD card you can invalidate the boot partition on the onboard eMMC. Then the AM335x processor will always fail back to the second boot option in the default order which is the microSD card. This can be done easily by booting your favourite Linux distribution on the Beagle Bone Black .

QUESTIONS

1. Explain Stand-Alone Processors.
2. Explain in detail Integrated Processors.
3. Differentiate RISC Vs CISC.
4. Explain Arm Architecture.
5. Explain Arm Assembly Language.

6. Explain data types of Arm Assembly Language.
7. Explain Instruction set and draw figure of instruction set.
8. Explain Conditional Execution with example.
9. Explain Data processing Instruction.
10. Explain Load and store instruction.
11. Explain Read-only and Read-write memory instruction.
12. Explain Multiple Register Load Store.

UNIT III

EMBEDDED LINUX KERNEL

3.0 INTRODUCTION

This chapter presents some basic information to help you Open Source Development Linux, different Tool chain Understanding. This chapter introduces a Linux Kernal Initialization. Many fundamental concepts can present challenges to newcomer to embedded systems development. We take a detailed look at the mechanisms and processes used during kernel initialization; it gives more valuable architectural features and the scope of this book.

3.1 LINUX STANDARD BASE (LSB)

- The **Linux Standard Base** (**LSB**) is a joint project by several Linux distributions. A Linux distribution (often called distro for short) is an operating system made as a collection of software based around the Linux kernel and often around a package management system.
- Linux distributions are available for a wide variety of systems, from embedded devices and personal computers up to the powerful supercomputers with specialised functionalities (for example, Rocks Cluster Distribution), or down to small embedded systems) under the organizational structure of the Linux Foundation to standardize the software system structure, including the file system hierarchy used in the GNU/Linux operating.
- The LSB is based on the POSIX specification, the Single UNIX Specification, and several other open standards, but extends them in certain areas.
- The Linux Standard Base was created to lower the overall costs of supporting the Linux platform. By reducing the differences between individual Linux distributions, the LSB greatly reduces the costs involved with porting applications to different distributions, as well as lowers the cost and effort involved in after-market support of those applications.
- The goal of the LSB is to develop and promote a set of open standards that will increase compatibility among Linux distributions and enable software applications to run on any compliant system even in binary form.
- In addition, the LSB will help coordinate efforts to recruit software vendors to port and write products for Linux Operating Systems.

The LSB Specifies for Example
- Standard libraries.
- A number of commands and utilities that extend the POSIX standard.

- The layout of the file system hierarchy.
- Run levels the printing system.
- Including spoolers such as CUPS.
- Tools like Foomatic.
- Several extensions to the X Window System.
  The command **lsb_release-a** is available in many systems to get the LSB version details, or can be made available by installing *lsb-release*.
- The LSB is designed to be binary-compatible and produce stable application binary interface (ABI) for independent software vendors. To achieve backward compatibility, each subsequent version is purely additive. In other words, interfaces are only added, not removed.
- The LSB adopted an interface deprecation policy to give application developers enough time in case an interface is removed from the LSB. This allows the developer to rely on every interface in the LSB for a known time and also to plan for changes, without being surprised. Interfaces are only removed after having been marked "deprecated" for at least three major versions, or roughly six years.

ISO Standard

The LSB is registered as an official ISO standard The main parts of it are :

- **ISO/IEC 23360-1 : 2006** Linux Standard Base (LSB) core specification 3.1 - Part 1: Generic specification
- **ISO/IEC 23360-2 : 2006** Linux Standard Base (LSB) core specification 3.1 - Part 2: Specification for IA-32 architecture
- **ISO/IEC 23360-3 : 2006** Linux Standard Base (LSB) core specification 3.1 - Part 3: Specification for IA-64 architecture
- **ISO/IEC 23360-4 : 2006** Linux Standard Base (LSB) core specification 3.1 - Part 4: Specification for AMD64 architecture
- **ISO/IEC 23360-5 : 2006** Linux Standard Base (LSB) core specification 3.1 - Part 5: Specification for PPC32 architecture
- **ISO/IEC 23360-6 : 2006** Linux Standard Base (LSB) core specification 3.1 - Part 6: Specification for PPC64 architecture
- **ISO/IEC 23360-7 : 2006** Linux Standard Base (LSB) core specification 3.1 - Part 7: Specification for S390 architecture
- **ISO/IEC 23360-8 : 2006** Linux Standard Base (LSB) core specification 3.1 - Part 8: Specification for S390X architecture
- There is also ISO/IEC TR 24715 : 2006 which identifies areas of conflict between ISO/IEC 23360 (the Linux Standard Base 3.1 specification) and the ISO/IEC 9945 : 2003 (POSIX) International Standard.
- ISO/IEC 23360 and ISO/IEC TR 24715 can be freely downloaded from ISO website.

3.2 OSDL (OPEN SOURCE DEVELOPMENT LAB)

Linus Torvalds, the creator of Linux - is dedicated to accelerating the growth and adoption of Linux. Founded in 2000 by CA, Hitachi, HP, IBM, Intel and NEC, OSDL is a non-profit organization at the center of Linux supported by a global consortium of more than 70 of the world's largest Linux customers and IT industry leaders. OSDL sponsors industry-wide initiatives around Linux in telecommunications, in the enterprise data center and on corporate desktops. The Lab also provides Linux expertise and computing and test facilities in the United States and Japan available to developers around the world. The Open Source Development Labs, Inc. (OSDL) is a non-profit organization whose purpose is to promote the growth and adoption of Linux and other open source software at the enterprise level.

In pursuit of this goal, the OSDL provides developers of open source software with enterprise-level hardware to support enterprise and telecommunications applications. It also reports on testing of open source software and sponsors key industry projects, including industry initiatives to enhance Linux for use in corporate data centers, in telecommunications networks and on the desktop.

In addition, the OSDL attempts to focus Linux-industry investment on areas of the greatest need to facilitate growth, and it provides practical guidance to its members on working effectively with the Linux development community. OSDL is a registered trademark of Open Source Development Labs, Inc. Linux is a registered trademark of Linus Torvalds. Third party marks and brands are the property of their respective holders.

3.3 OSDL'S MOBILE LINUX INITIATIVE

OSDL Targets Next-Generation Handsets with Mobile Linux Initiative New working group supports growing opportunity for Linux in mobile market; more than 2.8 billion mobile phones expected to be in use by 2009. BEAVERTON, Ore., October 17, 2005.

- The Open Source Development Labs (OSDL), a global consortium dedicated to accelerating the adoption of Linux the Mobile Linux Initiative (MLI), focused on accelerating the adoption of Linux in the rapidly-growing mobile market. OSDL is creating MLI in response to input from its membership and the growing global demand for Linux-based mobile platform requirements.

- "Linux provides mobile device manufacturers with a powerful platform and Unmatched interoperability to deliver new capabilities in advanced handsets," said Stuart Cohen, CEO of OSDL.

- In much the same way that the OSDL Carrier Grade Linux working group helped accelerate Linux adoption in telecommunications network infrastructure, we believe that MLI will create the ideal forum where device manufacturers, network operators and developers can focus specifically on Linux and open source applications to move mobile handsets to the next level of functionality and profitability."

- The MLI working group is designed to maximize the market opportunity for Linux-based devices. MLI participants will work on operating system technical challenges, foster development of applications for Linux-based mobile devices, deliver requirements definition documents and use cases, and host complementary open source projects that support the initiative. OSDL is a proven launch pad for Linux technology and collaboration.
- Carrier Grade Linux is a perfect example of an OSDL initiative that has been widely accepted by the industry.

3.3.1 OSDL MLI - Bridging Gaps

In October 2005, OSDL launched its fourth and latest working group, the Mobile Linux Initiative. MLI includes members from all levels of the mobile telephony ecosystem chipset makers, Linux distribution and platform suppliers, middleware ISVs, handset manufacturers, integrators, carriers, and operators. Dubbed "Carrier Grade Linux for handsets" by several OSDL members, MLI will strive to address the platform challenges described in this article "from the kernel up" to accelerate Linux adoption on mobile phones and other converged voice and data devices.

In contrast to other industry groups, MLI intends to focus on solution creation, not merely publishing APIs and new standards that can end up as unfunded mandates. To that end, MLI members are today marshaling resources to create unique implementations to meet handset OEM, carrier, and operator needs, to foster the advance of existing Open Source projects, and to open existing internal technologies for the benefit of the MLI audience and the community in general.

3.3.2 Technical Challenges

Experienced handset makers like Motorola, NEC, and Panasonic have clearly demonstrated that Linux-based mobile telephony is a reality. However, these companies and other established OEMs, as well as new entrants in the handset market, want the process of building Linux-based handsets to be easier, with faster time-to-market and better price-performance. In particular, they want to reduce the hardware BOM (Bill of Materials) burden needed to support a Linux-based phone stack, and to optimize the performance of key technologies. As a result, at its most recent face-to-face meeting in Tokyo, OSDL's MLI agreed to focus on the following technical areas :

- Development Tools.
- I/O and Networking.
- Memory Management.

- Multimedia.
- Performance.
- Power Management.
- Security.
- Storage.

3.3.3 Security

Mobile device security breaks out into several distinct areas, and mobile OEM seek standard solutions to the following issues :

Wireless Network Security

While the wireless networks that carry mobile traffic are theoretically "closed," they can be compromised, both in terms of access to client and infrastructure devices, and to the streams of voice and data that they carry. This area, however, is usually the purview of carriers and operators, who present fairly well-defined requirements to handset OEMs. At present, OEMs seem content with how a Linux-based phone fits into their wireless (GPRS/CDMA) security implementations. However, with the addition of Wi-Fi and Bluetooth to handsets, a new set of concerns arise, especially after accounts of phonebook cracking and other skullduggery via Bluetooth.

Content Security

Handset suppliers have requirements to protect both users personal content (phonebooks, e-mail etc.) and commercial content (movies music, and other copyrighted material) that are increasingly ubiquitous on smart phones. While a range of strong encryption technology is readily available for Linux, OEMs aver that the same is not true for broader DRM and other content protection needs.

Physical Access

Unlike the remote servers and clients that populate other networks, phones are by definition "handy" – that is, the so-called "black hats" can use physical means to crack device integrity and security. Opening the "clamshell" plastic that protects a phone's innards can also expose peripheral interface pins and allow probing and malicious signal injection. Phones can also be baked – literally heated up – and dropped, shocked, or similarly abused to induce failure modes that further enable circumvention of security precautions.

Exploit Resilience

Security measures focus on limiting access, often creating a false sense of security on the devices themselves. Moreover, embedded tool kit makers usually ship their tools and platforms with the security minimized or disabled to facilitate development, leaving the final secure configuration and deployment up to OEMs, integrators, and their customers. Misconfiguring firewalls, failing to apply up-to-date security patches, leaving a single physical port exposed, or running multiple functions as root (all common with embedded applications) can lead to deploying easily exploitable devices, and both leaving the phones and networks open to compromise.

3.3.4 Storage

Local storage on mobile devices resides in a mix of Flash, RAM, and remote stores. Linux does present a range of embedded file systems – CramFS, JFFS2, YAFFS, RAMFS, pRAMFS and also semi-proprietary Flash file schemata from Intel, M-Systems, etc. However, device OEMs report a range of performance issues around journaling, mount time, wear leveling, and support for both NAND and NOR devices.

3.3.5 Memory Management

Mobile device memory management has its own unique, non-standard requirements. These include non-contiguous physical memory; heterogeneous memory types like volatile DRAM, battery-backed RAM, NAND and NOR Flash; application and OS execute in place; strong protection of base software, and field upgradable downloads of both platform and application software. Another key memory management concern is out-of-memory handling. In enterprise Linux systems, low memory invokes a "reaper" that terminates "stale" processes to free up RAM; criteria for reaping in a phone must disallow disruption of phone service or other compromised handset performance.

3.3.6 Multimedia

For smart phones and many mid-tier phones, OEMs need to port or fully reimplement complex audio and video capabilities to a Linux platform. Barriers to building next-generation multimedia start with the lack of a unified multimedia framework for Linux (which competing platforms have) and also include the lack of Linux-based DRM software, as well as issues surrounding patent-bearing media formats. Eschewing DRM and using patent-free open media formats isn't a realistic alternative for device OEMs.

3.3.7 Performance

For both the GPRS interface, and for other capabilities like multi-media, Linux still needs to move in the direction of RTOS like responsiveness. Linux must meet deadlines and switch context adroitly in systems where clocks can slow to conserve battery power from 400 MHz peak performance down to 40 MHz (or even 0 MHz) and back in response to policies and hardware events. The current generation of ARM-based phone chipsets also feature silicon crammed with peripherals. So C peripherals and secondary cores can be highly stateful with hard-to-program shared memory interfaces connecting them. These channels constitute a troublesome.

3.3.8 MLI Goals/ Mission

To accelerate Linux adoption in the mobile space

- Identify and address technical and non-technical industry requirements.
- Create and foster implementations in Open Source.
- Advocate and explain industry needs to the kernel/Open Source community.
- Promote mobile Linux (including educating carriers about the benefits of Open Source).
- Clarify legal and regulatory issues surrounding mobile phones as they relate to Linux and Open Source.
- Enable and foster pre-platform developer ecosystem.

3.4 LINUX BACKGROUND

Linus Torvalds wrote the original version of Linux while he was a student at the University of Helsinki in Finland. His work began in 1991. In August of that year, Torvalds posted this now-famous announcement on comp.os.minix :

Special About Linux

- Multiple choices vs. sole source.
- Source code freely available.
- Robust and reliable.
- Modular, configurable, scalable.
- Superb support for networking and Internet.
- No runtime licenses.
- Large pool of skilled developers.

Since that initial release, Linux has matured into a full-featured operating system with reliability, robustness, open source and high-end features that competitor those of the best commercial operating systems. By some estimates, more than half of the Internet servers on the Web are powered by Linux servers. It is no secret that the online search giant Google uses a large collection of low-cost PCs running a fault-tolerant version of Linux to implement its popular search engine.

3.4.1 Kernel Versions

You can obtain the source code for a Linux kernel and complementary components in numerous places. Your local bookstore might have several versions as companion CDROMs in books about Linux. You can also download the kernel itself or even complete Linux distributions from numerous locations on the Internet. The official home for the Linux kernel is www.kernel.org. You will often hear the terms mainline source or mainline kernel, referring to the source trees found at kernel.org.

For quite some time now, Linux version 2.6 has been the current version. Early in the development cycle, the developers chose a numbering system designed to differentiate between kernel source trees intended for development and experimentation and source trees intended to be stable, production-ready kernels. The numbering scheme contains a major version number, a minor version number, and a sequence number.

Before Linux version 2.6, if the minor version number is even, it denotes a production Kernel; if it is odd, it denotes a development kernel. For example:

- **Linux 2.4.x**-Production kernel
- **Linux 2.5.x**-Experimental (development)
- **Linux 2.6.x**-Production kernel

Currently, the Linux 2.6 kernel has no separate development branch. All new features, Enhancements, and bug fixes are funneled through a series of gatekeepers who Ultimately filter and push changes to the top-level Linux source trees maintained by Andrew Morton and Linus Torvalds. It is easy to tell what kernel version you are working with. The first few lines of the top-level *makefile*4 in a kernel source tree detail the exact kernel version represented by a given instance. It looks like this for the 2.6.30 kernel release:

VERSION = 2

PATCHLEVEL = 6

SUBLEVEL = 30

EXTRAVERSION =

NAM E = Man-Eating Seals of Antiquity

Later in the same make file, these macros are used to form a version-level macro, like this ***KERNELVERSION=$(VERSION).$(PATCHLEVEL).$(SUBLEVEL)$(EXTRAVERSION).***

This macro is used in several places in the kernel build system to indicate the kernel version. Its use has diminished in more recent kernels to a few locations in the scripts directory.

It has been replaced by a more complete descriptive string called KERNELRELEASE. This string contains the kernel version as well as a tag that correlates to a source control revision level that comes from git, the source control system adopted for Linux. KERNELRELEASE is used in several places within the kernel source tree. This macro is also built into the kernel image so that it can be queried from the console. You can check the kernel release string from a command prompt on a running Linux system like this :

$ cat /proc/version

Linux version 2.6.13 (chris@pluto) (gcc version 4.0.0 (DENX ELDK 4.0

4.0.0)) #2 Thu Feb 16 19:30:13 EST 2006

One final note about kernel versions: You can make it easy to keep track of the kernel version in your own kernel project by customizing the EXTRAVERSION field. For example, if you are developing enhancements for some new kernel feature, you might set EXTRAVERSION to something like this:

EXTRAVERSION=-foo

Later, when you use cat /proc/version, Later, when you use cat /proc/version, you would see Linux version 2.6.13-foo, and this would help you distinguish between development versions of your own kernel.

3.4.2 Kernel Source Repositories

- The official home of the Linux kernel source code is www.kernel.org.
- There you can find both current and historical versions of the Linux kernel, as well as numerous patches.
- The primary FTP repository, found at ftp.kernel.org, contains subdirectories going all the way back to Linux version 1.0. kernel.org is the primary focus of the ongoing development activities within the Linux kernel.
- If you download a recent Linux kernel from kernel.org, you will find files in the source tree for over 20 different architectures and sub-architectures. Several other development trees support the major architectures. One of the reasons is simply the sheer volume of developers and changes to the kernel.
- If every developer on every architecture submitted patches to a single source tree, the maintainers would be inundated with changes and patch management and would never get to do any feature development.
- Several other public source trees exist outside the mainline kernel.org source, mostly for architecture-specific development.
  For example, a developer working on the MIPS architecture might find a suitable kernel at *www.linux-mips.org*. Normally, work done in an architecture tree is eventually submitted to the mainline kernel maintainers.
- If you are wondering how to find a kernel for your particular application, the bestway to proceed is to obtain the latest stable Linux source tree. Check to see if support for your particular processor exists, and then search the Linux kernel mailing lists for any patches or issues related to your application. Also find the mailing list that most closely matches your interest, and search that archive as well.

3.4.3 Using Git to Download a Kernel

To download the latest Linux kernel a simple way is to use git.

This utility has become the tool of choice for source control management in the Linux kernel community. The repositories of most modern desktop distributions contain a version of git.

For example, on Ubuntu,5 enter the following command to install git on your desktop or laptop PC.

```
$ sudo apt-get install git-core
```

After git has been properly installed on your system, you can use the git clone command to *lone* a git source tree:

```
$ git clone
git://git.kernel.org/pub/scm/linux/kernel/git/torvalds/linux-2.6.git linux-2.6
```

3.5 LINUX KERNEL CONSTRUCTIONS

- In few sections explore the layout, organization, and construction of the Linux kernel. Armed with this knowledge, you will find it much easier to navigate this large, complex source code base. Over time, significant improvements have been made to the organization of the source tree, especially in the architecture branch, which contains support for numerous architectures and machine types.

3.5.1 Top-Level Source Directory

- In every case, we are referring to the highest-level directory contained in the kernel source tree. On any given machine, it might be located anywhere, but on a desktop Linux workstation, it is often found in /usr/src/linux-x.y.z, where x.y.z represents the kernel version.
- We use the shorthand .../ to represent the top-level kernel source directory. The top-level kernel source directory contains the following subdirectories. (We have omitted the no directory entries in this listing, as well as directories used for source control, for clarity and brevity.)

  ```
  arch / firmware/ kernel/ scripts/
  block / fs/ lib/ security/
  crypto / include/ mm/ sound/
  Documentation/ init/ net/ usr/
  Drivers / ipc/ samples/ virt/
  ```

- Many of these directories contain several additional levels of subdirectories containing source code, make files, and configuration files. By far the largest branch of the Linux kernel source tree is found under .../drivers.
- Here you can find support for the various Ethernet network cards, USB controllers, and the numerous hardware devices that the Linux kernel supports. As you might imagine, the .../arch subdirectory is the next largest, containing support for more than 20 unique processor architectures.
- Additional files found in the top-level Linux subdirectory include the top-level makefile, a hidden configuration file (*dot-config*, introduced in the kernel build system "The Dot-Config"), and various other informational files not involved in the build itself.

Finally, two important build targets are found in the top-level kernel source tree after a successful build: System.map and the kernel proper, vmlinux.

3.5.2 Compiling the Kernel

- Understanding a large body of software such as Linux can be a daunting task. It is too large to simply "step through" the code to follow what is happening. Multithreading and preemption add to the complexity of analysis. In fact, even locating the entry point (the first line of code to be executed upon entry to the kernel) can be challenging.
- One of the more useful ways to understand the structure of a large binary image is to examine its build components.
- The output of the kernel build system produces several common files, as well as one or more architecture-specific binary modules. Common files are always built regardless of the architecture. Two of the common files are System.map and vmlinux.
- The former is useful during kernel debug and is particularly interesting. It contains a human-readable list of the kernel symbols and their respective addresses. The latter is an architecture-specific *ELF* 7 file in executable format.
- It is produced by the top-level kernel makefile for every architecture. If the kernel was compiled with symbolic debug information, it will be contained in the vmlinux image. In practice, although it is an ELF executable, this file is virtually never booted directly, as you will see shortly.
- Listing 3-1 is a snippet of output resulting from executing make in a recent kernel tree configured for the ARM XScale architecture. The kernel source tree was configured for the ADI Engineering Coyote reference board based on the Intel IXP425 network processor using the following command

$ make ARCH=arm CROSS_COMPILE=xscale_be- ixp4xx_defconfig

- This command does not build the kernel; it prepares the kernel source tree for the XScale architecture, including an initial default configuration for this architecture and Processor,
- It builds a default configuration (the dot-config file) that drives the kernelbuild, based on the defaults found in the ixp4xx_defconfig file.

In Listing 3-1, only the first few and last few lines of the build output are shown for this discussion.

LISTING 3-1 Kernel Build Output

```
$ make ARCH=arm CROSS_COMPILE=xscale_be- zImage
CHK      include/linux/version.h
UPD      include/linux/version.h
Generating include/asm-arm/mach-types.h
CHK      include/linux/utsrelease.h
UPD      include/linux/utsrelease.h
SYMLINK include/asm -> include/asm-arm
CC       kernel/bounds.s
GEN      include/linux/bounds.h
CC       arch/arm/kernel/asm-offsets.s
.
. <hundreds of lines of output omitted here>
.
LD       vmlinux
SYSMAP   System.map
SYSMAP   .tmp_System.map
OBJCOPY arch/arm/boot/Image
Kernel:  arch/arm/boot/Image is ready
AS       arch/arm/boot/compressed/head.o
GZIP     arch/arm/boot/compressed/piggy.gz
AS       arch/arm/boot/compressed/piggy.o
CC       arch/arm/boot/compressed/misc.o
AS       arch/arm/boot/compressed/head-xscale.o
AS       arch/arm/boot/compressed/big-endian.o
LD       arch/arm/boot/compressed/vmlinux
OBJCOPY arch/arm/boot/zImage
Kernel:  arch/arm/boot/zImage is ready
```

- Both the desired architecture (ARCH=arm) and the toolchain (CROSS_COMPILE=xscale_be-) are specified on the command line.
- This forces the make utility to use the XScale toolchain9 to build the kernel image and to use the arm-specific branch of the kernel source tree for architecture-dependent portions of the build.

- We also specify a target called zImage. This target is used in "Kernel Initialization." Modern kernels today build the proper default targets without specifying the make target, so you might not need to specify zImage or any other targets.
- The next thing you might notice is that the actual commands used for each step have been hidden and replaced with a shorthand notation.
- The motivation behind this was to clean up the build output to draw more attention to intermediate build issues, particularly compiler warnings. In earlier kernel source trees, each compilation or link command was output to the console verbosely, which often required several lines for each step. The end result was virtually unreadable, and compiler warnings slipped by unnoticed in the noise. The new system is definitely an improvement, because any anomaly in the build process is easily spotted. If you want or need to see the complete build step, you can force verbose output by defining V=1 on the make command line:

    $ **make ARCH=arm CROSS_COMPILE=xscale_be- V=1 zImage**
- We have omitted most of the actual compilation and link steps in Listing 3-1 for clarity. (This particular build contained more than 1,000 individual compile, link, and other commands. That would have made for a long listing indeed.) After all the intermediate files and library archives have been built and compiled, they are put together in one large ELF build target called vmlinux. Although it is architecture-specific, vmlinux is a common target. It is produced for all supported Linux architectures, and it lands in the top-level kernel source directory for easy reference.

3.5.3 The Kernel Proper : vmlinux

The vmlinux file is the actual *kernel proper*. It is a fully stand-alone, monolithic ELF image. That is, the vmlinux binary contains no unresolved external references. When caused to execute in the proper context (by a bootloader designed to boot the Linux kernel), it boots the board on which it is running, leaving a completely functional kernel. Actually, this vmlinux ELF target is rarely used directly. It is almost always used in compressed form, which is produced from the final steps shown in Listing 3-1. In keeping with the philosophy that to understand a system you must first understand its parts, let's look at the construction of the vmlinux kernel object. Listing 3-1. reproduces the actual link stage of the build process that resulted in the vmlinux ELF object. We have formatted it with line breaks (indicated by the UNIX line-continuation character, \) to make it more readable, but otherwise it is the exact output produced by the vmlinux link step in the build process from Listing 3-1. If you were building the kernel by hand, this is the link command you would issue from the command line.

LISTING 3-2 Link Stage: vmlinux

```
$ xscale_be-ld -EB -p --no-undefined -X -o vmlinux   \
-T arch/arm/kernel/vmlinux.lds                       \
arch/arm/kernel/head.o                               \
arch/arm/kernel/init_task.o                          \
init/built-in.o                                      \
--start-group                                        \
usr/built-in.o                                       \
arch/arm/kernel/built-in.o                           \
arch/arm/mm/built-in.o                               \
arch/arm/common/built-in.o                           \
arch/arm/mach-ixp4xx/built-in.o                      \
arch/arm/nwfpe/built-in.o                            \
kernel/built-in.o                                    \
mm/built-in.o                                        \
fs/built-in.o                                        \
ipc/built-in.o                                       \
security/built-in.o                                  \
crypto/built-in.o                                    \
block/built-in.o                                     \
arch/arm/lib/lib.a                                   \
lib/lib.a                                            \
arch/arm/lib/built-in.o                              \
lib/built-in.o                                       \
drivers/built-in.o                                   \
sound/built-in.o                                     \
firmware/built-in.o                                  \
net/built-in.o                                       \
--end-group                                          \
.tmp_kallsyms2.o
```

3.5.4 Kernel Image Components

You can see that the vmlinux image consists of several composite binary from Listing 3-2, images.

- Important is to understand the top-level view of what components makeup the kernel. The first line of the link command in Listing 3-2 specifies the output file (-o vmlinux). The second line specifies the *linker script* file (-T vmlinux.lds), a detailed recipe for how the kernel binary image should be linked. The third and subsequent lines in Listing 3-2 specify the object modules that form the resulting binary image. Notice that the first object specified is head.o.
- This object was assembled from .../arch/arm/kernel/head. S, an architecture-specific assembly language source file that performs very low-level kernel initialization. If you were searching for the first line of code to be executed by the kernel, it would make sense to start your search here, because it will ultimately be the first code found in the binary image created by this link stage.
- The next object, *init_task.o*, sets up initial thread and task structures that the kernel requires. Following this is a large collection of object modules, each having a common name: built-in.o. You will notice, however, that each built-in.o object comes from a specific part of the kernel source tree, as indicated by the path component preceding the *built-in.o* object name.
- These are the binary objects that are included in the kernel image. An illustration might help make this more clear. Fig. 3.1 illustrates the binary makeup of the vmlinux image. It contains a section for each line of the link stage. It is not to scale because of space considerations, but you can see the relative sizes of each functional component.
- Some components are tiny. For example, sound and firmware are each 8 bytes in this build, because they are empty object files. (Sound is compiled as modules, and this build has no firmware.)
- It might come as no surprise that the three largest binary components are the file system code, network code, and all the built-in drivers. If you take the kernel code and the architecture-specific kernel code together, this is the next-largest binary component.
- The scheduler, process and thread management, timer management, and other core kernel functionality. Naturally, the kernel contains some architecture-specific functionality, such as low-level context switching, hardware-level interrupt and timer processing, processor exception handling, and more. This is found in .../arch/arm/kernel. you will find it easy to navigate others.

To help you understand the breakdown of functionality in the kernel source tree, Table 3.1 lists each component in Fig. 3.1 and describes each binary element that makes up the vmlinux image.

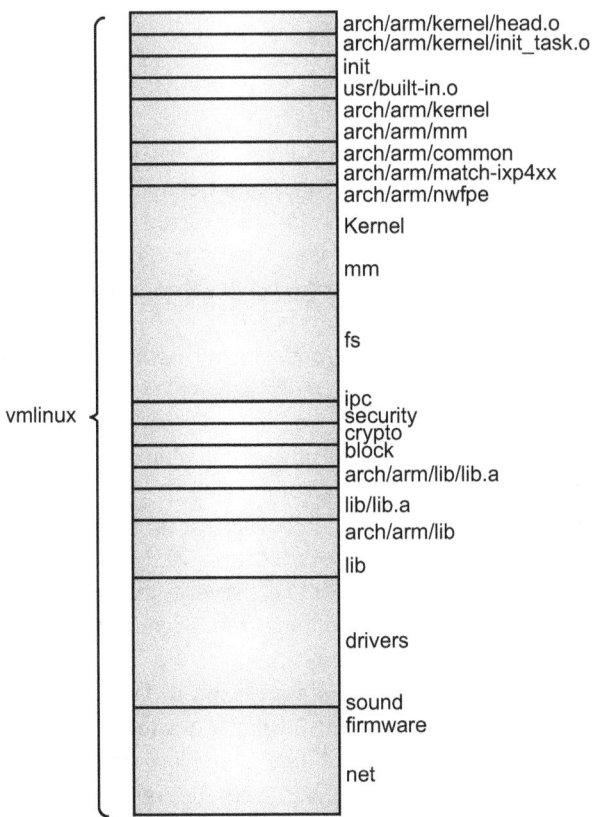

Fig. 3.1 : Vmlinux image components

Table 3.1 : Vmlinux Image Components

Sr. No	Component	Description
1.	arch/arm/kernel/head.o	Kernel-architecture-specific startup code.
2.	arch/arm/kernel/init_task.o	Initial thread and task structs required by the kernel.
3.	init/built-in.o	Main kernel initialization code.
4.	usr/built-in.o	Built-in initramfs image.
5.	arch/arm/kernel/built-in.o	Architecture-specific kernel code
6.	arch/arm/mm/built-in.o	Architecture-specific memory-management code.
7.	arch/arm/common/built-in.o	Architecture-specific generic code. Varies by architecture.

…Cont.

8.	arch/arm/mach-ixp4xx/built-in.o	Machine-specific code, usually initialization.
9.	arch/arm/nwfpe/built-in.o	Architecture-specific floating-point emulation code.
10.	kernel/built-in.o	Common components of the kernel itself.
11.	mm/built-in.o	Common components of memory-management code.
12.	fs/built-in.o	File system code.
13.	ipc/built-in.o	Interprocess communications, such as SysV IPC.
14.	security/built-in.o	Linux security components.
15.	crypto/built-in.o	Cryptographic API.
16.	block/built-in.o	Kernel blocks layer core code.
17.	arch/arm/lib/lib.	a Architecture-specific common facilities. Varies by Archi
18.	lib/lib.a	Common kernel helper functions.
19.	arch/arm/lib/built-in.o	Architecture-specific helper routines.
20.	lib/built-in.o	Common library functions.
21.	drivers/built-in.o	All the built-in drivers. Does not include loadable modules.
22.	sound/built-in.o	Sound drivers.
23.	firmware/built-in.o	Driver firmware objects.
24.	net/built-in.o	Linux networking.
25.	.tmp_kallsyms2.o	Kernel Symbol table.

When we speak of the kernel proper, this vmlinux image (found at the top-level kernel directory) is being referenced. As mentioned earlier, very few platforms boot this image directly. For one thing, the image that we use to boot is almost universally compressed.

At a bare minimum, a boot loader must decompress the image. Many platforms require some type of stub bolted onto the image to perform the decompression.

3.5.5 Subdirectory Layout

Now that you have seen the components that make up the kernel image, let's take a look at a representative kernel subdirectory. Listing 3-3 details the contents of the *mach-ixp4xx* subdirectory. This directory exists under the .../arch/arm architecture-specific branch of the source tree.

LISTING 3-3 Kernel Subdirectory

```
$ ls -l ./arch/arm/mach-ixp4xx
total 204
-rw-r--r-- 1 chris chris 1817   2009-11-19 17:12 avila-pci.c
-rw-r--r-- 1 chris chris 4610   2009-11-19 17:12 avila-setup.c
-rw-r--r-- 1 chris chris 11812  2009-11-19 17:12 common.c
-rw-r--r-- 1 chris chris 12979  2009-11-19 17:12 common-pci.c
-rw-r--r-- 1 chris chris 1459   2009-11-19 17:12 coyote-pci.c
-rw-r--r-- 1 chris chris 3158   2009-11-19 17:12 coyote-setup.c
-rw-r--r-- 1 chris chris 1898   2009-11-19 17:12 dsmg600-pci.c
-rw-r--r-- 1 chris chris 7030   2009-11-19 17:12 dsmg600-setup.c
-rw-r--r-- 1 chris chris 1625   2009-11-19 17:12 fsg-pci.c
-rw-r--r-- 1 chris chris 6622   2009-11-19 17:12 fsg-setup.c
-rw-r--r-- 1 chris chris 1490   2009-11-19 17:12 gateway7001-pci.c
-rw-r--r-- 1 chris chris 2646   2009-11-19 17:12 gateway7001-setup.c
-rw-r--r-- 1 chris chris 12280  2009-11-19 17:12 goramo_mlr.c
-rw-r--r-- 1 chris chris 2623   2009-11-19 17:12 gtwx5715-pci.c
-rw-r--r-- 1 chris chris 3935   2009-11-19 17:12 gtwx5715-setup.c
drwxr-xr-x 3 chris chris 4096   2009-11-19 17:12 include

-rw-r--r-- 1 chris chris 1794   2009-11-19 17:12 ixdp425-pci.c
-rw-r--r-- 1 chris chris 7430   2009-11-19 17:12 ixdp425-setup.c
-rw-r--r-- 1 chris chris 1354   2009-11-19 17:12 ixdpg425-pci.c
-rw-r--r-- 1 chris chris 21560  2009-11-19 17:12 ixp4xx_npe.c
-rw-r--r-- 1 chris chris 9350   2009-11-19 17:12 ixp4xx_qmgr.c
-rw-r--r-- 1 chris chris 6422   2009-11-19 17:12 Kconfig
-rw-r--r-- 1 chris chris 1319   2009-11-19 17:12 Makefile
-rw-r--r-- 1 chris chris 57     2009-11-19 17:12 Makefile.boot
-rw-r--r-- 1 chris chris 1751   2009-11-19 17:12 nas100d-pci.c
-rw-r--r-- 1 chris chris 7764   2009-11-19 17:12 nas100d-setup.c
-rw-r--r-- 1 chris chris 1561   2009-11-19 17:12 nslu2-pci.c
-rw-r--r-- 1 chris chris 6732   2009-11-19 17:12 nslu2-setup.c
-rw-r--r-- 1 chris chris 1468   2009-11-19 17:12 wg302v2-pci.c
-rw-r--r-- 1 chris chris 2585   2009-11-19 17:12 wg302v2-setup.c
```

This chapter provides an overview of the Linux capabilities you should be familiar with in order to develop embedded Linux systems. It covers aspects such as cross-development tool chains, configuring and building the Linux kernel, development of a simple character device driver and provides an overview of some key kernel services that can be used within your device drivers.

3.5.6 Why Tool Chain?

- Necessary to build OS and apps.
- Most common are the GNU tools.
- Normally the target and host machine compile and build with the same environment.
  - **Host :** the machine on which you develop your applications.
  - **Target :** the machine for which you develop your applications.
  - Native development (same) or cross development (different).
  - In order to build the operating system and applications, you need a tool chain. The tool chain provides the assembler, compiler, and linker, along with a number of other utilities needed to develop a Linux based system.
  - The most common tool chain used in Linux systems are the GNU tools. The compiler is provided by GNU Compiler Collection (GCC) *(http://gcc.gnu.org/)*, and the assembler, linker, library, and object manipulation tools are provided by the GNU binutils project *(http://www.gnu.org/software/binutils/)*.
  - These tool chains are available in source form but in many cases are also available in binary form. It is simple to install GNU tool chains on a Linux desktop distribution.
  - Desktop distributions include a software package manager such as apt for debian-based hosts or yum for rpm type distributions. The command sudo apt-get install gcc will install the IA-32 GCC binary tool chain for a *debian/Ubuntu-based* system.
  - When you install a tool chain as shown above, you are downloading a binary version of the tool chain from a repository.
  - The binaries were configured and built from a source for the target system you are downloading to. This build process and hosting is carried out by the repository maintainer.
  - Normally, the tool chain being installed has been configured to compile and build applications with the same environment (processor type, 32/64 bit, and so on) as the host downloading the tool chain.
  - The host machine is the machine you develop your applications on. In most cases today that will be an IA-32-based machine running a desktop distribution of Linux such as *Fedora/Centos, Ubuntu, or SUSE/OpenSuse*. In most examples used in the text, we have used an Ubuntu desktop distribution (with no real rationale or preference).
  - The target device is the actual embedded device that you are developing the software for. The device could be based on *IA-32, ARM_, MIPS_, PowerPC_*, or any of

- the other CPU architecture supported by Linux. When the host and target architecture are the same, you are said to be doing native development; however, the target platform architecture does not have to be the same as the host platform architecture (for example, CPU IA-32). When the host and target platforms differ, you are said to be doing cross development.
- In this case, the tool chain that you download and run on your host must be a specialized version capable of executing on the host CPU architecture but building for the target CPU architecture. All of the GNU tools support both native host development and cross-development configurations. If your target embedded device is IA-32 and your host is IA-32, it is still advisable to create a tool chain dedicated to your target and not to rely on your host tools chains. It is convenient for early development, but can cause getting the Tools You can download the source code for binutils and gcc and build the tool chain yourself.
- This can often be very tricky and takes many separate stages (consider the problem of creating a compiler without first having a compiler). There are a number of scripts that greatly simplify the generation of the tool chain.
- At the time of writing, the cross tool-NG is a good option if you just require a tool chain. It cross-builds the tool chain for all architectures supported by GCC. The ct-ng menuconfig line is where you select the target CPU architecture. Below is a Mercurial source code control command to get the source from the source repository system.

```
>hg clone http://crosstool-ng.org/hg/crosstool-ng
>./configure --prefix=/some/place>make
>make install
>export PATH="${PATH}:/some/place/bin"
>cd /your/development/directory
>ct-ng help
>ct-ng menuconfig
>ct-ng build
```

There are four key attributes of the target tool chain that must be selected :
- The target CPU architectures (for example, IA-32, ARM).
- The application binary interface (ABI)/calling conventions (for example, fast call, X.32, System VAMD64 ABI convention and EABI).
- Object format (for example, ELF).
- Target operating system (for example, bare metal/Linux). This is important for calling conventions used to interact with the system.

The output of the build process is placed in your home directory in an x-tools folder. Each tool chain that you select is placed in a configuration specific folder. For example, a generic IA-32 tool chain is placed in the *~/x-tool/i386-unknown-elf/* folder, and a generic ARM tool chain is placed in *~/x-tools/arm-unknown-eabi* folder. In addition to the target architectures, the target application binary interface must also be selected for the tool chain to use. The ABI defines all semantics associated with the construction of binary objects, libraries; inter function calling mechanisms, calls to operating system services, register usage.

There are two versions of ABIs in use on IA-32 systems, a 32-bit and a 64-bit version. The 32-bit version of standard can be found at *http://www.sco.com/developers/devspecs/abi386-4.pdf* and the 64-bit version http://www.x86-64.org/documentation/abi.pdf.

The default ARM tool chain application binary interface is the Embedded Application Binary Interface (EABI). It defines the conventions for files, data types, register mapping, stack frame and parameter passing rules. The EABI is commonly used on ARM and Power PC CPUs. The ARM EABI specification can be found at *http://www.arm.com*.

The primary object format is defined by the Tool Interface Standard – Executable and Linking Format (ELF) *(http://refspecs.freestandards.org/elf/elf.pdf.)*. The standard is composed of books that define the generic ELF format, alongwith extensions of processor architectures and target operating systems. In some cases, there is no target operating system specified or used; this is in effect a generic target. Most tool chains support a non-OS-specific processor-specific target option. This is sometimes known as bare metal.

Table 3.2 : Cross-Tool Chain Program

Executable	Description
add2line	Converts an address into a file name and file line number. It uses debug information to figure out the file name/line number from the executable. This is very useful for debugging crashes, as it can be used to narrow down and finf the cause.
ar	Creates, modifies, and extracts from archives. An archive is a collection of objects or libraries. It provides a simple way to distribute a large number of objects/libraries in a single file.
as	The GNU assembler. The assembler can be used natively and is used to assembly the output of the GCC compiler.
C++filt	Demangles C++ and Jave symbols. C++ and Java languages provide function overloading. This demangless the auto-generated (managed) names produced by the compiler into a human-readable form.
cpp	The C preprocessor, the MACRO preprocessor used by the C compiler prior to compilation. it expands macros, definitions, and so on in the code. The C preprocessor can also be used as a standalone tool.
gcc	The GNU C and C++ compiler. The default invocation of cc performs preprocessing compilation assembly, and linking to generate an executable image.

...Cont.

gcov	Coverage testing tool. Use this tool to analyze your programs, create more efficient code, and discover untested portions of code (from http://gcc.cnu.org/onlinedocs/gcc/Gcov-Introl.html#Gcov-Intro).
gdb	The GNU debugger. It can be used for application/user space and kernel space debugging; it can also be used to communicate with target debug hardware such as JTAG ICEs. IDE wrappers such as DDD also exist to improve usability.
gprof	Display call graph profile data. Profiling allows you to examine the amount of time spent in certain function and frequency of function calls being made.
Id	The GNU linker. The linker combines objects and archives, relocates their data, and resolves symbol references. A map file of the resulting output can be generated and is very useful in understanding the layout of the application.
nm	Lists all the symbols from objects.
objdump	Displays information from objects files: objdump –S <file> dumps the entire object and displays the disassembly object and where possible interleaves this with the source code; objdump -0s vm 1nu × generates a useful file for debugging kernel oops (at least for the statically linder kernel elements).
ranlib	Generates an index to the contents of an archive and stores it in the archive.
readelf	Displays information about ELF files, similar to objdump but displays additional information.
size	Lists the size of sections and to the total size of an object/executable. The sections are text, data and bss. The text section is where the code resides, data is where global and static variables that are program initialized such as char str[] = 'hello world' are stored, and bss are uninitialized variables, such as a global or statics that are not initialized or initialized to zero. The startup code for an application clears the bss section.
strings	Displays any human-readable strings from a file. For an executable or object, it displays strings in the code and any symbol strings in the object.
strip	Removes symbol information from object files.

3.6 KERNEL BUILD SYSTEM

The Linux kernel configuration and build system is rather complicated, as you would expect of software projects containing more than 10 million lines of code. This section covers the foundation of the kernel build system in case you need to customize your build environment.

A recent Linux kernel snapshot showed more than 1,200 makefiles in the kernel source tree, when you understand the structure and operation of the build system. The Linux kernel build system has been significantly updated since the days of Linux 2.4 and earlier. If you are familiar with the older kernel build system, we are sure you will find the new Kbuild system to be a huge improvement.

3.6.1 The Dot-Config

- Introduced earlier, the dot-config file is the configuration blueprint for building a Linux kernel image. You will likely spend significant effort at the start of your Linux project building a configuration that is appropriate for your embedded platform. Several editors, both text-based and graphical, are designed to edit your kernel configuration.
- The output of this configuration exercise is written to a configuration file named .config, located in the top-level Linux source directory that drives the kernel build. You have likely invested a significant amount of time in perfecting your kernel configuration, so you will want to protect it. Several *make* commands delete this configuration.
- File without warning. The most common is *make distclean*. This make target is designed to return the kernel source tree to its pristine, unconfigured state. This includes removing all configuration data from the source tree and, yes, it deletes your preexisting *.config*.

    As you might know, any filename in a Linux file system preceded by a dot is a hidden file in Linux.

- It is unfortunate that such an important file is marked as hidden; this has brought considerable grief to more than one developer. If you execute make dist clean or make improper without having a backup copy of your .config file, you too will share our grief. (You have been warned back up your *.config* file!)
- To understand the .config file, you need to understand a fundamental aspect of the Linux kernel. Linux has a monolithic structure. In other words, the entire kernel is compiled and linked as a single statically linked executable. However, it is possible to compile and *incrementally link*12 a set of sources into a single object module suitable for dynamic insertion into a running kernel. This is the usual method for supporting most common device drivers. In Linux, these are called *loadable modules*.

- They are also generically called device drivers. After the kernel is booted, a special application program is invoked to insert the loadable module into a running kernel. Armed with that knowledge, let's look again at listing 3-4. This snippet of the configuration file (.config) shows a portion of the USB subsystem configuration. The first configuration option, CONFIG_USB=m, declares that the USB subsystem is to be listing 3-4.

LISTING 3-4 Snippet from Linux 2.6 .config

```
...
# USB support
#
CONFIG_USB=m
# CONFIG_USB_DEBUG is not set
# Miscellaneous USB options
#
CONFIG_USB_DEVICEFS=y
# CONFIG_USB_BANDWIDTH is not set
# CONFIG_USB_DYNAMIC_MINORS is not set
# USB Host Controller Drivers
#
CONFIG_USB_EHCI_HCD=m
# CONFIG_USB_EHCI_SPLIT_ISO is not set
# CONFIG_USB_EHCI_ROOT_HUB_TT is not set
CONFIG_USB_OHCI_HCD=m
CONFIG_USB_UHCI_HCD=m
```

Included in this kernel configuration and that it will be compiled as a *dynamically loadable module* (=m), to be loaded sometime after the kernel has booted. The other choice would have been =y, in which case the USB module would be compiled and statically linked as part of the kernel image itself. It would end up in the .../drivers/built-in.o composite binary. The astute reader will realize that if a driver is configured as a loadable module, its code is not included in the kernel proper, but rather exists as a stand-alone object module, a *loadable module*, to be inserted into the running kernel after boot.

Notice in Listing 3-4 the *CONFIG_USB_DEVICEFS=y* declaration. This configuration option behaves in a slightly different manner. In this case, USB_DEVICEFS (as configuration options are commonly abbreviated) is not a stand-alone module, but rather a feature to be enabled or disabled in the USB driver. It does not necessarily result in a module that is compiled into the kernel proper (=y). Instead, it enables one or more features, often represented as additional object modules to be included in the overall USB device driver module. Usually, the help text in the configuration editor, or the hierarchy presented by the configuration editor, makes this distinction clear.

3.6.2 Configuration Editor(s)

- Early kernels used a simple command-line-driven script to configure the kernel.
- This was cumbersome even for early kernels, in which the number of configuration parameters was much smaller.
- This command-line-style interface is still supported, but using it is tedious, to say the least. A typical configuration from a recent kernel requires you to answer more than 900 questions from the command line.
- You enter your choice and then press Enter for each query in the script. Furthermore, if you make a mistake, there is no way to back up; you must start from the beginning. That can be profoundly frustrating if you make a mistake on the 899th entry.
- In some situations, such as building a kernel on an embedded system without graphics, using the command-line configuration utility may be unavoidable, but this author would go to great lengths to find a way around it. The kernel configuration subsystem has several configuration targets. In fact, a recent Linux kernel release included 11 such configuration targets. They are summarized here, from text taken from the output of *make help*:
- *config* - Update current config using a line-oriented program
- *menuconfig* - Update current config using a menu-based program
- *xconfig* - Update current config using a QT-based front end
- *gconfig* - Update current config using a GTK-based front end
- *oldconfig* - Update current config using a provided .config as the base
- *silentoldconfig* - Same as oldconfig but silently
- *randconfig* - New config with random answer to all options
- *defconfig* - New config with default answer to all options
- *allmodconfig* - New config that selects modules, when possible
- *allyesconfig* - New config in which all options are accepted with yes
- *allnoconfig* - New minimal config

The first four of these makefile configuration targets invoke a form of configuration editor, as described in the list. Because of space considerations, we focus our discussion in this chapter and the rest of this book only on the GTK-based graphical front end. Realize that you can use the configuration editor of your choice with the same results. You invoke the configuration editor by entering the command make gconfig from the top-level kernel directory.

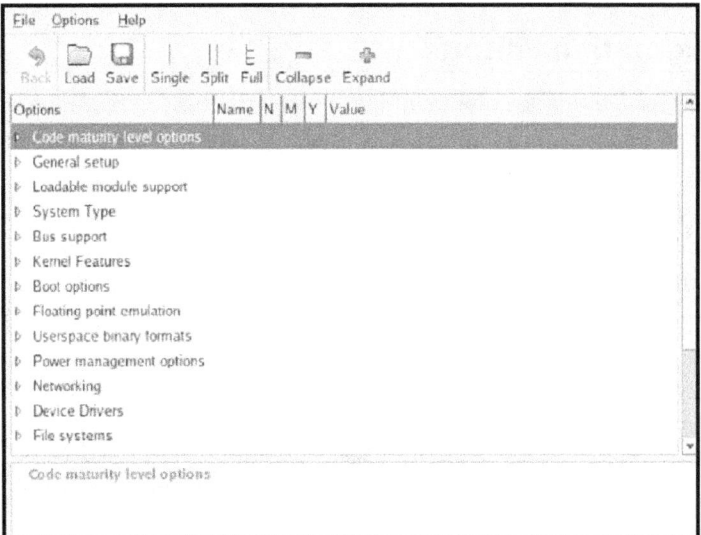

Fig. 3.2 : Top-level kernel configuration

When you exit the configuration editor, you are prompted to save your changes. If you elect to save your changes, the global configuration file .config is updated (or created, if it does not already exist). This .config file, introduced earlier, drives the kernel build via the top-level makefile. Most kernel software modules also read the configuration indirectly via the .config file as follows. During the build process, the .config file is processed into a C header file found in the .../include/linux directory, called autoconf.h. This file is generated automatically. You should never edit it directly, because edits are lost each time a configuration is changed and a new build is started. Many kernel source files include this file directly using the #include preprocessor directive. Listing 3-5 reproduces a section of this header file related to USB support. The kernel build files include this autoconf.h file into every kernel compile command line, using the -include gcc directive as follows :

gcc ... -include include/linux/autoconf.h ... <somefile.c>

This is how the kernel config is accessed by various kernel modules.

LISTING 3-5 Linux autoconf.h

```
$ cat include/linux/autoconf.h | grep CONFIG_USB
#define CONFIG_USB_ARCH_HAS_EHCI 1
#define CONFIG_USB_HID 1
```

```
#define CONFIG_USB_EHCI_BIG_ENDIAN_DESC 1
#define CONFIG_USB_ARCH_HAS_OHCI 1
#define CONFIG_USB_EHCI_BIG_ENDIAN_MMIO 1
#define CONFIG_USB_STORAGE 1
#define CONFIG_USB_SUPPORT 1
#define CONFIG_USB_EHCI_HCD 1
#define CONFIG_USB_DEVICEFS 1
#define CONFIG_USB_OHCI_HCD 1
#define CONFIG_USB_UHCI_HCD 1
#define CONFIG_USB_OHCI_LITTLE_ENDIAN 1
#define CONFIG_USB_ARCH_HAS_HCD 1
#define CONFIG_USB 1
```

If you have not already done so, execute make gconfig in your top-level kernel source directory and poke around this configuration utility to see the large number of subsections and configuration options available to the Linux developer. As long as you do not explicitly save your changes, they will be lost when you exit the configuration editor, so you can safely explore without modifying your kernel configuration.14 Many configuration parameters contain helpful explanatory text, which can add to your understanding of the various configuration options.

3.6.3 Makefile Targets

- If you type make help at the top-level Linux source directory, you are presented with a list of targets that can be generated from the source tree. The most common use of make is to specify no target.
- This generates the kernel ELF file vmlinux and the default binary image for your chosen architecture (for example, bzImage for x86). Specifying make with no target also builds all the device driver modules (kernel loadable modules) specified by the configuration. Many architectures and machine types require binary targets specific to the architecture and bootloader in use. One of the more common architecture-specific targets is zImage.
- In many architectures, this is the default target image that can be loaded and run on the target embedded system. One of the common mistakes that newcomers make is to specify bzImage as the make target.
- The bzImage target is specific to the x86/PC architecture. Contrary to popular myth, the bzImage is not a bzip2-compressed image. It is a big zImage. Without going into the details of legacy PC architecture, it is enough for you to know that a bzImage is suitable only for PC-compatible machines with an industry-standard PC-style BIOS.

- Upon power-on, the bootloader in an embedded system is the first software to get processor control. After the bootloader has performed some low-level hardware initialization, control is passed to the Linux kernel. This can be a manual sequence of events to facilitate the development process (for example, the user types interactive load/boot commands at the bootloader prompt), or it can be an automated startup sequence typical of a production environment.
- Recall that one of the common files built for every architecture is the ELF binary named *vmlinux*. This binary file is the monolithic kernel itself, or what we have been calling the *kernel proper*. In fact, when we looked at its construction in the link stage of *vmlinux*, we pointed out where we might look to see where the first line of code might be found. In most architecture, it is found in an assembly language source file called head.S or a similar filename. In the Power Architecture (powerpc) branch of the kernel, several versions of head. S are present, depending on the processor. For example, the AMCC 440 series processors are initialized from a file called head_44x.S.
- Some architectures and bootloaders can directly boot the vmlinux kernel image.

For example, platforms based on Power Architecture and the U-Boot bootloader usually can boot the *vmlinux* image directly1 (after conversion from ELF to binary, as you will see shortly). In other combinations of architecture and bootloader, additional functionality might be needed to set up the proper context and provide the necessary utilities to load and boot the kernel.

LISTING 3-6 Final Kernel Build Sequence: ARM/IXP425 (Coyote)

$ make ARCH=arm CROSS_COMPILE=xscale_be- zImage

... < many build steps omitted for clarity>
LD vmlinux
SYSMAP System.map
SYSMAP .tmp_System.map
OBJCOPY arch/arm/boot/Image
Kernel: arch/arm/boot/Image is ready
AS arch/arm/boot/compressed/head.o
GZIP arch/arm/boot/compressed/piggy.gz
AS arch/arm/boot/compressed/piggy.o
CC arch/arm/boot/compressed/misc.o
AS arch/arm/boot/compressed/head-xscale.o
AS arch/arm/boot/compressed/big-endian.o
LD arch/arm/boot/compressed/vmlinux
OBJCOPY arch/arm/boot/zImage
Kernel: arch/arm/boot/zImage is ready

The vmlinux image is linked. This includes *head.o,piggy.o* and the Architecture specific *head-xscale.o*.

Table 3.3

Vmlinux	Kernel proper, in ELF format, including symbols, comments, debug info (if compiled with g), and architecture-generic components.
System.map	Text-based kernel symbol table for the vmlinux module. .tmp System.map generated only to sanity-check System.map; otherwise, not used in the final build image.
Image	Binary kernel module stripped of symbols, notes, and comments.
head.o	ARM-specific startup code generic to ARM processors. This object is passed control by the bootloader.
piggy.gz	The file Image compressed with gzip.
piggy.o	The file piggy.gz in assembly language format so that it can be linked with a subsequent object, misc.o (see the text).
misc.o	Routines used to decompress the kernel image (piggy.gz) and the source of the familiar boot message Uncompressing Linux . . . Done on some architectures.
head xscale.o	Processor initialization specific to the XScale processor family.
big endian.o	Tiny assembly language routine to switch the XScale processor into big-endian mode.
vmlinux	Composite kernel image. This is an unfortunate choice of names, because it duplicates the name for the kernel proper; the two are not the same. This binary image is the result when the kernel proper is linked with the objects in this table. See the text for an explanation.
zImage	Final composite kernel image loaded by bootloader. See the following text.

The image components and their metamorphosis during the build process leading up to a bootable kernel image. The following sections describe the components and process in detail.

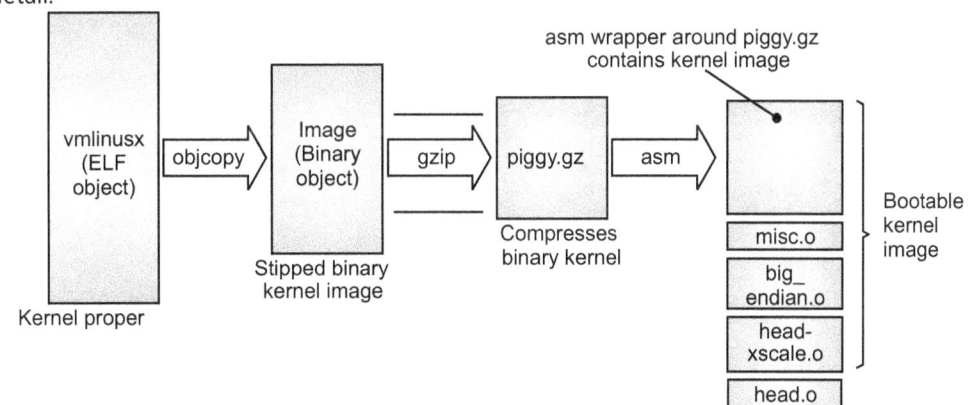

Fig. 3.3 : Composite kernel image construction

3.6.4 The Image Object

After the vmlinux kernel ELF file has been built, the kernel build system continues to process the targets described in Table 3.3. The Image object is created from the *vmlinux* object. Image is basically the vmlinux ELF file stripped of redundant sections (notes and comments) and also stripped of any debugging symbols that might have been present. The following command is used for this purpose: *xscale_be-objcopy -O binary -R .note -R .note.gnu.build-id -R .comment –S* vmlinux arch/arm/boot/Image The -O option tells objcopy to generate a binary file; the -R option removes the ELFsections named .note, .note.gnu.build-id, and .comment; and the -S option is the flag to strip debugging symbols. Notice that objcopy takes the vmlinux ELF image as input and generates the target binary file called Image. In summary, Image is nothing more than the kernel proper converted from ELF to binary form and stripped of debug symbols and the aforementioned .note* and .comment sections.

3.6.5 Architecture Objects

Following the build sequence further, a number of small modules are compiled. These include several assembly language files (head.o, head-xscale.o, and so on) that perform low-level architecture and processor-specific tasks. Each of these objects is summarized in Table 3.3. Of particular note is the sequence creating the object called piggy.o. First, the Image file (binary kernel image) is compressed using this gzip command: cat Image | gzip -f -9 > piggy.gz. This creates a new file called piggy.gz, which is simply a compressed version of the binary kernel Image. You can see this graphically in Fig. 3.3. What comes next is rather interesting. An assembly language file called piggy.S is assembled, which contains a reference to the compressed piggy.gz. In essence, the binary kernel image is being piggybacked as payload into a low-level assembly language *bootstrap loader*. This bootstrap loader initializes the processor and required memory regions, decompresses the binary kernel image, and loads it into the proper place in system memory before passing control to it.

LISTING 3-7 Assembly File Piggy.S

```
.section .piggydata,#alloc
.globl input_data
input_data:
.incbin "arch/arm/boot/compressed/piggy.gz"
.globl input_data_end
input_data_end:
```

This small assembly-language file is simple yet produces a complexity that is not immediately obvious. The purpose of this file is to cause the compressed binary kernel image to be emitted by the assembler as an ELF section called .piggy data. It is triggered by the .incbin assembler preprocessor directive, which can be viewed as the assembler's version of an #include file, except that it expects binary data. In summary, the net result of this assembly language file is to contain the compressed binary kernel image as a payload within another image the bootstrap loader. Notice the labels input data and input_data_end. The bootstrap loader uses these to identify the boundaries of the binary payload the kernel image itself.

3.6.6 Bootstrap Loader

In many architectures use a *bootstrap loader* (or second-stage loader) to load the Linux kernel image into memory. Some bootstrap loaders perform checksum verification of the kernel image, and most decompress and relocate the kernel image. The difference between a bootloader and a bootstrap loader in this context is simple: The bootloader controls the board upon power-up and does not rely on the Linux kernel in any way. In contrast, the bootstrap loader's primary purpose is to act as the *glue* between a bare metal bootloader and the Linux kernel. It is the bootstrap loader's responsibility to provide a proper context for the kernel to run in, as well as perform the necessary steps to decompress and relocate the kernel binary image. It is similar to the concept of a primary and secondary loader found in the PC architecture. Fig. 3.4 makes this concept clear. The bootstrap loader is concatenated to the kernel image for loading.

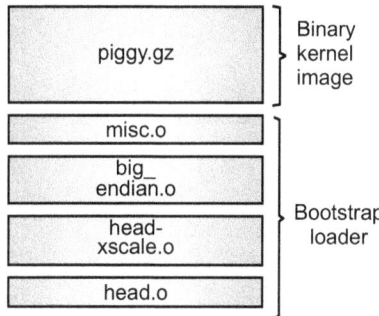

Fig. 3.4 : Composite kernel image for ARM XScale

In the example we have been studying, the bootstrap loader consists of the binary images shown in Fig. 3.4.

The functions performed by this bootstrap loader include the following :

- Low-level assembly language processor initialization, which includes support for enabling the processor's internal instruction and data caches, disabling interrupts, and setting up a C runtime environment.

These include head.o and head-xscale.o.

- Decompression and relocation code, embodied in misc.o.
- Other processor-specific initialization, such as big-endian.o, which enables big endian mode for this particular processor.

It is worth noting that the details we have been examining are specific to the *ARM/XScale* kernel implementation. Each architecture has different details, although the Concepts are similar. Using an analysis similar to that presented here, you can learn the requirements of your own architecture.

3.6.7 Boot Messages

Perhaps you have seen a PC workstation booting a desktop Linux distribution such as Red Hat or SUSE Linux. After the PC's own BIOS messages, you see Linux display a flurry of console messages as it initializes the various kernel subsystems. Significant portions of the output are common across disparate architectures and machines. Two of the more interesting early boot messages are the kernel version string and the *kernel command line*, which is described shortly. Listing 3-8 reproduces the kernel boot messages for the ADI Engineering Coyote Reference Platform booting Linux on the Intel XScale IXP425 processor. The listing has been formatted with line numbers for easy reference.

LISTING 3-8 Linux Boot Messages on IPX425

Using base address 0x01000000 and length 0x001ce114

Uncompressing Linux....... done, booting the kernel.

Linux version 2.6.32-07500-g8bea867 (chris@brutus2) (gcc version 4.2.0
    20070126 (prerelease) (MontaVista 4.2.0-3.0.0.0702771 2007-03-10)) #12 Wed Dec 16
    23:07:01 EST 2009

CPU: XScale-IXP42x Family [690541c1] revision 1 (ARMv5TE), cr=000039ff

CPU: VIVT data cache, VIVT instruction cache

Machine: ADI Engineering Coyote

Memory policy: ECC disabled, Data cache writeback

Built 1 zonelists in Zone order, mobility grouping on. Total pages: 16256

Kernel command line: console=ttyS0,115200 root=/dev/nfs ip=dhcp

PID hash table entries: 256 (order: -2, 1024 bytes)

Dentry cache hash table entries: 8192 (order: 3, 32768 bytes)

Inode-cache hash table entries: 4096 (order: 2, 16384 bytes)

Memory: 64MB = 64MB total

Memory: 61108KB available (3332K code, 199K data, 120K init, 0K highmem)

SLUB: Genslabs=11, HWalign=32, Order=0-3, MinObjects=0, CPUs=1, Nodes=1

Hierarchical RCU implementation.

RCU-based detection of stalled CPUs is enabled.

NR_IRQS:64

Calibrating delay loop... 532.48 BogoMIPS (lpj=2662400)

Mount-cache hash table entries: 512

```
CPU: Testing write buffer coherency: ok
NET: Registered protocol family 16
IXP4xx: Using 16MiB expansion bus window size
PCI: IXP4xx is host
PCI: IXP4xx Using direct access for memory space
PCI: bus0: Fast back to back transfers enabled
SCSI subsystem initialized
usbcore: registered new interface driver usbfs
usbcore: registered new interface driver hub
usbcore: registered new device driver usb
NET: Registered protocol family 8
NET: Registered protocol family 20
NET: Registered protocol family 2
IXP4xx Queue Manager initialized.
NetWinder Floating Point Emulator V0.97 (double precision)
JFFS2 version 2.2. (NAND) (c) 2001-2006 Red Hat, Inc.
io scheduler noop registered
io scheduler deadline registered
o scheduler cfq registered (default)
Serial: 8250/16550 driver, 2 ports, IRQ sharing disabled
serial8250.0: ttyS0 at MMIO 0xc8001000 (irq = 13) is a XScale
console [ttyS0] enabled
Uniform Multi-Platform E-IDE driver
ide-gd driver 1.18
IXP4XX-Flash.0: Found 1 x16 devices at 0x0 in 16-bit bank
Intel/Sharp Extended Query Table at 0x0031
Intel/Sharp Extended Query Table at 0x0031
Using buffer write method
Searching for RedBoot partition table in IXP4XX-Flash.0 at offset 0xfe0000
5 RedBoot partitions found on MTD device IXP4XX-Flash.0
Creating 5 MTD partitions on "IXP4XX-Flash.0":
0x000000000000-0x000000060000 : "RedBoot"
0x000000100000-0x000000260000 : "MyKernel"
0x000000300000-0x000000900000 : "RootFS"
0x000000fc0000-0x000000fc1000 : "RedBoot config"
```

0x000000fe0000-0x000001000000 : "FIS directory"

e100: Intel(R) PRO/100 Network Driver, 3.5.24-k2-NAPI

e100: Copyright(c) 1999-2006 Intel Corporation

ehci_hcd: USB 2.0 'Enhanced' Host Controller (EHCI) Driver

ohci_hcd: USB 1.1 'Open' Host Controller (OHCI) Driver

uhci_hcd: USB Universal Host Controller Interface driver

Initializing USB Mass Storage driver...

usbcore: registered new interface driver usb-storage

USB Mass Storage support registered.

IXP4xx Watchdog Timer: heartbeat 60 sec

usbcore: registered new interface driver usbhid

usbhid: USB HID core driver

TCP cubic registered

NET: Registered protocol family 17

XScale DSP coprocessor detected.

drivers/rtc/hctosys.c: unable to open rtc device (rtc0)

e100 0000:00:0f.0: firmware: using built-in firmware e100/d101m_ucode.bin

e100: eth0 NIC Link is Up 100 Mbps Full Duplex

IP-Config: Complete:

device=eth0, addr=192.168.0.29, mask=255.255.255.0, gw=255.255.255.255,

host=coyote1, domain=, nis-domain=(none),

bootserver=192.168.0.103, rootserver=192.168.0.103, rootpath=

Looking up port of RPC 100003/2 on 192.168.0.103

Looking up port of RPC 100005/1 on 192.168.0.103

VFS: Mounted root (nfs filesystem) on device 0:11.

Freeing init memory: 120K

INIT: version 2.86 booting

... <some userland init messages omitted>

coyote1 login:

The kernel produces much useful information during startup, as shown in Listing 3-8. We study this output in some detail in the next few sections. Line 1 is produced by the Reboot boot loader on the board. Line 2 is produced by the bootstrap loader we presented earlier in this chapter. This message was produced by the decompression loader found in .../arch/arm/boot/compressed/misc.c, in a function called *decompress_kernel()*.

Line 3 of Listing 3-8 is the kernel version string. It is the first line of output from the kernel itself. One of the first lines of C code executed by the kernel *(in .../init/ main.c)* upon entering start_kernel() is as follows:

printk(KERN_NOTICE "%s", linux_banner);

This line produces the output just described—the kernel version string, line 3 of Listing 3-8.

This version string contains a number of pertinent data points related to the kernel image :

- Kernel version: Linux version 2.6.32-07500-g8bea8674.
- Username/machine name where the kernel was compiled.
- Toolchain info: gcc version 4.2.0, supplied by MontaVista Software.
- Build number.
- Date and time the kernel image was compiled.

This is useful information both during development and later in production. All but one of the entries is self-explanatory. The *build number* is simply a tool that the developers added to the version string to indicate that something more substantial than the date and time changed from one build to the next. It is a way for developers to keep track of the build in a generic and automatic fashion. You will notice in this example that this was the twelfth build in this series, as indicated by the #12 on line 3 of listing 3-8. The build number is stored in a hidden file in the top-level Linux directory and is called .version. It is automatically incremented by a build script found in .../scripts/mkversion. In short, it is a numeric string tag that is automatically incremented whenever anything substantial in the kernel is rebuilt. Note that it is reset to #1 on execution of make mrproper.

3.7 KERNEL INITIALIZATION

When the Linux kernel begins execution, it spews out numerous status messages during its rather comprehensive boot process. In the example being discussed here, the Linux kernel displayed approximately 200 printk4 lines before it issues the login prompt. The goal of this exercise is not to delve into the details of the kernel initialization. The goal is to gain a high-level understanding of what is happening and what components are required to boot a Linux kernel on an embedded system.

3.7.1 BIOS Versus Bootloader

- When power is first applied to the desktop computer, a software program called the BIOS immediately takes control of the processor. (Historically, BIOS was an acronym Meaning Basic Input/output Software, but the term has taken on a meaning of its own as the functions it performs have become much more complex than the original implementations.) The BIOS might actually be stored in Flash memory (described shortly)to facilitate field upgrade of the BIOS program itself.

- The BIOS is a complex set of system-configuration software routines that have knowledge of the low-level details of the hardware architecture.
- Most of us are unaware of the extent of the BIOS and its functionality, but it is a critical piece of the desktop computer.
- The BIOS first gains control of the processor when power is applied. Its primary responsibility is to initialize the hardware, especially the memory subsystem, and load an operating system from the PC's hard drive.
- In a typical embedded system (assuming that it is not based on an industry standard x86 PC hardware platform), a bootloader is the software program that performs the equivalent functions. In your own custom embedded system.

Here are some of the more important tasks your bootloader performs on power-up :

- Initializes critical hardware components, such as the SDRAM controller, I/O controllers, and graphics controllers.
- Initializes system memory in preparation for passing control to the operating system.
- Allocates system resources such as memory and interrupt circuits to peripheral controllers, as necessary. Provides a mechanism for locating and loading your operating system image.
- Loads and passes control to the operating system, passing any required startup information. This can include total memory size, clock rates, serial port speeds, and other low-level hardware-specific configuration data. If your embedded system will be based on a custom-designed platform, these bootloader functions must be supplied by you, the system designer. If your embedded system is based on a Commercial Off-The-Shelf (COTS) platform such as an ATCA chassis, 1.

3.7.2 U-Boot

- Many open source and commercial bootloaders are available, and many more one of a kind homegrown design is in widespread use today.
- Most of these have some level of commonality of features. For example, all of them have some capability to load and execute other programs, particularly an operating system. Most interact with the user through a serial port. Support for various networking subsystems (such as Ethernet) is a very powerful but less common feature.
- Many bootloaders are specific to a particular architecture. The capability of a bootloader to support a wide variety of architectures and processors can be an important feature to larger development organizations. It is not uncommon for a single development organization to have multiple processors spanning more than one architecture.
- Investing in a single bootloader across multiple platforms ultimately results in lower development costs.

- This section studies an existing bootloader that has become very popular in the embedded Linux community. The official name of this bootloader is Das U-Boot. It is maintained by Wolfgang Denx and hosted at *www.denx.de/wiki/U-Boot*. U-Boot supports multiple architectures and has a large following of embedded developers and hardware manufacturers who have adopted it for use in their projects and who have contributed to its development.

Obtaining U-Boot

The simplest way to get the U-Boot source code is via git. If you have git installed on your desktop or laptop, simply issue this command:

```
$ git clone git://git.denx.de/u-boot.git
```

This creates a directory called u-boot in the directory in which you executed this command. If you do not have git, or you prefer to download a snapshot instead, you can do so through the git server at denx.de. Point your browser to *http://git.denx.de/* and click the "summary" link on the first project, *u-boot.git*. This takes you to a summary screen and provides a "snapshot" link, which generates and downloads a tarball that you can install on your system. Select the most recent snapshot, which is at the top of the "shortlog" list.

Configuring U-Boot

This configures the U-Boot source tree with the appropriate soft links to select ARM as the target architecture, the ARM926 core, and the 5912 OSK as the target platform.

The next step in configuring U-Boot for this platform is to edit the configuration file specific to this board. This file is found in the U-Boot ../include/configs subdirectory and is called omap5912osk.h. The README file that comes with the U-Boot source code describes the details of configuration and is the best source of this information. (For existing boards that are already supported by U-Boot, it may not be necessary to edit this board-specific configuration file. The defaults may be sufficient for your needs. Sometimes minor edits are needed to update memory size or flash size, because many reference boards can be purchased with varying configurations.) U-Boot is configured using configuration variables defined in a board-specific header file. Configuration variables have two forms. Configuration options are selected using macros in the form of *CONFIG_XXXX*. Configuration settings are selected using macros in the form of CONFIG_SYS_*XXXX*. In general, configuration *options (CONFIG_XXX)* are user-configurable and enable specific U-Boot operational features. Configuration *settings (CONFIG_SYS_XXX)* usually are hardware-specific and require detailed knowledge of the underlying processor and/or hardware platform

U-Boot Monitor Commands

U-Boot supports more than 70 standard command sets that enable more than 150 unique commands using *CONFIG_CMD_** macros. A command set is enabled in U-Boot through the use of configuration setting *(CONFIG_*)* macros. For a complete list from a recent U-Boot snapshot, consult Appendix B, *"U-Boot Configurable Commands."*

Table 3.4 shows just a few, to give you an idea of the capabilities available.

Table 3.4 : Some U-Boot Configurable Commands

Command Set	Description Commands
CONFIG_CMD_FLASH	Flash memory commands
CONFIG_CMD_MEMORY	Memory dump, fill, copy, compare, and so on
CONFIG_CMD_DHCP	DHCP support
CONFIG_CMD_PING	Ping support
CONFIG_CMD_EXT2	EXT2 file system support

To enable a specific command, define the macro corresponding to the command you want. These macros are defined in your board-specific configuration file.

.here you see *CONFIG_CMD_USB, CONFIG_CMD_FAT,* and *CONFIG_CMD_EXT2* being defined conditionally if the board is a 440EP. Instead of specifying each individual CONFIG_CMD_* macro in your own board specific configuration header, you can start from the full set of commands defined *in .../include/config_cmd_all.h*. This header file defines every command available. A second header file, *.../include/config_cmd_default.h,* defines a list of useful default U-Boot command sets such as tftpboot (boot an image from a tftpserver), bootm (boot an image from memory), memory utilities such as md (display memory), and so on. To enable your specific combination of commands, you can start with the default and add and subtract as necessary. the *USB, FAT, and EXT2* command sets to the default. You can subtract in a similar fashion, starting from config_cmd_all.h:

```
#include "condif_cmd_all.h"
#undef CONFIG_CMD_DHCP
#undef CONFIG_CMD_FAT
#undef CONFIG_CMD_FDOS
<...>
```

Take a look at any board-confi guration header file in .../include/configs/ for examples.

Network Operations
- Many bootloaders include support for Ethernet interfaces. In a development environment, this is a huge time saver.
- Loading even a modest kernel image over a serial port can take minutes versus a few seconds over an Ethernet link, especially if your board supports Fast or Gigabit Ethernet. Furthermore, serial links are more prone to errors from poorly behaved serial terminals, line noise, and so on.
- Some of the more important features to look for in a bootloader include support for the BOOTP, DHCP, and TFTP protocols.

- If you're unfamiliar with these, BOOTP (Bootstrap Protocol) and DHCP (Dynamic Host Configuration Protocol) enable a target device with an Ethernet port to obtain an IP address and other network-related configuration information from a central server. TFTP (Trivial File Transfer Protocol) allows the target device to download files (such as a Linux kernel image) from a TFTP server.

Fig. 3.5 illustrates the flow of information between the target device and a BOOTP server. The client (U-Boot, in this case) initiates the exchange by sending a broadcast packet searching for a BOOTP server. The server responds with a reply packet that includes the client's IP address and other information. The most useful data includes a filename used to download a kernel image.

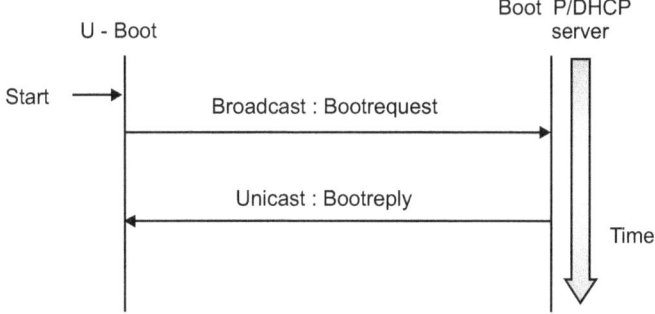

Fig. 3.5 : Bootp client/server handshake

In practice, dedicated BOOTP servers no longer exist as stand-alone servers. DHCP servers included with your favorite Linux distribution also support BOOTP protocol packets and are almost universally used for BOOTP operations. The DHCP protocol builds on BOOTP. It can supply the target with a wide variety of configuration information. In practice, the information exchange is often limited by the target/bootloader DHCP client implementation.

3.8 ANATOMY OF AN EMBEDDED SYSTEM

The Fig. 3.6 is a block diagram of a typical embedded system. This is a simple example of a high-level hardware architecture that might be found in a wireless access point. The system is architected around a 32-bit RISC processor. Flash memory is used for non-volatile program and data storage. Main memory is synchronous dynamic random-access memory (SDRAM) and might contain anywhere from a few megabytes to hundreds of megabytes, depending on the application. A real-time clock module, often backed up by battery, keeps the time of day (calendar/wall clock, including date). This example includes an Ethernet and USB interface, as well as a serial port for console access via RS-232. The 802.11 chipset or module implements the wireless modem function. Often the processor in an embedded system performs many functions beyond the traditional core instruction stream processing. The hypothetical processor shown in Fig. 3.6 contains an integrated UART for a serial interface and integrated USB and Ethernet controllers. Many processors contain integrated peripherals. Sometimes they are referred to as system on chip (SOC).

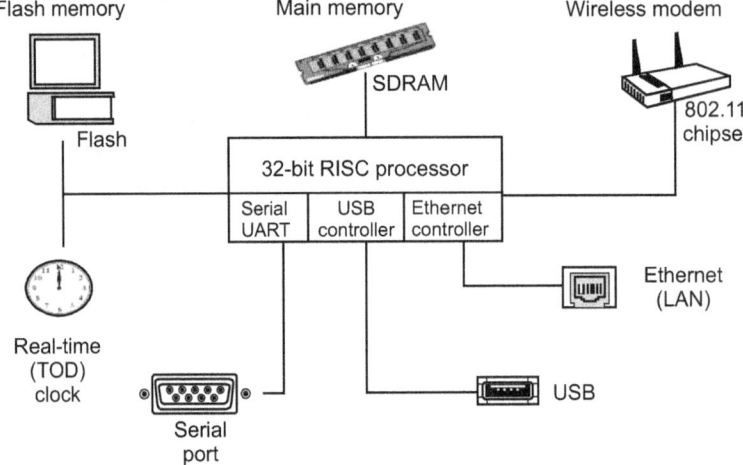

Fig. 3.6 : Embedded system

3.8.1 Post and Boot Process Linux Boot Process for Embedded Systems

This provides an insight in to the Embedded Linux Boot Process. Reader should have a basic Knowledge of Boot Process in general and should be familiar with Embedded Linux BootProcess.

Part - A

(1) **Software components Involved in Embedded Linux Boot Process**
    (a) Bootloader
    (b) kernel Image
    (c) root file system - either an initrd image or a NFS location.

(2) **Steps during Booting process of a conventional PC**
    (a) System Startup - PC-BIOS/BootMonitor
    (b) Stage 1 bootloader – MBR
    (c) Stage2 bootloader- LILO, GRUB etc.
    (d) Kernel – Linux
    (e) init - The User Space

(3) **Booting process for an Embedded Systems**
    (a) Instead of BIOS you will run program from a fixed location in Flash.
    (b) The components involved in the first steps of PC boot process are combined in to a single "boot strap firmware", called "boot loader".

(c) Bootloader also provides additional features useful for development and debugging.

(4) What is System Startup? [Exact process depends on the Target Hardware]
   (a) CPU starts executing BIOS at address 0xFFFF0.
   (b) POST (Power On Self Test) - is the first step of BIOS.
   (c) Run time services - involve local device enumeration and initialization.
   (d) After the POST is complete, POST related code is flushed out of memory. But BIOS runtime services remain in memory and are available to the target OS.
   (e) The runtime searches for devices that are both active and bootable in order of preference defined in CMOS settings.
   (f) The primary boot loader is loaded and BIOS returns control to it.

(5) The Primary boot loader
   (a) Performs few optional initializations.
   (b) Its main job is to Load the secondary boot loader.

(6) Secondary boot loader
   (a) The Second Stage boot loader loads the Linux & an optional initial RAM disk in to the memory.
   (b) On PC, the initrd is used as a temporary root files system, before final root file system gets mounted. However, on embedded systems, the initrd is generally the final root file system.
   (c) The secondary loader passes control to the kernel image - kernel is decompressed and initialized.
   (d) So, the secondary boot loader is the kernel Loader, can also load optional initial RAM disk (initrd), and then invokes the kernel image.

(7) Kernel Invocation
   (a) As the kernel is invoked, it performs the checks on system hardware, enumerates the attached hardware devices, mounts the root device.
   (b) Next it loads the necessary kernel modules.
   (c) First user-space program (init) now starts and high-level system initialization is performed.
   (d) The Kernel Invocation Process is similar on Embedded Linux Systems as well as on PC. We will discuss this in detail in following text.

(8) Kernel Image
   (a) Is typically a compressed image [zlib compression] ?
   (b) Typical named a zImage (<512 KB) or bzImage (> 512 kB).
   (c) At the head of this image (in file head.S) is a routine that does some minimal amount of hardware set up and then decompresses the kernel contained in the kernel image and places in to high memory (high memory & low memory).

Part-B

(1) Kernel Invocation Process - A Summary
   (a) zImage Entry Point.
   (b) Perform Basic Hardware Set Up.
   (c) Perform Basic Environment Set Up (stack etc.).
   (d) Clear Bss   [Now we have set up the run time environment for the code to be executed next].
   (e) Decompress the Kernel Image.
   (f) Execute the decompressed Kernel Image - Initialize Page Tables - ENABLE MMU - DETECT CPU (& optional FPU) TYPE & SAVE THIS INFO   [With above set up, we are now ready to execute a general CCode. Till now we only executed asm routines.].
   (g) The First Kernel C function - do further initializations - load initrd [The above code is being executed by swapper process, the one with pid 0].
   (h) The Init Process - fork init process - Init process is with pid 1 - Invoke Scheduler - relinquish control to scheduler.

(2) zImage Entry point
   (a) This is a call to the absolute physical address by boot loader - Refer to file arch/***/boot/compressed/head.S: start() in kernel source. - For the ARM process this is "arch/arm/boot/compressed/head.S: start()" .
   (b) start() performs - basic hardware set up - basic environment set up - clears bss - calls the decompress_kernel().

(3) Decompressing Kernel Image
   (a) This is a call to arch/***/boot/compressed/misc.c: decompress_kernel() - This function decompresses the kernel image, stores it in to the RAM & returns the address of decompressed image in RAM.
   (b) on ARM processor this maps to "arch/arm/boot/compressed/misc.c: decompress_kernel()" routine.

(4) Execute the decompressed Kernel Image
   (a) After we have got the (uncompressed) kernel image in RAM, we execute it.
   (b) Execution starts with call_kernel() function call [from start.
   (c) call_kernel() will start executing the kernel code, from Kernelentry point.
   (d) arch/***/kernel/head.S contains the kernel entry point. - separate entry points for Master CPU and Secondary CPUs (for SMPsystems). - This code is in asm - Page Tables are Initialized & MMU is enabled. - type of CPU alongwith optional FPU is detected and stored - For Master CPU; start_kernel(), which is the first C function to be executed in kernel, is called. - For secondary CPUs (on an SMP system); secondary_start_kernel()is the first C function to be called.
   (e) On ARM process it maps to "arch/arm/kernel/head.S - Contains kernel ENTRY points for master and secondary CPU. - For Master CPU "mmap_switched()" is

called as soon as mmu gets enabled. The mmap_switched() saves the CPU info makes a call to start_kernel() - For Secondary CPU "secondary_start_kernel()" is called as soon as MMU gets enabled.

(5) The first kernel C function
(a) The start_kernel() function is being executed by the swapper process.
(b) Refer to init/main.c: start_kernel() in the kernel source.
(c) start_kernel(): - a long list of initialization functions are called: this sets up interrupts, performs further memory configuration & loads the initrd. - calls rest_init() in the End.
(d) econdary_start_kernel() for secondary CPUs (on SMP systems). – arch /***/ kernel/smp.c: secondary_start_kernel() – for ARM, arch/arm/kernel/smp.c - there is not rest_init() call for secondary CPUs.

(6) Init process
(a) Refer to init/main.c: rest_init() in kernel source.
(b) Executed only on the Master CPU
(c) rest_init() forks new process by calling kernel_thread() function
(d) kernel_thread(kern_init,*,*); kern_init has PID-1
(e) kern_init() will call the initialization scripts.
(f) kernel_thread() defined in "arch/***/kernel/process.c: kernel_thread()".
(g) on ARM, arch/arm/kernel/process.c

(7) Invoke scheduler
(a) The rest_init() calls cpu_idle() in end [after it is done creating the init process]
(b) For the Secondary CPUs (on SMP systems), CPU_idle is directly called from secondary_start_kernel [no step-5 & hence no init process].
(c) cpu_idle() defined in "arch/***/kernel/process.c: cpu_idle()".
(d) on ARM, arch/arm/kernel/process.c

(8) initrd image
(a) The initrd serves as a temporary root file system in RAM & allows the kernel to fully boot without having to mount and physical disks. Since the necessary modules needed to interface with peripherals can be part of initrd the kernel can be very small.
(b) pivot_root() routine: the root files system is pivoted where the initrd root file system is unmounted & the real root file system is mounted.
(c) In any embedded system, the initrd could be the root file system.

3.8.2 Kernel Initialization : Overview

When the Linux kernel begins execution, it spews out numerous status messages during its rather comprehensive boot process. The Linux kernel displayed approximately 200 printk4 lines before it issues the login prompt. (We omitted them from the listing to clarify the point being discussed.) Listing 3-9 reproduces the last several lines of output before the login prompt. The goal of this exercise is not to delve into the details of the kernel initialization.

The goal is to gain a high-level understanding of what is happening and what components are required to boot a Linux kernel on an embedded system.

LISTING 3-9 Linux Final Boot Messages

Looking up port of RPC 100005/1 on 192.168.0.9

VFS: Mounted root (nfs file system).

Freeing unused kernel memory: 152k init

INIT: version 2.86 booting

...

freescale-8548cds login:

Shortly before issuing a login prompt on the serial terminal, Linux *mounts* a *root file system*. In LISTING 3-10 Linux goes through the steps required to mount its root file system remotely (via Ethernet) from an NFS5 server on a machine with the IP address 192.168.0.9. Usually, this is your development workstation. The root file system contains the application programs, system libraries, and utilities that make up a Linux system. The important point in this discussion should not be understated: *Linux requires a file system*. Many legacy embedded operating systems did not require a file system. This fact is a frequent surprise to engineers making the transition from legacy embedded OSs to embedded Linux. A file system consists of a predefined set of system directories and files in a specific layout on a hard drive or other medium that the Linux kernel *mounts* as its root file system. Linux can mount a root file system from other devices. The most common, of course, is to mount a partition from a hard drive as the root file system, as is done on your Linux laptop or workstation. Indeed, NFS is pretty useless when you ship your embedded Linux widget out the door and away from your development environment. However, as you progress through this book, you will come to appreciate the power and flexibility of NFS root mounting as a development environment.

3.8.3 First User Space Process : init

Another important point should be made before we move on. Notice in Listing 3-9 this line:

INIT: version 2.86 booting

Until this point, the kernel itself was executing code, performing the numerous initialization steps in a context known as *kernel context*. In this operational state, the kernel owns all system memory and operates with full authority over all system resources. The kernel has access to all physical memory and to all I/O subsystems. It executes code in kernel virtual address space, using a stack created and owned by the kernel itself.

When the Linux kernel has completed its internal initialization and mounted its root file system, the default behavior is to spawn an application program called init. When the kernel starts init, it is said to be running in *user space* or user space context. In this operational mode, the user space process has restricted access to the system and must use kernel system calls to request kernel services such as device and file I/O. These user space processes, or programs, operate in a virtual memory space picked at random6 and managed by the kernel. The kernel, in co-operation with specialized memory management hardware in the processor, performs virtual-to-physical address translation for the user space process. The single biggest benefit of this architecture is that an error in one process can not trash the memory space of another. This is a common pitfall in legacy embedded OSs that can lead to bugs that are some of the most difficult to track down.

3.9 STORAGE CONSIDERATIONS

- In embedded linux development system most tricky task is embedded systems have limited physical resources. Although the Core 2 Duo machine on your desktop might have 500 GB of hard drive space, it is not uncommon to find embedded systems with a fraction of that amount.
- In many cases, the hard drive typically is replaced by smaller and less expensive nonvolatile storage devices. Hard drives are bulky, have rotating parts, are sensitive to physical shock, and require multiple power supply voltages, which makes them unsuitable for many embedded systems.

3.9.1 Flash Memory

- Now-a-days everyone is familiar with SD cards and Compact flash used in a wide variety of consumer devices.

  For example : digital cameras and PDAs (both great examples of embedded Systems). These modules, based on *Flash* memory technology, can be thought of as solid-state hard drives, capable of storing many megabytes and even gigabytes of data in a tiny footprint.

- It contains no moving parts, is relatively rugged, and operates on a single common power supply voltage. Several manufacturers of Flash memory exist. Flash memory comes in a variety of electrical formats, physical packages, and capacities.
- It is common to see embedded systems with as little as 4 MB or 8 MB of nonvolatile storage. More typical storage requirements for embedded Linux systems range from 16 MB to 256 MB or more.
- An increasing number of embedded Linux systems have non-volatile storage into the gigabyte range.
- Flash memory can be written to and erased under software control. Rotational Hard drive technology remains the fastest writable medium.

- Flash writing and erasing speeds have improved considerably over time, although Flash write and erase time is still considerably slower.
- You must understand some fundamental differences between hard drive and Flash memory technology to properly use the technology.
- Flash memory is divided into relatively large erasable units, referred to as erase blocks. One of the defining characteristics of Flash memory is how data in Flash is written and erased.
- In a typical NOR7 Flash memory chip, data can be changed from a binary 1 to a binary 0 under software control using simple data writes directly to the cell's address, one bit or word at a time.
- A typical NOR Flash memory device contains many erase blocks. For example, 4MB Flash chip might contain 64 erase blocks of 64KB each. Flash memory is also available with non-uniform erase block sizes, to facilitate flexible data-storage layouts. These are commonly called boot block or boot sector Flash chips. Often the bootloader is stored in the smaller blocks, and the kernel and other required data are stored in the larger blocks. Fig. 3.7 illustrates the block size layout for a typical top boot Flash.

3.9.2 NAND Flash

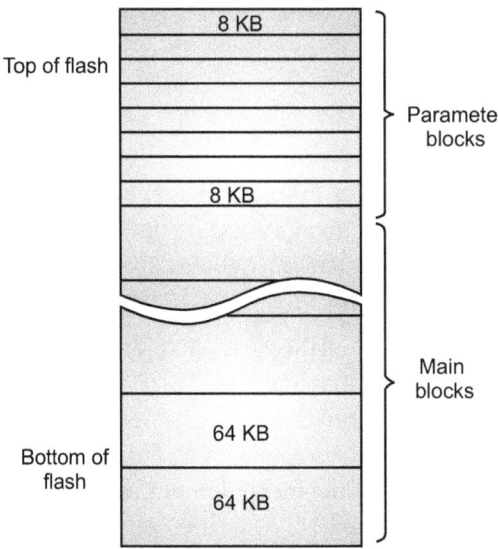

Fig. 3.7 : Boot block flash architecture

- To modify data stored in a Flash memory array, the block in which the modified data resides must be completely erased.

- Even if only 1 byte in a block needs to be changed, the entire block must be erased and rewritten. Flash block sizes are relatively large compared to traditional hard-drive sector sizes. In comparison, a typical high performance hard drive has writable sectors of 512 or 1024 bytes. The ramifications of this might be obvious: Write times for updating data in Flash memory can be many times that of a hard drive, due in part to the relatively large quantity of data that must be erased and written back to the Flash for each update. In the worst case, these write cycles can take several seconds.
- Another limitation of Flash memory that must be considered is Flash memory cell write lifetime. A NOR Flash memory cell has a limited number of write cycles before failure.

3.9.3 NAND Flash

- NAND Flash is a relatively new Flash technology. When NAND Flash hit the market, traditional Flash memory such as that described in the preceding section was called NOR Flash.
- These distinctions relate to the internal Flash memory cell architecture. NAND Flash devices improve on some of the limitations of traditional (NOR) Flash by offering smaller block sizes, resulting in faster and more efficient writes and generally more efficient use of the Flash array.
- NOR Flash devices interface to the microprocessor in a fashion similar to many microprocessor peripherals.
- That is, they have a parallel data and address bus that are connected directly9 to the microprocessor data/address bus. Each byte or word in the Flash array can be individually addressed in a random fashion.
- In contrast, NAND devices are accessed serially through a complex interface that varies among vendors.
- NAND devices present an operational model more similar to that of a traditional hard drive and associated controller. Data is accessed in serial bursts, which are far smaller than NOR Flash block size.
- Write cycle lifetime for NAND Flash is an order of magnitude greater than for NOR Flash, although erase times are significantly smaller.

3.9.4 Flash Usage

- In embedded system there are many options in through layout and use of Flash memory. In the simplest of systems, in which resources are not overly constrained, raw binary data (perhaps compressed) can be stored on the Flash device.
- When booted, a file system image stored in Flash is read into a Linux ramdisk block device, mounted as a file system, and accessed only from RAM.

- This is often a good design choice when the data in Flash rarely needs to be updated. Any data that does need to be updated is relatively small compared to the size of the ramdisk.
- It is important to realize that any changes to files in the ramdisk are lost upon reboo or power cycle.

Fig. 3.8 illustrates a common Flash memory organization that is typical of a simple embedded system in which nonvolatile storage requirements of dynamic data are small and infrequent

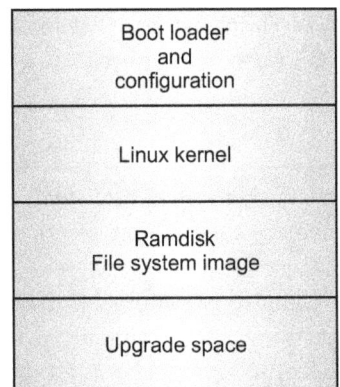

Fig. 3.8 : Typical flash memory layout

- The bootloader is often placed in the top or bottom of the Flash memory array. Following the bootloader, space is allocated for the Linux kernel image and the ramdisk file system image, which holds the root file system. Typically, the Linux kernel and ramdisk file system images are compressed, and the bootloader handles the decompression task during the boot cycle. For dynamic data that needs to be saved between reboots and power cycles, another small area of Flash can be dedicated, or another type of nonvolatile storage can be used. This is a typical configuration for embedded systems that have requirements to store configuration data, as might be found in a wireless access point aimed at the consumer market, for example.

3.9.5 Flash File Systems

- The limitations of the simple Flash layout scheme just described can be overcome by using a Flash file system to manage data on the Flash device in a manner similar to how data is organized on a hard drive.
- Early implementations of file systems for Flash devices consisted of a simple block device layer that emulated the 512-byte sector layout of a common hard drive. These simple emulation layers allowed access to data in file format rather than unformatted bulk storage, but they had some performance limitations.

- Flash blocks are subject to a finite write lifetime. Wear leveling algorithms are used to distribute writes evenly over the physical erase blocks of the Flash memory in order to extend the life of the Flash memory chip.
- Another limitation that arises from the Flash architecture is the risk of data loss during a power failure or premature shut down.
- Consider that the Flash block sizes are relatively large and that average file sizes being written are often much smaller relative to the block size.
- Therefore, to write a small 8KB file, you must erase and rewrite an entire Flash block, perhaps 64 kB or 128 kB in size; in the worst case, this can take several seconds to complete.
- This opens a significant window to risk of data loss due to power failure. One of the more popular Flash file systems in use today is JFFS2, or Journaling Flash File System
- It has several important features aimed at improving overall Performance, increasing Flash lifetime, and reducing the risk of data loss in the case of power failure.
- The more significant improvements in the latest JFFS2 file system include improved wear leveling, compression and decompression to squeeze more data into a given Flash size, and support for Linux hard links.

3.9.6 Memory Space

- Virtually all legacy embedded operating systems view and manage system memory as a single large, flat address space. That is, a microprocessor's address space exists from 0 to the top of its physical address range. For example, if a microprocessor had 24 physical address lines, its top of memory would be 16 MB. Therefore, its hexadecimal address would range from 0x00000000 to 0x00ffffff.
- Hardware designs commonly place DRAM starting at the bottom of the range, and Flash memory from the top down.
- Unused address ranges between the top of DRAM and bottom of Flash would be allocated for addressing of various peripheral chips on the board.
- This design approach is often dictated by the choice of microprocessor. Fig. 3.9 shows a typical memory layout for a simple embedded system.
- In traditional embedded systems based on legacy operating systems, the OS and all the tasks12 had equal access rights to all resources in the system. A bug in one process could wipe out memory contents anywhere in the system, whether it belonged to itself, the OS, another task, or even a hardware register somewhere in the address space. Although this approach had simplicity as its most valuable characteristic, it led to bugs that could be challenging to diagnose.
- High-performance microprocessors contain complex hardware engines called Memory Management Units (MMUs). Their purpose is to enable an operating system to exercise a high degree of management and control over its address space and the

address space it allocates to processes. This control comes in two primary forms: *access rights* and *memory translation*.

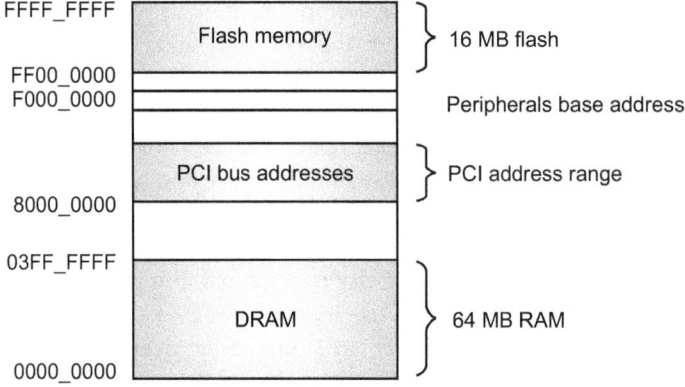

Fig. 3.9 : Typical embedded system memory map

- Access rights allow an operating system to assign specific memory-access privileges to specific tasks. Memory translation allows an operating system to virtualize its address space, which has many benefits.
- The Linux kernel takes advantage of these hardware MMUs to create a *virtual memory* operating system. One of the biggest benefits of virtual memory is that it can make more efficient use of physical memory by presenting the appearance that the system has more memory than is physically present.
- The other benefit is that the kernel can enforce access rights to each range of system memory that it allocates to a task or process, to prevent one process from errantly accessing memory or other resources that belong to another process or to the kernel itself.

3.9.7 Execution Contexts

- One of the very first chores that Linux performs is to configure the hardware MMU on the processor and the data structures used to support it, and to enable address translation. When this step is complete, the kernel runs in its own virtual memory space.
- The virtual kernel address selected by the kernel developers in recent Linux kernel versions defaults to 0xC0000000. In most architecture, this is a configurable parameter. If we looked at the kernel's symbol table, we would find kernel symbols linked at an address starting with 0xC0xxxxxx. As a result, any time the kernel executes code in kernel space, the processor's instruction pointer (program counter) contains values in this range.
- In Linux, we refer to two distinctly separate operational contexts, based on the environment in which a given thread is executing.

- Threads executing entirely within the kernel are said to be operating in *kernel context*. Application programs are said to operate in *user space context*. A user space process can access only memory it owns, and it is required to use kernel system calls to access privileged resources such as file and device I/O. An example might make this more clear.
- The read function call begins in user space, in the C library read() function. The C library then issues a read request to the kernel. The read request results in a context switch from the user's program to the kernel, to service the request for the file's data. Inside the kernel, the read request results in a hard-drive access requesting the sectors containing the file's data.

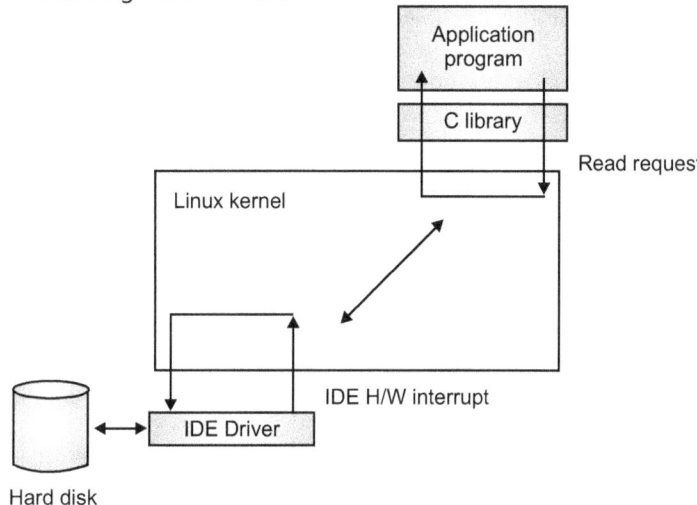

Fig. 3.10 : Simple file read request

- Usually the hard-drive read request is issued asynchronously to the hardware itself. That is, the request is posted to the hardware, and when the data is ready, the hardware interrupts the processor.
- The application program waiting for the data is *blocked* on a wait queue until the data is available. Later, when the hard disk has the data ready, it posts a hardware interrupt. (This description is intentionally simplified for the purposes of this illustration.) When the kernel receives the hardware interrupt, it suspends whatever process was executing and proceeds to read the waiting data from the drive.

we have identified two general execution contexts

- user space and kernel space. When an application program executes a system call that results in a context switch and enters the kernel, it is executing kernel code on behalf of a process.

- You will often hear this referred to as *process context* within the kernel. In contrast, the interrupt service routine (ISR) handling the IDE drive (or any other ISR, for that matter) is kernel code that is not executing on behalf of any particular process. This is typically called *interrupt context*.
- Several limitations exist in this operational context, including the limitation that the ISR cannot block (sleep) or call any kernel functions that might result in blocking.

3.10 BUSYBOX

- Busy Box has gained tremendous popularity in the embedded Linux community. It is remarkably easy to configure, compile, and use.
- In addition, it has the potential to significantly reduce the overall system resources required to support a wide collection of common Linux utilities.
- BusyBox provides compact replacements for many traditional full-blown utilities found on most desktop and embedded Linux distributions.
  Examples include the file utilities such as ls, cat, cp, dir, head, and tail; general utilities such as dmesg, kill, halt, fdisk, mount, and umount; and many more. BusyBox also provides support for more-complex operations, such asifconfig, netstat, route, and other network utilities.
- BusyBox combines tiny versions of many common UNIX utilities into a single small executable.
- It provides replacements for most of the utilities you usually find in GNU fileutils, shellutils, etc.
- The utilities in BusyBox generally have fewer options than their full-featured GNU cousins; however, the options that are included provide the expected functionality and behave very much like their GNU counterparts.
- BusyBox provides a fairly complete environment for any small or embedded system.
- **BusyBox Is Easy**
  If you can configure and build the Linux kernel, you will find BusyBox quite straightforward to configure, build, and install.

The steps are similar

1. Execute a configuration utility and enable your choice of features.
2. Run make to build the package.
3. Install the binary and a series of *symbolic links*1 on your target system

You can build and install BusyBox on your development workstation or your target embedded system. BusyBox works equally well in both environments. However, you must take care when installing on your development workstation that you keep it isolated in a working directory, to avoid overwriting your system's startup files or primary utilities.

3.10.1 BusyBox Configuration

To initiate the Busy Box configuration, the command is the same as that used with the Linux kernel for the ncurses library-based configuration utility. Note that, in a similar fashion to the Linux kernel, make help produces much useful information on available make targets. The command to configure is:

$ **make menuconfig**

Space does not permit coverage of each configuration option. However, some of the options deserve mention. Some of the more important BusyBox configuration options appear under *Busybox Settings* ---> Build Options. Here you will find configuration options necessary to cross-compile the BusyBox application. Listing 3-10 details the options found under Build Options in a recent BusyBox snapshot. Select Build Options from the top-level Busy Box configuration utility to navigate to this screen.

LISTING 3-10 BusyBox Build Options

[ ] Build BusyBox as a static binary (no shared libs)

[ ] Build BusyBox as a position independent executable

[ ] Force NOMMU build

[ ] Build shared libbusybox

[*] Build with Large File Support (for accessing files > 2 GB)

() Cross Compiler prefix

The first option is useful for building very minimal embedded systems. It allows BusyBox to be compiled and linked statically so that no dynamically loaded libraries *(libc-*, for example)* are required at runtime on the target system. Without this option, BusyBox requires various libraries so that it can run. We can easily determine what libraries BusyBox (or any other binary) requires on our target system by using the ldd command. Listing 3-11 is the output of ldd cross-compiled for ARM xscale.

LISTING 3-11 BusyBox Library Dependencies

$ xscale_be-ldd busybox

linux-gate.so.1 => (0xb8087000)

libm.so.6 => /lib/tls/i686/cmov/libm.so.6 (0xb804d000)

libc.so.6 => /lib/tls/i686/cmov/libc.so.6 (0xb7efe000)

/lib/ld-linux.so.2 (0xb8088000)

The BusyBox utility, as compiled using the default configuration, requires the four shared libraries shown in Listing 3-11. Had we elected to build Busy-Box as a static binary, ldd would simply issue a message telling us that the BusyBox binary is not a dynamic executable. In other words, it requires no shared libraries to resolve any unresolved dependencies in the executable. Static linking yields a smaller overall footprint on a root file system because no shared libraries are required. However, building an embedded application without shared libraries means that none of the familiar C library functions are available to your applications. To give you an idea of the relative size difference between a statically linked BusyBox and the same configuration compiled against shared libraries, a statically linked busybox is about 1.5MB versus 778kB for a dynamically linked image for a recent version of BusyBox.

Cross-Compiling BusyBox
- In earlier versions of BusyBox the only requirement was to specify the prefix to the cross-compiler by selecting the option to build BusyBox with a cross-compiler. This has been superseded by the more standard method of specifying an environment variable similar to building other packages such as the Linux kernel.
- To cross-compile with a specific cross-compiler on your development workstation, simply define *CROSS_COMPILE* in your environment. Some examples of *CROSS_COMPILE* values are *arm5vt_le-, xscale_be-, and ppc_linux-*.

3.10.2 BusyBox Operation

When you build BusyBox, you end up with a binary called you guessed it BusyBox. BusyBox can be invoked from the binary name itself, but it is usually launched via a *symlink*. When BusyBox is invoked without command-line parameters, it produces a list of the functions that were enabled via the configuration. Listing 11-3 shows such an output (it has been formatted to fit the page width).

BusyBox init
- The kernel attempts to execute a program called */sbin/init* as the last step in kernel initialization.
- There is no reason why BusyBox can't emulate the init functionality, and that's exactly how the system illustrated in Listing 11-5 is configured. BusyBox handles the init functionality.
- BusyBox handles system initialization differently from standard System V init.
- BusyBox also reads an init tab file, but the syntax of the init tab file is different.

BusyBox Target Installation
- The Purpose of symlinks when we understand then we can proceed BusyBox installation.
- The BusyBox makefile contains a target called install.
- Executing make install creates a directory structure containing the BusyBox executable and a symlink tree.
- This environment needs to be migrated to your target embedded system's root directory, complete with the symlink tree.
- The symlink tree eliminates the need to type busybox *command* for each command.

BusyBox Applets
- In a recent BusyBox snapshot, 282 commands (also called applets) were documented in the man page. Sufficient support exists for reasonably complex shell scripts, including support for Bash shell scripting.
- BusyBox supports awk and sed, frequently found in Bash scripts. BusyBox supports network utilities such as ping, ifconfig, traceroute, and netstat. Some commands are specifically included for scripting support, including true, false, and yes.
- Spend a few moments perusing Appendix C, *"BusyBox Commands,"* where you can find a summary of each BusyBox command. After you have done so, you will have a better appreciation of the capabilities of BusyBox and how it might be applicable to your own embedded Linux project.
- Many of the BusyBox commands contain a limited subset of features and options compared to their full-featured counterparts.

In general, you can get help on any given BusyBox command at runtime by invoking the command with the-help option. This produces a usage message with a brief description of each supported command option. The BusyBox gzip applet is a useful example of a BusyBox command that supports a limited set of options. Listing 3-12 displays the output from gzip -help on a BusyBox target.

LISTING 3-12 BusyBox *gzip* Applet Usage

```
/ # gzip --help
BusyBox v1.13.2 (2010-02-24 16:04:14 EST) multi-call binary
Usage: gzip [OPTION]... [FILE]...
Compress FILEs (or standard input)
Options:
-c Write to standard output
-d Decompress
-f Force
```

- The BusyBox version of gzip supports just three command-line options. Its full featured counterpart supports more than 15 different command-line options. For example, the full-featured gzip utility supports a --list option that produces compression statistics for each file on the command line.
- No such support exists for BusyBoxgzip. This is usually not a significant limitation for embedded systems. We present this information so that you can make an informed choice when deciding on BusyBox.
- When the full capabilities of a utility are needed, the solution is simple: Delete support for that particular utility in the BusyBox configuration, and add the standard Linux utility to your target system.

In this way you can mix BusyBox utilities and the standard Linux utilities on the same embedded system

3.11 PROCESS VIRTUAL MEMORY

When a process is spawned for example, when the user types ls at the Linux command prompt the kernel allocates memory for the process and assigns a range of virtual-memory addresses to the process. The resulting address values bear no fixed relationship to those in the kernel, nor to any other running process. Furthermore, there is no direct correlation between the physical memory addresses on the board and the virtual memory as seen by the process. In fact, it is not uncommon for a process to occupy multiple different physical addresses in main memory during its lifetime as a result of paging and swapping. Listing 3-13 is the venerable "Hello world," modified to illustrate the concepts just discussed. The goal of this example is to illustrate the address space that the kernel assigns to the process. This code was compiled and run on an embedded system containing 256 MB of DRAM memory.

LISTING 3-13 : Hello world, Embedded Style

```
include <stdio.h>
int bss_var; /* Uninitialized global variable */
int data_var = 1; /* Initialized global variable */
int main(int argc, char **argv)
{

void *stack_var; /* Local variable on the stack */
stack_var = (void *)main; /* Don't let the compiler */
/* optimize it out */
printf("Hello world! Main is executing at %p\n", stack_var);
printf("This address (%p) is in our stack frame\n", &stack_var);
/* bss section contains uninitialized data */
printf("This address (%p) is in our bss section\n", &bss_var);
/* data section contains initializated data */
printf("This address (%p) is in our data section\n", &data_var);
return 0;
}
```

Listing 3-13 shows the console output that this program produces. Notice that the process called Good thinks it is executing somewhere in high RAM just above the 256 MB boundary (0x10000418). Notice also that the stack address is roughly halfway into a 32-bit address space, well beyond our 256 MB of RAM (0x7ff8ebb0). How can this be? DRAM is usually contiguous in systems like these. To the casual observer, it appears that we have nearly 2 GB of DRAM available for our use. These *virtual addresses* were assigned by the kernel and are backed by physical RAM somewhere within the 256 MB range of available memory on our embedded board.

LISTING 3-13 Hello world Output

root@192.168.4.9:~#. /Hello
Hello world!! Main is executing at 0x10000418
This address (0x7ff8ebb0) is in our stack frame
This address (0x10010a1c) is in our bss section
This address (0x10010a18) is in our data section
root@192.168.4.9:~#

3.11.1 Cross-Development Environment

- Before we can develop applications and device drivers for an embedded system, we need a set of tools (compiler, utilities, and so on) that will generate binary executables in the proper format for the target system.
- Consider a simple application written on your desktop PC, such as the traditional "Hello world" example. After you have created the source code on your desktop, you invoke the compiler that came with your desktop system (usually GNU gcc) to generate a binary executable image. That image file is properly formatted to execute on the machine on which it was compiled.
- This is referred to as *native* compilation. In other words, using compilers on your desktop system, you generate code that will execute on that desktop system.
- If you have a tool chain that runs on your target board, you can natively compile applications for your target's architecture.
- In fact, one great way to stress-test a new embedded kernel and custom board is to repeatedly compile the Linux kernel on it.
- Developing software in a cross-development environment requires that the compiler running on your development host output a binary executable that is incompatible with the desktop development workstation on which it was compiled.
- The primary reason these tools exist is that it is often impractical or impossible to develop and compile software natively on the embedded system because of resource (typically memory and CPU horsepower) constraints.

Numerous hidden traps to this approach often catch the unwary newcomer to embedded development. When a given program is compiled, the compiler often knows how to find include files, and where to find libraries that might be required for the compilation to succeed.

3.11.2 Embedded Linux Distributions

- After the Linux kernel boots, it expects to find and mount a root file system. When a suitable root file system has been mounted, startup scripts launch a number of programs and utilities that the system requires.

- These programs often invoke other programs to do specific tasks, such as spawn a login shell, initialize network interfaces, and launch a user's applications. Each of these programs has specific requirements (often called dependencies) that must be satisfied by other components in the system.
- Most Linux application programs depend on one or more system libraries. Other programs require configuration and log files, and so on.
- Even a small embedded Linux system needs many dozens of files populated in an appropriate directory structure on a *root file system*.
- Full-blown desktop systems have many thousands of files on the root file system.
  These files come from *packages* that are usually grouped by functionality. The packages typically are installed and managed using a package manager.
- Red Hat's Package Manager (rpm) is a popular example and is widely used to install, remove, and update packages on a Linux system. If your Linux workstation is based on Red Hat, including the Fedora series, typing rpm -qa at a command prompt lists all the packages installed on your system. If you are using a distribution based on Debian, such as Ubuntu, typing dpkg -l has the same result.
- A package can consist of many files; indeed, some packages contain hundreds of files. A complete Linux distribution can contain hundreds or even thousands of packages.

These are some examples of packages you might find on an embedded Linux distribution, and their purpose

- initscripts contains basic system startup and shutdown scripts.
- apache implements the popular Apache web server.
- telnet-server contains files necessary to implement telnet server functionality, which allows you to establish telnet sessions to your embedded target.
- glibc implements the Standard C library.
- busybox contains compact versions of dozens of popular command-line utilities commonly found on *UNIX/Linux systems*.
  - This is the purpose of a Linux *distribution*, as the term has come to be used. A typical Linux distribution comes with several CD-ROMs full of useful programs, libraries, tools, utilities, and documentation. Installation of a distribution typically leaves the user with a fully functional system based on a reasonable set of default configuration options, which can be tailored to suit a particular set of requirements. You may be familiar with one of the popular desktop Linux distributions, such as Red Hat or Ubuntu.
  A Linux distribution for embedded targets differs in several significant ways. First, the executable target binaries from an embedded distribution will not run on your PC, but are targeted to the architecture and processor of your embedded system. (Of course, if your embedded Linux distribution targets the x86 architecture, this statement does not necessarily apply.)

- A desktop Linux distribution tends to have many GUI tools aimed at the typical desktop user, such as fancy graphical clocks, calculators, personal time-management tools, e-mail clients, and more. An embedded Linux distribution typically omits these components in favor of specialized tools aimed at developers, such as memory analysis tools, remote debug facilities, and many more.
- Another significant difference between desktop and embedded Linux distributions is that an embedded distribution typically contains cross tools, as opposed to native tools. For example, the gcc tool chain that ships with an embedded Linux distribution runs on your x86 desktop PC but produces binary code that runs on your target system, often a non-x86 architecture. Many of the other tools in the toolchain are similarly configured: They run on the development host (usually an x86 PC) but are designed to emit or manipulate objects targeted at foreign architectures such as ARM or Power Architecture.

3.11.3 Do-It-Yourself Linux Distributions

- You can choose to assemble all the components you need for your embedded project on your own. You have to decide whether the risks are worth the effort. If you find yourself involved with embedded Linux purely for the pleasure of it, such as for a hobby or college project, this approach might be a good one. However, plan to spend a significant amount of time assembling all the tools and utilities your project needs and making sure they all interoperate.
- For starters, you need a *toolchain. gcc* and binutils are available from *www.fsf.org* and other mirrors around the world. Both are required to compile the kernel and user space applications for your project. These are distributed primarily in source code form, and you must compile the tools to suit your particular cross-development environment.
- Patches are often required to the most recent "stable" source trees of these utilities, especially when they will be used beyond the *x86/IA32* architecture. The patches usually
  can be found at the same location as the base packages. The challenge is to discover which collections of patches you need for your particular problem or architecture.
- As soon as your tool chain is working, you need to download and compile many applications packages along with the dependencies they require. This can be a formidable challenge, since many packages even today do not lend themselves to cross-compiling.
  Many still have build or other issues when moved away from their native x86 environment where they were developed.
- Beyond these challenges, you might want to assemble a competent development environment, containing tools such as graphical debuggers, memory analysis tools, system tracing and profiling tools, and more. You can see from this discussion that building your own embedded Linux distribution can be quite challenging.

3.12 INITIALIZATION FLOW OF CONTROL

Now that you understand the structure and components of the composite kernel image, let's examine the flow of control from the bootloader to the kernel in a complete boot cycle. Operating system image loading and system diagnostics. It might contain memory dump and fill routines for examining and modifying the contents of memory. It might also contain low-level board self-test routines, including memory and I/O tests. Finally, a bootloader contains logic for loading and passing control to another program, usually an operating system such as Linux. The ARM XScale platform used as a basis for the examples in this chapter contains the Redboot bootloader. When power is first applied, this bootloader is invoked and proceeds to load the operating system (OS). When the bootloader locates and loads the OS image (which could be resident locally in Flash, on a hard drive, or via a local area network or other device), control is passed to that image. On this particular XScale platform, the bootloader passes control to our head.o module at the label start in the bootstrap loader, as shown in Fig. 3.11.

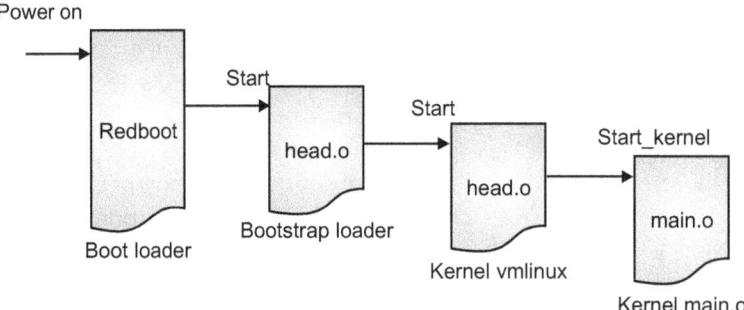

Fig. 3.11 : ARM boot control flow

As discussed earlier, the bootstrap loader pretended to the kernel image has a single primary responsibility: to create the proper environment to decompress and relocate the kernel and pass control to it. Control is passed from the bootstrap loader directly to the kernel proper, to a module called head.o for most architecture. It is an unfortunate historical artifact that both the bootstrap loader and the kernel proper contain a module called head.o, because it is a source of confusion for the new embedded Linux developer. The head.o module in the bootstrap loader might be more appropriately called *kernel_bootstrap_loader_head.o,* although I doubt that the kernel developers would accept this patch! In fact, a recent Linux 2.6 source tree contains more than 25 source files named head.S and almost 70 named *head*.S* This is another reason why you need to know your way around the kernel source tree.

3.12.1 Kernel Entry Point : head.o

The intention of the kernel developers was to keep the architecture-specific head.o module very generic, without any specific machine5 dependencies. This module, derived from the assembly language file head.S, is *located at .../arch/<ARCH>/kernel/ head.S*, where *<ARCH>* is replaced by the given architecture. The examples in this chapter are based on the *ARM/XScale*, as you have seen, with *<ARCH>=arm*. The head.o module performs architecture- and often CPU-specific initialization in preparation for the main body of the kernel. CPU-specific tasks are kept as generic as possible across processor families. Machine-specific initialization is performed elsewhere, as you will discover shortly. Among other low-level tasks, head.o does the following:

- Checks for valid processor and architecture.
- Creates initial page table entries.
- Enables the processor's memory management unit (MMU).
- Establishes limited error detection and reporting.
- Jumps to the start of the kernel proper, start_kernel() in main.c.

These functions contain some hidden complexities. Many novice embedded developers have tried to single-step through parts of this code, only to find that the debugger becomes hopelessly lost. Although a discussion of the complexities of assembly language and the hardware details of virtual memory is beyond the scope of this book, a few things are worth noting about this complicated module.

3.12.2 Kernel Startup : main.c

The final task performed by the kernel's own head.o module is to pass control to the primary kernel startup file written in C. We spend a good portion of the rest of this chapter on this important file. Each architecture has a different syntax and methodology, but every architecture's head.o module has a similar construct for passing control to the kernel proper. For the ARM architecture, it looks as simple as this :

b start_kernel8

For Power Architecture, it looks similar to this:

lis r4,start_kernel@h

ori r4,r4,start_kernel@l

lis r3,MSR_KERNEL@h

ori r3,r3,MSR_KERNEL@l

mtspr SRR0,r4

mtspr SRR1,r3

rfi

Without going into the details of the specific assembly language syntax, both of these examples result in the same thing. Control is passed from the kernel's first object module (head.o) to the C language routine start_kernel() located in .../init/ main.c. Here the kernel begins to develop a life of its own.

The file main.c should be studied carefully by anyone seeking a deeper understanding of the Linux kernel, what components make it up, and how they are initialized and/or instantiated. main.c does the bulk of the post-assembly-language startup work for the Linux kernel, from initializing the first kernel thread all the way to mounting a root file system and executing the very first user space Linux application program. The function start_kernel() is by far the largest function in main.c. Most of the Linux kernel initialization takes place in this routine. Our purpose here is to highlight the particular elements that will prove useful in the context of embedded systems development. It is worth repeating that studying main.c is a great way to spend your time if you want to develop a better understanding of the Linux kernel as a system.

3.12.3 Architecture Setup

Among the first few things that happen in .../init/main.c in the start_kernel() function is the call to setup_arch() found in .../arch/arm/kernel/setup.c. This function takes a single parameter-a pointer to the kernel command line *setup_arch(&command_line);* This statement calls an architecture-specific setup routine responsible for performing initialization tasks common across each major architecture. Among other functions, setup_arch() calls functions that identify the specific CPU and provides a mechanism for calling high-level CPU-specific initialization routines. One such function, called directly by setup_arch(), is setup_processor(), found in .../arch/arm/kernel/setup.c. This function verifies the CPU ID and revision, calls CPU-specific initialization functions, and displays several lines of information on the console during boot. An example of this output can be found in Listing 5-3, lines 4 through 6, reproduced here for your convenience :

CPU : XScale-IXP42x Family [690541c1] revision 1 (ARMv5TE), cr=000039ff

CPU : VIVT data cache, VIVT instruction cache

Machine : ADI Engineering Coyote

Here you can see the CPU type, ID string, and revision read directly from the processor core. This is followed by details of the processor cache and machine type. In this example, the IXP425-based Coyote board has an XScale-IXP42x revision 1 processor, ARMv5TE architecture, virtually indexed, virtually tagged (VIVT) data, and instruction caches. One of the final actions of the architecture setup routines is to perform any machine- dependent initialization. The exact mechanism for this varies across different architectures. For ARM, you will find machine-specific initialization in the .../arch/ arm/mach-* series of directories, depending on your machine type. MIPS architecture also contains directories specific to supported reference platforms. With Power Architecture, a platforms directory contains machine-specific routines. 3 Kernel Command-Line Processing :

In this simple example, the kernel being booted is instructed to open a console device on serial port device ttyS0 (usually the first serial port) at a baud rate of 115 Kbps. It is being instructed to obtain its initial IP address information from a DHCP server and to mount a root file system via the NFS protocol. Linux typically is launched by a bootloader (or bootstrap loader) with a series of parameters that have come to be called the *kernel command line*. Although you don't actually invoke the kernel using a command prompt from a shell, many bootloaders can pass parameters to the kernel in a fashion that resembles this well-known model.

On some platforms whose bootloaders are not Linux-aware, the kernel command line can be defined at compile time and becomes hard-coded as part of the kernel binary image. On other platforms (such as a desktop PC running Red Hat Linux), the user can modify the command line without having to recompile the kernel. The bootstrap loader (Grub or Lilo in the desktop PC case) builds the kernel command line from a configuration file and passes it to the kernel during the boot process. These command line parameters are a boot mechanism to set the initial configuration necessary for proper boot on a given machine. Numerous command-line parameters are defined throughout the kernel. The .../Documentation subdirectory in the kernel source contains a file called kernel parameters. txt containing a list of kernel command-line parameters in dictionary order. Remember the previous warning about kernel documentation: The kernel changes far faster than the documentation. Use this file as a guide, but not a definitive reference. Hundreds of distinct kernel command-line parameters are documented in this file, but it cannot be considered a comprehensive list. For that, you must refer directly to the source code. The basic syntax for kernel command-line parameters is fairly simple and mostly evident from the example in line 9 of Listing 5-3. Kernel commandline parameters can be either a single text word, a *key=value* pair, or a *key=value1,value2,....* key and multi-value format. It is up to the consumer of this information to process the data as delivered. The command line is available globally and is processed by as many modules as needed. As noted earlier, *setup_arch()* in main.c is called with the kernel command line as its only argument. This is to pass architecture-specific parameters and configuration directives to the relevant portions of architecture- and machine-specific code. Device driver writers and kernel developers can add additional kernel commandline parameters for their own specific needs. Let's take a look at the mechanism. Unfortunately, some complications are involved in using and processing kernel commandline parameters. The first of these is that the original mechanism is being deprecated in favor of a much more robust implementation. The second complication is that you need to comprehend the complexities of a linker script file to fully understand the mechanism.

3.12.4 The Setup Macro

As an example of the use of kernel command-line parameters, consider the specification of the console device. We want a console initialized early in the boot cycle so that we have a destination for messages during boot. This initialization takes place in a kernel object called printk.o. The C source file for this module is found in *.../kernel/m printk.c.* The console initialization routine is called console_setup() and takes the kernel command-line parameter string as its only argument. The challenge is to communicate the console parameters specified on the kernel command line to the setup and device driver routines that require this data in a modular and general fashion. Further complicating the issue is that typically the command-line parameters are required early, before (or in time for) the modules that need them. The startup code in main.c, where the main processing of the kernel command line takes place, cannot possibly know the destination functions for each of hundreds of kernel command-line parameters without being hopelessly polluted with knowledge from every consumer of these parameters. What is needed is a flexible and generic way to pass these kernel command-line parameters to their consumers. A special macro defined in *.../include/linux/init.h* is used to associate a portion of the kernel command-line string with a function that will act on that portion of the string.

3.13 SUBSYSTEM INITIALIZATION

Many kernel subsystems are initialized by the code found in main.c. Some are initialized explicitly, as with the calls to init_timers() and console_init(), which need to be called very early. Others are initialized using a technique very similar to that described earlier for the setup macro. In short, the linker builds lists of function pointers to various initialization routines, and a simple loop is used to execute each inturn. Listing 3-14 shows how this works.

LISTING 3-14 Sample Initialization Routine

```
static int __init customize_machine(void)
{
/* customizes platform devices, or adds new ones */
if (init_machine)
init_machine();
return 0;
}
arch_initcall(customize_machine);
```

This code snippet comes from *.../arch/arm/kernel/setup.c.* It is a simple routine designed to provide a customization hook for a particular board.

3.13.1 The *__initcall Macros

Two important things about the initialization routine shown in Listing 3-14 First, it is defined with the __init macro. As we saw earlier, this macro applies a section attribute to declare that this function gets placed in a section called .init.text in the vmlinux ELF file. Recall that the purpose of placing this function in a special section of the object file is so that the memory space it occupies can be reclaimed when it is no longer needed. The second thing to notice is the macro immediately following the definition of the function: arch_initcall(customize_machine). This macro is part of a family of macros defined in .../include/linux/init.h. These macros are reproduced here as :

LISTING 3-15 initcall Family of Macros

```
#define __define_initcall (level,fn,id) \
Static initcall_t __initcall_##fn##id __used \
__attribute__((__section__(".initcall" level ".init"))) = fn
/*
* Early initcalls run before initializing SMP.
*
* Only for built-in code, not modules.
*/
#define early_initcall(fn) __define_initcall("early",fn,early)
/*
* A "pure" initcall has no dependencies on anything else, and purely
* initializes variables that couldn't be statically initialized.
*
* This only exists for built-in code, not for modules.
*/
#define pure_initcall(fn) __define_initcall("0",fn,0)
#define core_initcall(fn) __define_initcall("1",fn,1)
#define core_initcall_sync(fn) __define_initcall("1s",fn,1s)
#define postcore_initcall(fn) __define_initcall("2",fn,2)
#define postcore_initcall_sync(fn) __define_initcall("2s",fn,2s)

#define arch_initcall(fn) __define_initcall("3",fn,3)
#define arch_initcall_sync(fn) __define_initcall("3s",fn,3s)
#define subsys_initcall(fn) __define_initcall("4",fn,4)
#define subsys_initcall_sync(fn) __define_initcall("4s",fn,4s)
#define fs_initcall(fn) __define_initcall("5",fn,5)
#define fs_initcall_sync(fn) __define_initcall("5s",fn,5s)
```

```
#define rootfs_initcall(fn) __define_initcall("rootfs",fn,rootfs)
#define device_initcall(fn) __define_initcall("6",fn,6)
#define device_initcall_sync(fn) __define_initcall("6s",fn,6s)
#define late_initcall(fn) __define_initcall("7",fn,7)

#define late_initcall_sync(fn) __define_initcall("7s",fn,7s)
#define __initcall(fn) device_initcall(fn)
...
```

In a similar fashion to the __setup macro described earlier, these macros declare a data item based on the function's name. They also use the section attribute to place this data item in a uniquely named section of the vmlinux ELF file. The benefit of this approach is that main.c can call an arbitrary initialization function for a subsystem that it has no knowledge of. The only other option, as mentioned earlier, is to pollute main.c with knowledge of every subsystem in the kernel. You can derive the section names from Listing 3-15 The name of the section is initcallN.init, where N is the level defined, between 1 and 7. Notice also that there is a section named for each of the seven levels with an s appended. This is intended to be a synchronous initcall. The data item is assigned the address of the function being named in the macro. The data itemwould be as follows (simplified by omitting the section attribute):

static initcall_t __initcall_customize_machine = customize_machine; This data item is placed in the kernel's object file in a section called .initcall3.init. The level (N) is used to provide an ordering of initialization calls. Functions declared using the *core_initcall()* macro are called before all others. Functions declared using the *postcore_initcall()* macros are called next, and so on, and those declared with late_initcall() are the last initialization functions to be called.

In a fashion similar to the __setup macro, you can think of this family of *_initcallmacros as registration functions for kernel subsystem initialization routines that need to be run once at kernel startup and never used again. These macros provide a mechanism for causing the initialization routine to be executed during system startup and a mechanism to discard the code and reclaim the memory after the routine has been executed. The developer is also provided up to seven levels of when to perform the initialization routines. Therefore, if you have a subsystem that relies on another subsystem's being available, you can enforce this ordering using these levels. If you grep (search) the kernel for the string [a-z]*_initcall, you will see that this family of macros is used extensively. One final note about the *_initcall family of macros: The use of multiple levels was introduced during the development of the 2.6 kernel series. Earlier kernel versions used the __initcall() macro for this purpose. This macro is still in widespread use, especially in device drivers. To maintain backward compatibility, this macro has been defined to *device_initcall()*, which has been defined as a level 6 initcall.

3.14 THE INIT THREAD

The code found in .../init/main.c is responsible for bringing the kernel to life. After *start_kernel()* performs some basic kernel initialization, calling early initialization functions explicitly by name, the very first kernel thread is spawned. This thread eventually becomes the kernel thread called *init()*, with a process ID (PID) of 1. As you will learn, *init()* becomes the parent of all Linux processes in user space. At this point in the boot sequence, two distinct threads are running: that represented by *start_ kernel()*, and now init(). The former goes on to become the idle process, having completed its work. The latter becomes the init process. This is shown in Listing 3-16.

LISTING 3-16 Creation of Kernel init Thread

```
Static noinline void __init_refok rest_init(void)
__releases(kernel_lock)
{
int pid;
rcu_scheduler_starting();
kernel_thread(kernel_init, NULL, CLONE_FS | CLONE_SIGHAND);
numa_default_policy();
pid = kernel_thread(kthreadd, NULL, CLONE_FS | CLONE_FILES);
kthreadd_task = find_task_by_pid_ns(pid, &init_pid_ns);
unlock_kernel();
/*
 * The boot idle thread must execute schedule()
 * at least once to get things moving:
 */
init_idle_bootup_task(current);
preempt_enable_no_resched();
schedule();
preempt_disable();
/* Call into cpu_idle with preempt disabled */
cpu_idle();
}
```

The start_kernel() function calls *rest_init()*, reproduced in Listing 3-16 The kernel's init process is spawned by the call to *kernel_thread()*, with the function kernel_init as its first parameter. init goes on to complete the rest of the system initialization, while the thread of execution started by *start_kernel()* loops forever in the call to *cpu_idle()*. The reason for this structure is interesting. You might have noticed that *start_ kernel()*, a relatively large function, was marked with *the __init macro*. This means that the memory it occupies will be reclaimed during the final stages of kernel initialization. It is necessary to exit this function and the address space it occupies before reclaiming its memory. The answer to this is for *start_kernel()* to call rest_init(), shown in Listing 3-16 a much smaller piece of memory that becomes the idle process.

3.14.1 Initialization Via initcalls

When kernel_init()is spawned, it eventually calls do_initcalls(), which is the function responsible for calling most of the initialization functions registered with the *_initcall family of macros. The code is reproduced in LISTING 3-17.

LISTING 3-17 Initialization Via initcalls

```
extern initcall_t __initcall_start[], __initcall_end[], __early_initcall_end[];
static void __init do_initcalls(void)
{
initcall_t *fn;
for (fn = __early_initcall_end; fn < __initcall_end; fn++)
do_one_initcall(*fn);
/* Make sure there is no pending stuff from the initcall sequence */
flush_scheduled_work();
}
```

Two similar blocks of code exist. Earlier in the initialization process, a similar function called *do_pre_smp_initcalls()* processes part of the list, from *__initcall_start to __early_initcall_end*. *This* code is self-explanatory, except for the two labels marking the loop boundaries: *__initcall_start and __initcall_end*. These labels are not found in any C source or header file. They are defined in the linker script file used during the link stage of vmlinux. These labels mark the beginning and end of the list of initialization functions populated using the *_initcall family of macros. You can see each of the labels by looking at the System.map file in the top-level kernel directory. They all begin with the *string __initcall,* as shown in Listing 3-18

3.14.2 Initcall_debug

A very interesting kernel command-line parameter allows you to watch these calls being executed during bootup. It is enabled by setting the kernel command-line parameter initcall_debug. Simply start your kernel with the kernel command-line parameter initcall_debug to enable this diagnostic output.12 Here is an example of what you will see when you enable these debug statements:

...

calling uhci_hcd_init+0x0/0x100 @ 1

uhci_hcd: USB Universal Host Controller Interface driver

initcall uhci_hcd_init+0x0/0x100 returned 0 after 5639 usecs

...

Here you see the USB Universal Host Controller Interface driver being called. The first line announces the intention to call the function uhci_hcd_init, which is a device driver initialization call from the USB driver. After this announcement is made, the call to the function is executed. The second line is printed by the driver itself. The trace information on the third line includes the return result and the call's duration. This is a useful way to see the details of kernel initialization, especially the order in which various subsystems and modules get called. More interesting is the call's duration. If you are concerned with system boot time, this is an excellent way to isolate where time is being consumed on boot. Even on a modestly configured embedded system, dozens of these initialization functions are invoked in this manner. This example is taken from an ARM XScale embedded target, compiled with a default configuration. The default configuration results in 206 such calls to various kernel initialization routines

3.14.3 Final Boot Steps

Having spawned the kernel_init() thread, and after all the various initialization calls have completed, the kernel performs its final steps in the boot sequence. These include freeing the memory used by the initialization functions and data, opening a system console device, and starting the first user space process. Listing 3-18 reproduces the last steps in the kernel's init process from main.c.

LISTING 3-18 Final Kernel Boot Steps from main.c

static noinline int init_post(void)

__releases(kernel_lock)

```
{

<... lines trimmed for clarity ...>
...
if (execute_command) {
run_init_process(execute_command);
printk(KERN_WARNING "Failed to execute %s. Attempting "
"defaults...\n", execute_command);
}

run_init_process("/sbin/init");
run_init_process("/etc/init");

run_init_process("/bin/init");
run_init_process("/bin/sh");

panic("No init found. Try passing init= option to kernel.");
```

If the code proceeds to the end of this function *(init_post())*, a kernel panic results. If you have spent any time experimenting with embedded systems or custom root file systems, you have undoubtedly encountered this very common error message as the last line of output on your console. One way or another, one of these *run_init_process()* commands must proceed without error. The run_init_process() function does not return on successful invocation. It overwrites the calling process with the new one, effectively replacing the current process with the new one. It uses the familiar execve() system call for this functionality. The most common system configurations spawn /sbin/init as the userland initialization process.

initcall_debug init=/sbin/myinit console=ttyS1,115200 root=/dev/hda1

This kernel command line instructs the kernel to display all the initialization routines as they are invoked, configures the initial console device *as /dev/ttyS1 at 115Kbps*, and executes a custom user space initialization process called myinit, which is located in *the /sbin directory* on the root file system. It directs the kernel to mount its root file system from the device */dev/hda1*, which is the first IDE hard drive. Note that, in general, the order of parameters given on the kernel command line is irrelevant.

3.15 SYSTEM INITIALIZATION

The routine performs the initialization of each module, such as processes and threads, initializing in the following order:
- Internal Process context structures
- Ready queues
- Pthread module
- Semaphore module Message queue module
- Shared memory module
- Memory allocation module
- software timers module
- Idle task creation
- Static pthread creation

After this steps, interrupts and exceptions are enabled, the kernel loops infinitely.

In the task, enabling the scheduler start scheduling processes.

QUESTIONS

1. Explain in detail LSB.
2. What is OSDL? Explain in detail OSDLs Mobile Linux Initiative.
3. Write short note on OSDL.
4. What is the Goal or Mission of MLI ?
5. Explain in detail 1Kernel Versions with example.
6. How to construct Linux Kernel Explain in detail ?
7. How to Compile Kernel explain with example ?
8. Explain with neat diagram kernel image components.
9. Write short note on Tool Chain.
10. Explain in detail Kernel Build System.
11. Write short note on The Dot-Config.
12. Write short note on Make file Targets.
13. What is kernel Initialization ?
14. Write short note on BIOS Versus Bootloader.
15. Explain in detail U-Boot Process.
16. How to obtain U-Boot ?

17. How to Configure U-Boot ?
18. What are the different U-Boot Monitor Commands ?
19. Explain in detail Anatomy of an Embedded System.
20. Explain in detail Linux Boot Process for Embedded Systems.
21. What is the importance of Busy box ?
22. Why Busy box is easy ?
23. Explain in detail BusyBox Configuration.
24. What are the different BusyBox Operation ?
25. Explain in detail Busybox.
26. Explain in detail Process Virtual Memory.
27. Write Short note on Cross-Development Environment.
28. What exactly is a Linux distribution ?
29. Explain in detail Subsystem Initialization.
30. Write steps for system initialization.

UNIT IV

BOOTLOADERS AND DEVICE DRIVERS

4.1 Introduction to Bootloaders

- Bootloader is a piece of code that runs before any operating system is running.
- Bootloader are used to boot other operating systems, usually each operating system has a set of bootloaders specific for it.
- Bootloaders usually contain several ways to boot the OS kernel and also contain commands for debugging and/or modifying the kernel environment.
- A critical component of an embedded system, the bootloader provides the foundation from which the primary system software is spawned.

4.1.1 Role of a Bootloader

- When power is first applied to a processor board, many elements of hardware must be initialized before even the simplest program can run.
- Each architecture and processor has a set of predefined actions and configurations upon release of reset, which includes fetching initialization code from an onboard storage device (usually Flash memory).
- This early initialization code is part of the bootloader and is responsible for breathing life into the processor and related hardware components. Most processors have a default address from which the first bytes of code are fetched upon application of power and release of reset.
- Hardware designers use this information to arrange the layout of Flash memory on the board and to select which address range(s) the Flash memory responds to. This way, when power is first applied, code is fetched from a well-known and predictable address, and software control can be established.
- The bootloader provides this early initialization code and is responsible for initializing the board so that other programs can run. This early initialization code is almost always written in the processor's native assembly language. This fact alone presents many challenges, some of which we examine here.
- After the bootloader has performed this basic processor and platform initialization, its primary role is fetching and booting a full-blown operating system. It is responsible for locating, loading, and passing control to the primary operating system.
- In addition, the bootloader might have advanced features, such as the capability to validate an OS image, upgrade itself or an OS image, or choose from among several OS images based on a developer defined policy. Unlike the traditional PC-BIOS model, when the OS takes control, the bootloader is overwritten and ceases to exist.

4.1.2 Bootloader Challenges

- DRAM Controller
- Flash Versus RAM
- Image Complexity
- Execution Context

4.1.2.1 DRAM Controller

- DRAM chips cannot be directly read from or written to like other microprocessor bus resources. They require specialized hardware controllers to enable read and write cycles.
- To further complicate matters, DRAM must be constantly refreshed, or the data contained within will be lost. Refresh is accomplished by sequentially reading each location in DRAM in a systematic manner within the timing specifications set forth by the DRAM manufacturer.
- Modern DRAM chips support many modes of operation, such as burst mode and dual data rate for high-performance applications. It is the DRAM controller's responsibility to configure DRAM, keep it refreshed within the manufacturer's timing specifications, and respond to the various read and write commands from the processor.
- Setting up a DRAM controller is the source of much frustration for the newcomer to embedded development. It requires detailed knowledge of DRAM architecture, the controller itself, the specific DRAM chips being used, and the overall hardware design.
- Very little can happen in an embedded system until the DRAM controller and DRAM itself have been properly initialized. One of the first things a bootloader must do is enable the memory subsystem.
- After it is initialized, memory can be used as a resource. In fact, one of the first actions many bootloaders perform after memory initialization is to copy themselves into DRAM for faster execution.

4.1.2.2 Flash Versus RAM

- Another complexity inherent in bootloaders is that they are required to be stored in nonvolatile storage but usually are loaded into RAM for execution. Again, the complexity arises from the level of resources available for the bootloader to rely on.
- In a fully operational computer system running an operating system such as Linux, it is relatively easy to compile a program and invoke it from nonvolatile storage. The runtime libraries, operating system, and compiler work together to create the infrastructure necessary to load a program from nonvolatile storage into memory and pass control to it.
- The aforementioned "Hello World" program is a perfect example. When compiled, it can be loaded into memory and executed simply by typing the name of the executable (hello) on the command line (assuming, of course, that the executable exists some where

on your PATH). This infrastructure does not exist when a bootloader gains control upon power-on. Instead, the bootloader must create its own operational context and move itself, if required, to a suitable location in RAM. Furthermore, additional complexity is introduced by the requirement to execute from a read-only medium.

4.1.2.3 Image Complexity

- As application developers, we do not need to concern ourselves with the layout of a binary executable file when we develop applications for our favorite platform. The compiler and binary utilities are preconfigured to build a binary executable image containing the proper components needed for a given architecture.
- The linker places startup (prologue) and shutdown (epilogue) code into the image. These objects set up the proper execution context for your application, which typically starts at main(). This is absolutely not the case with a typical bootloader. When the bootloader gets control, there is no context or prior execution environment.
- A typical system might not have any DRAM until the bootloader initializes the processor and related hardware.

4.1.2.4 Execution Context

The other primary reason for bootloader image complexity is the lack of execution context. When the sequence of instructions starts executing, the resources available to the running program are nearly zero. Default values designed into the hardware ensure that fetches from Flash memory work properly. This also ensures that the system clock has some default values, but little else can be assumed. The reset state of each processor is usually well defined by the manufacturer, but the reset state of a board is defined by the hardware designers.

Indeed, most processors have no DRAM available at startup for temporary storage of variables or, worse, for a stack that is required to use C program calling conventions. If you were forced to write a "Hello World" program with no DRAM and, therefore, no stack, it would be quite different from the traditional "Hello World" example.

This limitation places significant challenges on the initial body of code designed to initialize the hardware. As a result, one of the first tasks the bootloader performs on startup is to configure enough of the hardware to enable at least some minimal amount of RAM. Some processors designed for embedded use have small amounts of on-chip static RAM available. This is the case with the 405 GP we've been discussing.

When RAM is available, a stack can be allocated using part of that RAM, and a proper context can be constructed to run higher-level languages such as C. This allows the rest of the processor and platform initialization to be written in something other than assembly language.

4.1.3 A Universal Bootloader (Das U-Boot)

- Investing in a single bootloader across multiple platforms ultimately results in lower development costs. This section studies an existing bootloader that has become very popular in the embedded Linux community. The official name of this bootloader is Das U-Boot. It is maintained by Wolfgang Denx.
- Das U-Boot (Universal Bootloader) is an open source, primary boot loader used in embedded devices. It is available for a number of computer architectures, including 68 k, ARM, AVR32, Blackfin, MicroBlaze, MIPS, Nios, PPC and x86.

Design Principles of a Universal Bootloader are as Follows
1. Easy to port to new architectures, new processors, and new boards.
2. Easy to debug : serial console output as soon as possible.
3. Features and commands configurable.
4. As small as possible.
5. As reliable as possible.

4.1.3.1 Obtaining U-Boot

The simplest way to get the U-Boot source code is via git. If you have git installed on your desktop or laptop, simply issue this command :

$ git clone git://git.denx.de/u-boot.git

4.1.3.2 Configuring U-Boot

For a bootloader to be useful across many processors and architectures, some method of configuring the bootloader is necessary. As with the Linux kernel itself, a bootloader is configured at compile time. This method significantly reduces the complexity of the binary bootloader image, which in itself is an important characteristic. In the case of U-Boot, board-specific configuration is driven by a single header file specific to the target platform, together with a few soft links in the source tree that select the correct subdirectories based on target board, architecture, and CPU.

- When configuring U-Boot for one of its supported platforms, issue this command :

$ make <platform>_config

Here, platform is one of the many platforms supported by U-Boot. These platform configuration targets are listed in the top-level U-Boot make file.

- For example, to configure for the Spectrum Digital OSK, which contains a TI OMAP 5912 processor, issue this command :

$ make omap5912osk_config

This configures the U-Boot source tree with the appropriate soft links to select ARM as the target architecture, the ARM926 core, and the 5912 OSK as the target platform.

- The next step in configuring U-Boot for this platform is to edit the configuration file specific to this board. This file is found in the U-Boot ../include/configs subdirectory and is called omap5912osk.h.
- The README file that comes with the U-Boot source code describes the details of configuration and is the best source of this information.
- U-Boot is configured using configuration variables defined in a board-specific header file. Configuration variables have two forms. Configuration options are selected using macros in the form of CONFIG_XXXX. Configuration settings are selected using macros in the form of CONFIG_SYS_XXXX.
- In general, configuration options (CONFIG_XXX) are user-configurable and enable specific U-Boot operational features. Configuration settings (CONFIG_SYS_XXX) usually are hardware-specific and require detailed knowledge of the underlying processor and/or hardware platform.
- Board-specific U-Boot configuration is driven by a header file dedicated to that specific platform that contains configuration options and settings appropriate for the underlying platform. The U-Boot source tree includes a directory where these board-specific configuration header files reside. They can be found in .../include/configs from the top-level U-Boot source directory.

4.1.3.3 U-Boot Monitor Commands
- U-Boot supports more than 70 standard command sets that enable more than 150 unique commands using CONFIG_CMD_* macros.
- A command set is enabled in U-Boot through the use of configuration setting (CONFIG_*) macros.

4.1.3.4 Network Operations
- Many bootloaders include support for Ethernet interfaces. In a development environment, this is a huge time saver.
- Loading even a modest kernel image over a serial port can take minutes versus a few seconds over an Ethernet link, especially if your board supports Fast or Gigabit Ethernet. Furthermore, serial links are more prone to errors from poorly behaved serial terminals, line noise, and so on.
- Some of the more important features to look for in a bootloader include support for the BOOTP, DHCP, and TFTP protocols. If you're unfamiliar with these, BOOTP (Bootstrap Protocol) and DHCP (Dynamic Host Configuration Protocol) enable a target device with an Ethernet port to obtain an IP address and other network-related configuration information from a central server.
- TFTP (Trivial File Transfer Protocol) allows the target device to download files (such as a Linux kernel image) from a TFTP server. Servers for these services are described in, "Embedded Development Environment."

- Fig. 4.1 illustrates the flow of information between the target device and a BOOTP server. The client (U-Boot, in this case) initiates the exchange by sending a broadcast packet searching for a BOOTP server.
- The server responds with a reply packet that includes the client's IP address and other information. The most useful data includes a filename used to download a kernel image.

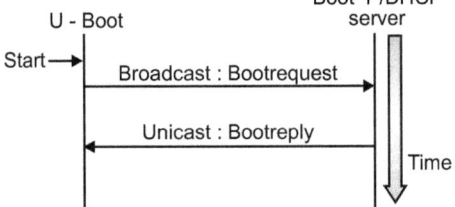

Fig. 4.1 : BOOTP client/server handshake

- In practice, dedicated BOOTP servers no longer exist as stand-alone servers. DHCP servers included with your favorite Linux distribution also support BOOTP protocol packets and are almost universally used for BOOTP operations.
- The DHCP protocol builds on BOOTP. It can supply the target with a wide variety of configuration information. In practice, the information exchange is often limited by the target/bootloader DHCP client implementation.

Table 4.1 : DHCP Target Parameters

Sr. No.	DHCP Target Parameter	Purpose	Description
1.	Host	Hostname	Symbolic label from the DHCP configuration file.
2.	Hardware Ethernet	Ethernet hardware address	Low-level ehterner hardware address of the targets Ethernet interface.
3.	Fixed-address	Target IP address	The IP address that the target will assume.
4.	Netmask	Target netmask	The IP netmask that the target will assume.
5.	Server-name	TFTP server IP address	The IP address to which the target will direct requests for file transfers, the root file system, and so on.
6.	Filename	TFTP filename	The filename that the bootloader can use to boot a secondary image (usually a linux kernel)
7.	Root-path	NFS root path	Defines the network path for the remote NFS root mount.

- When the bootloader on the target board has completed the BOOTP or DHCP exchange, these parameters are used for further configuration. For example, the bootloader uses the target IP address (fixed-address) to bind its Ethernet port to this IP address.
- The bootloader then uses the server-name field as a destination IP address to request the file contained in the filename field, which, in most cases, represents a Linux kernel image. Although this is the most common use, this same scenario could be used to download and execute manufacturing test and diagnostics firmware.
- It should be noted that the DHCP protocol supports many more parameters than those detailed in Table 4.1. These are simply the more common parameters you might encounter for embedded systems. See the DHCP specification referenced at the end of this section for complete details.

4.1.3.5 Storage Subsystems

- Many bootloaders support the capability of booting images from a variety of nonvolatile storage devices in addition to the usual Flash memory.
- The difficulty in supporting these types of devices is the relative complexity in both hardware and software.
- To access data on a hard drive, for example, the bootloader must have device driver code for the IDE controller interface, as well as knowledge of the underlying partition scheme and file system. This is not trivial and is one of the tasks more suited to full-blown operating systems.
- Even with the underlying complexity, methods exist for loading images from this class of device. The simplest method is to support the hardware only. In this scheme, no knowledge of the file system is assumed.
- The bootloader simply raw-loads from absolute sectors on the device. This scheme can be used by dedicating an unformatted partition from sector 0 on an IDE-compatible device (such as CompactFlash) and loading the data found there without any structure imposed on the data. This is a simple configuration for loading a kernel image or other binary image from a block storage device.
- Additional partitions on the device can be formatted for a given file system and can contain complete file systems. After the kernel boots, Linux device drivers can be used to access the additional partitions. U-Boot can load an image from a specified raw partition or from a partition with a file system structure.
- Of course, the board must have a supported hardware device (an IDE subsystem), and U-Boot must be so configured. Adding CONFIG_CMD_IDE to the board-specific configuration file enables support for an IDE interface, and adding CONFIG_CMD_BOOTD enables support for booting from a raw partition. If you are porting U-Boot to a custom board, you will likely have to modify U-Boot to understand your particular hardware.

4.1.3.6 Booting from Disk

- As just described, U-Boot supports several methods for booting a kernel image from a disk subsystem. This simple command illustrates one of the supported methods :

  diskboot 0x400000 0:0

- To understand this syntax, you must first understand how U-Boot numbers disk devices. The 0:0 in this example specifies the device and partition.
- In this simple example, U-Boot performs a raw binary load of the image found on the first IDE device (IDE device 0) from the first partition (partition 0) found on this device. The image is loaded into system memory at physical address 0x400000.
- After the kernel image has been loaded into memory, the U-Boot bootm command (boot from memory) is used to boot the kernel

  bootm 0x400000

4.1.4 Porting U-Boot

- One of the reasons U-Boot has become so popular is the ease with which new platforms can be supported.
- Each board port must supply a subordinate makefile that supplies board-specific definitions to the build process.
- These files are all given the name config.mk. They exist in the .../board/vendor/boardname subdirectory under the U-Boot top-level source directory, where boardname specifies a particular board. As of a recent U-Boot snapshot, more than 460 different board configuration files are named config.mk under the .../boards subdirectory.
- In this same U-Boot version, 49 different CPU configurations are supported (counted in the same manner). Note that, in some cases, the CPU configuration covers a family of chips, such as ppc4xx, that supports several processors in the Power Architecture 4xx family.
- U-Boot supports a large variety of popular CPUs and CPU families in use today, and a much larger collection of reference boards based on these processors. If your board contains one of the supported CPUs, porting U-Boot is straight forward. If you must add a new CPU, plan on substantially more effort.
- The good news is that someone before you has probably done the bulk of the work. Whether you are porting to a new CPU or a new board based on an existing CPU, study the existing source code for specific guidance. Determine what CPU is closest to yours, and clone the functionality found in that CPU-specific directory. Finally, modify the resulting sources to add the specific support for your new CPU's requirements.

4.1.4.1 EP405 U-Boot Port

- The same logic used in porting to a different CPU applies to porting U-Boot to a new board. Let's look at an example. We will use the Embedded Planet EP405 board, which contains the AMCC Power Architecture 405GP processor. The particular board used for this example was provided courtesy of Embedded Planet and came with 64 MB of SDRAM and 16 MB of on-board Flash. Numerous other devices complete the design.
- The first step is to see how close we can come to an existing board. Many boards in the U-Boot source tree support the 405GP processor. A quick grep of the board configuration header files narrows the choices to those that support the 405GP processor :

  $ cd .../u-boot/include/configs
  $ grep -l CONFIG_405GP *

- In a recent U-Boot snapshot, 28 board configuration files are configured for the 405GP. After examining a few, we choose the AR405.h configuration as a baseline. It supports the LXT971 Ethernet transceiver, which is also on the EP405.
- The goal is to minimize any development work by borrowing from similar architectures in the spirit of open source. We'll tackle the easy steps first. We need a custom board configuration header file for our EP405 board. Copy the board configuration file to a new file with a name appropriate for your board. We'll call ours EP405.h. These commands are issued from the top-level U-Boot source tree :

  $ cp .../include/configs/AR405.h .../include/configs/EP405.h

- After you have copied the configuration header file, you must create the board specific directory and make a copy of the AR405 board files. We don't know yet if we need all of them. That step will come later. After copying the files to your new board directory, edit the filenames appropriately for your board name :

  $ cd board <<< from top-level U-Boot source directory
  $ mkdir ep405
  $ cp esd/ar405/* ep405

- Now comes the hard part. Jerry Van Baren, a developer and U-Boot contributor, detailed a humorous but realistic process for porting U-Boot in an e-mail posting to the U-Boot mailing list. His complete process, documented in pseudo-C, can be found in the U-Boot README file. The following summarizes the hard part of the porting process in Jerry's style and spirit :

```
while (!running)
{
do
{
```

```
Add / modify source code
} until (compiles);
Debug;
...
}
```

- Jerry's process, as summarized here, is the simple truth. When you have selected a baseline from which to port, you must add, delete, and modify source code until it compiles, and then debug it until it is running without error! There is no magic formula.
- Porting any bootloader to a new board requires knowledge of many areas of hardware and software. Some of these disciplines, such as setting up SDRAM controllers, are rather specialized and complex.
- Virtually all of this work involves detailed knowledge of the underlying hardware. Therefore, be prepared to spend many entertaining hours poring over your processor's hardware reference manual, along with the data sheets of numerous other components that reside on your board.

4.1.4.2 U-Boot Makefile Configuration Target

- Now that we have a code base to start from, we must make some modifications to the top-level U-Boot makefile to add the configuration steps for our new board.
- Upon examining this makefile, we find a section for configuring the U-Boot source tree for the various supported boards. This section can be found starting with the unconfig target in the top-level makefile.
- We now add support for our new board to allow us to configure it. Because we derived our board from the ESD AR405, we will use that rule as the template for building our own.
- If you follow along in the U-Boot source code, you will see that these rules are placed in the makefile in alphabetical order according to their configuration names. We will be good open-source citizens and follow that lead. We call our configuration target EP405_config, again in concert with the U-Boot conventions.
- Edit the top-level makefile using your favorite editor.
- Upon completing the steps just described, we have a U-Boot source tree that represents a starting point. It probably will not compile cleanly, so that should be our first step. At least the compiler can give us some guidance on where to start.

4.1.4.3 EP405 First Build

We now have a U-Boot source tree with our candidate files. Our first step is to configure the build tree for our newly installed EP405 board. Using the configuration target we just added to the top-level makefile, we configure the tree.

4.1.4.4 EP405 Processor Initialization

- The first task that your new U-Boot port must do correctly is initialize the processor and the memory (DRAM) subsystems. After reset, the 405GP processor core is designed to fetch instructions starting from 0xFFFF_FFFC.
- The core attempts to execute the instructions found here. Because this is the top of the memory range, the instruction found here must be an unconditional branch instruction. This processor core is also hard-coded to configure the upper 2 MB memory region so that it is accessible without programming the external bus controller, to which Flash memory is usually attached. This forces the requirement to branch to a location within this address space, because the processor is incapable of addressing memory anywhere else until our bootloader code initializes additional memory regions.
- We must branch to somewhere at or above 0xFFE0_0000. How do we know all this? Because we read the 405GP user manual!
- The behavior of the 405GP processor core, as just described, places requirements on the hardware designer to ensure that, on power-up, nonvolatile memory (Flash) is mapped to the required upper 2 MB memory region.
- Certain attributes of this initial memory region assume default values on reset.
- For example, this upper 2 MB region will be configured for 256 wait states, three cycles of address to chip select delay, three cycles of chip select to output enable delay, and seven cycles of hold time. This allows maximum freedom for the hardware designer to select appropriate devices or methods of getting instruction code to the processor directly after reset.

4.1.4.5 Board-Specific Initialization

- The first opportunity for any board-specific initialization comes in .../cpu/ppc4xx/ start.S just after the cacheable regions have been initialized. Here we find a call to an external assembler language routine called ext_bus_cntlr_init :
  bl ext_bus_cntlr_init /* Board-specific bus cntrl init */
- This routine is defined in .../board/ep405/init.S, in the new board-specific directory for our board. It provides a hook for very early hardware-based initialization. This is one of the files that has been customized for our EP405 platform. This file contains the board-specific code to initialize the 405GP's external bus controller for our application.

4.1.4.6 Porting Summary

- By now, you can appreciate some of the difficulties of porting a bootloader to a hardware platform. There is simply no substitute for detailed knowledge of the underlying hardware.
- Of course, we'd like to minimize our investment in time required for this task. After all, we usually are not paid based on how well we understand every hardware detail of a given processor, but rather on our ability to deliver a working solution in a timely manner.

- Indeed, this is one of the primary reasons open source has flourished. You just saw how easy it is to port U-Boot to a new hardware platform not because you're an expert on the processor, but because many before us have done the bulk of the hard work already.

4.1.4.7 U-Boot Image Format
- Now that we have a working bootloader for our EP405 board, we can load and run programs on it.
- Ideally, we want to run an operating system such as Linux. To do this, we need to understand the image format that U-Boot requires.
- U-Boot expects a small header on the image file that identifies several attributes of the image. U-Boot provides the mkimage tool (part of the U-Boot source code) to build this image header.
- Recent Linux kernel distributions have built-in support for building images directly bootable by U-Boot. Both the arm and powerpc branches of the kernel source tree support a target called uImage.

4.1.5 Device Tree Blob (Flat Device Tree)
- One of the more challenging aspects of porting Linux (and U-Boot) to your new board is the recent requirement for a device tree blob (DTB).
- It is also referred to as a flat device tree, device tree binary, or simply device tree. Throughout this discussion, these terms are used interchangeably.
- The DTB is a database that represents the hardware components on a given board. It is derived from the IBM Open Firmware specifications and has been chosen as the default mechanism to pass low-level hardware information from the bootloader to the kernel.
- Prior to the requirement for a DTB, U-Boot would pass a board information structure to the kernel, which was derived from a header file in U-Boot that had to exactly match the contents of a similar header file in the kernel.
- It was very difficult to keep them in sync, and it didn't scale well. This was, in part, the motivation for incorporating the flat device tree as a method to communicate low-level hardware details from the bootloader to the kernel.
- Similar to U-Boot or other low-level firmware, mastering the DTB requires complete knowledge of the underlying hardware.
- By now, you are probably wondering where the DTB came from. The easy answer is that it was provided as a courtesy by the board/architecture developers as part of the Linux kernel source tree.

4.1.5.1 Device Tree Source
- The device tree blob is "compiled" by a special compiler that produces the binary in the proper form for U-Boot and Linux to understand.
- The dtc compiler usually is provided with your embedded Linux distribution, or it can be found at http://jdl.com/ software.

4.1.5.2 Device Tree Compiler

- Introduced earlier, the device tree compiler (dtc) converts the human-readable device tree source into the machine-readable binary that both U-Boot and the Linux kernel understand.
- Although a git tree is hosted on kernel.org for dtc, the device tree source has been merged into the kernel source tree and is built along with any Power Architecture kernel from the .../arch/powerpc branch. It is quite straight forward to use the device tree compiler. A typical command to convert source to binary looks like this :

  $ dtc -O dtb -o myboard.dtb -b 0 myboard.dts

- In this command, myboard.dts is the device tree human-readable source, and myboard.dtb is the binary created by this command invocation. The -O flag specifies the output format in this case, the device tree blob binary. The -o flag names the output file, and the -b 0 parameter specifies the physical boot CPU in the multicore case.
- Note that the dtc compiler allows you to go in both directions. The command example just shown performs a compile from source to device tree binary, whereas a command like this produces source from the binary :

  $ dtc -I dtb -O dts mpc8548.dtb >mpc8548.dts

- You can also build the DTB for many well-known reference boards directly from the kernel source. The command looks similar to the following :

  $ make ARCH=powerpc mpc8548cds.dtb

- This produces a binary device tree blob from a source file with the same base name (mpc8548cds) and the dts extension. These are found in .../arch/powerpc/boot/dts.
- A recent kernel source tree had 120 such device tree source files for a range of Power Architecture boards.

4.1.6 Other Bootloaders

Here we introduce the more popular bootloaders, describe where they might be used, and summarize their features. This is not intended to be a thorough tutorial; doing so would require a book of its own.

4.1.6.1 Lilo

- The Linux Loader, or Lilo, was widely used in commercial Linux distributions for desktop PC platforms; as such, it has its roots in the Intel x86/IA32 architecture. Lilo has several components.
- It has a primary bootstrap program that lives on the first sector of a bootable disk drive. The primary loader is limited to a disk sector size, usually 512 bytes. Therefore, its primary purpose is simply to load and pass control to a secondary loader. The secondary loader can span multiple sectors and does most of the bootloader's work.

- Lilo is driven by a configuration file and utility that is part of the Lilo executable. This configuration file can be read or written to only under control of the host operating system. That is, the configuration file is not referenced by the early boot code in either the primary or secondary loaders.
- Entries in the configuration file are read and processed by the Lilo configuration utility during system installation or administration.
- Configuration file instructs the Lilo configuration utility to use the master boot record of the first hard drive (/dev/hda). It contains a delay instruction to wait for the user to press a key before the time out (5 seconds, in this case). This allows the system operator to select from a list of OS images to boot.
- If the system operator presses the Tab key before the timeout, Lilo presents a list to choose from. Lilo uses the label tag as the text to display for each image. The images are defined with the image tag in the configuration file.
- Lilo loads this image from the hard drive. It then loads a second file to be used as an initial ramdisk. Lilo constructs a kernel command line containing the string "root=LABEL=/" and passes this to the Linux kernel upon execution. This instructs Linux where to get its root file system after boot.

4.1.6.2 GRUB

- Many current commercial Linux distributions now ship with the GRUB bootloader. GRUB, or GR and Unified Bootloader, is a GNU project. It has many enhanced features not found in Lilo.
- The biggest difference between GRUB and Lilo is GRUB's capability to understand file systems and kernel image formats. Furthermore, GRUB can read and modify its configuration at boot time.
- GRUB also supports booting across a network, which can be a tremendous asset in an embedded environment. GRUB offers a command-line interface at boot time to modify the boot configuration.
- Like Lilo, GRUB is driven by a configuration file. Unlike Lilo's static configuration, however, the GRUB bootloader reads this configuration at boot time. This means that the configured behavior can be modified at boot time for different system configurations.
- The GRUB configuration file is called grub.conf and usually is placed in a small partition dedicated to storing boot images.
- Unlike Lilo, GRUB can actually read a file system on a given partition to load an image from.
- Notice that the GRUB syntax has the kernel command-line parameters on the same line as the kernel file specification.

4.1.6.3 Still More Bootloaders

- Numerous other bootloaders have found their way into specific niches. For example, Redboot is another open source bootloader that Intel and the XScale community have adopted for use on various evaluation boards based on the Intel IXP and Marvel PXA processor families.
- Micromonitor is in use by board vendors such as Cogent and others. YAMON has found popularity in MIPs circles.
- Linux BIOS is used primarily in X86 environments. In general, when you consider a boot loader, you should consider some important factors up front :
  - Does it support my chosen processor?
  - Has it been ported to a board similar to my own?
  - Does it support the features I need?
  - Does it support the hardware devices I intend to use?
  - Is there a large community of users where I might get support?
  - Are there any commercial vendors from which I can purchase support?
- These are some of the questions you must answer when considering what bootloader to use in your embedded project.
- Unless you are doing something on the "bleeding edge" of technology using a brand-new processor, you are likely to find that someone has already done the bulk of the hard work in porting a bootloader to your chosen platform.

4.2 DEVICE DRIVER BASICS

- One of the more challenging aspects of system design is partitioning functionality in a rational manner. The familiar device driver model found in UNIX and Linux provides a natural partitioning of functionality between your application code and hardware or kernel devices.
- A device driver is a hides the details of a particular peripheral and provides a slightly high-level programming interface to it. A device driver is typically specific to a given operating system.
- Device drivers allow application software to attach to, read and write data from, and change the behavior of the peripheral device. This section helps you understand this model and the basics of Linux device driver architecture.

4.2.1 Device Driver Concepts

- A device driver or software driver is a computer program allowing higher-level computer programs to interact with a hardware device.
- Device drivers are integral components of operating systems.

- One of the fundamental purposes of a device driver is to isolate the user programs from ready access to critical kernel data structures and hardware devices. Furthermore, a well-written device driver hides from the user the complexity and variability of the hardware device.
- For example, a program that wants to write data to the hard disk doesn't need to know if the disk drive uses 512-byte or 1024-byte sectors. The user simply opens a file and issues a write command. The device driver handles the details and isolates the user from the complexities and perils of hardware device programming.
- The device driver provides a consistent user interface to a large variety of hardware devices. It provides the basis for the familiar UNIX/Linux convention that everything must be represented as a file.

Why a Device Driver ?
- A device driver simplifies programming by acting as an abstraction layer between a hardware device and the applications or operating systems that use it.
- The higher-level application code can be written independently of whatever specific hardware device it will ultimately control, as it can interface with it in a standard way, regardless of the underlying hardware.
- The device-driver accepts the generic high-level commands and breaks them into a series of low-level device-specific commands as required by the device being driven.
- Device Drivers can provide a level of security as they can run in kernel-mode, thereby protecting the operating system from applications running in user mode.

4.2.1.1 Loadable Modules

- Unlike some other operating systems, Linux lets you add and remove kernel components at runtime.
- Linux is structured as a monolithic kernel with a well-defined interface for adding and removing device driver modules dynamically after boot time.
- This feature not only provides flexibility for the user, but it also has proven invaluable to the device driver developer. Assuming that your device driver is reasonably well behaved, you can insert and remove the device driver from a running kernel at will during the development cycle instead of rebooting the kernel every time you want to test a change.
- Loadable modules have particular importance to embedded systems. Loadable modules enhance field upgrade capabilities. For example, the module itself can be updated in a live system without the need for a reboot.
- Modules can be stored on media other than the root (boot) device, which can be space-constrained. Of course, device drivers can also be statically compiled into the kernel, and, for many drivers, this is completely appropriate.
- Consider, for example, a kernel configured to mount a root file system from a network attached NFS server. In this scenario, you configure the network-related drivers (TCP/IP

and the network interface card driver) to be compiled into the main kernel image so that they are available during boot for mounting the remote root file system.
- Loadable modules are installed after the kernel has booted. Startup scripts can load device driver modules, and modules can also be "demand loaded" when needed.
- Linux can request a module when a service is requested that requires a particular module. Terminology has never been standardized when discussing kernel modules.
- Many terms have been and continue to be used interchangeably when discussing Linux device drivers. Throughout this and later section, the terms device driver, Loadable Kernel Module (LKM), loadable module, and module are all used to describe a kernel device driver module.

4.2.1.2 Device Driver Architecture

- The basic Linux device driver model is familiar to UNIX/Linux system developers. Although the device driver model continues to evolve, some fundamental constructs have remained nearly constant over the course of UNIX/Linux evolution.
- The devices in UNIX fall in two categories- Character devices and Block devices.
- Character devices can be compared to normal files in that we can read/write arbitrary bytes at a time (although for most part, seeking is not supported).
- They work with a stream of bytes.
- Block devices, on the other hand, operate on blocks of data, not arbitrary bytes.
- Usual block size is 512 bytes or larger powers of two. However, block devices can be accessed the same was as character devices, the driver does the block management. (Networking devices do not belong to these categories, the interface provided by these drivers in entirely different from that of char/block devices).
- The beauty of UNIX is that devices are represented as files. Both character devices and block devices are represented by respective files in the /dev directory. This means that you can read and write into the device by manipulating those file using standard system calls like open, read, write, close etc.
- For example you could directly write or read the hard disk by accessing /dev/sd* file a dangerous act unless you know what you are doing (for those interested, try hexdump C /dev/sda –n 512 – what you see then is the boot sector of your hard disk !). As another example, you could directly see the contents of the RAM by reading /dev/mem.
- Every device file represented in this manner is associated with the device driver of that device which is actually responsible for interacting with the device on behalf of the user request. So when you access a device file, the request is forwarded to the respective device driver which does the processing and returns the result.

Character Device Vs. Block Device
- A Character ('c') Device is one with which the Driver communicates by sending and receiving single characters (bytes, octets).

- A Block ('b') Device is one with which the Driver communicates by sending entire blocks of data.
- Examples for Character Devices : serial ports, parallel ports, sounds cards.
- Examples for Block Devices : hard disks, USB cameras, Disk-On-Key.
- For the user, the type of the Device (block or character) does not matter you just care that this is a hard disk partition or a sound card.
- Driver programmers, however, do care, but that's beyond our scope.

4.2.1.3 Minimal Device Driver Example

Because Linux supports loadable device drivers, it is relatively easy to demonstrate a simple device driver skeleton. Listing 4-1 shows a loadable device driver module that contains the bare minimum structure to be loaded and unloaded by a running kernel.

LISTING 4–1 Minimal Device Driver

```
/* Example Minimal Character Device Driver */
#include <linux/module.h>
static int __init hello_init(void)
{
printk(KERN_INFO "Hello Example Init\n");
return 0;
}
static void __exit hello_exit(void)
{
printk("Hello Example Exit\n");
}
module_init(hello_init);
module_exit(hello_exit);
MODULE_AUTHOR("Chris Hallinan");
MODULE_DESCRIPTION("Hello World Example");
MODULE_LICENSE("GPL");
```

- The skeletal driver shown in Listing 4–1 contains enough structure for the kernel to load and unload the driver and to invoke the initialization and exit routines. Let's look at how this is done, because it illustrates some important high-level concepts that are useful for device driver development.
- A device driver is a special kind of binary module. Unlike a stand-alone binary executable application, a device driver cannot simply be executed from a command prompt.
- The 2.6 kernel series requires that the binary be in a special "kernel object" format. When properly built, the device driver binary module contains a .ko suffix.

- The build steps and compiler options required to create the .ko module object can be complex. Here we outline a set of steps to harness the power of the Linux kernel build system without requiring you to become an expert in it, which is beyond the scope of this book.

4.2.1.4 Module Build Infrastructure

- A device driver must be compiled against the kernel on which it will execute. Although it is possible to load and execute kernel modules built against a different kernel version, it is risky to do so unless you are certain that the module does not rely on any features of your new kernel.
- The easiest way to do this is to build the module within the kernel's own source tree. This ensures that as the developer changes the kernel configuration, his custom driver is automatically rebuilt with the correct kernel configuration. It is certainly possible to build your drivers outside the kernel source tree.
- However, in this case, you are responsible for making sure that your device driver build configuration stays in sync with the kernel you want to run your driver on. This typically includes compiler switches, the location of kernel header files, and kernel configuration options.
- For the sample driver introduced in Listing 4–1, the following changes were made to the stock Linux kernel source tree to enable building this sample driver. We'll explain each step in detail :
  (1) Starting from the top-level Linux source directory, create a directory under .../drivers/char called examples.
  (2) Add a menu item to the kernel configuration to enable building examples and to specify a built-in or loadable kernel module.
  (3) Add the new examples subdirectory to the .../drivers/char/Makefile conditional on the menu item created in step 2.
  (4) Create a makefile for the new examples directory, and add the hello1.o module object to be compiled conditional on the menu item created in step 2.
  (5) Create the driver hello1.c source file from Listing 4–1. Adding the examples directory under the .../drivers/char subdirectory is self explanatory. After this directory is created, two files are created in this directory : the module source file itself from Listing 4-1, and the makefile for the examples directory.

4.2.1.5 Installing a Device Driver

- Now that this driver is built, we can load and unload it on a running kernel to observe its behavior. Before we can load the module, we need to copy it to an appropriate location on our target system.

- Although we could put it anywhere we want, a convention is in place for kernel modules and where they are populated on a running Linux system. As with module compilation, it is easiest to let the kernel build system do that for us.
- The makefile target modules_install automatically places modules in the system in a logical layout.
- You simply need to supply the desired location as a prefix to the default path.
- In a standard Linux workstation installation, you might already know that the device driver modules live in /lib/modules/<kernel-version>/... ordered in a manner similar to the device driver directory hierarchy in the Linux kernel tree. The <kernel-version> string is produced by executing the command uname -r on your target Linux system.
- If you do not provide an installation prefix to the kernel build system, by default your modules are installed in your own workstation's /lib/ modules/... directory.
- Since we are embedded developers, and we are crosscompiling, this is probably not what you intended. You can point to a temporary location in your home directory and manually copy the modules to your target's file system.
- Alternatively, if your target embedded system uses NFS root mount to a directory on your local development workstation, you can install the modules directly to the target file system. The following example assumes the latter :

```
$ make ARCH=arm CROSS_COMPILE=xscale_be- \
INSTALL_MOD_PATH=/home/chris/sandbox/coyote-target \
modules_install
```

- This places all your modules in the directory coyote-target, which on this sample system is exported via NFS and mounted as root on the target system.

4.2.1.6 Loading a Module

- Having completed all the necessary steps, we are now in a position to load and test the device driver module.
- Listing 4–2 shows the output resulting from loading and subsequently unloading the device driver on the embedded system.

LISTING 4–2 Loading and Unloading a Module

```
# modprobe hello1 <<< Load the driver, must be root
Hello Example Init
# modprobe -r hello1 <<< Unload the driver, must be root
Hello Example Exit
```

- When the module is loaded, the module-initialization function is called.

- We specify the initialization function that will be executed on module insertion using the module_init() macro. We declare it as follows:

  module_init(hello_init);

  In our initialization function, we simply print the obligatory hello message and return.
- In a real device driver, this is where you would perform any initial resource allocation for our module. In a similar fashion, when we unload the module (using the modprobe -r command), our module exit routine is called. As shown in Listing 4-1, the exit routine is specified using the module_exit() macro. In a real driver, this is where you undo everything that was done on entry, such as freeing any memory or returning the device to a known, harmless state.
- That's all there is to a skeletal device driver capable of live insertion in an actual kernel. The following sections introduce additional functionality to our loadable device driver module that illustrates how a user space program would interact with a device driver module.

4.2.1.7 Module Parameters

- Many device driver modules can accept parameters to modify their behavior. Examples include enabling debug mode, setting verbose reporting, and specifying module specific options.
- The insmod utility (and the modprobe utility, introduced later) accepts module parameters (also called options in some contexts) by specifying them after the module name.

4.2.2 Driver Methods

- We've covered much ground in our short treatment of module utilities. The remaining sections describe the basic mechanism for communicating with a device driver from a user space program (your application code).
- We have introduced the two fundamental methods responsible for the module's one-time initialization and exit processing.
- Now we need some methods to interface with our device driver from our application program. After all, two of the more important reasons we use device drivers are to isolate the user from the perils of writing code in kernel space and to present a unified method to communicate with hardware or kernel-level devices.

4.2.2.1 Driver File System Operations

- After the device driver is loaded into a live kernel, the first action we must take is to prepare the driver for subsequent operations.
- The open() method is used for this purpose. After the driver has been opened, we need routines for reading and writing to the driver.

- A *release()* routine is provided to clean up after operations are complete (basically, a close() call). Finally, a special system call is provided for nonstandard communication with the driver. This is called *ioctl()*.

4.2.2.2 Allocation of Device Numbers
- Usually you will not specify a device number in your driver. You will use methods that allow the kernel to specify a device number for you.
- This avoids collisions with device numbers and scales much better than manually assigning your own device number.

4.2.2.3 Device Nodes and mknod
- To understand how an application binds its requests to a specific device represented by our device driver, we must understand the concept of a device node.
- A device node is a special file type in Linux that represents a device.
- Virtually all Linux distributions keep device nodes in a common location (specified by the Filesystem Hierarchy Standard7), in a directory called /dev.
- A dedicated utility is used to create a device node on a file system. This utility is called mknod.
- An example of node creation is the best way to illustrate its functionality and the information it conveys. In keeping with our simple device driver example, let's create the proper device node to exercise it :

    $ mknod /dev/hello1 c 234 0

- After executing this command on our target embedded system, we end up with a new file called /dev/hello1 that represents our device driver module. If we list this file, it looks like this :

    $ ls -l /dev/hello1
    crw-r--r-- 1 root root 234, 0 Jul 14 2005 /dev/hello1

- The parameters we passed to mknod include the name, type, and major and minor numbers for our device driver. The name we chose was hello1. Because we are demonstrating the use of a character driver, we use c to indicate that. The major number is 234, the number we chose for this example, and the minor number is 0.
- By itself, the device node is just another file on our file system. However, because of its special status as a device node, we use it to bind to an installed device driver. If an application process issues an open() system call with our device node as the path parameter, the kernel searches for a valid device driver registered with a major number that matches the device node, in this case, 234. This is the mechanism by which the kernel associates our particular device to the device node.
- As most C programmers know, the open() system call, or any of its variants, returns a reference (file descriptor) that our applications use to issue subsequent file system

operations, such as read, write, and close. This reference is then passed to the various file system operations, such as read and write, or their variants. If you're curious about the purpose of the minor number, it is a mechanism for handling multiple devices or subdevices with a single device driver. It is not used by the operating system; it is simply passed to the device driver.
- The device driver can use the minor number in any way it sees fit. For example, with a multiport serial card, the major number would specify the driver. The minor number might specify one of the multiple ports handled by the same driver on the multiport card. Consult one of the excellent texts on device drivers for further details.

4.2.3 Device Drivers and the GPL

- Much discussion and debate surround the issue of device drivers and how the terms of the GNU Public License apply to device drivers.
- The first test is well understood : If your device driver (or any software, for that matter) is based, even in part, on existing GPL software, it is considered a derived work. For example, if you start with a current Linux device driver and modify it to suit your needs, this is certainly considered a derived work.
- Therefore, you are obligated to license this modified device driver under the terms of the work it was derived from, presumably the GPL, observing all its requirements.
- This is where the debate comes in. Some of these concepts have not yet been tested in court.
- The prevailing opinion of the legal and open source communities is that if a work can be proven to be independently derived, and a given device driver does not assume "intimate knowledge" of the Linux kernel, the developers are free to license it in any way they see fit.
- If modifications are made to the kernel to accommodate a special need of the driver, it is considered a derived work and therefore is subject to the GPL.
- A large and growing body of information exists in the open source community regarding these issues. It seems likely that, at some point in the future, these concepts will be tested in a court of law, and a precedent will be established.

4.3 CHARACTER DEVICE

- An infinite stream of bytes, with no beginning, no end, no size. For example serial port.
- Used for serial ports, terminals etc.
- Most of the devices that are not block devices are represented by linux kernel as character device.

4.3.1 Major and Minor Numbers

- Now how does Linux know which driver is associated with which file? For that, each device and its device file has associated with it, a unique Major number and a Minor number. No two devices have the same major number.
- When a device file is opened, Linux examines its major number and forwards the call to the driver registered for that device. Subsequent calls for read/write/close too are processed by the same driver.
- As far as kernel is concerned, only major number is important. Minor number is used to identify the specific device instance if the driver controls more than one device of a type.
- Char devices are accessed through names in the file system. Those names are called special files or device files or simply nodes of the file system tree; they are conventionally located in the /dev directory.
- Special files for char drivers are identified by a "c" in the first column of the output of ls –l. Block devices appear in /dev as well, but they are identified by a "b". The focus of this section is on char devices, but much of the following information applies to block devices as well.
- If you issue the (ls l) command, you'll see two numbers (separated by a comma) in the device file entries before the date of the last modification, where the file length normally appears.
- These numbers are the major and minor device number for the particular device. The following listing shows a few devices as they appear on a typical system. Their major numbers are 1, 4, 7, and 10, while the minors are 1, 3, 5, 64, 65, and 129.

  ```
  crw-rw-rw- 1 root root 1, 3 Apr 11 2002 null
  crw------- 1 root root 10, 1 Apr 11 2002 psaux
  crw------- 1 root root 4, 1 Oct 28 03:04 tty1
  crw-rw-rw- 1 root tty 4, 64 Apr 11 2002 ttys0
  crw-rw---- 1 root uucp 4, 65 Apr 11 2002 ttyS1
  crw--w---- 1 vcsa tty 7, 1 Apr 11 2002 vcs1
  crw--w---- 1 vcsa tty 7, 129 Apr 11 2002 vcsa1
  crw-rw-rw- 1 root root 1, 5 Apr 11 2002 zero
  ```

- Traditionally, the major number identifies the driver associated with the device. For example, /dev/null and /dev/zero are both managed by driver 1, whereas virtual consoles and serial terminals are managed by driver 4; similarly, both vcs1 and vcsa1 devices are managed by driver 7.
- Modern Linux kernels allow multiple drivers to share major numbers, but most devices that you will see are still organized on the one-major, one-driver principle.

- The minor number is used by the kernel to determine exactly which device is being referred to. Depending on how your driver is written (as we will see below), you can either get a direct pointer to your device from the kernel, or you can use the minor number yourself as an index into a local array of devices.
- Either way, the kernel itself knows almost nothing about minor numbers beyond the fact that they refer to devices implemented by your driver.
- The Internal Representation of Device Numbers Within the kernel, the dev_t type (defined in <linux/types.h>) is used to hold device numbers both the major and minor parts.
- As of Version 2.6.0 of the kernel, *dev_t* is a 32-bit quantity with 12 bits set aside for the major number and 20 for the minor number. Your code should, of course, never make any assumptions about the internal organization of device numbers; it should, instead, make use of a set of macros found in <*linux/kdev_t.h*>. To obtain the major or minor parts of a *dev_t*, use :

  MAJOR(dev_t dev);

  MINOR(dev_t dev);

  If, instead, you have the major and minor numbers and need to turn them into a *dev_t*, use :

  MKDEV(int major, int minor);

- Note that the 2.6 kernel can accommodate a vast number of devices, while previous kernel versions were limited to 255 major and 255 minor numbers. One assumes that the wider range will be sufficient for quite some time, but the computing field is littered with erroneous assumptions of that nature. So you should expect that the format of *dev_t* could change again in the future; if you write your drivers carefully, however, these changes will not be a problem.

4.3.2 Allocating and Freeing Device Numbers

- One of the first things your driver will need to do when setting up a char device is to obtain one or more device numbers to work with. The necessary function for this task is register_chrdev_region, which is declared in <*linux/fs.h*> :

  int register_chrdev_region(dev_t first, unsigned int count, char *name);

- Here, first is the beginning device number of the range you would like to allocate. The minor number portion of first is often 0 , but there is no requirement to that effect. Count is the total number of contiguous device numbers you are requesting.
- Note that, if count is large, the range you request could spill over to the next major number; but everything will still work properly as long as the number range you request is available.
- Finally, name is the name of the device that should be associated with this number range; it will appear in */proc/devices* and *sysfs*. As with most kernel functions, the return value

from *register_chrdev_region* will be 0 if the allocation was successfully performed. In case of error, a negative error code will be returned, and you will not have access to the requested region. *register_chrdev_region* works well if you know ahead of time exactly which device numbers you want.
- Often, however, you will not know which major numbers your device will use; there is a constant effort within the Linux kernel development com- munity to move over to the use of dynamicly allocated device numbers. The kernel will happily allocate a major number for you on the fly, but you must request this allocation by using a different function :

int alloc_chrdev_region(dev_t *dev, unsigned int firstminor, unsigned int count, char *name);
- With this function, dev is an output-only parameter that will, on successful completion, hold the first number in your allocated range. First minor should be the requested first minor number to use; it is usually 0. The count and name parameters work like those given to *request_chrdev_region*.
- Regardless of how you allocate your device numbers, you should free them when they are no longer in use. Device numbers are freed with :

void unregister_chrdev_region(dev_t first, unsigned int count);
- The usual place to call *unregister_chrdev_region* would be in your module's cleanup function.
- The above functions allocate device numbers for your driver's use, but they do not tell the kernel anything about what you will actually do with those numbers. Before a user-space program can access one of those device numbers, your driver needs to connect them to its internal functions that implement the device's operations. We will describe how this connection is accomplished shortly, but there are a couple of necessary digressions to take care of first.

4.3.3 Dynamic Allocation of Major Numbers

Some major device numbers are statically assigned to the most common devices. A list of those devices can be found in Documentation/devices.txt within the kernel source tree. The chances of a static number having already been assigned for the use of your new driver are small, however, and new numbers are not being assigned. So, as a driver writer, you have a choice : you can simply pick a number that appears to be unused, or you can allocate major numbers in a dynamic manner. Picking a number may work as long as the only user of your driver is you; once your driver is more widely deployed, a randomly picked major number will lead to conflicts and trouble. Thus, for new drivers, we strongly suggest that you use dynamic allocation to obtain your major device number, rather than choosing a number randomly from the ones that are currently free. In other words, your drivers should almost certainly be using *alloc_chrdev_region* rather than *register_chrdev_region*. The disadvantage of

dynamic assignment is that you can't create the device nodes in advance, because the major number assigned to your module will vary. For normal use of the driver, this is hardly a problem, because once the number has been assigned, you can read it from
/proc/devices
.
*

To load a driver using a dynamic major number, therefore, the invocation of insmod can be replaced by a simple script that, after calling insmod , reads
/proc/devices in order to create the special file(s). A typical */proc/devices*
file looks like the following :

Character Devices
1 mem
2 pty
3 ttyp
4 ttyS
6 lp
7 vcs
10 misc
13 input
14 sound
21 sg
180 usb

Block Devices
2 fd
8 sd
11 sr
65 sd
66 sd

The script to load a module that has been assigned a dynamic number can, therefore, be written using a tool such as awk to retrieve information from */proc/devices* in order to create the files in */dev*

4.3.4 Implementing a Character Driver

Four major steps :
- Implement operations corresponding to the system calls an application can apply to a file : file operations.

- Define a "file_operations" structure containing function pointers to system call functions in your driver.
- Reserve a set of major and minors for your driver.
- Tell the kernel to associate the reserved major and minor to your file operations.
- This is a very common design scheme in the Linux kernel.
- A common kernel infrastructure defines a set of operations to be implemented by a driver and functions to register your driver.
- Your driver only needs to implement this set of well-defined operations.

4.3.5 File Operations

- Before registering character devices, you have to define file_operations (called fops) for the device files.
- The file_operations structure is generic to all files handled by the Linux kernel.
- Here are the most important operations for a character driver. All of them are optional.

```
#(include/$linux/fs.h)
struct file_operations {
ssize_t (*read) (struct file *, char __user *, size_t, loff_t *);
ssize_t (*write) (struct file *, const char __user *, size_t, loff_t *);
long (*unlocked_ioctl) (struct file *, unsigned int, unsigned long);
int (*open) (struct inode *, struct file *);
int (*release) (struct inode *, struct file *);
[...]
};
```

4.3.5.1 File Operation Definition Example

```
#include <linux/fs.h>
static const struct file_operations sample_device_fops = {
.owner = THIS_MODULE,
.open = sample_device_open,
.release = sample_device_release,
.unlocked_ioctl = sample_device_ioctl,
};
```

- You need to fill the fops with function your device needs to be supported.

4.3.5.2 File Operations

1. **open :** For opening the device(allocating resources).
2. **release :** For closing the device (releasing resources).
3. **write :** For writing data to the device.
4. **read :** For reading data from the device.
5. **ioctl :** For query the device statistics and passing configuration parameters to device.
6. **mmap :** For potentially faster but more complex direct access to the device.

(1) Open() and release()

- int open(struct inode *i, struct file *f)
  - Called when user-space opens the device file.
  - Inode is a structure that uniquely represent a file in the system.
  - File is a structure created every time a file is opened. Several file structures can point to the same inode structure.
- Contains info like the current position, the opening mode, etc.
- Has a *void *private_data* pointer to store driver specific data.
  - The open method is provided by the driver to do any initialization in preparation to later operations such as allocating memory resources.
- int release(struct inode *i, struct file *f)
  - Called when user-space closes the file.
  - The role of release is reverse of *open()*. It performs all the operation to undo the tasks done in *open()* such as de-allocating the memory resources allocated at time of *open()*.

(2) read( ) function

- ssize_t read (struct file *file, __user char *buf, size_t size, loff_t *off)
  - Called when user-space uses the read() system call on the device.
  - Must read data from the device,
  - Write at most 'size' bytes in the user-space buffer buf, and
  - Update the current position in the file off.
  - "File " is a pointer to the same file structure that was passed in the *open()* operation.
  - Must return the number of bytes read.
  - On UNIX/Linux, *read()* operations typically block when there isn't enough data to read from the device.

(3) Write( )

- ssize_t foo_write(struct file *file, __user const char *buf, size_t size ,loff_t *off)

- Called when user-space uses the write() system call on the device
- The opposite of read, must read at most 'size' bytes from buf,
- Write it to the device,
- Update off and
- Return the number of bytes written.

(4) ioctl
- *static long ioctl(struct file *file, unsigned int cmd, unsigned long arg)*
  - Associated with the ioctl system call.
  - Allows to extend drivers capabilities beyond read/write API.
  - Example :
- changing the speed of a serial port,
- Setting video output format,
- querying a device serial number.
  - *cmd* is a number identifying the operation to perform.
  - *arg* is the optional argument passed as third argument of the ioctl() system call. Can be an integer, an address, etc.
  - The semantic of *cmd* and *arg* is driver-specific.

(5) dev_t Data Types
- The kernel data type *dev_t* represent a major/ minor number pair also called a device number.
  - Defined in <linux/kdev_t.h>
    Linux 2.6 : 32-bit size (major: 12-bits, minor : 20-bits)
  - Macro to compose the device number :
    MKDEV(int major, int minor);
  - Macro to extract the minor and major numbers :
    MAJOR(dev_t dev);
    MINOR(dev_t dev);

4.3.6 Registering Device Numbers

#include <linux/fs.h>
int register_chrdev_region(
dev_t from, /* Starting device number */
unsigned count, /* Number of device numbers */
const char *name); /* Registered name */
Returns 0 if the allocation was successful.

- If you don't have fixed device numbers assigned to your driver.
  - Better not to choose arbitrary ones. There could be conflicts with other drivers.
  - The kernel API offers an *alloc_chrdev_region* function to have the kernel allocate free ones for you. You can find the allocated major number *in/proc/devices*.

4.3.7 Information of Registered Devices

Registered devices are visible in /proc/devices :

- **Character Devices**
  - 1 mem
  - 4 /dev/vc/0
  - 4 tty
  - 4 ttyS
  - 5 /dev/tty
  - 5 /dev/console
  - 5 /dev/ptmx
  - 6 lp
- **Block Devices**
  - 1 ramdisk
  - 259 blkext
  - 7 loop
  - 8 sd
  - 9 md
  - 11 sr
  - 65 sd
  - 66 sd

Major number Registered name.

4.3.8 Character Device Registration

- The kernel represents character drivers with a cdev structure.
- Declare this structure globally (within your module) :
  #include <linux/cdev.h>
  static struct cdev char_cdev;
- In the init function, initialize the structure.
  void cdev_init(struct cdev *cdev, struct file_operations *fops);
  cdev_init(&char_cdev, &fops);

4.3.9 Character Device Unregistration

- First delete your character device :
  void cdev_del(struct cdev *p);
- Then, and only then, free the device number :
  void unregister_chrdev_region(dev_t from, unsigned count);
- Example :
  cdev_del(&char_cdev);
  unregister_chrdev_region(char_dev, count);

4.4 PCI DEVICES DRIVERS

Peripheral Component Interconnect (PCI), as its name implies is a standard that describes how to connect the peripheral components of a system together in a structured and controlled way. The standard describes the way that the system components are electrically connected and the way that they should behave.

4.4.1 The PCI Interface

- Although many computer users think of PCI as a way of laying out electrical wires, it is actually a complete set of specifications defining how different parts of a computer should interact.
- The PCI specification covers most issues related to computer interfaces. We are not going to cover it all here; in this section, we are mainly concerned with how a PCI driver can find its hardware and gain access to it.

4.4.2 PCI Addressing

- Each PCI peripheral is identified by a bus number, a device number, and a function number. The PCI specification permits a single system to host up to 256 buses, but because 256 buses are not sufficient for many large systems, Linux now supports PCI domains.
- Each PCI domain can host up to 256 buses. Each bus hosts up to 32 devices, and each device can be a multifunction board (such as an audio device with an accompanying CD-ROM drive) with a maximum of eight functions.
- Therefore, each function can be identified at hardware level by a 16-bit address, or key. Device drivers written for Linux, though, do not need to deal with those binary addresses, because they use a specific data structure, called pci_dev, to act on the devices. Most recent workstations feature at least two PCI buses.

- Plugging more than one bus in a single system is accomplished by means of Bridges, special-purpose PCI peripherals whose task is joining two buses. The overall layout of a PCI system is a tree where each bus is connected to an upper-layer bus, up to bus 0 at the root of the tree.
- The CardBus PC-card system is also connected to the PCI system via bridges. A typical PCI system is represented in Fig. 4.2, where the various bridges are highlighted.

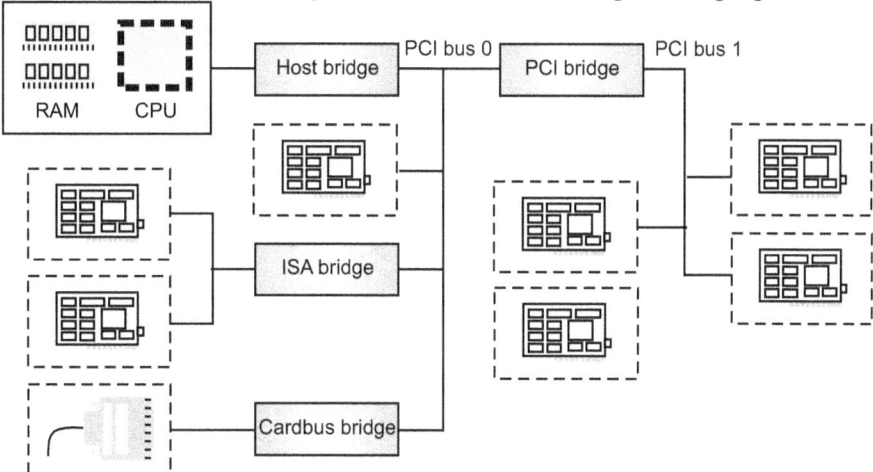

Fig. 4.2 : Layout of a typical PCI system

- The 16-bit hardware addresses associated with PCI peripherals, although mostly hidden in the *struct pci_dev object*, are still visible occasionally, especially when lists of devices are being used. One such situation is the output of lspci(part of the pciutils package, available with most distributions) and the layout of information in */proc/pci* and */proc/bus/pci*. The sysfs representation of PCI devices also shows this addressing scheme, with the addition of the PCI domain information.
- When the hardware address is displayed, it can be shown as two values (an 8-bit bus number and an 8-bit device and function number), as three values (bus, device, and function), or as four values (domain, bus, device, and function); all the values are usually displayed in hexadecimal.

4.4.3 PCI-PCI Bridges

- PCI-PCI bridges are special PCI devices that glue the PCI buses of the system together. Simple systems have a single PCI bus but there is an electrical limit on the number of PCI devices that a single PCI bus can support.
- Using PCI-PCI bridges to add more PCI buses allows the system to support many more PCI devices. This is particularly important for a high performance server. Of course, Linux fully supports the use of PCI-PCI bridges.

4.4.4 Linux PCI Initialization

The PCI initialisation code in Linux is broken into three logical parts :
- **PCI Device Driver**

This pseudo-device driver searches the PCI system starting at Bus 0 and locates all PCI devices and bridges in the system. It builds a linked list of data structures describing the topology of the system. Additionally, it numbers all of the bridges that it finds.
- **PCI BIOS**

This software layer provides the services described in, PCI BIOS ROM specification. Even though Alpha AXP does not have BIOS services, there is equivalent code in the Linux kernel providing the same functions,
- **PCI Fixup**

System specific fixup code tidies up the system specific loose ends of PCI initialization.

4.4.5 PCI Device Driver

- The PCI device driver is not really a device driver at all but a function of the operating system called at system initialisation time. The PCI initialisation code must scan all of the PCI busses in the system looking for all PCI devices in the system (including PCI-PCI bridge devices).
- It uses the PCI BIOS code to find out if every possible slot in the current PCI bus that it is scanning is occupied. If the PCI slot is occupied, it builds a *pci_dev* data structure describing the device and links into the list of known PCI devices (pointed at by *pci_devices*).
- The PCI initialisation code starts by scanning PCI Bus 0. It tries to read the Vendor Identification and Device Identification fields for every possible PCI device in every possible PCI slot. When it finds an occupied slot it builds a *pci_dev* data structure describing the device. All of the *pci_dev* data structures built by the PCI initialisation code (including all of the PCI-PCI Bridges) are linked into a singly linked list; *pci_devices*.
- If the PCI device that was found was a PCI-PCI bridge then a pci_bus data structure is built and linked into the tree of *pci_bus* and *pci_dev* data structures pointed at by *pci_root*. The PCI initialisation code can tell if the PCI device is a PCI-PCI Bridge because it has a class code of *0x060400*.
- The Linux kernel then configures the PCI bus on the other (down stream) side of the PCI-PCI Bridge that it has just found. If more PCI-PCI Bridges are found then these are also configured. This process is known as a depth wise algorithm; the system's PCI topology is fully mapped depth wise before searching breadth wise.

4.5 FILE SYSTEMS

- Perhaps one of the most important decisions an embedded developer makes is which file system(s) to deploy. Some file systems optimize for performance, whereas others optimize for size. Still others optimize for data recovery after device or power failure.
- This section introduces the major file systems in use on Linux systems and examines the characteristics of each as they apply to embedded designs.
- Starting with the most popular file system in use on earlier Linux desktop distributions, we introduce concepts from the Second Extended File System (ext2) to lay a foundation for further discussion.
- Next we look at its successor, the Third Extended File System (ext3), which has enjoyed much popularity as the default file system for many Linux desktop and server distributions. We then describe the improvements that led to ext4. After introducing some fundamentals, we examine a variety of specialized file systems, including those optimized for data recovery and storage space, and those designed for use on Flash memory devices. The Network File System (NFS) is presented, followed by a discussion of the more important pseudo file systems, including the */proc* file system and *sysfs*.

4.5.1 Linux File System Concepts

Before delving into the details of the individual file systems, let's look at the big picture of how data is stored on a Linux system. In our study of device drivers Device Driver Basics, we looked at the structure of a character device. In general, character devices store and retrieve data in serial streams. The most basic example of a character device is a serial port or mouse. In contrast, block devices store and retrieve data in equal-sized chunks of data at a time, in random locations on an addressable medium. For example, a typical IDE hard disk controller can transfer 512 bytes of data at a time to and from a specific, addressable location on the physical medium.

4.5.1.1 Partitions

- Before we begin our discussion of file systems, we start by introducing partitions, the logical division of a physical device on which a file system exists. At the highest level, data is stored on physical devices in partitions.
- A partition is a logical division of the physical medium (hard disk, Flash memory) whose data is organized following the specifications of a given partition type. A physical device can have a single partition covering all its available space, or it can be divided into multiple partitions to suit a particular task.
- A partition can be thought of as a logical disk onto which a complete file system can be written. Fig. 4.1 shows the relationship between partitions and file systems.
- Linux uses a utility called fdisk to manipulate partitions on block devices. A recent fdisk utility found on many Linux distributions has knowledge of more than 90 different

partition types. In practice, only a few are commonly used on Linux systems. Some common partition types are Linux, FAT32, and Linux Swap.

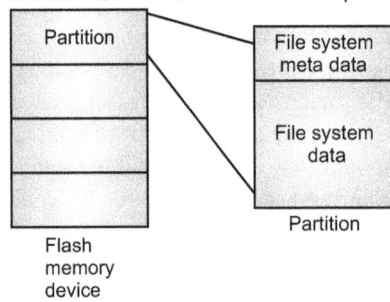

Fig. 4.3 : Partitions and file systems

LISTING 4–3

fdisk /dev/sdb

Command (m for help): p

Disk /dev/sdb: 49 MB, 49349120 bytes

4 heads, 32 sectors/track, 753 cylinders

Units = cylinders of 128 * 512 = 65536 bytes

Table 4.2 : Displaying Partition Information Using Fdisk

Device	Boot	Start	End	Blocks	Id	System
/dev/sdb1	*	1	180	11504	83	Linux
/dev/sdb2		181	360	11520	83	Linux
/dev/sdb3		361	540	11520	83	Linux
/dev/sdb4		541	753	13632	83	Linux

- For this discussion, we have created four partitions on the device using the fdisk utility. One of them is marked bootable, as indicated by the asterisk in the Boot column. This reflects a boot indicator flag in the data structure that represents the partition table on the device. As you can see from the listing, the logical unit of storage used by fdisk is a cylinder. On this device, a cylinder contains 64KB. On the other hand, Linux represents the smallest unit of storage as a logical block.
- You can deduce from this listing that a block is a unit of 1024 bytes. After the Compact Flash has been partitioned in this manner, each device representing a partition can be formatted with the file system of your choice.
- When a partition is formatted with a given file system type, Linux can mount the corresponding file system from that partition.

4.5.2 ext2

Building on Listing 4–3, we need to format the partitions created with fdisk. To do so, we use the Linux *mkfs.ext2* utility. *mkfs.ext2* is similar to the familiar DOS format command. This utility makes a file system of type ext2 on the specified partition. *mkfs. ext2* is specific to the ext2 file system; other file systems have their own versions of these utilities. Listing 4–4 captures the output of this process.

LISTING 4–4 Formatting a Partition Using mkfs.ext2

mkfs.ext2 /dev/sdb1 -L CFlash_Boot_Vol

mke2fs 1.40.8 (13-Mar-2008)

Filesystem label=CFlash_Boot_Vol

OS type: Linux

Block size=1024 (log=0)

Fragment size=1024 (log=0)

2880 inodes, 11504 blocks

575 blocks (5.00%) reserved for the super user

First data block=1

Maximum filesystem blocks=11796480

2 block groups

8192 blocks per group, 8192 fragments per group

1440 inodes per group

Superblock backups stored on blocks :

8193

Writing inode tables : done

Writing superblocks and filesystem accounting information: done

This filesystem will be automatically checked every 33 mounts or 180

days, whichever comes first. Use tune2fs -c or -i to override.

- Listing 4–4 contains much detail relating to the ext2 file system. It's an excellent way to begin understanding the operational characteristics of ext2. This partition was formatted as type ext2 (we know this because we used the ext2 mkfs utility) with a volume label of *CFlash_Boot_Vol*. It was created on a Linux partition (OS Type:) with a block size of 1024 bytes.
- Space was allocated for 2,880 inodes, occupying 11,504 blocks. An inode is the fundamental data structure representing a single file.
- Looking at the output of *mkfs.ext2* in Listing 4–4, we can ascertain certain characteristics of how the storage device is organized. We already know that the block size is 1024

bytes. If necessary for your particular application, *mkfs.ext2* can be instructed to format an ext2 file system with different block sizes. Current implementations allow block sizes of 1,024, 2,048, and 4,096 blocks. Block size is always a compromise for best performance.
- On one hand, large block sizes waste more space on disks with many small files, because each file must fit into an integral number of blocks. Any leftover fragment above *block_size * n* must occupy another full block, even if only 1 byte. On the other hand, very small block sizes increase the file system overhead of managing the metadata that describes the blockto-file mapping. Benchmark testing on your particular hardware implementation and data formats is the only way to be sure you have selected an optimum block size.

4.5.2.1 Mounting a File System
- After a file system has been created, we can mount it on a running Linux system. The kernel must be compiled with support for our particular file system type, either as a compiled in module or as a dynamically loadable module.
- The following command mounts the previously created ext2 file system on a mount point that we specify :

  # mount /dev/sdb1 /mnt/flash

- This example assumes that we have a directory created on our target Linux machine called */mnt/flash*. This is called the mount point because we are installing (mounting) the file system rooted at this point in our file system hierarchy.
- We are mounting the Flash device described earlier that was assigned to the device */dev/sdb1*. On a typical Linux desktop (development) machine, we need to have root privileges to execute this command.
- The mount point is any directory path on your file system that you decide, which becomes the top level (root) of your newly mounted device. In the preceding example, to reference any files on your Flash device, you must prefix the path with */mnt/flash*.
- The mount command has many options. Several options that mount accepts depend on the target file system type. Most of the time, mount can determine the type of file system on a properly formatted file system known to the kernel.

4.5.2.2 Checking File System Integrity
- The e2fsck command is used to check the integrity of an ext2 file system. A file system can become corrupted for several reasons. By far the most common reason is an unexpected power failure. Linux distributions close all open files and unmount file systems during the shut down sequence (assuming an orderly shutdown of the system).
- However, when we are dealing with embedded systems, unexpected power-downs are common, so we need to provide some defensive measures against these cases. e2fsck is our first line of defense.

- Listing 4–5 shows the output of e2fsck run on our Compact Flash from the previous examples. It has been formatted and properly unmounted, so no errors should occur.

LISTING 4–5 Clean File System Check

e2fsck /dev/sdb1

e2fsck 1.40.8 (13-Mar-2008)

CFlash_Boot_Vol: clean, 11/2880 files, 471/11504 blocks

- The e2fsck utility checks several aspects of the file system for consistency. If no issues are found, e2fsck issues a message similar to that shown in Listing 4-5. Note that e2fsck should be run only on an unmounted file system. Although it is possible to run it on a mounted file system, doing so can cause significant damage to internal file system structures on the disk or Flash device.
- Of course, in a real system, you might not be this lucky. Some types of file system errors cannot be repaired using e2fsck. Moreover, the embedded system designer should understand that if power has been removed without proper shut down, the boot cycle can be delayed by the length of time it takes to scan your boot device and repair any errors. Indeed, if these errors are not repairable, the system boot is halted, and manual intervention is indicated. Furthermore, it should be noted that if your file system is large, the file system check (fsck) can take minutes or even hours for large multigigabyte file systems.
- Another defense against file system corruption is to ensure that writes are committed to disk immediately when written. The sync utility can be used to force all queued I/O requests to be committed to their respective devices.
- One strategy to minimize the window of vulnerability for data corruption from unexpected power loss or drive failure is to issue the sync command after every file write or strategically as needed by your application requirements. The trade-off is, of course, a performance penalty. Deferring disk writes is a performance optimization used in all modern operating systems. Using sync effectively defeats this optimization.
- The ext2 file system has matured as a fast, efficient, and robust file system for Linux systems.
- However, if you need the additional reliability of a journaling file system, or if boot time after unclean shut down is an issue in your design, you should consider the ext3 file system.

4.5.3 ext3

- The ext3 file system has become a powerful, high-performance, and robust journaling file system. It is currently the default file system for many popular desktop Linux distributions.

- The ext3 file system is basically an extension of the ext2 file system with added journaling capability. Journaling is a technique in which each change to the file system is logged in a special file so that recovery is possible from known journaling points. One of the primary advantages of the ext3 file system is its ability to be mounted directly after an unclean shut down.
- As stated in the preceding section, when a system shuts down unexpectedly, such as during a power failure, the system forces a file system consistency check, which can be a lengthy operation. With ext3 file systems, a consistency check is unneeded, because the journal can simply be played back to ensure the file system's consistency.
- Without going into design details that are beyond the scope of this book, we will quickly explain how a journaling file system works. A journaling file system contains a special file, often hidden from the user, that is used to store file system metadata5 and file data itself. This special file is referred to as the journal.
- Whenever the file system is subject to a change (such as a write operation), the changes are first written to the journal. The file system drivers make sure that this write is committed to the journal before the actual changes are posted and committed to the storage medium (disk or Flash, for example).
- After the changes have been logged in the journal, the driver posts the changes to the actual file and metadata on the medium. If a power failure occurs during the media write and a reboot occurs, all that is necessary to restore consistency to the file system is to replay the changes in the journal.
- One of the most significant design goals for the ext3 file system was that it be both backward and forward compatible with the ext2 file system.
- It is possible to convert an ext2 file system to an ext3 file system and back again without reformatting or rewriting all the data on the disk.
- Notice that first we mounted the file system on */mnt/flash* for illustrative purposes only. Normally, we would execute this command on an unmounted ext2 partition. The design behavior for tune2fs when the file system is mounted is to create the journal file called .journal, a hidden file.
- A file in Linux preceded by a period (.) is considered a hidden file; most Linux command-line file utilities silently ignore files of this type.

4.5.4 ext4

- The ext4 file system builds on the success of the ext3 file system. Like its predecessor, it is a journaling file system.
- It was developed as a series of patches designed to remove some of the limitations of the ext3 file system.
- It is likely that ext4 will become the default file system for a number of popular Linux distributions.

- The ext4 file system removed the 16-terabyte limit for file systems, increasing the size to 1 exbibyte (260 bytes, if you can count that high!) and supports individual file sizes up to 1024 gigabytes. (I can't pronounce exbibyte, much less comprehend that quantity!)
- Several other improvements have been made to increase performance for the types of loads expected on large server and database systems, where ext4 is expected to be the default.
- If your embedded system requirements include support for large, high-performance journaling file systems, you might consider investigating ext4.

4.5.5 ReiserFS

- The ReiserFS file system has enjoyed popularity among some desktop distributions such as SuSE and Gentoo.
- Reiser4 is the current incarnation of this journaling file system. Like the ext3 file system, ReiserFS guarantees that either a given file system operation completes in its entirety, or none of it completes.
- Unlike ext3, Reiser4 has introduced an API for system programmers to guarantee the atomicity of a file system transaction.
- Consider the following example : A database program is busy updating records in the database. Several writes are issued to the file system. Power is lost after the first write but before the last one has completed.
- A journaling file system guarantees that the metadata changes have been stored to the journal file so that when power is again applied to the system, the kernel can at least establish a consistent state of the file system. That is, if file A was reported as having 16 KB before the power failure, it will be reported as having 16 KB afterward, and the directory entry representing this file (actually, the inode) properly records the file's size. This does not mean, however, that the file data was properly written to the file; it indicates only that there are no errors on the file system. Indeed, it is likely that data was lost by the database program in the previous scenario, and it would be up to the database logic to recover the lost if, in fact, recovery is even possible.
- Reiser4 implements high-performance "atomic" file system operations designed to protect both the state of the file system (its consistency) and the data involved in a file system operation.
- Reiser4 provides a user-level API to enable programs such as database managers to issue a file system write command that is guaranteed to either succeed in its entirety or fail in a similar manner. This guarantees not only that file system consistency is maintained, but also that no partial data or garbage data remains in files after a system crash.

4.5.6 JFFS2 (Journaling Flash File System)

- Flash memory has been used extensively in embedded products. Because of the nature of Flash memory technology, it is inherently less efficient and more prone to data corruption caused by power loss.
- This is due to much larger write times. The inefficiency stems from the block size. Block sizes of Flash memory devices are often measured in the tens or hundreds of kilobytes.
- Flash memory can be erased only a block at a time, although writes usually can be executed 1 byte or word at a time.
- To update a single file, an entire block must be erased and rewritten. It is well known that the distribution of file sizes on any given Linux machine (or other OS) contains many more smaller files than larger files.

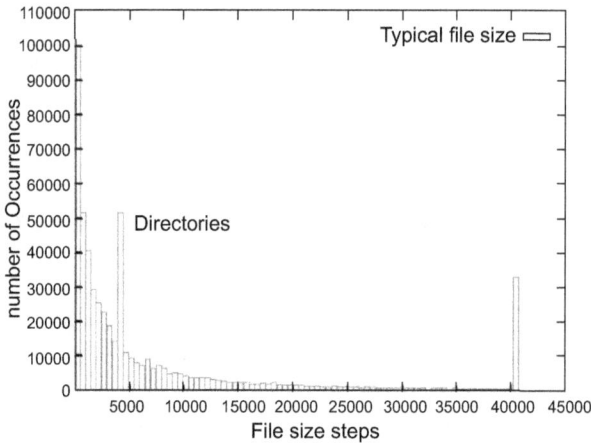

Fig. 4.4 : File size steps

- Fig. 4.4 shows that the majority of file sizes are well below approximately 5 KB. The spike at 4096 represents directories. Directory entries (also files themselves) are exactly 4096 bytes in length, and there are many of them. The spike above 40,000 bytes is an artifact of the measurement. It is a count of the number of files greater than approximately 40 KB, the end of the measurement quantum. It is interesting to note that the vast majority of files are very small.
- Small file sizes present a unique challenge to the Flash file system designer. Because Flash memory must be erased an entire block at a time, and the size of a Flash block is often many multiples of the smaller file sizes, Flash is subject to time-consuming block rewriting operations. For example, assume that a 128 KB block of Flash is being used to hold a couple dozen files of 4096 bytes or less.

- Now assume that one of those files needs to be modified. This causes the Flash file system to invalidate the entire 128 KB block and rewrite every file in the block to a newly erased block. This can be a time consuming process.
- Because Flash writes can be time-consuming (much slower than hard disk writes), this increases the window where data corruption can occur due to a sudden loss of power. Unexpected power loss is a common occurrence in embedded systems. For instance, if power is lost during the rewrite of the 128 KB data block just mentioned, all of the couple dozen files potentially could be lost.
- Enter the second-generation Journaling Flash File System (JFFS2). The issues just discussed and other problems have been largely reduced or eliminated by the design of JFFS2. The original JFFS was designed by Axis Communications AB of Sweden and was targeted specifically at the commonly available Flash memory devices of the time.
- The JFFS had knowledge of the Flash architecture and, more important, architectural limitations imposed by the devices. Another problem with Flash file systems is that Flash memory has a limited lifetime.
- Typical Flash memory devices are specified for a minimum of 100,000 write cycles, and, more recently, 1,000,000-cycle devices have become common. This specification is applicable to each block of the Flash device. This unusual limitation imposes the requirement to spread the writes evenly across the blocks of a Flash memory device. JFFS2 uses a technique called wear leveling to accomplish this function.

4.5.6.1 Building a JFFS2 Image

- Building a JFFS2 image is relatively straightforward. Although you can build a JFFS2 image on your workstation without kernel support, you cannot mount it.
- Before proceeding, ensure that your kernel has support for JFFS2 and that your development workstation contains a compatible version of the *mkfs.jffs2* utility. These utilities can be downloaded and built from source code, ftp://ftp.infradead.org/pub/mtd-utils/.
- Preferably, they should be available from your desktop Linux package maintainer. For example, on Ubuntu, they can be installed by executing this command :
  $ sudo apt-get install mtd-tools
- Your distribution may call them something different, such as mtd-utils. Consult the documentation that came with your desktop Linux distribution. JFFS2 images are built from a directory that contains the desired files on the file system image.
- It should be pointed out that any Flash-based file system that supports write operations is subject to conditions that can lead to premature failure of the underlying Flash device.
- For example, enabling system loggers *(syslogd and klogd)* configured to write their data to Flash-based file systems can easily overwhelm a Flash device with continuous writes. Some categories of program errors can also lead to continuous writes. Care must be taken to limit Flash writes to values within the lifetime of Flash devices.

4.5.7 cramfs

- From the README file in the cramfs project, the goal of cramfs is to "cram a file system into a small ROM". The cramfs file system is very useful for embedded systems that contain a small ROM or FLASH memory that holds static data and programs.
- Borrowing again from the cramfs README file, "cramfs is designed to be simple and small, and compress things well". The cramfs file system is read-only. It is created with a command-line utility called mkcramfs.
- As with JFFS2, mkcramfs builds a file system image from a directory specified on the command line. Following is the procedure for building a cramfs image.

mkcramfs Command Example
```
# mkcramfs
usage: mkcramfs [-h] [-v] [-b blksize] [-e edition] [-i file] [-n name]
dirname outfile
-h print this help
-E make all warnings errors (non-zero exit status)
-b blksize use this blocksize, must equal page size
-e edition set edition number (part of fsid)
-i file insert a file image into the filesystem (requires >= 2.4.0)
-n name set name of cramfs filesystem
-p pad by 512 bytes for boot code
-s sort directory entries (old option, ignored)
-v be more verbose
-z make explicit holes (requires >= 2.3.39)
dirname root of the directory tree to be compressed
outfile output file
# mkcramfs . ../cramfs.image
warning: gids truncated to 8 bits (this may be a security concern)
# ls -l ../cramfs.image
-rw-rw-r-- 1 chris chris 1019904 Sep 19 18:06 ../cramfs.image
```

- The mkcramfs command was initially issued without any command-line parameters to reproduce the usage message. Because this utility has no man page, this is the best way to understand its usage. We subsequently issued the command specifying the current directory (.) as the source of the files for the cramfs file system, and a file called cramfs.image as the destination. Finally, we listed the file just created, and we see a new file called *cramfs.image*.
- Note that if your kernel is configured with cramfs support, you can mount this file system image on your Linux development workstation and examine its contents. Of course, because it is a read-only file system, you cannot modify it.

4.5.8 Network File System

- If you have developed in the UNIX environment, you undoubtedly are familiar with the Network File System (NFS).
- Properly configured, NFS enables you to export a directory on an NFS server and mount that directory on a remote client machine as if it were a local file system. This is useful in general for large networks of UNIX/Linux machines, and it can be a panacea to the embedded developer.
- Using NFS on your target board, an embedded developer can have access to a huge number of files, libraries, tools, and utilities during development and debugging, even if the target embedded system is resource-constrained.
- As with the other file systems, your kernel must be configured with NFS support, for both the server-side functionality and the client side. NFS server and client functionality is independently configured in the kernel configuration.
- Detailed instructions for configuring and tuning NFS are beyond the scope of this book, but a short introduction will help illustrate how useful NFS can be during development in the embedded environment.
- On your development workstation with NFS enabled, a configuration file contains a list specifying each directory that you want to export via the Network File System. On Red Hat, Ubuntu, and most other distributions, this file is located in the */etc* directory and is named exports.
- This file contains the names of two directories on a Linux development workstation. The first directory contains a target file system for an ADI Engineering Coyote reference board. The second directory is a general workspace that contains projects targeted for an embedded system.
- This is arbitrary; you can configure NFS any way you choose. On an embedded system with NFS enabled, the following command mounts the *.../workspace* directory exported by the NFS server on a mount point of our choosing :

mount -t nfs pluto:/home/chris/workspace /workspace

- Notice some important points about this command. We are instructing the mount command to mount a remote directory (on a machine named pluto, our development workstation in this example) onto a local mount point called */workspace*.
- For the command semantics to work, two requirements must be met on the embedded target. First, for the target to recognize the symbolic machine name pluto, it must be able to resolve the symbolic name.
- The easiest way to do this is to place an entry in the */etc/ hosts* file on the target. This allows the networking subsystem to resolve the symbolic name to its corresponding IP address. The entry in the target's */etc/hosts* file would look like this :

192.168.11.9 pluto.

- The second requirement is that the embedded target must have a directory in its root directory called */workspace*. (You may choose any pathname you wish. For example, you could mount it on */mnt/mywork*.) This is called a mount point.
- The requirement is that the target must have a directory created with the same name as given on the mount command. The mount command in the preceding example causes the contents of the NFS server's */home/chris/workspace* directory to be available on the embedded system's */workspace* path.
- Using NFS in the manner just described, assuming that you are working in the NFS exported directory on your host, the changes are immediately available on your target embedded system without the need to upload the newly compiled project files. This can speed development considerably.

4.5.8.1 Root File System on NFS

- Mounting your project workspace on your target embedded system is very useful for development and debugging because it facilitates rapid access to changes and source code for source-level debugging. This is especially useful when the target system is severely resource-constrained.
- NFS really shines as a development tool when you mount your embedded system's root file system entirely from an NFS server. The leading embedded Linux distributions targeted at embedded systems ship tens of thousands of files compiled and tested for the chosen target architecture.

4.5.9 Pseudo File Systems

A number of file systems fall under the category of Pseudo File Systems in the kernel configuration menu. Together they provide a range of facilities useful in a wide range of applications.

4.5.9.1 /proc File System

- The */proc* file system takes its name from its original purpose : an interface that allows the kernel to communicate information about each running process on a Linux system.
- Over the course of time, it has grown and matured to provide much more than process information. We introduce the highlights here; a complete tour of the */proc* file system is left as an exercise for you.
- The */proc* file system has become a virtual necessity for all but the simplest of Linux systems, even embedded ones.
- Many user level functions rely on the contents of the */proc* file system to do their job.
- For example, the mount command, issued without any parameters, lists all the currently active mount points on a running system, from the information delivered by */proc/mounts*. If the */proc* file system is unavailable, the mount command silently returns.

4.5.9.2 sysfs
- Like the */proc* file system, *sysfs* is not representative of an actual physical device.
- Instead, sysfs models specific kernel objects such as physical devices and provides a way to associate devices with device drivers. Some agents in a typical Linux distribution depend on the information on *sysfs*. We can get some idea of what kinds of objects are exported by looking directly at the directory structure exported by *sysfs*.

4.5.10 Other File Systems

Linux supports numerous file systems. Space does not permit us to cover all of them. However, you should be aware of some important file systems frequently found in embedded systems.
- The ramfs file system is best considered from the context of the Linux source code module that implements it. The tmpfs file system is similar to and related to ramfs. Like ramfs, everything in tmpfs is stored in kernel virtual memory, and the contents of tmpfs are lost on power down or reboot.
- The tmpfs file system is useful for fast temporary file storage. A good example of tmpfs use is to mount your */tmp* directory on a tmpfs. It improves performance for applications that use many small temporary files. This is also a great way to keep your */tmp* directory clean, because its contents are lost on every reboot. Mounting tmpfs is similar to any other virtual file system : # **mount -t tmpfs /tmpfs /tmp**
- As with other virtual file systems such as */proc*, the first tmpfs parameter in this mount command is a "no-op." In other words, it could be the word none and still function. However, it is a good reminder that you are mounting a virtual file system called tmpfs.

4.5.11 Building a Simple File System

It is straight forward to build a simple file system image. Here we demonstrate the use of the Linux kernel's loopback device. The loopback device enables the use of a regular file as a block device. In short, we build a file system image in a regular file and use the Linux loopback device to mount that file in the same way any other block device is mounted.

To build a simple root file system, start with a fixed-sized file containing all 0s :

dd if=/dev/zero of=./my-new-fs-image bs=1k count=512

This command creates a file of 512KB containing nothing but 0s. We fill the file with 0s to aid in compression later and to have a consistent data pattern for uninitialized data blocks within the file system. Exercise caution when using the dd command. Executing dd with no boundary (count=) or with an improper boundary can fill up your hard drive and possibly crash your system. dd is a powerful tool; use it with the respect it deserves. Simple typos in commands such as dd, executed as root, have destroyed countless file systems. When we have the new image file, we actually format the file to contain the data structures defined by a given file system.

4.6 Device Tree

- The Device Tree is a data structure for describing hardware. Rather than hard coding every detail of a device into an operating system, many aspect of the hardware can be described in a data structure that is passed to the operating system at boot time. The device tree is used both by Open Firmware, and in the standalone Flattened Device Tree (FDT) form.
- The data structure itself is a simple tree of named nodes and properties. Nodes contain properties and child nodes. Properties are simple name-value pairs. The structure can hold any kind of data.
- However, in order to be useful, device tree data must be laid out in a structure that operating systems can understand. A "bindings" is a description of how a device is described in the device tree. Bindings for a lot of devices are well established and documented.

4.6.1 History of Device Tree

- The DT was originally created by Open Firmware as part of the communication method for passing data from Open Firmware to a client program (like an operating system). An operating system used the Device Tree to discover the topology of the hardware at runtime, and thereby support a majority of available hardware without hard coded information (assuming drivers were available for all devices).
- Since Open Firmware is commonly used on PowerPC and SPARC platforms, the Linux support for those architectures has for a long time used the Device Tree.
- In 2005, when PowerPC Linux began a major cleanup and to merge 32-bit and 64-bit support, the decision was made to require DT support on all powerPC platforms, regardless of whether or not they used Open Firmware. To do this, a DT representation called the Flattened Device Tree (FDT) was created which could be passed to the kernel as a binary blob without requiring a real Open Firmware implementation. U-Boot, kexec, and other bootloaders were modified to support both passing a Device Tree Binary (dtb) and to modify a dtb at boot time.
- Some time later, FDT infrastructure was generalized to be usable by all architectures. At the time of this writing, 6 mainlined architectures (arm, microblaze, mips, powerpc, sparc, and x86) and 1 out of mainline (nios) have some level of DT support.

4.6.2 High Level View

- The most important thing to understand is that the DT is simply a data structure that describes the hardware.
- It provides a language for decoupling the hardware configuration from the board and device driver support in the Linux kernel (or any other operating system for that matter).

- Using it allows board and device support to become data driven; to make setup decisions based on data passed into the kernel instead of on per-machine hard coded selections.
- Ideally, data driven platform setup should result in less code duplication and make it easier to support a wide range of hardware with a single kernel image.
- The device tree source (.dts) format is used to express device trees in human-editable format.
- The device tree compiler tool (.dtc) can be used to translate device trees between the .dts format and the binary device tree blob (.dtb) format needed by an operating system.
- The device tree is a simple tree structure of nodes and properties.
- Properties are key-value pairs, and node may contain both properties and child nodes.
- For example, the following is a simple tree in the .dts format :

```
/ {
    node1 {
        a-string-property = "A string";
        a-string-list-property = "first string", "second string";
        a-byte-data-property = [0x01 0x23 0x34 0x56];
        child-node1 {
            first-child-property;
            second-child-property = <1>;
            a-string-property = "Hello, world";
        };
        child-node2 {
        };
    };
    node2 {
        an-empty-property;
        a-cell-property = <1 2 3 4>; /* each number (cell) is a uint32 */
        child-node1 {
        };
    };
};
```

- This tree shows the structure of nodes an properties. There is :
  A single root node: "/"
  A couple of child nodes: "node1" and "node2"
  A couple of children for node1: "child-node1" and "child-node2"

A bunch of properties scattered through the tree.
- Properties are simple key-value pairs where the value can either be empty or contain an arbitrary byte stream. While data types are not encoded into the data structure, there are a few fundamental data representations that can be expressed in a device tree source file. Text strings (null terminated) are represented with double quotes :
  string-property = "a string"
  'Cells' are 32-bit unsigned integers delimited by angle brackets :
  cell-property = <0xbeef 123 0xabcd1234>
- binary data is delimited with square brackets :
  binary-property = [0x01 0x23 0x45 0x67];
- Data of differing representations can be concatenated together using a comma :
  mixed-property = "a string", [0x01 0x23 0x45 0x67], <0x12345678>;
- Commas are also used to create lists of strings :
  string-list = "red fish", "blue fish";

4.6.3 Basic Concepts

To understand how the device tree is used, we will start with a simple machine and build up a device tree to describe it step by step.

4.6.3.1 Sample Machine

Consider the following imaginary machine (loosely based on ARM Versatile), manufactured by "Acme" and named "Coyote's Revenge" :
- One 32 bit ARM CPU.
- Processor local bus attached to memory mapped serial port, SPI bus controller, I2C controller, interrupt controller, and external bus bridge.
- 256MB of SDRAM based at 0.
- 2 Serial ports based at 0x101F1000 and 0x101F2000.
- GPIO controller based at 0x101F3000.
- SPI controller based at 0x10170000 with following devices.
  - MMC slot with SS pin attached to GPIO #1
  - External bus bridge with following devices.
  - SMC SMC91111 Ethernet device attached to external bus based at 0x10100000.
  - I2C controller based at 0x10160000 with following devices.
  - Maxim DS1338 real time clock. Responds to slave address 1101000 (0x58).
  - 64 MB of NOR flash based at 0x30000000.

4.6.3.2 Initial Structure

The first step is to lay down a skeleton structure for the machine. This is the bare minimum structure required for a valid device tree. At this stage you want to uniquely identify the machine.

```
/ {
    compatible = "acme,coyotes-revenge";
};
```

compatible specifies the name of the system. It contains a string in the form "<manufacturer>,<model>. It is important to specify the exact device, and to include the manufacturer name to avoid namespace collisions. Since the operating system will use the compatible value to make decisions about how to run on the machine, it is very important to put correct data into this property.

Theoretically, compatible is all the data an OS needs to uniquely identify a machine. If all the machine details are hard coded, then the OS could look specifically for "acme,coyotes-revenge" in the top level compatible property.

4.6.3.3 CPUs

Next step is to describe for each of the CPUs. A container node named "cpus" is added with a child node for each CPU. In this case the system is a dual-core Cortex A9 system from ARM.

```
/ {
    compatible = "acme,coyotes-revenge";

    cpus {
        cpu@0 {
            compatible = "arm,cortex-a9";
        };
        cpu@1 {
            compatible = "arm,cortex-a9";
        };
    };
};
```

The compatible property in each CPU node is a string that specifies the exact CPU model in the form <manufacturer>,<model>, just like the compatible property at the top level.

More properties will be added to the CPU nodes later, but we first need to talk about more of the basic concepts.

4.6.3.4 Node Names

It is worth taking a moment to talk about naming conventions. Every node must have a name in the form <name>[@<unit-address>]. <name> is a simple ASCII string and can be up to

31 characters in length. In general, nodes are named according to what kind of device it represents. ie. A node for a 3com Ethernet adapter would be use the name ethernet, not 3com509. The unit-address is included if the node describes a device with an address. In general, the unit address is the primary address used to access the device, and is listed in the node's reg property. We'll cover the reg property later in this document. Sibling nodes must be uniquely named, but it is normal for more than one node to use the same generic name so long as the address is different (i.e., serial@101f1000 & serial@101f2000).

4.6.3.5 Devices

Every device in the system is represented by a device tree node. The next step is to populate the tree with a node for each of the devices. For now, the new nodes will be left empty until we can talk about how address ranges and irqs are handled.

```
/ {
    compatible = "acme,coyotes-revenge";
    cpus {
        cpu@0 {
            compatible = "arm,cortex-a9";
        };
        cpu@1 {
            compatible = "arm,cortex-a9";
        };
    };
    serial@101F0000 {
        compatible = "arm,pl011";
    };
    serial@101F2000 {
        compatible = "arm,pl011";
    };
    gpio@101F3000 {
        compatible = "arm,pl061";
    };
    interrupt-controller@10140000 {
        compatible = "arm,pl190";
    };
    spi@10115000 {
```

```
        compatible = "arm,pl022";
    };
    external-bus {
      ethernet@0,0 {
        compatible = "smc,smc91c111";
      };
      i2c@1,0 {
        compatible = "acme,a1234-i2c-bus";
        rtc@58 {
          compatible = "maxim,ds1338";
        };
      };
      flash@2,0 {
        compatible = "samsung,k8f1315ebm", "cfi-flash";
      };
    };
  };
};
```

- In this tree, a node has been added for each device in the system, and the hierarchy reflects the how devices are connected to the system. ie. devices on the extern bus are children of the external bus node, and I2C devices are children of the I2C bus controller node. In general, the hierarchy represents the view of the system from the perspective of the CPU.
- This tree isn't valid at this point. It is missing information about connections between devices. That data will be added later.
- Some things to notice in this tree :
    - Every device node has a compatible property.
    - The flash node has 2 strings in the compatible property. Read on to the next section to learn why.
    - As mentioned earlier, node names reflect the type of device, not the particular model. Understanding the compatible Property.
- Every node in the tree that represents a device is required to have the compatible property. compatible is the key an operating system uses to decide which device driver to bind to a device.

- compatible is a list of strings. The first string in the list specifies the exact device that the node represents in the form "<manufacturer>,<model>". The following strings represent other devices that the device is compatible with.

4.6.3.6 How Addressing Works

- Devices that are addressable use the following properties to encode address information into the device tree :
  - reg
  - #address-cells
  - #size-cells
- Each addressable device gets a reg which is a list of tuples in the form reg = <address1 length1 [address2 length2] [address3 length3] ... >. Each tuple represents an address range used by the device. Each address value is a list of one or more 32 bit integers called cells. Similarly, the length value can either be a list of cells, or empty.
- Since both the address and length fields are variable of variable size, the #address-cells and #size-cells properties in the parent node are used to state how many cells are in each field. Or in other words, interpreting a reg property correctly requires the parent node's #address-cells and #size-cells values. To see how this all works, lets add the addressing properties to the sample device tree, starting with the CPUs.

4.6.3.7 CPU Addressing

- The CPU nodes represent the simplest case when talking about addressing. Each CPU is assigned a single unique ID, and there is no size associated with CPU IDs.

```
cpus {
    #address-cells = <1>;
    #size-cells = <0>;
    cpu@0 {
        compatible = "arm,cortex-a9";
        reg = <0>;
    };
    cpu@1 {
        compatible = "arm,cortex-a9";
        reg = <1>;
    };
};
```

- In the CPUs node, #address-cells is set to 1, and #size-cells is set to 0. This means that child reg values are a single Unit 32 that represent the address with no size field. In this

case, the two CPUs are assigned addresses 0 and 1. #size-cells is 0 for cpu nodes because each CPU is only assigned a single address.
- You'll also notice that the reg value matches the value in the node name. By convention, if a node has a reg property, then the node name must include the unit address, which is the first address value in the reg property.

4.6.3.8 Memory Mapped Devices
- Instead of single address values like found in the CPU nodes, a memory mapped device is assigned a range of addresses that it will respond to. #size-cells is used to state how large the length field is in each child reg tuple. In the following example, each address value is 1 cell (32 bits), and each length value is also 1 cell, which is typical on 32 bit systems. 64-bit machines may use a value of 2 for #address-cells and #size-cells to get 64-bit addressing in the device tree.

```
/ {
    #address-cells = <1>;
    #size-cells = <1>;

    ...

    serial@101f0000 {
        compatible = "arm,pl011";
        reg = <0x101f0000 0x1000 >;
    };

    serial@101f2000 {
        compatible = "arm,pl011";
        reg = <0x101f2000 0x1000 >;
    };

    gpio@101f3000 {
        compatible = "arm,pl061";
        reg = <0x101f3000 0x1000
               0x101f4000 0x0010>;
    };

    interrupt-controller@10140000 {
```

```
    compatible = "arm,pl190";
    reg = <0x10140000 0x1000 >;
  };

  spi@10115000 {
    compatible = "arm,pl022";
    reg = <0x10115000 0x1000 >;
  };

  ...

};
```

- Each device is assigned a base address, and the size of the region it is assigned. The GPIO device address in this example is assigned two address ranges; 0x101f3000...0x101f3fff and 0x101f4000..0x101f400f.
- Some devices live on a bus with a different addressing scheme. For example, a device can be attached to an external bus with discrete chip select lines.
- Since each parent node defines the addressing domain for its children, the address mapping can be chosen to best describe the system. The code below show address assignment for devices attached to the external bus with the chip select number encoded into the address.

```
external-bus {
  #address-cells = <2>
    #size-cells = <1>;

  ethernet@0,0 {
    compatible = "smc,smc91c111";
    reg = <0 0 0x1000>;
  };

  i2c@1,0 {
    compatible = "acme,a1234-i2c-bus";
    reg = <1 0 0x1000>;
    rtc@58 {
      compatible = "maxim,ds1338";
```

```
    };
  };

  flash@2,0 {
    compatible = "samsung,k8f1315ebm", "cfi-flash";
    reg = <2 0 0x4000000>;
  };
};
```

- The external-bus uses 2 cells for the address value; one for the chip select number, and one for the offset from the base of the chip select. The length field remains as a single cell since only the offset portion of the address needs to have a range. So, in this example, each reg entry contains 3 cells; the chipselect number, the offset, and the length.
- Since the address domains are contained to a node and its children, parent nodes are free to define whatever addressing scheme makes sense for the bus. Nodes outside of the immediate parent and child nodes do not normally have to care about the local addressing domain, and addresses have to be mapped to get from one domain to another.

4.6.3.9 Non Memory Mapped Devices

- Other devices are not memory mapped on the processor bus. They can have address ranges, but they are not directly accessible by the CPU. Instead the parent device's driver would perform indirect access on behalf of the CPU.
- To take the example of I2C devices, each device is assigned an address, but there is no length or range associated with it. This looks much the same as CPU address assignments.

```
i2c@1,0 {
    compatible = "acme,a1234-i2c-bus";
    #address-cells = <1>;
      #size-cells = <0>;
    reg = <1 0 0x1000>;
    rtc@58 {
      compatible = "maxim,ds1338";
      reg = <58>;
    };
};
```

4.6.3.10 Ranges (Address Translation)

- The root node always describes the CPU's view of the address space. Child nodes of the root are already using the CPU's address domain, and so do not need any explicit mapping. For example, the serial@101f0000 device is directly assigned the address 0x101f0000.
- Nodes that are not direct children of the root do not use the CPU's address domain. In order to get a memory mapped address the device tree must specify how to translate addresses from one domain to another. The ranges property is used for this purpose.
- Here is the sample device tree with the ranges property added.

```
/ {
    compatible = "acme,coyotes-revenge";
    #address-cells = <1>;
    #size-cells = <1>;
    ...
    external-bus {
        #address-cells = <2>
        #size-cells = <1>;
        ranges = <0 0  0x10100000  0x10000     // Chipselect 1, Ethernet
                  1 0  0x10160000  0x10000     // Chipselect 2, i2c controller
                  2 0  0x30000000  0x1000000>; // Chipselect 3, NOR Flash

        ethernet@0,0 {
            compatible = "smc,smc91c111";
            reg = <0 0 0x1000>;
        };

        i2c@1,0 {
            compatible = "acme,a1234-i2c-bus";
            #address-cells = <1>;
            #size-cells = <0>;
            reg = <1 0 0x1000>;
            rtc@58 {
                compatible = "maxim,ds1338";
                reg = <58>;
```

```
        };
    };

    flash@2,0 {
        compatible = "samsung,k8f1315ebm", "cfi-flash";
        reg = <2 0 0x4000000>;
    };
  };
};
```

- Ranges is a list of address translations. Each entry in the ranges table is a tuple containing the child address, the parent address, and the size of the region in the child address space.
- The size of each field is determined by taking the child's #address-cells value, the parent's #address-cells value, and the child's #size-cells value. You should also notice that there is no ranges property in the i2c@1,0 node. The reason for this is that unlike the external bus, devices on the I2C bus are not memory mapped on the CPU's address domain.
- Instead, the CPU indirectly accesses the rtc@58 device via the i2c@1,0 device. The lack of a ranges property means that a device cannot be directly accessed by any device other than it's parent.

4.6.4 How Interrupts Work

Unlike address range translation which follows the natural structure of the tree, Interrupt signals can originate from and terminate on any device in a machine. Unlike device addressing which is naturally expressed in the device tree, interrupt signals are expressed as links between nodes independent of the tree. Four properties are used to describe interrupt connections :

- **Interrupt Controller :** An empty property declaring a node as a device that receives interrupt signals
- **Interrupt-Cells :** This is a property of the interrupt controller node. It states how many cells are in an interrupt specifier for this interrupt controller (Similar to #address-cells and #size-cells).
- **Interrupt-Parent :** A property of a device node containing a phandle to the interrupt controller that it is attached to. Nodes that do not have an interrupt-parent property can also inherit the property from their parent node.
- **Interrupts :** A property of a device node containing a list of interrupt specifiers, one for each Interrupt output signal on the device.

An interrupt specifier is one or more cells of data (as specified by #interrupt-cells) that specifies which interrupt input the device is attached to. Most devices only have a single interrupt output as shown in the example below, but it is possible to have multiple interrupt outputs on a device. The meaning of an interrupt specifier depends entirely on the binding for the interrupt controller device. Each interrupt controller can decide how many cells it need to uniquely define an interrupt input.

Some things to notice :
- The machine has a single interrupt controller, interrupt-controller@10140000.
- The label 'intc:' has been added to the interrupt controller node, and the label was used to assign a phandle to the interrupt-parent property in the root node. This interrupt-parent value becomes the default for the system because all child nodes inherit it unless it is explicitly overridden.
- Each device uses an interrupt property to specify a different interrupt input line.
- #interrupt-cells is 2, so each interrupt specifier has 2 cells. This example uses the common pattern of using the first cell to encode the interrupt line number, and the second cell to encode flags such as active high vs. active low, or edge vs. level sensitive. For any given interrupt controller, refer to the controller's binding documentation to learn how the specifier is encoded.

4.6.5 Device Specific Data

Beyond the common properties, arbitrary properties and child nodes can be added to nodes. Any data needed by the operating system can be added as long as some rules are followed.

4.6.6 Special Nodes

4.6.6.1 Aliases Node

A specific node is normally referenced by the full path, like */external-bus/ethernet@0,0*, but that gets cumbersome when what a user really wants to know is, "which device is eth0?" The aliases node can be used to assign a short alias to a full device path. For example :

```
aliases {
   ethernet0 = &eth0;
   serial0 = &serial0;
};
```

The operating system is welcome to use the aliases when assigning an identifier to a device.

You'll notice a new syntax used here. The *property = &label;* syntax assigns the full node path referenced by the label as a string property.

This is different from the *phandle = < &label >;* form used earlier which inserts a phandle value into a cell.

4.6.6.2 Chosen Node

The chosen node doesn't represent a real device, but serves as a place for passing data between firmware and the operating system, like boot arguments. Data in the chosen node does not represent the hardware. Typically the chosen node is left empty in .dts source files and populated at boot time.

In our example system, firmware might add the following to the chosen node :

```
chosen {
    bootargs = "root=/dev/nfs rw nfsroot=192.168.1.1 console=ttyS0,115200";
};
```

4.6.7 Purpose of Device Tree

Linux uses DT data for three major purposes :

1. Platform identification,
2. Runtime configuration, and
3. Device population.

1. Platform Identification

First and foremost, the kernel will use data in the DT to identify the specific machine. In a perfect world, the specific platform shouldn't matter to the kernel because all platform details would be described perfectly by the device tree in a consistent and reliable manner. Hardware is not perfect though, and so the kernel must identify the machine during early boot so that it has the opportunity to run machine-specific fixups.

2. Runtime Configuration

In most cases, a DT will be the sole method of communicating data from firmware to the kernel, so also gets used to pass in runtime and configuration data like the kernel parameters string and the location of an initrd image.

Most of this data is contained in the /chosen node, and when booting Linux it will look something like this :

```
chosen {
    bootargs = "console=ttyS0,115200 loglevel=8";
    initrd-start = <0xc8000000>;
    initrd-end = <0xc8200000>;
};
```

The bootargs property contains the kernel arguments, and the initrd-* properties define the address and size of an initrd blob. Note that initrd-end is the first address after the initrd image, so this doesn't match the usual semantic of struct resource. The chosen node may also optionally contain an arbitrary number of additional properties for platform-specific configuration data.

3. Device Population
- After the board has been identified, and after the early configuration data has been parsed, then kernel initialization can proceed in the normal way. At some point in this process, *unflatten_device_tree()* is called to convert the data into a more efficient runtime representation.
- This is also when machine specific setup hooks will get called, like *the machine_desc .init_early(), .init_irq() and .init_machine()* hooks on ARM. The remainder of this section uses examples from the ARM implementation, but all architectures will do pretty much the same thing when using a DT.
- As can be guessed by the names, *.init_early()* is used for any machine specific setup that needs to be executed early in the boot process, and *.init_irq()* is used to set up interrupt handling. Using a DT doesn't materially change the behaviour of either of these functions. If a DT is provided, then both *.init_early()* and *.init_irq()* are able to call any of the DT query functions *(of_* in include/linux/of*.h)* to get additional data about the platform.
- The most interesting hook in the DT context is *.init_machine()* which is primarily responsible for populating the Linux device model with data about the platform. Historically this has been implemented on embedded platforms by defining a set of static clock structures, platform_devices, and other data in the board support .c file, and registering it en-masse in *.init_machine()*. When DT is used, then instead of hard coding static devices for each platform, the list of devices can be obtained by parsing the DT, and allocating device structures dynamically.
- The simplest case is when *.init_machine()* is only responsible for registering a block of *platform_devices*. A *platform_device* is a concept used by Linux for memory or I/O mapped devices which cannot be detected by hardware, and for 'composite' or 'virtual' devices (more on those later).
- While there is no 'platform device' terminology for the DT, platform devices roughly correspond to device nodes at the root of the tree and children of simple memory mapped bus nodes.

4.7 MTD Subsystem

The Memory Technology Device (MTD) subsystem grew out of the need to support a wide variety of memory-like devices such as Flash memory chips. Many different types of Flash chips are available, along with numerous methods to program them, partly because of the many specialized and high-performance modes that are supported. The MTD layer architecture enables the separation of the low-level device complexities from the higher-layer data organization and storage formats that use memory and flash devices. This section introduces the MTD subsystem and provides some simple examples of its use. First we look at what is required of the kernel to support MTD services. We show some simple operations on a development workstation with MTD enabled to help you understand the basics of this subsystem. This section also integrates MTD and the JFFS2 file system. Then this section discusses the concept of partitions as they relate to the MTD layer. We examine the details of building partitions from a bootloader and how the Linux kernel detects them. The section continues with a brief introduction to the MTD utilities. We conclude by putting it all together and booting a target board using an in-Flash JFFS2 file system image.

4.7.1 MTD Overview

- Simply stated, MTD is a device driver layer that provides a uniform API for interfacing with raw Flash devices.
- MTD supports a wide variety of Flash devices. However, MTD is not a block device. MTD deals with devices in units of erase blocks that are not always a uniform size, whereas block devices operate on fixed-size read/write blocks called sectors.
- Block devices have two primary operations read and write to a sector and MTDs have three : read, write, and erase.
- MTD devices have a limited write life cycle, and MTD has logic to spread the write operations over the device's life span to increase the device's life span. This is called wear leveling. Contrary to popular belief, SD/MMC cards, CompactFlash cards, USB Flash drives, and other popular devices are not MTD devices. These devices all contain internal Flash translation layers that handle MTD-like functions such as block erasure and wear leveling. Therefore, these devices appear to the system as traditional block devices and do not require the specialized handling of MTD.
- Most device drivers in Linux are either character or block devices. MTD is neither. Although translation mechanisms can make MTD look like a character or block device, MTD is unique in Linux driver architecture. This is because MTD drivers must perform Flash-specific operations such as the erase block and wear leveling operations, which have no parallel in traditional block drivers.

4.7.1.1 Enabling MTD Services

- To use MTD services, your kernel must be configured with MTD enabled. This applies equally to your development workstation and your embedded system. For simplicity, we'll demonstrate MTD operations on your development workstation. To follow along, you must have MTD enabled on your workstation as described here.
- In a similar fashion, you must also have MTD enabled on your embedded target to use MTD capabilities there. MTD has many configuration options, some of which can be confusing.
- The best way to understand the myriad choices is simply to begin working with them. To illustrate the mechanics of the MTD subsystem and how it fits in with the system, we'll

begin with some simple that you can perform on your Linux development workstation. Fig. 4.5 shows the kernel configuration (invoked per the usual make ARCH=<arch> gconfig) necessary to enable the bare-minimum MTD functionality.

- Listing 4-6 displays the .config file entries resulting from the selections shown in Fig. 4.5. These configuration options are found under Device drivers in the kernel configuration utility.

LISTING 4–6 Basic MTD Configuration from .config

CONFIG_MTD=y
CONFIG_MTD_CHAR=y
CONFIG_MTD_BLOCK=y
CONFIG_MTD_MTDRAM=m
CONFIG_MTDRAM_TOTAL_SIZE=8192
CONFIG_MTDRAM_ERASE_SIZE=128

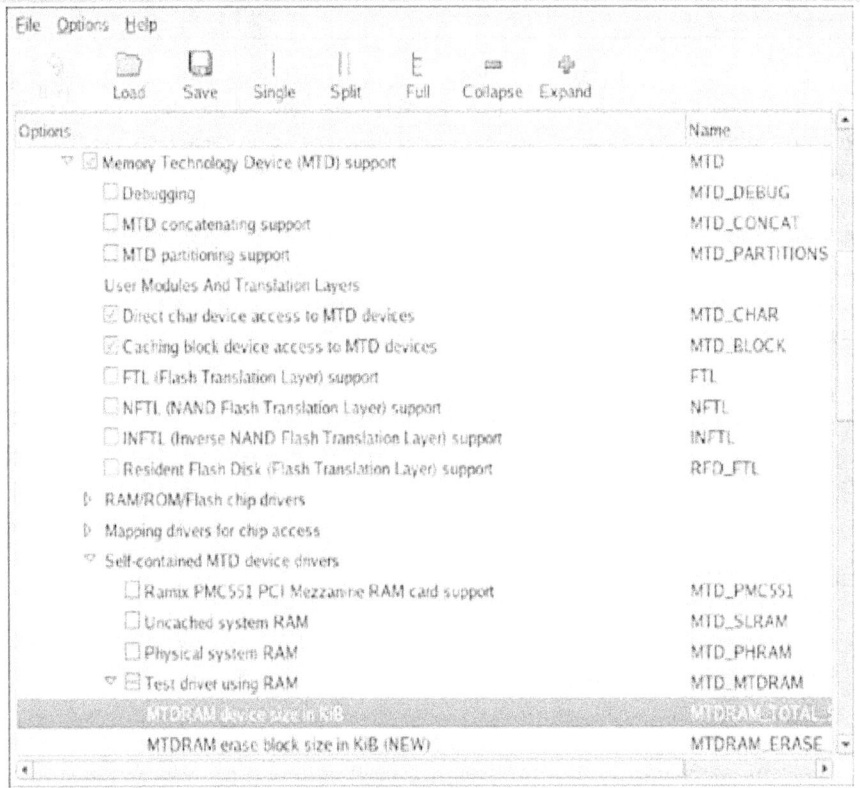

Fig. 4.5 : MTD configuration

- The MTD subsystem is enabled through the first configuration option, which you select by checking the first box shown in Fig. 4.5, Memory Technology Device (MTD) Support. The next two entries from the configuration shown in Fig. 4.6 enable special device-level access to the MTD devices, such as Flash memory, from user space.
- The first one (CONFIG_MTD_CHAR) enables character device mode access, essentially a sequential access characterized by byte-at-a-time sequential read and write access.
- The second (CONFIG_MTD_BLOCK) enables access to the MTD device in block device mode, the access method used for disk drives, in which blocks of multiple bytes of data are read or written at one time.
- These access modes allow the use of familiar Linux commands to read and write data to Flash memory, as you will see shortly. The CONFIG_MTD_MTDRAM element enables a special test driver that allows us to examine the MTD subsystem on our development host even if no MTD devices (such as Flash memory) are available.
- Remember, we are working with MTD on our development workstation in these examples as a convenient way to get familiar with the MTD subsystem. You would rarely if ever do this on an embedded target.
- Coupled with this configuration selection are two parameters associated with the RAM-based test driver : the device size and the erase size. For this example, we have specified 8192KB total size and 128KB erase size. The objective of this test driver is to emulate a Flash device, primarily to facilitate MTD subsystem testing and development. Because Flash memory is architected using fixed-size erase blocks, the test driver also contains the concept of erase blocks. You will see how these parameters are used shortly.

4.7.1.2 MTD Basics
- Recent Linux kernel releases have MTD integrated, so you don't need to apply MTD patches to enable it. Of course, in either case, MTD must be enabled in your kernel configuration, as shown in Fig. 4.6.
- After MTD is enabled, we can examine how this subsystem works on our Linux development workstation. Using the test RAM driver we just configured, we can mount a JFFS2 image using an MTD device.

4.7.1.3 Configuring MTD on Your Target
To use MTD with the Flash memory on your board, you must have MTD configured correctly. You must do the following to configure MTD for your board, Flash, and Flash layout :
- Specify the partitioning on your Flash device.
- Specify the type of Flash and location.
- Configure the proper Flash driver for your chosen chip.
- Configure the kernel with the appropriate driver(s).
- Each of these steps is explored in the following sections.

4.7.2 MTD Partitions

- Most Flash devices on a given hardware platform are divided into several sections, called partitions, similar to the partitions found on a typical desktop workstation hard drive. The MTD subsystem supports such Flash partitions.
- The MTD subsystem must be configured for MTD partitioning support. Fig. 4.6 shows the configuration options for MTD partitioning support from a recent Linux kernel snapshot.
- You can communicate the partition data to the Linux kernel in several ways. You can see the configuration options for each in Fig. 4.6 under "MTD partitioning support." The following methods currently are supported :
  - Redboot partition table parsing.
  - Kernel command-line partition table definition.
  - Board-specific mapping drivers.
  - TI AR7 partitioning support.

MTD also allows configurations without partition data. In this case, MTD simply treats the entire Flash memory as a single device.

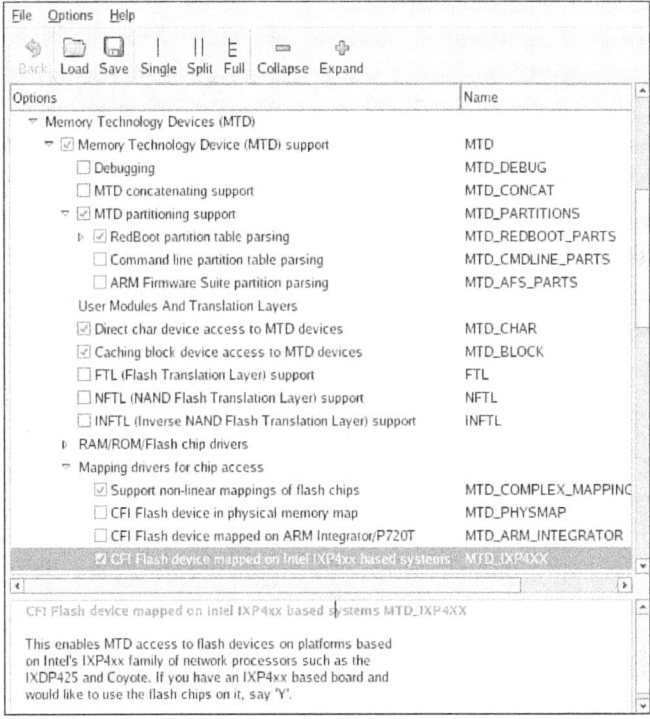

Fig. 4.6 : Kernel configuration for MTD partitioning support

4.7.2.1 Redboot Partition Table Partitioning

- One of the more common methods of defining and detecting MTD partitions stems from one of the original implementations : Redboot partitions. Redboot is a bootloader found on many embedded boards, especially ARM XScale boards such as the ADI Engineering Coyote Reference Platform.
- The MTD subsystem defines a method for storing partition information on the Flash device itself, similar in concept to a partition table on a hard disk. In the case of the Redboot partitions, the developer reserves and specifies a Flash erase block that holds the partition definitions.
- A mapping driver is selected that calls the partition parsing functions during boot to detect the partitions on the Flash device.

4.7.2.2 Kernel Command-Line Partitioning

As detailed in Section 4.7.2, "MTD Partitions," the raw Flash partition information can be communicated to the kernel using other methods. Indeed, possibly the most straightforward way, though perhaps not the simplest, is to manually pass the partition information directly on the kernel command line.

- Of course, as you have learned, some bootloaders make that easy (such as U-Boot), whereas others do not have a facility to pass a kernel command line to the kernel upon boot. In these cases, the kernel command line must be configured at compile time and therefore is more difficult to change, requiring a recompile of the kernel itself each time the partitions are modified.
- To enable command-line partitioning in the MTD subsystem, your kernel must be configured for this support. You can see this configuration option in Fig. 4.6 under "MTD partitioning support." Select the option for command-line partition table parsing, which defines the CONFIG_MTD_CMDLINE_PARTS option.

4.7.2.3 Mapping Driver

The final method for defining your board-specific Flash layout is to use a dedicated board-specific mapping driver. The Linux kernel source tree contains many examples of mapping drivers, located in .../drivers/mtd/maps. The implementation details vary by architecture. The mapping driver is a proper kernel module, complete with *module_init()* and *module_exit()* calls, as described in Chapter "Device Driver Basics." A typical mapping driver is small and easy to navigate, often containing fewer than a couple dozen lines of C.

4.7.2.4 Flash Chip Drivers

MTD supports a wide variety of Flash chips and devices. Chances are very good that your chosen chip is also supported. The most common Flash chips support the Common Flash

Interface (CFI) mentioned earlier. Older Flash chips might have JEDEC support, which is an older Flash compatibility standard. Fig. 4.6 shows the kernel configuration from a recent Linux kernel snapshot. This version supports many Flash types.

If your Flash chip is not supported, you must provide a device file yourself. Using one of the many examples in .../drivers/mtd/chips as a starting point, customize or create your own Flash device driver. Better yet, unless the chip was just introduced with some newfangled interface, someone probably has already produced a driver.

4.7.2.5 Board-Specific Initialization

Along with a mapping driver, your board-specific (platform) setup must provide the underlying definitions for proper MTD Flash system operation.

4.7.3 MTD Utilities

- The MTD package contains a number of system utilities useful for setting up and managing your MTD subsystem. The utilities are built separately from the primary MTD subsystem, which should be built from within your Linux kernel source tree. These utilities can be built in a manner similar to any other cross-compiled user space code.
- You must exercise caution when using these utilities, because Linux provides no protection from mistakes. A single-digit typo can wipe out the bootloader on your hardware platform. This can ruin your day unless you've backed it up and know how to reprogram it using a JTAG Flash programmer. In keeping with a common practice throughout this book, we cannot devote sufficient space to cover every MTD utility. We highlight the most common and useful ones and leave it as an exercise for you to explore the rest.
- A recent MTD snapshot contained more than 20 binary utilities. The flash_* family of utilities is useful for raw device operations on an MTD partition.
- These include flashcp, flash_erase, flash_info, flash_lock, flash_unlock, and others. Hopefully their names are descriptive enough to give you some idea of their function. After partitions are defined and enumerated as kernel devices, any of these user space utilities can be run on a partition.
- We repeat the warning we issued earlier : If you execute flash_erase on the partition containing your bootloader, you'll be the proud owner of a silicon paperweight. If you intend to experiment like this, it's a good idea to have a backup of your bootloader image and to know how to re-Flash it using a hardware JTAG emulator or another Flash programming tool.
- Here you can see the new partition we created instantiated as the kernel device mtd1.

LISTING 4-7 Kernel MTD Partition List

```
root@coyote:~# cat /proc/mtd
dev: size erasesize name
mtd0: 00060000 00020000 "RedBoot"
mtd1: 00160000 00020000 "MyKernel"
mtd2: 00001000 00020000 "RedBoot config"
mtd3: 00020000 00020000 "FIS directory"
```

- Using the MTD utilities, we can perform a number of operations on the newly created partition. The following is the result of a flash_erase command on the partition :
  # flash_erase /dev/mtd1
  Erase Total 1 Units
  Performing Flash Erase of length 131072 at offset 0x0 done
- To copy a new kernel image to this partition, use the flashcp command :
  root@coyote:~# **flashcp /workspace/coyote-40-zImage /dev/mtd1**
- It gets a bit more interesting working with a root file system partition. We have the option of using the bootloader or the Linux kernel to place the initial image on the Redboot Flash partition.
- First, we use Redboot to create the new partition that will hold our root file system. The following command creates a new partition on the Flash device called RootFS starting at physical memory address 0x50300000, with a length of 30 blocks.
- Remember, a block, generically called an erase unit, is 128KB on this Flash chip.
  RedBoot> **fis create -f 0x50300000 -l 0x600000 -n RootFS**
- Next, we boot the kernel and copy the root file system image into the new partition we have named RootFS. This is accomplished with the following command from a Linux command prompt on your target board.
- Note that this assumes you have already placed your file system image in a directory accessible to your board. As mentioned many times throughout this book, NFS root mount is your best friend during development.
  root@coyote:~# **flashcp /rootfs.ext2 /dev/mtd2**
- The file system can be anywhere from a couple megabytes up to the largest size we have allowed on this partition, so this can take some time. Remember, this operation involves programming (sometimes called flashing) the image into the Flash memory. After copying, we can mount the partition as a file system. Listing 4-8 displays the sequence.

LISTING 4-8 Mounting the MTD Flash Partition as an ext2 File System

```
root@coyote:~# mount -t ext2 /dev/mtdblock2 /mnt/remote ro
root@coyote:~# ls -l /mnt/remote/
total 16
```

```
LISTING 4-8 Continued
drwxr-xr-x 2 root root 1024 Nov 19 2005 bin
drwxr-xr-x 2 root root 1024 Oct 26 2005 boot
drwxr-xr-x 2 root root 1024 Nov 19 2005 dev
drwxr-xr-x 5 root root 1024 Nov 19 2005 etc
drwxr-xr-x 2 root root 1024 Oct 26 2005 home
drwxr-xr-x 3 root root 1024 Nov 19 2005 lib
drwxr-xr-x 3 root root 1024 Nov 19 2005 mnt
drwxr-xr-x 2 root root 1024 Oct 26 2005 opt
drwxr-xr-x 2 root root 1024 Oct 26 2005 proc
drwxr-xr-x 2 root root 1024 Oct 26 2005 root
drwxr-xr-x 2 root root 1024 Nov 19 2005 sbin
drwxr-xr-x 2 root root 1024 Oct 26 2005 srv
drwxr-xr-x 2 root root 1024 Oct 26 2005 sys
drwxr-xr-x 2 root root 1024 Oct 26 2005 tmp
drwxr-xr-x 6 root root 1024 Oct 26 2005 usr
drwxr-xr-x 2 root root 1024 Nov 19 2005 var
root@coyote:~#
```

- Listing 4-8 has two important subtleties. Notice that we have specified */dev/mtdblock2* on the mount command line. This is the MTD block driver that enables us to access the MTD partition as a block device.
- Specifying */dev/mtd2* instructs the kernel to use the MTD character driver. Both mtdchar and mtdblock are pseudo drivers used to provide either character-based or block-oriented access to the underlying Flash partition. Because mount expects a block device, you must use the block-device specifier. Fig. 4.5 shows the kernel configuration that enables these access methods.
- The respective kernel configuration macros are CONFIG_MTD_CHAR and CONFIG_MTD_BLOCK. The second subtlety is the use of the read-only (ro) command-line switch on the mount command.
- It is perfectly acceptable to mount an ext2 image from Flash using the MTD block emulation driver for read-only purposes. However, there is no support for writing to an ext2 device using the mtdblock driver. This is because ext2 has no knowledge of Flash erase blocks. For write access to a Flash-based file system, we need to use a file system with Flash knowledge, such as JFFS2.

4.7.3.1 JFFS2 Root File System
- Creating a JFFS2 root file system is a straightforward process. In addition to compression, JFFS2 supports wear leveling, a feature designed to increase Flash lifetime by fairly distributing the write cycles across the blocks of the device.
- Flash memory is subject to a limited number of write cycles. Wear leveling should be considered a mandatory feature in any Flash-based file system you employ. Flash memory as a write occasional medium. Specifically, you should avoid allowing any processes that require frequent writes to target the Flash file system. Be especially aware of any logging programs, such as syslogd.
- We can build a JFFS2 image on our development workstation using the ext2 image we used on our Redboot RootFS partition. The compression benefits will be immediately obvious. The image we used in the previous RootFS example was an ext2 file system image. Here is the listing in long (-l) format :

    # ls -l rootfs.ext2

    -rw-r--r-- 1 root root 6291456 Nov 19 16:21 rootfs.ext2
- Now let's convert this file system image to JFFS2 using the mkfs.jffs2 utility found in the MTD package. Listing 4-9 shows the command and results.

LISTING 4-9 Converting RootFS to JFFS2

    # mount -o loop rootfs.ext2 /mnt/flash/
    # mkfs.jffs2 -r /mnt/flash -e 128 -b -o rootfs.jffs2
    # ls -l rootfs.jffs2

    -rw-r--r-- 1 root root 2401512 Nov 20 10:08 rootfs.jffs2

- First we mount the ext2 file system image on a loopback device on an arbitrary mount point on our development workstation. Next we invoke the MTD utility *mkfs. jffs2* to create the JFFS2 file system image. The -r flag tells mkfs.jffs2 where the root file system image is located.
- The -e instructs *mkfs.jffs2* to build the image while assuming a 128 KB block size. The default block size is 64 KB. JFFS2 does not exhibit its most efficient behavior if the Flash device contains a different block size than the block size of the image.
- Finally, we display a long listing and discover that the resulting JFFS2 root file system image has been reduced in size by more than 60 percent. When you are working with limited Flash memory, this is a substantial reduction in precious Flash resource usage.
- Take note of an important command-line flag passed to *mkfs.jffs2*. The -b flag is the big-endian flag.

- It instructs the *mkfs.jffs2* utility to create a JFFS2 Flash image suitable for use on a big-endian target. Because we are targeting the ADI Engineering Coyote board, which contains an Intel IXP425 processor running in big-endian mode, this step is crucial for proper operation.
- If you fail to specify big-endian, you will get several screens full of complaints from the kernel as it tries to negotiate the superblock of a JFFS2 file system that is essentially gibberish. Would you like to guess how I remembered this important detail? In a manner similar to the previous example, we can copy this image to our Redboot RootFS Flash partition using the flashcp utility. Then we can boot the Linux kernel using a JFFS2 root file system. Listing 4-10 provides the details, running the MTD utilities on our target hardware.

LISTING 4-10 Copying JFFS2 to the RootFS Partition

```
root@coyote:~# cat /proc/mtd
dev: size erasesize name
mtd0: 00060000 00020000 "RedBoot"
mtd1: 00160000 00020000 "MyKernel"
mtd2: 00600000 00020000 "RootFS"
mtd3: 00001000 00020000 "RedBoot config"
mtd4: 00020000 00020000 "FIS directory"
root@coyote:~# flash_erase /dev/mtd2
Erase Total 1 Units
Performing Flash Erase of length 131072 at offset 0x0 done
root@coyote:~# flashcp /rootfs.jffs2 /dev/mtd2
root@coyote:~#
```

- It is important to note that you must have the JFFS2 file system enabled in your kernel configuration. Execute make ARCH=<arch> gconfig and select JFFS2 under File Systems, Miscellaneous File Systems.
- Another useful hint is to use the -v (verbose) flag on the MTD utilities. This provides progress updates and other useful information during the Flash operations.
- We have already seen how to boot a kernel with the Redboot exec command. Listing 4-11 details the sequence of commands to load and boot the Linux kernel with our new JFFS2 file system as root.

LISTING 4-11 Booting with JFFS2 as the Root File System

```
RedBoot> load -r -v -b 0x01008000 coyote-zImage
Using default protocol (TFTP)
```

```
Raw file loaded 0x01008000-0x0114decb, assumed entry at 0x01008000
RedBoot> exec -c "console=ttyS0,115200 rootfstype=jffs2 root=/dev/mtdblock2"
Using base address 0x01008000 and length 0x00145ecc
Uncompressing Linux...... done, booting the kernel.
...
```

4.7.4 UBI File System

The Unsorted Block Image (UBI) File System was designed to overcome some of the limitations of the JFFS2 file system. It can be considered the successor to JFFS2, although JFFS2 remains in widespread use on embedded Linux devices containing Flash memory. The UBI File System (UBIFS) is layered on top of UBI devices, which in turn depends on MTD devices. UBIFS improves on one of the more significant limitations of the JFFS2 file system. mount time. JFFS2 maintains its indexing metadata in system memory and must read this index to build a complete directory tree each time the system boots. This can require reading a significant portion of the Flash device. In contrast, UBIFS maintains its indexing metadata on the Flash device itself, negating the need to scan and rebuild this data on each mount. Therefore, UBIFS mounts many times faster than JFFS2. UBIFS also supports write caching, which can be a significant performance enhancement.

4.7.4.1 Configuring for UBIFS

To use UBIFS, your kernel needs to have UBI support enabled. Two different kernel configuration menu items must be enabled in your kernel configuration to enable UBIFS. First, enable support for MTD_UBI. This option can be found in your kernel configuration under Device Drivers --> Memory Technology Device (MTD) support --> UBI Unsorted Block Images --> Enable UBI. After this item is chosen, it enables the file system support configuration options found under File Systems --> Miscellaneous filesystems --> UBIFS file system support.

4.7.4.2 Building a UBIFS Image

- Building a UBIFS image is a little more tricky than building a JFFS2 image. The additional complexity comes from the NAND Flash technology. Building a UBIFS image requires that you have knowledge of the NAND Flash architecture on your target system. This will become clear in a moment.
- You will also need a fairly recent version of MTD Utils installed on your development workstation. MTD Utils can be found at *git://git.infradead.org/mtd-utils.git*. Listing 4-12 details the process for creating the UBIFS image on your development workstation.
- Assume for this exercise that you have the desired contents of your file system in a directory called rootfs.

LISTING 4-12 Building the UBIFS Image

```
$ mkfs.ubifs -m 2048 -e 129024 -c 1996 -o ubifs.img -r ./rootfs
$ ubinize -m 2048 -p 128KiB -s 512 -o ubi.img ubinize.cfg
$ ls -l
total 200880
drwxr-xr-x 17 chris chris 4096 2010-03-01 11:33 rootfs
-rw-r--r-- 1 chris chris 101799936 2010-03-01 11:55 ubifs.img
-rw-r--r-- 1 chris chris 103677952 2010-03-01 11:58 ubi.img
-rw-r--r-- 1 chris chris 112 2010-03-01 11:54 ubinize.cfg
```

- The raw UBIFS image is built using the mkfs.ubifs utility, from the mtd-utils package. This produces the target file ubifs.img. It is critical that the correct parameters are passed to *mkfs.ubifs*.
- These parameters come from your hardware design and NAND Flash architecture. The -m specifies the minimum I/O unit size in this case, 2KB. The -e specifies the logical erase block (LEB) size for the image.
- The maximum number of LEBs for the image is specified by -c. The name of the output image is specified using -o. For this example, we have named it ubifs.img. Now that we have the UBIFS image, we must generate the UBI volume image.
- We use the ubinize tool (part of the mtd-utils package) for this. Once again, we must use the correct parameters for our target environment. In addition, you will notice that ubinize requires a configuration file.
- The ubinize.cfg file contains the volume name, among other things, as we will see shortly.
- Listing 4-12 specifies the minimum I/O size, as in mkfs.ubifs, as 2 KB. Here we specify the physical erase block size, given by the -p parameter. In our case, we are using NAND Flash with a 128 KB physical erase block size.
- The -s parameter specifies a subpage size, which is the minimum I/O unit. We name the target output file using -o ubi.img. We will flash this image into our device. The configuration file used by ubinize specifies the volumes to be generated by the ubinize tool. Listing 4-13 details the simple configuration we used for Listing 4-12.

LISTING 4-13 ubinize Configuration File

```
$ cat ubinize.cfg
[ubifs]
mode=ubi
image=ubifs.img
vol_id=0
```

```
vol_size=200MiB
vol_type=dynamic
vol_name=rootfs
```

- Here you can see that we named the volume rootfs and that the raw image comes from the file called ubifs.img. Recall from Listing 4-12 that this was the image produced by the mkfs.ubifs utility.
- Once we have the final image, we can flash it to our device. We will use the ubiformat command for that.
- You cannot simply flash the raw image to the device. This is because NAND Flash as used by the UBI layer contains special headers that record the erase count, among other things, for each physical erase block.
- This is used for wear leveling. Using ubiformat preserves these error count headers. Listing 4-14 shows the details.

LISTING 4-14 Using the UBIFS Image

```
root@beagleboard:~# flash_eraseall /dev/mtd4
Erasing 128 Kibyte @ f980000 -- 100 % complete.
root@beagleboard:~# ubiformat /dev/mtd4 -s 512 -f /ubi.img
ubiformat: mtd4 (NAND), size 261619712 bytes (249.5 MiB), 131072 eraseblocks of
131072 bytes (128.0 KiB), min. I/O size 2048 bytes
<...>
root@beagleboard:~# ubiattach /dev/ubi_ctrl -m 4
UBI device number 0, total 1996 LEBs (257531904 bytes, 245.6 MiB), available 0
LEBs (0 bytes), LEB size 129024 bytes (126.0 KiB)
root@beagleboard:~# mount -t ubifs ubi0:rootfs /mnt/ubifs
root@beagleboard:~# ls /mnt/ubifs
bin dev home linuxrc mnt sbin sys usr
boot etc lib media proc srv tmp var
```

- Here you can see the sequence of events leading to mounting of the UBIFS file system. First, we erase the Flash device, using flash_eraseall, one of the utilities from mtd-utils. Consider your need to use this erase utility, because it does not preserve error counters. This would be a first-time-use scenario.
- The ubiformat command places the image on the NAND Flash in our example. The -s specifies the subpage size, which must agree with the image, and the -f is used to select the image file.

- After this operation completes, we can attach the UBI device, which is required before the UBI device is mounted. ubiattach requires the UBI control device *(/dev/ubi_ctrl)* and a specifier to select which MTD device to attach.
- Because we wrote the image to MTD partition 4 *(/dev/mtd4)*, we specify this to ubiattach using the -m 4 parameter.With all of this in place, we can now mount the UBIFS image. Notice in Listing 4-14 that we pass the volume name specified in the *ubinize.cfg* configuration file to the mount command.

4.7.4.3 Using UBIFS as the Root File System

Now that we have an image in place on /dev/mtd4, we can instruct the kernel to mount this file system as its root file system. To do so, pass the following kernel command-line parameters to the kernel : ubi.mtd=4 root=ubi0:rootfs rw rootfstype=ubifs.

This set of kernel command-line parameters instructs the kernel to attach the mtd4 device to ubi0 and to mount the resulting UBI device as the root file system. If you run into difficulties, make sure you include an appropriate rootdelay option on your kernel command line. For this exercise, rootdelay=1 was required to allow time for the UBI and UBIFS layers to be ready when it came time to mount the UBIFS as the root file system.

4.8 EMBEDDED DEVELOPMENT ENVIRONMENT

The configuration and services available on your host development system can have a huge impact on your success as an embedded developer. This section examines the unique requirements of a cross-development environment and some of the tools and techniques that an embedded developer needs to know to be productive. We begin by examining a typical cross-development environment. Using the familiar "Hello World" example, we detail the important differences between host-based applications and those targeted for embedded systems.

We also look at differences in the toolchains for native versus embedded application development. Then present host system requirements and detail the use of some important elements of your host system. We conclude this section with an example of a target board being hosted by a network-based host.

4.8.1 Cross-Development Environment

- Developers new to embedded development often struggle with the concepts of and differences between native and cross-development environments.
- Debugging an application on your target embedded system can be difficult without the right tools and host-based utilities. You must manage and keep separate the files and

utilities designed to run on your host system from those you intend to use on your target.
- When we use the term host in this context, we are referring to the development workstation that is sitting on your desktop and running your favorite Linux desktop distribution. Conversely, when we use the term target, we are referring to your embedded hardware platform.
- Therefore, native development denotes the compilation and building of applications on and for your host system. Cross-development denotes the compilation and building of applications on the host system that will be run on the embedded system.
- Fig. 4.7 shows the layout of a typical cross-development environment. A host PC is connected to a target board through one or more physical connections. It is most convenient if both serial and Ethernet ports are available on the target. Later, when we discuss kernel debugging, you will realize that a second serial port can be a valuable asset.

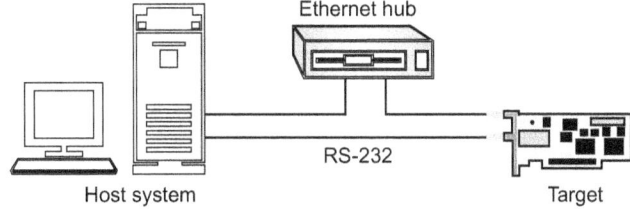

Fig. 4.7 : Cross-development setup

- In the most common scenario, the developer has a serial terminal on the host connected to the RS232 serial port, possibly one or more telnet or SSH terminal sessions to the target board, and potentially one or more debug sessions using Ethernet as the connection medium. This cross-development setup provides a great deal of flexibility.
- The basic idea is that the host system provides the horse power to run the compilers, debuggers, editors, and other utilities, and the target executes only the applications designed for it. You can certainly run compilers and debuggers on the target system, but we assume that your host system has more resources available, including processor horse power, RAM, disk storage, and Internet connectivity. In fact, it is not uncommon for a target embedded board to have no human-input devices or output displays.

4.8.1.1 "Hello World" Embedded

- A properly configured cross-development system hides a great deal of complexity from the average application developer. Looking at a simple example will help uncover and explain some of the mystery.

- When we compile a simple "Hello World" program, the toolchain (compiler, linker, and associated utilities) makes many assumptions about the host system we are building on and the program we are compiling.
- Actually, they are not assumptions, but a collection of rules that the compiler references to build a proper binary.

LISTING 4-15 Reproduces a Simple "Hello World" Program.

Host System
Ethernet Hub
RS-232
Target
LISTING 4-15 Hello World Again

```
#include <stdio.h>
int main(int argc, char **argv)
{
printf("Hello World\n");
return 0;
}
```

- Even the casual application developer will realize some important points about this C source file. First, the function printf() is referenced but not defined in this file. If we omit the #include directive containing the prototype for the printf() function, the compiler emits this familiar message :

    hello.c:5 : warning : implicit declaration of function 'printf'

This introduces some interesting questions :

- Where is the file stdio.h located, and how is it found?
- Where is the printf() function object code stored on your system, and how is this reference resolved in the binary executable?
- Somehow it seems that the compiler just knows how to put together a proper binary file that can be executed from the command line. To further complicate matters, the final executable contains startup and shut down prologue code that we never see but that the linker automatically includes.
- This prologue deals with details such as the environment and arguments passed to your program, startup and shut down house-keeping, exit handling, and more. To build the "Hello World" application, we can use a simple command-line invocation of the compiler, similar to this :

$ gcc -o hello hello.c
- This produces the binary executable file called hello, which we can execute directly from the command line.
- Defaults referenced by the compiler provide guidance on where include files will be found. In a similar fashion, the linker knows how to resolve the reference to the printf() function by including a reference to the library where it is defined. This, of course, is the standard C library.
- We can query the toolchain to see some of the defaults that were used. Listing 4-16 is a partial listing of the output from cpp when passed the -v flag. You might already know that cpp is the C preprocessor component of the GNU gcc toolchain. We have added some formatting (white space only) to improve readability.

LISTING 4-16 Default Native cpp Search Directories

```
$ cpp -v /dev/null
Reading specs from /usr/lib/gcc-lib/i386-redhat-linux/3.3.3/specs
Configured with: ../configure --prefix=/usr
--mandir=/usr/share/man --infodir=/usr/share/info
--enable-shared --enable-threads=posix --disable-checking
--disable-libunwind-exceptions --with-system-zlib
--enable-__cxa_atexit -host=i386-redhat-linux
Thread model: posix
gcc version 3.3.3 20040412 (Red Hat Linux 3.3.3-7)
/usr/lib/gcc-lib/i386-redhat-linux/3.3.3/cc1 -E -quiet -v -
ignoring nonexistent directory "/usr/i386-redhat-linux/include"
#include "..." search starts here:
#include <...> search starts here:
/usr/local/include
/usr/lib/gcc-lib/i386-redhat-linux/3.3.3/include
/usr/include
End of search list.
/usr/lib/
```

- This simple query produces some useful information. First, we can see how the compiler was configured using the familiar *./configure* utility.
- The default thread model is posix, which determines the thread library your application gets linked against if you employ threading functions. Finally, you see the default search directories for *#include* directives.

- But what if we want to build hello.c for a different architecture, such as Power Architecture? When we compile an application program for a Power Architecture target using a cross-compiler on our host machine, we must make sure that the compiler does not use the default host include directories or library paths.
- Using a properly configured cross-compiler is the first step, and having a well-designed cross-development environment is the second.
- Listing 4-17 is the output from a popular open-source cross-development toolchain known as the Embedded Linux Development Kit (ELDK), assembled and maintained by Denx Software Engineering. This particular installation was configured for the Power Architecture 82xx toolchain. Again, we have added some white space to the output for readability.

LISTING 4-17 Default Cross-Search Directories

```
$ ppc_82xx-cpp -v /dev/null
Reading specs from /opt/eldk/usr/bin/..
/lib/gcc-lib/ppc-linux/3.3.3/specs
Configured with: ../configure --prefix=/usr
--mandir=/usr/share/man --infodir=/usr/share/info
--enable-shared --enable-threads=posix --disable-checking
--with-system-zlib --enable-__cxa_atexit --with-newlib
--enable-languages=c,c++ --disable-libgcj
--host=i386-redhat-linux -target=ppc-linux
Thread model: posix
gcc version 3.3.3 (DENX ELDK 3.1.1 3.3.3-10)
/opt/eldk/usr/bin/../lib/gcc-lib/ppc-linux/3.3.3/cc1
-E -quiet -v -iprefix /opt/eldk/usr/bin/..
/lib/gcc-lib/ppc-linux/3.3.3/ -D__unix__ -D__gnu_linux__
-D__linux__ -Dunix -D__unix -Dlinux -D__linux -Asystem=unix
-Asystem=posix - -mcpu=603
ignoring nonexistent directory "/opt/eldk/usr/ppc-linux/sys-include"
ignoring nonexistent directory "/opt/eldk/usr/ppc-linux/include"
#include "..." search starts here:
#include <...> search starts here:
/opt/eldk/usr/lib/gcc-lib/ppc-linux/3.3.3/include
/opt/eldk/ppc_82xx/usr/include
End of search list.
```

- Here you can see that the default search paths for include directories are now adjusted to point to your cross versions instead of the native include directories. This seemingly obscure detail is critical to being able to develop applications and compile open source packages for your embedded system. It is one of the most confusing topics to even experienced application developers who are new to embedded systems.

4.8.2 Host System Requirements

- Your development workstation must include several important components and systems. First, you need a properly configured cross toolchain. You can download and compile one yourself or obtain one of the many commercial toolchains available.
- Building one yourself is beyond the scope of this book; however, several good references are available. The next major item you need is a Linux distribution targeted for your embedded system architecture. This includes hundreds to potentially thousands of files that will populate your embedded system's file system(s).
- Again, the choices are to build your own or to obtain one of the commercial ones. One of the more popular open source embedded system distributions is the aforementioned ELDK. The ELDK is available for many Power Architecture, ARM, and other embedded targets. The topic of building an embedded Linux distribution from scratch would require a book of this size in itself; therefore, it's beyond the scope of our discussion. In summary, your development host requires four separate and distinct capabilities :
    - Cross toolchain and libraries.
    - Target system packages, including programs, utilities, and libraries.
    - Host tools such as editors, debuggers, and utilities.
    - Servers for hosting your target board, as covered in the next section.
- If you install a ready-built embedded Linux development environment on your workstation, either a commercial variety or one freely available in the open source community, the toolchain and components have already been preconfigured to work together. For example, the toolchain has been configured with default directory search paths that match the location of the target header files and system libraries on your development workstation. The situation becomes much more complex if your requirements include support for multiple architectures and processors on your development workstation. This is the reason that commercial embedded Linux distributions exist.

4.8.2.1 Hardware Debug Probe

In addition to the components just listed, you should consider some type of hardware assisted debugging. This consists of a hardware probe connected to your host (often via Ethernet) and connected to your target via a debug connector on the board. Many solutions are available.

4.8.3 Hosting Target Boards

- Referring to Fig. 4.7, you will notice an Ethernet connection from the target embedded board to the host-development system. This is not strictly necessary; indeed, some smaller embedded devices do not have an Ethernet interface.
- However, this is the exception rather than the rule. Having an Ethernet connection available on your target board is worth its cost in silicon! This enables the NFS root mount configuration, which can save you days or weeks of development time.
- While developing your embedded Linux kernel, you will compile and download kernels and root file systems to your embedded board many times. Many embedded development systems and bootloaders support TFTP and assume that the developer will use it. TFTP is a lightweight protocol for moving files between a TFTP server and TFTP client over Ethernet, similar to FTP.
- Using TFTP from your bootloader to load the kernel will save you countless hours waiting for serial downloads, even at higher serial baud rates. And loading your root file system or ramdisk image can take much longer, because these images can grow to many tens of megabytes or more, depending on your requirements. The investment in your time to configure and use TFTP will definitely pay off and is highly recommended. Very few designs can't afford the real estate to include an Ethernet port during development, even if it is depopulated for production.

4.8.3.1 TFTP Server

- Configuring TFTP on your Linux development host is not difficult. Of course, the details might vary, depending on which Linux distribution you choose for your development workstation. The guidelines presented here are based on popular desktop Linux distributions.
- TFTP is a TCP/IP service that must be enabled on your workstation. To enable the TFTP service, you must instruct your workstation to respond to incoming TFTP packets. The easiest way to do this is to run a TFTP server daemon. Most modern desktop Linux distributions have multiple packages available to provide this service. HPA's TFTP server will be used as the basis for the examples here. It can be obtained from *ftp://ftp.kernel.org/pub/software/network/tftp*. On modern Ubuntu and other Debian-based systems, the HPA TFTP server can be installed as follows :

    $ sudo apt-get install tftpd-hpa

- Configuring this TFTP server is easy. There is a single configuration file on Ubuntu and other distributions called */etc/default/tftpd-hpa*. This file needs to be customized to your particular requirements. Listing 4-18 shows a typical example of this configuration file.

LISTING 4-18 TFTP Configuration

```
#Defaults for tftpd-hpa
RUN_DAEMON="yes"
OPTIONS="-l -c -s /tftpboot"
```

- The first thing you must do is enable the service. When you first install the tftpd-hpa package, RUN_DAEMON defaults to "no". To enable the service, you must change the default "no" to "yes", as shown in Listing 4-18. The second line defines the command-line options to the daemon itself, usually */usr/sbin/in.tftpd*. The -s switch tells *in.tftpd* to switch to the specified directory *(/tftpboot)* upon startup, which causes this directory to be the root of your TFTP server.
- The -c flag allows the creation of new files. This is useful to write files to the server from the target. The BDI-3000 (covered later in this book) has such a capability, and it will not work without the -c. The -l argument instructs the TFTP daemon to run in the background and listen on the TFTP port for incoming TFTP packets. Once the changes are made to this configuration file, you must restart the TFTP server so that they take effect :

$ **sudo /etc/init.d/tftpd-hpa restart**

4.8.3.2 BOOTP/DHCP Server

- Having a DHCP server on your development host simplifies the configuration management for your embedded target. We have already established the reasons why an Ethernet interface on your target hardware is a good idea.
- When Linux boots on your target board, it needs to configure the Ethernet interface before the interface will be useful.
- Moreover, if you are using an NFS root mount configuration on your target board, Linux needs to configure your target's Ethernet interface before the boot process can complete.
- In general, Linux can use two methods to initialize its Ethernet/IP interface during boot :
  - Hard-code the Ethernet interface parameters either on the Linux kernel command line or in the default configuration, such as a static IP configuration.
  - Configure the kernel to automatically detect the network settings at boot time. For obvious reasons, the second choice is more flexible. DHCP or BOOTP is the protocol your target and server use to accomplish the automatic detection of network settings.
- A DHCP server controls the IP address assignments for IP subnets for which it has been configured, and for DHCP or BOOTP clients that have been configured to participate. A DHCP server listens for requests from a DHCP client (such as your target board) and assigns addresses and other pertinent information to the client as part of the boot process. A typical DHCP exchange (see Listing 4-19) can be examined by starting your

DHCP server with the -d debug switch and observing the output when a target machine requests configuration.

LISTING 4-19 Typical DHCP Exchange

```
tgt> DHCPDISCOVER from 00:09:5b:65:1d:d5 via eth0
svr> DHCPOFFER on 192.168.0.9 to 00:09:5b:65:1d:d5 via eth0
tgt> DHCPREQUEST for 192.168.0.9 (192.168.0.1) from \
00:09:5b:65:1d:d5 via eth0
svr> DHCPACK on 192.168.0.9 to 00:09:5b:65:1d:d5 via eth0
```

- The sequence starts with the client (target) transmitting a broadcast frame attempting to discover a DHCP server. This is shown by the DHCPDISCOVER message. The server responds (if it has been so configured and enabled) by offering an IP address for the client. This is evidenced by the DHCPOFFER message. The client then responds by testing this IP address locally.
- The testing includes sending the DHCPREQUEST packet to the DHCP server, as shown. Finally, the server responds by acknowledging the IP address assignment to the client, thus completing the automatic target configuration. It is interesting to note that a properly configured client will remember the last address it was assigned by a DHCP server. The next time it boots, it will skip the DHCPDISCOVER stage and proceed directly to the DHCPREQUEST stage, assuming that it can reuse the same IP address that the server previously assigned.
- A booting Linux kernel does not have this capability and emits the same sequence every time it boots. Configuring your host's DHCP server is not difficult. As usual, our advice is to consult the documentation that came with your desktop Linux distribution. On a Red Hat or Fedora distribution, the configuration entry for a single target might look like

LISTING 4-20 Sample DHCP Server Configuration

```
# Example DHCP Server configuration
allow bootp;
subnet 192.168.1.0 netmask 255.255.255.0 {
default-lease-time 1209600; # two weeks
option routers 192.168.1.1;
option domain-name-servers 1.2.3.4;
group {
host pdna1 {
hardware ethernet 00:30:bd:2a:26:1f;
fixed-address 192.168.1.68;
filename "uImage-pdna";
```

option root-path "/home/chris/sandbox/pdna-target";
}
}
}

- This is a simple example, meant only to show the kind of information you can pass to your target system. A one-to-one mapping of the target MAC address to its assigned IP address is defined by this host definition. In addition to its fixed IP address, you can pass other information to your target.
- In this example, the default router and DNS server addresses are passed to your target, along with the filename of a file of your choice, and a root path for your kernel to mount an NFS root file system from.
- The filename might be used by your bootloader to load a kernel image from your TFTP server. You can also configure your DHCP server to hand out IP addresses from a predefined range, but it is very convenient to use a fixed address. You must first enable the DHCP server on your Linux development workstation.
- This is typically done through your main menu or at the command line. Consult the documentation for your Linux distribution for details suitable for your environment. For example, to enable the DHCP server on a Fedora Core Linux distribution, simply type the following command from a root command prompt :

   $ /etc/init.d/dhcpd start

   or

   $ /etc/init.d/dhcpd restart

- You must do this each time you start your development workstation, unless you configure it to start automatically. Consult the documentation associated with your distribution for instructions on how to do this. You will usually find a reference to enabling services or something similar. In this example, dhcpd is considered a system service.
- Many nuances are involved with installing a DHCP server, so unless your server is on a private network, it is advisable to check with your system administrator before going live with your own. If you coexist with a corporate LAN, it is very possible that you will interfere with its own DHCP service.

4.8.3.3 NFS Server

Using an NFS root mount for your target board is a very powerful development tool. Here are some of the advantages of this configuration for development : Your root file system is not size-restricted by your board's own limited resources, such as Flash memory.

- Changes made to your application files during development are immediately available to your target system.
- You can debug and boot your kernel before developing and debugging your root file system.

The steps for setting up an NFS server vary depending on which desktop Linux distribution you are using. As with the other services described in this section, you must consult the documentation for your Linux distribution for the details appropriate to your configuration. The NFS service must be started from either your startup scripts, a graphical menu, or the command line. For example, the command to start NFS services from a root command prompt for a Fedora Core Linux desktop is as follows :

$ /etc/init.d/nfs start

or

$ /etc/init.d/nfs restart

Note that on later Ubuntu and other distributions this command has been changed to */etc/init.d/nfs-kernel-server*.

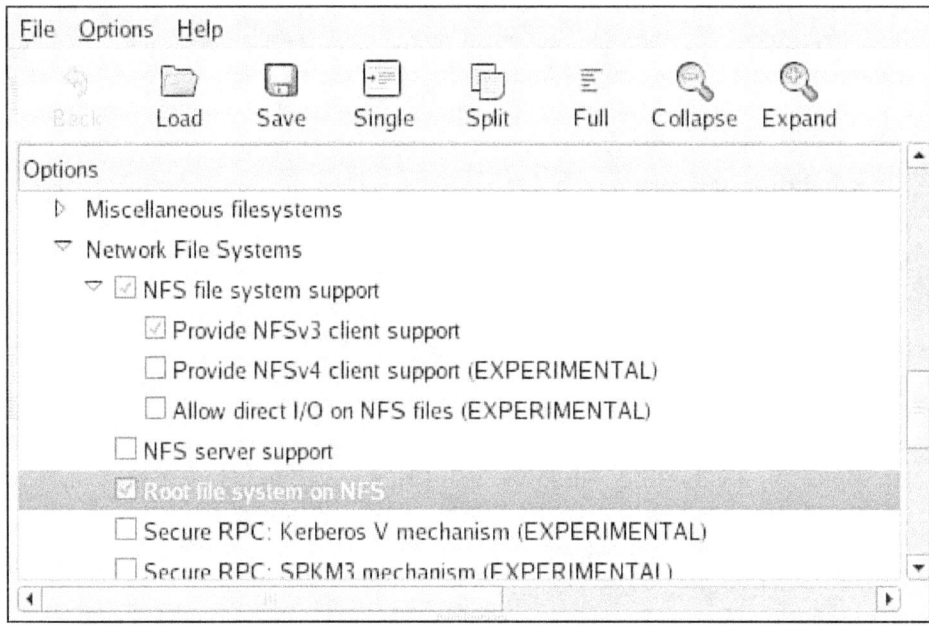

Fig. 4.8 : NFS kernel configuration

You must do this each time you start your desktop Linux work station. (This and other services can be started automatically on booting. Consult the documentation for your desktop Linux distribution.) In addition to enabling the service, your kernel must be compiled with support for NFS. Although DHCP and TFTP are both user space utilities, NFS requires kernel support. This is true on both your development workstation and your target board. Fig. 4.8 shows the configuration options for NFS in the kernel. Notice that there are configuration options for both NFS server and client support. Note also the option "Root file system on NFS." Your target kernel must have this option configured for NFS root mount operation. The NFS server gets its instructions from an exports file located on your development workstation. It is commonly found in /etc/exports. Listing 4-21 is an example of a simple exports entry.

LISTING 4-21 Simple NFS exports File

$ cat /etc/exports
# /etc/exports
/home/chris/sandbox/coyote-target *(rw,sync,no_root_squash,no_all_squash,no_subtree_check)
/home/chris/sandbox/pdna-target \ *(rw,sync,no_root_squash,no_all_squash,no_subtree_check)
/home/chris/workspace \ *(rw,sync,no_root_squash,no_all_squash,no_subtree_check)

These entries allow a client to remotely mount any of the three directories shown. The attributes following the directory specification instruct the NFS server to allow connections from any IP address (*) and to mount the respective directories with the given attributes (read/write with *no_root_squash)*. The latter attribute enables a client with root privileges to exercise those privileges on the given directory. It is usually required when working with embedded systems because they often have only root accounts.

The *no_all_squash* attribute ensures that the uid and gid of an incoming NFS request are honored, instead of being mapped to a default anonymous account. The *no_subtree_check* attribute disables subtree checking on your server. This can improve performance and reliability in some circumstances. Consult your NFS server documentation and the man page describing the exports file for more details. You can test your NFS configuration right from your work station. Assuming that you have NFS services enabled (which requires that both the NFS server and client components are enabled), you can mount a local NFS export as you would mount any other file system :

mount -t nfs localhost:/home/chris/workspace /mnt/remote

If this command succeeds and the files in .../workspace are available on */mnt/ remote*, your NFS server configuration is working.

4.8.3.4 Target NFS Root Mount

Mounting your target through NFS root mount is not difficult, and, as mentioned elsewhere, it is a very useful development configuration. However, a set of details must be correct before it will work. The steps required are as follows :

1. Configure your NFS server, and export a proper target file system for your architecture.
2. Configure your target kernel with NFS client services and root file system on NFS.
3. Enable kernel-level autoconfiguration of your target's Ethernet interface.
4. Provide your target Ethernet IP configuration using the kernel command line or static kernel configuration option.
5. Provide a kernel command line enabled for NFS.

We presented the kernel configuration in Fig. 4.8 when we explained the NFS server configuration. You must make sure that your target kernel configuration has NFS client services enabled, and, in particular, you must enable the option for Root file system on NFS. Specifically, make sure that your kernel has CONFIG_NFS_FS=y and CONFIG_ROOT_NFS=y. Obviously, you cannot configure NFS as loadable modules if you intend to boot via NFS root mount. Kernel-level autoconfiguration is a TCP/IP configuration option found under the Networking tab in the kernel configuration utility. Enable CONFIG_IP_PNP on your target kernel. When this is selected, you are presented with several options for automatic configuration. Select either BOOTP or DHCP, as described earlier. Fig. 4.9 illustrates the kernel configuration for kernel-level autoconfiguration.

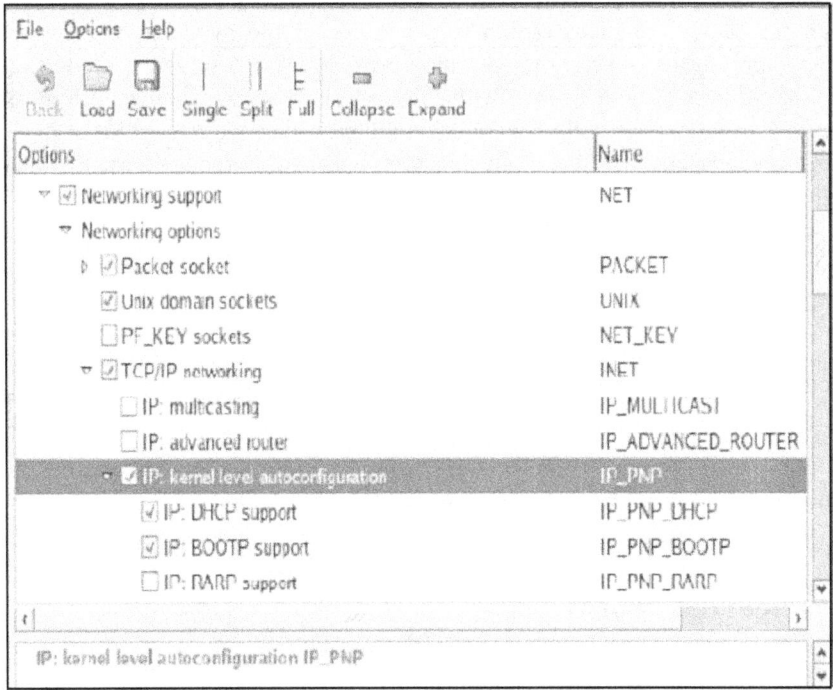

Fig. 4.9 : Kernel-level autoconfiguration

When your server and target kernel are configured, you need to provide your target Ethernet configuration using one of the methods described earlier. If your bootloader supports a kernel command line, that is the easiest method. Here is what a kernel command line to support NFS root mount might look like :

console=ttyS0,115200 root=/dev/nfs rw ip=dhcp \
nfsroot=192.168.1.9:/home/chris/sandbox/pdna-target

4.8.3.5 U-Boot NFS Root Mount Example

- U-Boot is a good example of a bootloader that supports a configurable kernel command line. Using U-Boot's nonvolatile environment feature, we can store our kernel command line in a parameter specially named for this purpose.
- To enable the NFS command line in U-Boot, we do the following (all on one line in our serial terminal) :

    setenv bootargs console=ttyS0,115200 root=/dev/nfs rw \
    ip=dhcp nfsroot=192.168.1.9:/home/chris/sandbox/pdna-target

- Then we load a kernel using our TFTP server. Listing 4-22 shows what this might look like on a Power Architecture embedded target.

LISTING 4-22 Loading a Kernel Using the TFTP Server

```
=> tftpboot 200000 uImage-pdna    <<< Entered at U-Boot prompt
Using FEC ETHERNET device
TFTP from server 192.168.1.9; our IP address is 192.168.1.68
Filename 'uImage-pdna'.
Load address: 0x200000
Loading:
#################################################################
#################################################################
##################################################
done
Bytes transferred = 911984 (dea70 hex)
=>
```

- When we boot the kernel, we see specific evidence of our NFS root mount configuration. Listing 4-23 reproduces selected output from the kernel boot messages to demonstrate this. This output has been formatted (with many lines omitted and white space added) for readability.

LISTING 4-23 Booting with NFS Root Mount

Uncompressing Kernel Image ... OK
Linux version 2.6.14 (chris@pluto) (gcc version 3.3.3
(DENX ELDK 3.1.1 3.3.3-10)) #1 Mon Jan 2 11:58:48 EST 2006
.
.
Kernel command line: console=ttyS0,115200 root=/dev/nfs rw
nfsroot=192.168.1.9:/home/chris/sandbox/pdna-target ip=dhcp
.
.
Sending DHCP requests ... OK
IP-Config: Got DHCP answer from 192.168.1.9, my address is 192.168.1.68
IP-Config: Complete:
device=eth0, addr=192.168.1.68, mask=255.255.255.0,
gw=255.255.255.255, host=192.168.1.68, domain=,
nis-domain=(none), bootserver=192.168.1.9,
rootserver=192.168.1.9,
rootpath=/home/chris/sandbox/pdna-target
.
.
Looking up port of RPC 100003/2 on 192.168.1.9
Looking up port of RPC 100005/1 on 192.168.1.9
VFS: Mounted root (nfs filesystem).
.
.
.
BusyBox v0.60.5 (2005.06.07-07:03+0000) Built-in shell (msh)
Enter 'help' for a list of built-in commands.
#

- In Listing 4-23, first we see the kernel banner, followed by the kernel command line. We specified four items in this kernel command line :
    - Console device *(/dev/console)*.
    - Root device *(/dev/nfs)*.

- NFS root path *(/home/chris/sandbox/pdna-target)*.
- IP kernel-level autoconfiguration method *(dhcp)*.
- Shortly thereafter, we see the kernel attempting kernel-level autoconfiguration via DHCP. This begins with the "Sending DHCP requests" console message. When the server responds and the DHCP exchange completes, the kernel displays the detected configuration in the following lines.
- You can see from this listing that the DHCP server has assigned the target the IP address 192.168.1.68. Compare the settings obtained via auto configuration with the DHCP server configuration in Listing 4-20. You can use a similar server configuration to assign the IP address and NFS root path to your target.
- When the kernel has completed the IP autoconfiguration, it can mount the root file system using the supplied parameters. You can see this from the three lines ending with the VFS (virtual file subsystem) message announcing that it has mounted the NFS root file system.
- After the NFS root file system has been mounted, initialization completes as described in Chapter, "Kernel Initialization." It is also possible to pass target IP settings to the kernel in a static fashion instead of having the kernel obtain IP settings from a DHCP or BOOTP server.
- IP settings can be passed using the kernel command line directly. In this case, the kernel command line might look similar to this :

console=console=ttyS0,115200 \
ip=192.168.1.68:192.168.1.9::255.255.255.0:pdna:eth0:off \
root=/dev/nfs rw nfsroot=192.168.1.9:/home/chris/pdna-target

SUMMARY

- This section provided the background to build and configure a development workstation suitable for embedded development work.
- Several key servers were introduced, along with information on how to install and configure them.
- We concluded this section by looking at one of the most powerful tools available to the embedded developer: the NFS server.

- Many features of a development environment greatly facilitate efficiency for embedded cross-development. Most of these fall under the category of tools and utilities. We cover this aspect in detail in the next section, where we describe development tools.
- A properly configured development host is a critical asset for the embedded developer.
- Toolchains employed for cross-development must be properly configured to match your host system's target Linux environment.
- Your development host must have target components installed that your toolchain and binary utilities can reference. These components include target header files, libraries, target binaries, and their associated configuration files. In short, you need to assemble or obtain an embedded Linux distribution.
- Configuring target servers such as TFTP, DHCP, and NFS will greatly increase your productivity as an embedded Linux developer. This section introduced configuration examples for each.

Bootloader Summary : This section examined the role of the bootloader and discovered the limited execution context in which a bootloader must exist. We covered one of the most popular bootloaders, U-Boot, in some detail. We walked through the steps of a typical port to a board with similar support in U-Boot. We briefly introduced additional bootloaders in use today so that you can make an informed choice for your particular requirements.

- The bootloader's role in an embedded system cannot be overstated. It is the first piece of software that takes control upon applying power.
- Das U-Boot has become a popular universal bootloader for many processor architectures. It supports a large number of processors, reference hardware platforms, and custom boards.
- U-Boot is configured using a series of configuration variables in a board-specific header file. Appendix B contains a list of all the standard U-Boot command sets supported in a recent U-Boot release.
- Porting U-Boot to a new board based on a supported processor is relatively straightforward.
- There is no substitute for detailed knowledge of your processor and hardware platform when bootloader modification or porting must be accomplished.
- You may need a device tree binary for your board, especially if it is Power Architecture and soon perhaps ARM.

Device Driver Summary :

- This section presented a high-level overview of device driver basics and how they fit into the architecture of a Linux system. Now that you're armed with the basics, if you're new to device drivers, you can jump into one of the excellent texts devoted to device driver writers, as listed in the last section. This section concluded by introducing the relationship between kernel device drivers and the Open Source GNU Public License.
- Device drivers enforce a rational separation between unprivileged user applications and critical kernel resources such as hardware and other devices. They present a well-known unified interface to applications.
- The minimum infrastructure to load a device driver is only a few lines of code. We presented this minimum infrastructure and built on the concepts to a simple shell of a driver module.
- Device drivers configured as loadable modules can be inserted into and removed from a running kernel after kernel boot.
- Module utilities are used to manage the insertion, removal, and listing of device driver modules. We covered the details of the module utilities used for these functions.
- Device nodes on your file system provide the glue between your user space application and the device driver.
- Driver methods implement the familiar open, read, write, and close functionality commonly found in UNIX/Linux device drivers. This mechanism was explained by example, including a simple user application to exercise these driver methods.

QUESTIONS

1. Explain Bootloader and role of Bootloader?
2. What are the challenges of Bootloader?
3. Explain U-Boot?
4. Explain Device Tree Blob?
5. Explain concept of Device Driver?
6. Differentiate between Character devices and Block devices?
7. Explain Character Devices?
8. Explain PCI & PCI Device Driver?

9. Explain Concept of File System?
10. Explain types of file system?
11. Explain partition of file system?
12. Explain JFFS2?
13. Explain in detail NSF?
14. Explain Device Tree?
15. Explain in detail concept of device tree with example ?
16. Explain Purpose of device tree?
17. Explain structure of device tree with example?
18. Explain Concept of MTD system ?
19. Explain MTD Partition and MTD Utilities?
20. Explain UBI File System?
21. Explain Embedded development environment ?
22. Explain cross development environment?
23. Explain Hosting Target Boards?

UNIT V

DEBUGGING TECHNIQUES FOR EMBEDDED LINUX

5.1 GNU DEBUGGER (GDB)

GDB is arguably the most important tool in the developer's toolbox. That is, the debugger itself runs on your development host, but it understands only binary executables in the architecture for which it was configured at compile time. The GDB debugger is a complex program that offers many configuration options during the build process.

5.1.1 Debugging a Core Dump

- One of the most common reasons to drag GDB out of the toolbox is to evaluate a core dump. This process is quick and easy and often leads to immediate identification of the offending code. A core dump is a file generated by the kernel when an application program generates a fault, such as accessing a memory location it does not own.
- Many conditions can trigger a core dump, but SIGSEGV (segmentation fault) is by far the most common. A SIGSEGV is a Linux kernel signal that is generated on illegal memory accesses by a user process. When this signal is generated, the kernel terminates the process. The kernel then dumps a core image if it is so enabled.
- To enable generation of a core dump, your process must have the authority to enable a core dump. This is achieved by setting the process's resource limits using the *setrlimit()* C function call, or from a BASH or BusyBox shell command prompt using ulimit. It is not uncommon to find the following line in the initialization scripts of an embedded system to enable the generation of core dumps on process errors
  ulimit -c unlimited
  This BASH built-in command is used to set the size limit of a core dump. In the receding instance, the size is set to unlimited. You can issue this command from the shell to how the current setting
  $ ulimit
  Unlimited
- When an application program generates a segmentation fault (for example, by writing to a memory address outside its permissible range), Linux terminates the process and generates a core dump, if so enabled. The core dump is a snapshot of the running process at the time the segmentation fault occurred.
  Listing 5-1 shows the results of a core dump analysis session using GDB.

LISTING 5–1 Core Dump Analysis Using GDB
$ xscale_be-gdb webs core
GNU gdb 6.3 (MontaVista 6.3-20.0.22.0501131 2005-07-23)

Copyright 2004 Free Software Foundation, Inc.

GDB is free software, covered by the GNU General Public

License, and you are welcome to change it and/or distribute copies of it under certain conditions.

Type "show copying" to see the conditions.

There is absolutely no warranty for GDB. Type "show warranty" for details.

This GDB was configured as "--host=i686-pc-linux-gnu

-target=armv5teb-montavista-linuxeabi"...

Core was generated by './webs'.

Program terminated with signal 11, Segmentation fault.

Reading symbols from /opt/montavista/pro/.../libc.so.6...done.

Loaded symbols for /opt/montavista/pro/.../libc.so.6

Reading symbols from /opt/montavista/pro/.../ld-linux.so.3...done.

Loaded symbols for /opt/montavista/pro/.../ld-linux.so.3

#0 0x00012ac4 in ClearBlock (RealBigBlockPtr=0x0, l=100000000) at led.c:43

43 *ptr = 0;

(gdb) l

38

39 static int ClearBlock(char * BlockPtr, int l)

40 {

41 char * ptr;

42 for (ptr = BlockPtr; (ptr - BlockPtr) < l; ptr++)

43 *ptr = 0;

44 return 0;

45 }

46 static int InitBlock(char * ptr, int n)

47 {

(gdb) **p ptr**

$1 = 0x0

(gdb)

5.1.2 Invoking GDB

- The first line of Listing 5-1 shows how GDB was invoked from the command line. Because we are doing cross-debugging, we need the cross-version of GDB that has been compiled for our host and target system. We invoke our version of cross-gdb as shown

- and pass xscale_be-gdb the name of the binary followed by the name of the core dump file in this case, simply core. After GDB prints several banner lines describing its configuration and other information, it displays the reason for the termination: signal 11, which indicates a segmentation fault.
- Several lines follow as GDB loads the binary, the libraries it depends on, and the core file. The last line printed upon GDB startup is the current location of the program when the fault occurred. The line preceded by the #0 string indicates the stack frame (stack frame zero in a function called ClearBlock() at virtual address 0x00012ac4).
- The following line starting with 43 is the line number of the offending source line from a file called led.c. From there, GDB displays its command prompt and waits for input.
- Here the program error begins to present itself. Here is the offending line, according to GDB's analysis of the core dump.

    43 *ptr = 0;
- Next we issue the gdb print command on the ptr variable, abbreviated as p. As you can see from Listing 5-1, the value of the pointer ptr is 0. So we conclude that the reason for the segmentation fault is the classic null pointer dereferences, a common programming error in many programming languages. From here, we can elect to use the backtrace command to see the call chain leading to this error, which might take us back to the source of the error. Listing 5-2 displays these results.

LISTING 5–2 Backtrace Command

(gdb) **bt**
#0 0x00012ac4 in ClearBlock (RealBigBlockPtr=0x0, l=100000000) at led.c:43
#1 0x00012b08 in InitBlock (ptr=0x0, n=100000000) at led.c:48
#2 0x00012b50 in ErrorInHandler (wp=0x325c8, urlPrefix=0x2f648 "/Error", webDir=0x2f660 "", arg=0, url=0x34f30 "/Error", path=0x34d68 "/Error", query=0x321d8 "") at led.c:61
#3 0x000126cc in websUrlHandlerRequest (wp=0x325c8) at handler.c:273
#4 0x0001f518 in websGetInput (wp=0x325c8, ptext=0xbefffc40, pnbytes=0xbefffc38) at webs.c:664
#5 0x0001ede0 in websReadEvent (wp=0x325c8) at webs.c:362
#6 0x0001ed34 in websSocketEvent (sid=1, mask=2, iwp=206280) at webs.c:319
#7 0x00019740 in socketDoEvent (sp=0x34fc8) at sockGen.c:903
#8 0x00019598 in socketProcess (sid=1) at sockGen.c:845
#9 0x00012be8 in main (argc=1, argv=0xbefffe14) at main.c:99
(gdb)

- The backtrace displays the call chain all the way back to main(), the start of the user's program. A stack frame number precedes each line of the backtrace. You can switch to any given stack frame using the gdb frame command. Listing 5-3 is an example of this.

Here we switch to stack frame 2 and display the source code in that frame. As in the previous examples, the lines preceded by the (gdb) command prompt are the commands we issue to GDB, and the other lines are the GDB output.

LISTING 5–3 Moving Around Stack Frames in GDB

```
(gdb) frame 2
#2 0x00012b50 in ErrorInHandler (wp=0x325c8, urlPrefix=0x2f648 "/Error",
webDir=0x2f660 "", arg=0, url=0x34f30 "/Error", path=0x34d68 "/Error",
query=0x321d8 "") at led.c:61
61 return InitBlock(p, siz);
(gdb) l
56
57 siz = 10000 * sizeof(BigBlock);
58
59 p = malloc(siz);
60 /* if (p) */
61 return InitBlock(p, siz);
62 /* else return (0); */
63 }
64
65
(gdb)
```

- As you can see, with a little help from the source code available using the list command, it would be a simple process to trace the code back to the source of the errant null pointer. In fact, notice the source of the segmentation fault we have produced for this example. In Listing 5-3, we see that the check of the return value in the call to *malloc()* has been commented out. In this example, the *malloc()* call failed, leading to the operation on a null pointer two frames later in the call chain. Although this example is both contrived and trivial, many crashes of this type are remarkably easy to track down using a similar method with GDB and core dumps. You can also see the null pointer by looking at the parameter values in the function call. This often leads you directly to the stack frame where the null pointer originated.

5.1.3 Debug Session in GDB

- Listing 5-4 details how we start GDB in preparation for a debug session. Note that the program must have been compiled with the debug flag enabled in the gcc command line for GDB to be useful in this context.

LISTING 5–4 Initiating a GDB Debug Session

```
$ xscale_be-gdb -silent webs
(gdb) target remote 192.168.1.21:2001
0x40000790 in ?? ()
(gdb) b main
Breakpoint 1 at 0x12b74: file main.c, line 78.
(gdb) c
Continuing.
Breakpoint 1, main (argc=1, argv=0xbefffe04) at main.c:78
78 bopen(NULL, (60 * 1024), B_USE_MALLOC);
(gdb) b ErrorInHandler
Breakpoint 2 at 0x12b30: file led.c, line 57.
(gdb) c
Breakpoint 2, ErrorInHandler (wp=0x311a0, urlPrefix=0x2f648 "/Error",
webDir=0x2f660 "", arg=0, url=0x31e88 "/Error", path=0x31918 "/Error",
query=0x318e8 "") at led.c:57
57 siz = 10000 * sizeof(BigBlock);
(gdb) next
59 p = malloc(siz);
(gdb) next
61 return InitBlock(p, siz);
(gdb) p p
$1 =(unsigned char *) 0x0
(gdb) p siz
$2 = 100000000
(gdb)
```

- Examining this simple debug session, first we connect to our target board using the gdb target command. When we are connected to our target hardware, we set a breakpoint at main() using the gdb break (abbreviated b) command.
- Then we issue the gdb continue (abbreviated c) command to resume program execution. If we had any program arguments, we could have issued them on the command line when we invoked GDB.

5.2 Data Display Debugger

- The Data Display Debugger (DDD), shown in Fig. 5.1, is a graphical front end to GDB and other command-line debuggers. DDD has many advanced features beyond simply viewing source code and stepping through a debug session.

Fig. 5.1 : Data display debugger

DDD is invoked as follows :

$ ddd --debugger xscale_be-gdb webs.

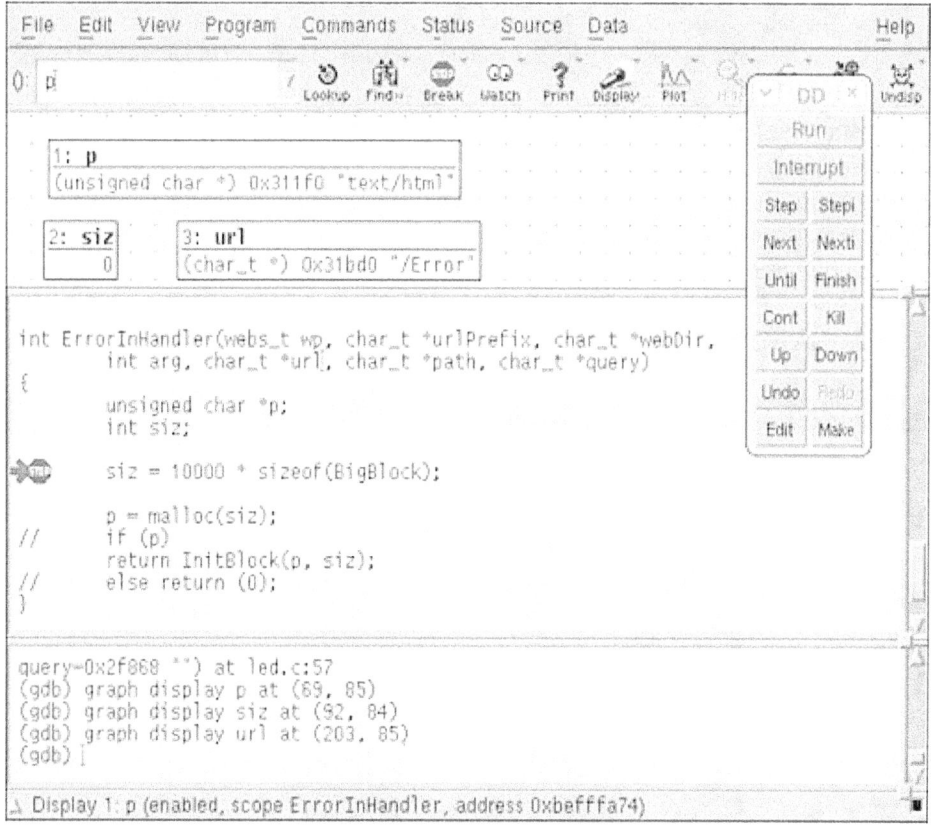

Fig. 5.2 : Debug session in DDD

- Without the --debugger flag, DDD would attempt to invoke the native GDB on your development host. This is not what you want if you are planning to debug an application on your target system. The second argument on the DDD command line is the program you will be debugging. See the DDD man page for additional details. Using the command tool as shown in Fig. 5.1, you can step through your program. You can set breakpoints either graphically or via the GDB console window at the bottom of the DDD screen. For target debugging, you must first connect your debugger to the target system as we did in Listing 5-4, using the target command. This command is issued in the GDB window of the DDD main screen.
- When you are connected to the target, you can execute commands similar to the sequence just shown to isolate the program failure. Fig. 5.2 shows the DDD display

during the later phase of this debugging session. DDD is a powerful graphical front end for GDB. It is relatively easy to use and widely supported for many development hosts.

5.3 C Browser/C Scope

- We introduce cbrowser because support for this handy tool has found its way into the Linux kernel source tree. cbrowser is a simple source-code browsing tool that makes it easy to navigate around a large source tree following symbols. Some distributions, such as Ubuntu, have cbrowser in their repository, but others, such as the recent Fedora, do not. On Ubuntu, simply type the following :

$ sudo apt-get install cbrowser

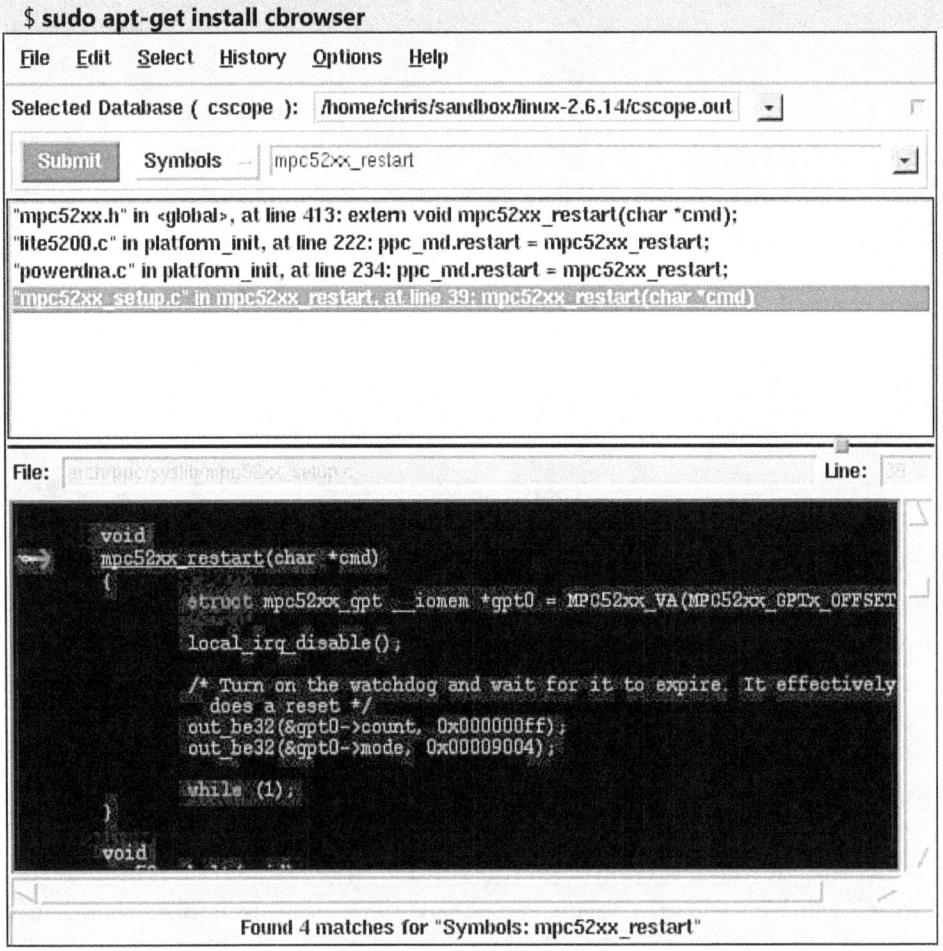

Fig. 5.3 : C browser in action

- The Linux kernel make file supports building the database that cbrowser uses. Here is a sample invocation from a recent Linux kernel snapshot :
  $ make ARCH=powerpc CROSS_COMPILE=ppc_82xx- cscope
- This produces the cscope symbol database that cbrowser uses. cscope is the engine; cbrowser is the graphical user interface. To invoke cbrowser, enter the directory that contains your cscope database, and simply type the cbrowser command without arguments. Fig. 5.3 shows a sample session.

5.4 TRACKING AND PROFILING TOOLS

5.4.1 Strace

- strace is a useful trace utility found in virtually all Linux distributions. strace captures and displays information for every kernel system call executed by a Linux application program. strace is especially handy because it can be run on programs for which no source code is available. It is not necessary to compile the program with debug symbols as it is with GDB. strace quickly identified the problem. Listing 5-5 shows the output from invoking strace on this application.

LISTING 5–5 *strace* Output : GoAhead Web Demo

```
01 root@coyote:$ strace ./websdemo
02 execve("./websdemo", ["./websdemo"], [/* 14 vars */]) = 0
03 uname({sys="Linux", node="coyote", ...}) = 0
04 brk(0) = 0x10031050
05 open("/etc/ld.so.preload", O_RDONLY) = -1 ENOENT (No such file or directory)
06 open("/etc/ld.so.cache", O_RDONLY) = -1 ENOENT (No such file or directory)
07 open("/lib/libc.so.6", O_RDONLY) = 3
08 read(3, "\177ELF\1\2\1\0\0\0\0\0\0\0\0\0\3\0\24\0\0\0\1\0\1\322"..., 1024) = 1024
09 fstat64(0x3, 0x7fffefc8) = 0
10 mmap(0xfe9f000, 1379388, PROT_READ|PROT_EXEC, MAP_PRIVATE, 3, 0) = 0xfe9f000
11 mprotect(0xffd8000, 97340, PROT_NONE) = 0
12 mmap (0xffdf000, 61440, PROT_READ|PROT_WRITE|PROT_EXEC,MAP_PRIVATE|MAP_FIXED, 3, 0x130000) = 0xffdf000
13 mmap(0xffee000, 7228, PROT_READ|PROT_WRITE|PROT_EXEC, MAP_PRIVATE|MAP_FIXED| MAP_ANONYMOUS, -1, 0) = 0xffee000
14 close(3) = 0
15 brk(0) = 0x10031050
```

```
16 brk(0x10032050) = 0x10032050
17 brk(0x10033000) = 0x10033000
18 brk(0x10041000) = 0x10041000
19 rt_sigaction(SIGPIPE, {SIG_IGN}, {SIG_DFL}, 8) = 0
20 stat("./umconfig.txt", 0x7ffff9b8) = -1 ENOENT (No such file or directory)
21 uname({sys="Linux", node="coyote", ...}) = 0
22 gettimeofday({3301, 178955}, NULL) = 0
23 getpid() = 156
24 open("/etc/resolv.conf", O_RDONLY) = 3
25 fstat64(0x3, 0x7fffd7f8) = 0
26 mmap(NULL, 4096, PROT_READ|PROT_WRITE, MAP_PRIVATE|MAP_ANONYMOUS, -1, 0) =
0x30017000
27 read(3, "#\n# resolv.conf This file is th"..., 4096) = 83
28 read(3, "", 4096) = 0
29 close(3) = 0
... <<< Lines 30-81 removed for brevity
82 socket(PF_INET, SOCK_DGRAM, IPPROTO_IP) = 3
83 connect(3, {sa_family=AF_INET, sin_port=htons(53), sin_addr=inet_addr("0.0.0.0")}, 28) = 0
84 send(3, "\267s\1\0\0\1\0\0\0\0\0\0\6coyotea\0\0\1\0\1", 24, 0) = 24
85 gettimeofday({3301, 549664}, NULL) = 0
86 poll([{fd=3, events=POLLIN, revents=POLLERR}], 1, 5000) = 1
87 ioctl(3, 0x4004667f, 0x7fffe6a8) = 0
88 recvfrom(3, 0x7ffff1f0, 1024, 0, 0x7fffe668, 0x7fffe6ac) = -1 ECONNREFUSED (Connection refused)
89 close(3) = 0
90 socket(PF_INET, SOCK_DGRAM, IPPROTO_IP) = 3
91 connect(3, {sa_family=AF_INET, sin_port=htons(53), sin_addr=inet_addr("0.0.0.0")}, 28) = 0
92 send(3, "\267s\1\0\0\1\0\0\0\0\0\0\6coyote\0\0\1\0\1", 24, 0) = 24
93 gettimeofday({3301, 552839}, NULL) = 0
94 poll([{fd=3, events=POLLIN, revents=POLLERR}], 1, 5000) = 1
95 ioctl(3, 0x4004667f, 0x7fffe6a8) = 0
96 recvfrom(3, 0x7ffff1f0, 1024, 0, 0x7fffe668, 0x7fffe6ac) = -1 ECONNREFUSED (Connection refused)
97 close(3) = 0
98 exit(-1) = ?
99 root@coyote:/home/websdemo#
```

- We see several *open()* system calls *to /etc/ld.so.*,* which is the Linux dynamic linker-loader *(ld.so)* doing its job. In fact, line 06 is a clue that this sample embedded board had not been properly configured.
- A linker cache file should be produced by running *ldconfig*. (The linker cache substantially speeds up searching for shared library references.) This was subsequently resolved by running *ldconfig* on the target. Down through line 19 is more basic housekeeping, mostly by the loader and *libc* initializing. Notice in line 20 that the program looks for a configuration file but does not find one. Starting with line 24, the program begins to set up and configure the appropriate networking resources it needs. Lines 24 through 29 open and read a Linux system file containing instructions for the DNS service to resolve hostnames. Local network configuration activity continues through line 81. Most of this activity consists of network setup and configuration necessary to build the networking infrastructure for the program itself.

5.4.2 Strace Variations

- The strace utility has many command-line options. One of the more useful is the ability to select a subset of system calls for tracing. For example, if you want to see only the network-related activity of a given process, issue the command as follows :

    $ strace -e trace=network process_name

    This produces a trace of all the network-related system calls, such as *socket()*, *connect()*, *recvfrom()*, and *send()*. This is a powerful way to view the network activity of a given program.
- strace can deal with tracing programs that spawn additional processes. Invoking strace with the -f option instructs strace to follow child processes that are created using the fork() system call. The strace command has numerous possibilities. The best way to become proficient with this powerful utility is to use it. Listing 5-6 is an example of running *strace -c* on the webs demo from the previous example.

LISTING 5–6 Profiling Using *strace*

root@coyote$ **strace -c ./webs**

% Time	Seconds	Usecs/Call	Calls	Errors Syscall
29.80	0.034262	189	181	send
18.46	0.021226	1011	21	10 open
14.11	0.016221	130	125	read
11.87	0.013651	506	27	8 stat64
5.88	0.006762	193	35	select
5.28	0.006072	76	80	fcntl64
3.47	0.003994	65	61	time
2.79	0.003205	3205	1	execve

1.71	0.001970	90	22	3 recv
1.62	0.001868	85	22	close
1.61	0.001856	169	11	shutdown
1.38	0.001586	144	11	accept
0.41	0.000470	94	5	mmap2
0.26	0.000301	100	3	mprotect
0.24	0.000281	94	3	brk
0.17	0.000194	194	1	1 access
0.13	0.000150	150	1	1 seek
0.12	0.000141	47	3	uname
0.11	0.000132	132	1	listen
0.11	0.000128	128	1	socket
0.09	0.000105	53	2	fstat64
0.08	0.000097	97	1	munmap
0.06	0.000064	64	1	getcwd
0.05	0.000063	63	1	bind
0.05	0.000054	54	1	setsockopt
0.04	0.000048	48	1	rt_sigaction
0.04	0.000046	46	1	gettimeofday
0.03	0.000038	38	1	getpid
100.00	0.114985	624	22	Total

- From Listing 5-6, we can see that the syscall with the longest duration was the *execve()*, which is the call that the shell used to spawn the application. As you can see, it was called only once. Another interesting observation is that the *send()* system call was the most frequently used syscall. This makes sense, because the application is a small web server.

5.4.3 ltrace

The ltrace and strace utilities are closely related. The ltrace utility does for library calls what strace does for system calls. It is invoked in a similar fashion. You precede the program to be traced by the tracer utility, as follows :

$ ltrace ./example

Listing 5-7 reproduces the output of ltrace on a small sample program that executes a handful of standard C library calls.

LISTING 5–7 Sample *ltrace* Output

```
$ ltrace ./example
__libc_start_main(0x8048594, 1,   0xbffff944,0x80486b4, 0x80486fc   <unfinished ...>
malloc(256)                                              = 0x804a008
getenv("HOME")                                           = "/home/chris"
strncpy(0x804a008, "/home", 5)                           = 0x804a008
fopen("foo.txt", "w")                                    = 0x804a110
printf("$HOME = %s\n", "/home/chris"$HOME = /home/chris) = 20
fprintf(0x804a110, "$HOME = %s\n", "/home/chris")        = 20
fclose(0x804a110)                                        = 0
remove("foo.txt")                                        = 0
free(0x804a008)                                          = <void>
+++ exited (status 0) +++
$
```

- Similar to strace, a variety of switches affect the behavior of ltrace. You can display the value of the program counter at each library call, which can be helpful in understanding your application's program flow. As with strace, you can use -c to accumulate and report count, error, and time statistics, making a useful, simple profiling tool. Listing 5-8 displays the results of simple sample program using the –c option.

LISTING 5–8 Profiling Using *ltrace*

```
$ ltrace -c ./example
$HOME = /home/chris
```

% Time	Seconds	Usecs/Call	Calls Function
24.16	0.000231	231	1 printf
16.53	0.000158	158	1 fclose
16.00	0.000153	153	1 fopen
13.70	0.000131	131	1 malloc
10.67	0.000102	102	1 remove
9.31	0.000089	89	1 fprintf
3.35	0.000032	32	1 getenv
3.14	0.000030	30	1 free
3.14	0.000030	30	1 strncypy
100.00	0.000956	9	Total

- The ltrace tool is available only for programs that have been compiled to use dynamically linked shared library objects. This is the usual default, so unless you explicitly specify static when compiling, you can use ltrace on the resulting binary. Also similar to strace, you must use an ltrace binary that has been compiled for your target architecture. These utilities are run on the target, not the host development system.

5.4.4 ps

- The ps utility lists all the running processes on a machine. However, it is quite flexible and can be tailored to provide much useful data on the state of a machine and the processes running on it. For example, ps can display the scheduling policy of each process. This is particularly useful for systems that employ real-time processes. Without any options, ps displays all processes that have the same user ID as the user who invoked the command, and only those processes associated with the terminal on which the command was issued.
- This is useful when many jobs have been spawned by that user and terminal. Passing options to ps can be confusing, because ps support a wide variety of standards (as in POSIX versus UNIX) and three distinct options styles : BSD, UNIX, and GNU. In general, BSD options are single or multiple letters, with no dash. UNIX options are the familiar dash-letter combinations, and GNU uses long argument formats preceded by double dashes. Refer to the main page for details of your ps implementation.
- Listing 5-9 is an example from a running embedded target board.

LISTING 5-9 Process Listing

$ **ps aux**

User	PID	% CPU	% MEM	VSZ	RSS	TTY	STAT	Start Time	Command
Root	1	0.0	0.8	1416	508	?	S	00:00 0:00	init [3]
Root	2	0.0	0.0	0	0	?	S<	00:00 0:00	[ksoftirqd/0]
Root	3	0.0	0.0	0	0	?	S<	00:00 0:00	[desched/0]
Root	4	0.0	0.0	0	0	?	S<	00:00 0:00	[events/0]
Root	5	0.0	0.0	0	0	?	S<	00:00 0:00	[khelper]
Root	10	0.0	0.0	0	0	?	S<	00:00 0:00	[kthread]
Root	21	0.0	0.0	0	0	?	S<	00:00 0:00	[kblockd/0]
Root	62	0.0	0.0	0	0	?	S	00:00 0:00	[pdflush]
Root	63	0.0	0.0	0	0	?	S	00:00 0:00	[pdflush]
Root	65	0.0	0.0	0	0	?	S<	00:00 0:00	[aio/0]

Root	36	0.0	0.0	0	0	?	S	00:00 0:00	[kapmd]
Root	64	0.0	0.0	0	0	?	S	00:00 0:00	[kswapd0]
Root	617	0.0	0.0	0	0	?	S	00:00 0:00	[mtdblockd]
Root	638	0.0	0.0	0	0	?	S	00:00 0:00	[rpciod]
Bin	834	0.0	0.7	1568	444	?	Ss	00:00 0:00	/sbin/portmap
Root	861	0.0	0.0	0	0	?	S	00:00 0:00	[lockd]
Root	868	0.0	0.9	1488	596	?	Ss	00:00 0:00	/sbin/syslogd-r
Root	876	0.0	0.7	1416	456	?	Ss	00:00 0:00	/sbin/klogd-x
Root	884	0.0	1.1	1660	700	?	Ss	00:00 0:00	/usr/sbin/rpc.statd
Root	896	0.0	0.9	1668	584	?	Ss	00:00 0:00	/usr/sbin/inetd
Root	909	0.0	2.2	2412	1372	?	Ss+	00:00 0:00	-bash
Telnetd	953	0.3	1.1	1736	732	?	S	0.5:58 0:00	in.telnetd
Root	954	0.2	2.1	2384	1348	Pts/0	Ss	0.5:58 0:00	-bash
Root	960	0.0	1.2	2312	772	Pts/0	R+	05:59 0:00	ps aux

- Most of the processes in this example are not associated with a controlling terminal. The ps command that generated Listing 5-9 was issued from a telnet session, as indicated by the pts/0 terminal device.
- The STAT field describes the state of the process at the time this snapshot was produced. S means that the process is sleeping, waiting on an event of some type, often I/O. R means that the process is in a runnable state (that is, the scheduler is free to give it control of the CPU if nothing of a higher priority is waiting). The angle bracket next to the state letter indicates that this process has a higher priority. The final column is the command name. Those listed in brackets are kernel threads.

5.4.5 top

- Whereas ps is a one-time snapshot of the current system, top takes periodic snapshots of the state of the system and its processes. Similar to ps, top has numerous command line and configuration options. It is interactive and can be reconfigured while running to customize the display to your particular needs. Entered without options, top displays all running processes in a fashion very similar to the ps aux command presented in Listing 5-9, updated every 3 seconds. Of course, this and many other aspects of top are user-configurable. The first few lines of the top screen display system information, also updated every 3 seconds. This includes the system uptime, the number of users, information on the number of processes and their state, and much more. Listing 5-10 shows top in its default configuration, resulting from executing top from the command line without parameters.

LISTING 5–10 Default *top* Display

top :   06:23:14 up 6:23, 2 users, load average: 0.00, 0.00, 0.00
Tasks: 24 total,   1 running,   23 sleeping,   0 stopped,   0 zombie
CPU(s): 0.0% us,   0.3% sy,   0.0% NI,   99.7% id,   0.0% wa, 0.0% hi, 0.0% si
Mem: 62060k total,   17292k used,   44768k free,   0k buffers
Swap: 0k total,   0k used,   0k free,   11840k cached

PID	User	PR	NI	VIRT	RES	SHR	S	%CPU	% MEM	Time+	Command
978	Root	16	0	1924	952	780	R	0.3	1.5	0.01.22	top
1	Root	16	0	1416	508	452	S	0.0	0.8	0:00.47	init
2	Root	5	–10	0	0	0	S	0.0	0.0	0:00.00	ksftirqd/0
3	Root	5	–10	0	0	0	S	0.0	0.0	0:00.00	desched/()
4	Root	–2	–5	0	0	0	S	0.0	0.0	0:00.00	events/()
5	Root	10	–5	0	0	0	S	0.0	0.0	0:00.09	khelper
10	Root	18	–5	0	0	0	S	0.0	0.0	0:00.00	kthread
21	Root	20	–5	0	0	0	S	0.0	0.0	0:00.00	kblockd/()
62	Root	20	0	0	0	0	S	0.0	0.0	0:00.00	pdflush
63	Root	15	0	0	0	0	S	0.0	0.0	0:00.00	pdflush
65	Root	19	–5	0	0	0	S	0.0	0.0	0:00.00	aio/()
36	Root	25	0	0	0	0	S	0.0	0.0	0:00.00	kapmd
64	Root	25	0	0	0	0	S	0.0	0.0	0:00.00	kswapd()
617	Root	25	0	0	0	0	S	0.0	0.0	0:00.00	mtdblockd
638	Root	15	0	0	0	0	S	0.0	0.0	0:00.34	rpciod
834	Bin	15	0	1568	444	364	S	0.0	0.7	0:00.00	portmap
861	Root	20	0	0	0	0	S	0.0	0.0	0:00.00	lockd
868	Root	16	0	1488	596	405	S	0.0	1.0	0:00.11	syslogd
876	Root	19	0	1416	456	396	S	0.0	0.7	0:00.00	klogd
884	Root	18	0	1660	700	612	S	0.0	1.1	0:00.02	rpc.statd
896	Root	16	0	1668	584	504	S	0.0	0.9	0:00.00	inetd
909	Root	15	0	2412	1372	1092	S	0.0	2.2	0:00.34	Bash
953	Telnetd	16	0	1736	736	616	S	0.0	1.2	0:00.27	in.telnetd
954	Root	15	0	2384	1348	1096	S	0.0	2.2	0:00.16	bash

- The default columns from Listing 5-10 are the PID, the user, the process priority, the process nice value, the virtual memory used by the process, the resident memory footprint, the amount of shared memory used by the task, and other fields that are identical to those described in the previous ps example.

5.4.6 mtrace

- mtrace is a simple utility that analyzes and reports on calls to *malloc()*, *realloc()*, and *free()* in your application. It is easy to use and can potentially help spot trouble in your application. As with other user land tools we have described in this chapter, mtrace must be configured and compiled for your target architecture. mtrace is a malloc replacement library that is installed on your target. Your application enables it with a special function call. Your embedded Linux distribution should contain the mtrace package.
- To demonstrate this utility, we created a simple program that creates dynamic data on a simple linked list. Each list item was dynamically generated, as was each data item we placed on the list. Listing 5–11 shows the simple list structure.

LISTING 5–11 Simple Linear Linked List

```
struct blist_s {
struct blist_s *next;
char *data_item;
int item_size;
int index;
};
```

Each list item was dynamically created using malloc() as follows and subsequently was placed at the end of the linked list :

```
struct blist_s *p = malloc( sizeof(struct blist_s) );
```

- Each variable-sized data item in the list was also dynamically generated and added to the list item before being placed at the end of the list. This way, every list item as created using two calls to *malloc()* one for the list item itself, represented by *struct blist_s*, just shown, and one for the variable data item. We then generated 10,000 records on the list containing variable string data, resulting in 20,000 calls to *malloc()*.

For you to use mtrace, three conditions must be satisfied :

- A header file, *mcheck.h*, must be included in the source file.
- The application must call *mtrace()* to install the handlers.
- The environment variable MALLOC_TRACE must specify the name of a writeable file to which the trace data is written.

5.4.7 dmalloc

dmalloc picks up where mtrace leaves off. The mtrace package is a simple, relatively nonintrusive package most useful for simple detection of malloc/free unbalance conditions. The dmalloc package lets you detect a much wider range of dynamic memory management errors. Compared to mtrace, dmalloc is highly intrusive. Depending on the configuration, dmalloc can slow your application to a crawl. It is definitely not the right tool if you suspect memory errors due to race conditions or other timing issues. dmalloc (and mtrace, to a lesser extent) will definitely change the timing of your application. dmalloc is a very powerful dynamic memory-analysis tool. It is highly configurable and, therefore, somewhat complex. It takes some time to learn and master this tool. However, from QA testing to bug squashing, it could become one of your favorite development tools. dmalloc is a debug malloc library replacement. These conditions must be satisfied for you to use dmalloc :

- Application code must include the dmalloc.h header file.
- The application must be linked against the dmalloc library.
- The dmalloc library and utility must be installed on your embedded target.
- Certain environment variables that the dmalloc library references must be defined before you run your application on the target.

5.4.8 Kernel OOPs

- Although not strictly a tool, a kernel OOPs contains much useful information to help you troubleshoot the cause. A kernel OOPs results from a variety of kernel errors, from simple memory errors produced by a process (fully recoverable, in most cases) to a hard kernel panic. Recent Linux kernels support display of symbolic information in addition to the raw hexadecimal address values. Listing 5–12 shows a kernel oops from a Power Architecture target.

LISTING 5–12 Kernel OOPs Display

```
$ modprobe loop
    Oops: kernel access of bad area, sig: 11 [#1]
    NIP: C000D058 LR: C0085650 SP: C7787E80 REGS: c7787dd0 TRAP: 0300 Not tainted
    MSR: 00009032 EE: 1 PR: 0 FP: 0 ME: 1 IR/DR: 11
    DAR: 00000000, DSISR: 22000000
    TASK = c7d187b0[323] 'modprobe' THREAD: c7786000
Last syscall: 128
    GPR00: 0000006C C7787E80 C7D187B0 00000000 C7CD25CC FFFFFFFF 00000000
80808081
    GPR08: 00000001 C034AD80 C036D41C C034AD80 C0335AB0 1001E3C0 00000000
00000000
```

GPR16: 00000000 00000000 00000000 100170D8 100013E0 C9040000 C903DFD8 C9040000

GPR24: 00000000 C9040000 C9040000 00000940 C778A000 C7CD25C0 C7CD25C0 C7CD25CC

NIP [c000d058] strcpy+0x10/0x1c
LR [c0085650] register_disk+0xec/0xf0
Call trace:
[c00e170c] add_disk+0x58/0x74
[c90061e0] loop_init+0x1e0/0x430 [loop]
[c002fc90] sys_init_module+0x1f4/0x2e0
[c00040a0] ret_from_syscall+0x0/0x44
Segmentation fault

Fig. 5.4 shows the configuration options under the General Setup main menu.

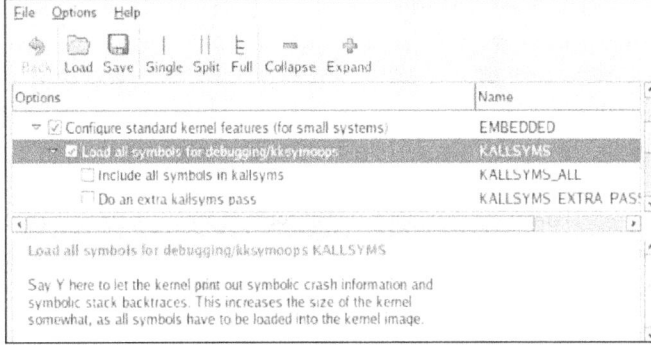

Fig. 5.4 : Symbol support for OOPs

- Analyzing the OOPs shown in Listing 5-12, we see right away that the OOPs was generated due to a "kernel access of bad area, sig : 11."
- In Listing 5–12, NIP is the next instruction pointer, which is decoded later in the OOPs message. This points to the offending code that led to the OOPs. LR is a Power Architecture register and usually indicates the return address for the currently executing subroutine. SP is the stack pointer. REGS indicates the kernel address for the data structure containing the register dump data. TRAP indicates the type of exception that this oops message relates to.
- On the third line of the OOPs message, we see additional Power Architecture machine registers, such as MSR (Machine State Register) and a decode of some of its bits. On the next line, we see the DAR (Data Access Register), which often contains the offending memory address. The DSISR register contents can be used in conjunction with the PowerPC architecture reference to discover much detail about the specific reason for the exception.

5.5 KERNEL DEBUGGING TECHNIQUES

5.5.1 Challenges to Kernel Debugging

Here are some of the challenges you will encounter while debugging Linux kernel code :
- Linux kernel code is highly optimized for speed of execution in many areas.
- Compilers use optimization techniques that complicate the correlation of C source to actual machine instruction flow. Inline functions are a good example of this.
- Single-stepping through compiler optimized code often produces unusual and unexpected results.
- Virtual memory isolates user space memory from kernel memory and can make various debugging scenarios especially difficult.
- Some code cannot be stepped through with traditional debuggers.
- Startup code can be especially difficult because of its proximity to the hardware and the limited resources available (for example, no console, limited memory mapping, and so on).
- The Linux kernel has matured into a very high-performance operating system that can compete with the best commercial operating systems. Many areas within the kernel do not lend themselves to easy analysis by simply reading the source code. Knowledge of the architecture and detailed design are often necessary to understand the code flow in a particular area. Several good books are available that describe the kernel design in detail. Refer to the last section of this chapter for recommendations. GCC is an optimizing compiler. By default, the Linux kernel is compiled with the -O2 compiler flag. This enables many optimization algorithms that can change the fundamental structure and order of your code.
- For example, the Linux kernel makes heavy use of inline functions. Inline functions are small functions declared with the inline keyword, which results in the function's being included directly in the execution thread instead of generating a function call with the associated overhead. Inline functions require a minimum of -O1 optimization level. Therefore, you cannot turn off optimization, which would be desirable to facilitate debugging.
- In many areas within the Linux kernel, single-stepping through code is difficult or impossible. The most obvious examples are code paths that modify the virtual memory settings. When your application makes a system call that result in entry into the kernel, this results in a change in address space as seen by the process. In fact, any transition that involves a processor exception changes the operational context and can be difficult or impossible to single-step through.

5.5.2 Kernel Debugging Techniques

- One of the more common reasons you might find yourself stepping through kernel code is to modify or customize the platform-specific code for your custom board. Let's see how this might be done using the AMCC Yosemite board. We place a breakpoint at the platform-specific architecture setup function and then continue until that breakpoint is encountered. Listing 5–13 shows the sequence.

LISTING 5–13 Debugging Architecture Setup Code

```
(gdb) b yosemite_setup_arch
Breakpoint 3 at 0xc021a488:
file arch/ppc/platforms/4xx/yosemite.c, line 308.
(gdb) c
Continuing.
Can't send signals to this remote system. SIGILL not sent.
Breakpoint 3, yosemite_setup_arch () at arch/ppc/platforms/4xx/yosemite.c:308
308 yosemite_set_emacdata();
(gdb) l
303 }
304
305 static void __init
306 yosemite_setup_arch(void)
307 {
308 yosemite_set_emacdata();
309
310 ibm440gx_get_clocks(&clocks, YOSEMITE_SYSCLK, 6 * 1843200);
311 ocp_sys_info.opb_bus_freq = clocks.opb;
312
(gdb)
```

When the breakpoint at *yosemite_setup_arch()* is encountered, control passes to GDB at line 308 of yosemite.c. The list (l) command displays the source listing centered on the breakpoint at line 308. The warning message about SIGILL displayed by GDB after the continue (c) command can be safely ignored. It is part of GDB's way of testing the capabilities of the remote system. It first sends a remote continue_with_ signal command to the target. The KGDB implementation for this target board does not support this command; therefore, it is NAKed by the target. GDB responds by displaying this informational message and issuing the standard remote continue command instead.

gdb Remote Serial Protocol

- GDB includes a debug switch that enables us to observe the remote protocol being used between GDB on your development host and the target. This can be very useful for understanding the underlying protocol, as well as for troubleshooting targets that exhibit unusual or errant behavior. To enable this debug mode, issue the following command :

(gdb) **set debug remote 1**

- With remote debugging enabled, it is instructive to observe the continue command in action and the steps taken by GDB. Listing 5–14 illustrates the use of the continue command with remote debugging enabled.

LISTING 5–14 Remote Protocol Example : continue Command

```
(gdb) c
Continuing.

Sending packet: $mc0000000,4#80...Ack
Packet received: c022d200
Sending packet: $Mc0000000,4:7d821008#68...Ack
Packet received: OK
Sending packet: $mc0016de8,4#f8...Ack
Packet received: 38600001
Sending packet: $Mc0016de8,4:7d821008#e0...Ack
Packet received: OK
Sending packet: $mc005bd5c,4#23...Ack
Packet received: 38600001
Sending packet: $Mc005bd5c,4:7d821008#0b...Ack
Packet received: OK
Sending packet: $mc021a488,4#c8...Ack
Packet received: 4bfffbad
Sending packet: $Mc021a488,4:7d821008#b0...Ack
Packet received: OK
Sending packet: $c#63...Ack
<<< program running, gdb waiting for event
```

In summary, GDB is restoring all its breakpoints on the target. We added a third breakpoint at *yosemite_setup_arch()*.

Thus, there are three active user-specified breakpoints. These can be displayed by issuing the GDB info breakpoints command. As usual, we use the abbreviated version :

(gdb) i b
Num Type Disp Enb Address What
1 breakpoint keep y 0xc0016de8 in panic at kernel/panic.c:74
2 breakpoint keep y 0xc005bd5c in sys_sync at fs/buffer.c:296
3 breakpoint keep y 0xc021a488 in yosemite_setup_arch at
arch/ppc/platforms/4xx/yosemite.c:308
breakpoint already hit 1 time
(gdb)

- Now compare the previous breakpoint addresses with the addresses in the GDB remote $m packet in Listing 5–14. The $m packet is a "read target memory" command, and the $M packet is a "write target memory" command. Once for each breakpoint, the address of the breakpoint is read from target memory, stored locally on the host by GDB (so that it can be restored later), and replaced with the Power Architecture trap instruction twge r2, r2 (0x7d821008). This results in control passing back to the debugger.

Debugging Optimized Kernel Code

The related Internet mail lists are strewn with questions about what appear to be broken tools. Sometimes the poster reports that his debugger is single-stepping backward or that his line numbers do not line up with his source code. Here we present an example to illustrate the complexities that optimizing compilers bring to source-level debugging. In this example, the line numbers that GDB reports when a breakpoint is hit do not match up with the line numbers in our source file due to function inlining. Listing 5–15 shows the results of this debugging session.

LISTING 5–15 Optimized Architecture-Setup Code

$ **ppc_44x-gdb --silent vmlinux**

(gdb) **target remote /dev/ttyS0**
Remote debugging using /dev/ttyS0
breakinst () at arch/ppc/kernel/ppc-stub.c:825
825 }
(gdb) **b panic**
Breakpoint 1 at 0xc0016b18: file kernel/panic.c, line 74.
(gdb) **b sys_sync**
Breakpoint 2 at 0xc005a8c8: file fs/buffer.c, line 296.
(gdb) **b yosemite_setup_arch**
Breakpoint 3 at 0xc020f438: file arch/ppc/platforms/4xx/yosemite.c, line 116.
(gdb) **c**

```
Continuing.
Breakpoint 3, yosemite_setup_arch ()
at arch/ppc/platforms/4xx/yosemite.c:116
116    def = ocp_get_one_device(OCP_VENDOR_IBM, OCP_FUNC_EMAC, 0);
(gdb) l
111 struct ocp_def *def;
112 struct ocp_func_emac_data *emacdata;
113
114 /* Set mac_addr and phy mode for each EMAC */
115
116    def = ocp_get_one_device(OCP_VENDOR_IBM, OCP_FUNC_EMAC, 0);
117    emacdata = def->additions;
118    memcpy(emacdata->mac_addr, __res.bi_enetaddr, 6);
119    emacdata->phy_mode = PHY_MODE_RMII;
120
(gdb) p yosemite_setup_arch
$1 = {void (void)} 0xc020f41c <yosemite_setup_arch>
```

- We hit the breakpoint, but GDB reports the breakpoint at file yosemite.c line 116. It appears at first glance to be a mismatch of line numbers between the debugger and the corresponding source code. Is this a GDB bug? First, let's confirm what the compiler produced for debug information.

```
$ ppc_44x-readelf --debug-dump=info vmlinux | grep -u6 \
yosemite_setup_arch | tail -n 7
    DW_AT_name : (indirect string, offset: 0x9c04): yosemite_setup_arch
    DW_AT_decl_file : 1
    DW_AT_decl_line : 307
    DW_AT_prototyped : 1
    DW_AT_low_pc : 0xc020f41c
    DW_AT_high_pc : 0xc020f794
    DW_AT_frame_base : 1 byte block: 51 (DW_OP_reg1)
```

GDB User-Defined Commands

You might already know that GDB looks for an initialization file on startup, called gdbinit. When first invoked, GDB loads this initialization file (usually found in the user's home directory) and acts on the commands within it. One of my favorite combinations is to connect to the target system and set initial breakpoints. In this case, the contents of gdbinit would look like Listing 5-16.

LISTING 5–16 Simple GDB Initialization File

```
$ cat ~/.gdbinit
set history save on
set history filename ~/.gdb_history
set output-radix 16
define connect
# target remote bdi:2001
target remote /dev/ttyS0
b panic
b sys_sync
end.
```

- There is no end to the creative uses of GDB user-defined commands. When debugging in the kernel, it is often useful to examine global data structures such as task lists and memory maps. Here we present several useful GDB user-defined commands that can display specific kernel data that you might need to access during your kernel debugging.

5.6 DEBUGGING EMBEDDED LINUX APPLICATIONS

5.6.1 Target Debugging

We explored several important debugging tools, "Development Tools." strace and ltrace can be used to observe and characterize a process's behavior and often isolate problems. dmalloc can help isolate memory leaks and profile memory usage. ps and top are useful for examining the state of processes. These relatively small tools are designed to run directly on the target hardware. Debugging Linux application code on an embedded system has its own unique challenges.

Resources on your embedded target are often limited. RAM and nonvolatile storage limitations might prevent you from running target-based development tools. You might not have an Ethernet port or other high-speed connection. Your target embedded system might not have a graphical display, keyboard, or mouse.

This is where your cross-development tools and an NFS root mount environment can yield large dividends. Many tools, especially GDB, have been architected to execute on your development host while actually debugging code on a remote target. GDB can be used to interactively debug your target code or to perform a postmortem analysis of a core file generated by an application crash.

5.6.2 Remote (Cross) Debugging

Cross-development tools were developed primarily to overcome the resource limitations of embedded platforms. A modest-size application compiled with symbolic debug information can easily exceed several megabytes. With cross debugging, the heavy lifting can be done on your development host. When you invoke your cross version of GDB on your development host, you pass it an ELF file compiled with symbolic debug information. On your target, you can strip the ELF file of all unnecessary debugging information to keep the resulting image to its minimum size.

Listing 5–17 contains the output of readelf for a relatively small web server application compiled for the ARM architecture.

LISTING 5–17 ELF File Debug Information for the Sample Program

$ **xscale_be-readelf -S websdemo**

There are 39 section headers, starting at offset 0x3dfd0 :

Section Headers :

[Nr] Name	Type	Addr	Off	Size	ES	Flg	Lk	Inf	Al
[0]	NULL	0000000	000000	000000	00		0	0	0
[1].interp	PROGBITS	00008154	000154	000013	00	A	0	0	1
[2].note.ABI-tag	NOTE	00008168	000168	000020	00	A	0	0	4
[3].note.numapolicy	NOTE	00008188	000188	000074	00	A	0	0	4
[4].hash	HASH	00081fc	0001fc	00022c	04	A	5	0	4
[5].dynsym	DYNSYM	00008428	000428	000460	10	A	6	1	4
[6].dynstr	STTAB	00008888	000888	000211	00	A	0	0	1
[7].gnu.version	VERSYM	00008a9a	000a9a	00008c	02	A	5	0	2
[8].gnu.version_r	VERNEED	00008b28	000b28	000020	00	A	6	1	4
[9].rel.plt	REL	00008b48	000b48	000218	08	A	6	1	4
[10].init	PROGBITS	00008d60	000d60	000018	00	AX	0	0	4
[11].plt	PROGBITS	00008d78	000d78	000338	04	AX	0	0	4
[12].text	PROGBITS	000090b0	0010b0	019fe4	00	AX	0	0	4
[13].fni	PROGBITS	00023094	01b094	000018	00	AX	0	0	4
[14].fodata	PROGBITS	000230b0	01b060	0023d0	00	A	0	0	8
[15].ARM.extab	PROGBITS	00025480	01d480	000000	00	A	0	0	1

(Contd.)

[Nr] Name	Type	Addr	Off	Size	ES	Flg	Lk	Inf	Al
[16].ARM exidx	ARM_EXIDX	00025480	01d480	000008	00	AL	12	0	4
[17].ec_frame_hdr	PROGBITS	00025488	01d488	00002c	00	A	0	0	4
[18].eh_frame	PROGBITS	000254b4	01d4b4	00007c	00	A	0	0	4
[19].init_array	INIT_ARRAY	0002d530	01d530	000004	00	W/A	0	0	4
[20].fini_array	FINI_ARRAY	0002d534	01d534	000004	00	WA	0	0	4
[21].jer	PROGBITS	0002d538	01d538	000004	00	WA	0	0	4
[22].dynamic	DYNAMIC	0002d53c	01d53c	0000d0	08	WA	6	0	4
[23].got	PROGBITS	0002d53c	01d53c	0000d0	08	WA	6	0	4
[24].data	PROGBITS	0002d728	01d728	0003c0	00	WA	0	0	4
[25].bss	NOBITS	0002dae8	01dae8	0001c8	00	WA	0	0	8
[26].comment	PROGBITS	00000000	01dae8	0001c8	00	WA	0	0	4
[27].debug_aranges	PROGBITS	00000000	01dae8	000940	00		0	0	1
[28].debug_pubnames	PROGBITS	00000000	01e8c8	001aae	00		0	0	1
[29].debig_info	PROGBITS	00000000	020376	013d27	00		0	0	1
[30].debug.abbrev	PROGBITS	00000000	03409d	002ede	00		0	0	1
[31].debug_line	PROGBITS	00000000	036f7b	0034a2	00		0	0	1
[32].debug_frame	PROGBITS	00000000	03a420	003380	00		0	0	4
[33].debug_str	PROGBITS	00000000	03d7a0	000679	00		0	0	1
[34].note.gnu.arm.ide	NOTE	00000000	03de19	00001c	00		0	0	1
[35].debug_ranges	PROGBITS	00000000	03de35	00018	00		0	0	1
[36].shstrtab	STRTAB	00000000	03de4d	000183	00		0	0	1
[37].symtab	SYMTAB	00000000	03e5e8	004bd9	10		38	773	4
[38].strtab	STRTAB	00000000	0431b8	0021bf	00		0	0	1

Key to Flags :

W (write), A (alloc), X (execute), M (merge), S (strings).

I (info), L (link order), G (group), x (unknown).

O (extra OS processing required) o (OS specific), p (processor specific).

$

- If we strip this file using our cross-strip utility, we can minimize its size to preserve resources on our target system. Listing 5–18 shows the results.

LISTING 5–18 Strip Target Application

```
$ xscale_be-strip -s -R .comment -o websdemo-stripped websdemo
$ ls -l websdemo*


-rwxrwxr-x 1 chris chris 283491 Apr 9 09:19 websdemo
-rwxrwxr-x 1 chris chris 123156 Apr 9 09:21 websdemo-stripped


$
```

- For debugging in this fashion, you place the stripped version of the binary on your target system and keep a local unstripped copy on your development workstation containing symbolic information needed for debugging. You use gdbserver on your target board to provide an interface back to your development host, where you run the full blown version of GDB (your cross-gdb, of course) on your unstripped binary.

5.6.2.1 gdbserver

- gdbserver is a small program that runs on the target board and allows remote debugging of a process on the board. It is invoked on the target board specifying the program to be debugged, as well as an IP address and port number on which it will listen for connection requests from GDB. Listing 5-18 shows the startup sequence for initiating a debug session on your target board.

LISTING 5-19 Starting gdbserver on Your Target Board

```
$ gdbserver localhost:2001 websdemo-stripped
Process websdemo-stripped created; pid = 197


Listening on port 2001
```

- This example starts gdbserver configured to listen for an Ethernet TCP/IP connection on port 2001, ready to debug our stripped binary program called websdemo-stripped.

5.6.3 Debugging with Shared Libraries

- Now that you understand how to invoke a remote debug session using GDB on the host and gdbserver on the target, we turn our attention to the complexities of shared libraries and debug symbols. Unless your application is a statically linked executable (linked with the -static linker command-line switch), many symbols in your application will reference code outside your application. Obvious examples include the use of standard C library routines such as fopen, printf, malloc, and memcpy. Less obvious examples might include calls to application-specific functions such as *jack_transport_locate()* (a routine from the JACK low-latency audio server), which calls a library function outside the standard C libraries.

To have symbols from these routines available, you must satisfy two requirements for GDB :

- You must have debug versions of the libraries available.
- GDB must know where to find them.

Given that, we can see the memory segments in use right after process startup, as shown in Listing 5–20.

LISTING 5–20 Initial Target Memory Segment Mapping

```
root@coyote:~# cat /proc/197/maps
00008000-00026000 r-xp 00000000 00:0e 4852444 ./websdemo-stripped
0002d000-0002e000 rw-p 0001d000 00:0e 4852444 ./websdemo-stripped
40000000-40017000 r-xp 00000000 00:0a 4982583 /lib/ld-2.3.3.so
4001e000-40020000 rw-p 00016000 00:0a 4982583 /lib/ld-2.3.3.so
bedf9000-bee0e000 rwxp bedf9000 00:00 0 [stack]
root@coyote:~#
```

- Here we see the target websdemo-stripped application occupying two memory segments. The first is the read-only executable segment at 0x8000, and the second is a read-write data segment at 0x2d000. The third memory segment is the one of interest.
- It is the Linux dynamic linker's executable code segment. Notice that it starts at address 0x40000000. If we investigate further, we can confirm that GDB is actually sitting at the first line of code for the dynamic linker, before any code from our own application has been executed. Using our cross version of readelf, we can confirm the linker's starting address as follows :

 # xscale_be-readelf -S ld-2.3.3.so | grep \.text

[9] .text PROGBITS 00000790 000790 012c6c 00 AX 0 0 16

- From this data, we conclude that the address that GDB reports on startup is the first instruction from ld-2.3.3. so, the Linux dynamic linker/loader. You can use this technique to get a rough idea of where your code is if you don't have symbolic debug information for a process or shared library.

5.6.4 Additional Remote Debug Options

Sometimes you might want to use a serial port for remote debugging. For other tasks, you might find it useful to attach the debugger to a process that is already running. These simple but useful operations are detailed here.

Debugging Using a Serial Port

- Debugging using a serial port is quite straightforward. Of course, you must have a serial port available on your target that is not being used by another process, such as a serial console. The same limitation applies to your host. A serial port must be available. If both of these conditions can be met, simply replace the *IP address : port number* specification passed to gdbserver with a serial port specification. Use the same technique when connecting to your target from your host-based GDB. On your target :

  root@coyote:/apps # **gdbserver /dev/ttyS0 ./tdemo**
  Process ./tdemo created; pid = 698
  Remote debugging using /dev/ttyS0

From your host :

$ **xscale_be-gdb -q tdemo**
(gdb) **target remote /dev/ttyS1**
Remote debugging using /dev/ttyS1
0x40000790 in ?? ()

Attaching to a Running Process

It is often advantageous to connect to a process to examine its state while it is running instead of killing the process and starting it again. With gdbserver, this task is trivial :

root@coyote:/apps # **ps ax | grep tdemo**
1030 pts/0 Sl+ 0:00 ./tdemo
root@coyote:/apps # **gdbserver localhost:2001 --attach 1030**
Attached; pid = 1030
Listening on port 2001

- When you are finished examining the process under debug, you can issue the GDB detach command. This detaches the gdbserver from the application on the target and terminates the debug session. The application continues where it left off. This is a very useful technique for examining a running program. Be aware, though, that when you attach to the process, it halts, waiting for instructions from you. It does not resume execution until instructed to do so, using either the continue or detach command. Also note that you can use the detach command at almost any time to end the debug session and leave the application running on the target.

5.7 STEPPER MOTOR

- A stepper motor is an electromechanical device which converts electrical pulses into discrete mechanical movements.
- The shaft or spindle of a stepper motor rotates in discrete step increments when electrical command pulses are applied to it in the proper sequence. The motors rotation has several direct relationships to these applied input pulses.
- The sequence of the applied pulses is directly related to the direction of motor shafts rotation. The speed of the motor shafts rotation is directly related to the frequency of the input pulses and the length of rotation is directly related to the number of input pulses applied.

5.7.1 BeagleBone Black

BeagleBone Black is a low-cost, community-supported development platform for developers and hobbyists. Boot Linux in under 10 seconds and get started on development in less than 5 minutes with just a single USB cable. The BeagleBone Black is the newest member of the BeagleBoard family. It is a lower-cost, high-expansion focused BeagleBoard using a low cost Sitara XAM3359AZCZ100 Cortex A8 ARM processor from Texas Instruments. It is similar to the Beaglebone, but with some features removed and some features added.

5.8 EMBEDDED GRAPHICS AND MULTIMEDIA

- Given that embedded applications often mix low power requirements and high-quality media, SOC devices often include dedicated hardware acceleration functions to support real-time decoding and encoding of high-definition compressed media streams such as MPEG4. In this chapter we will describe the frameworks and APIs for video capture, encoding, and decoding.
- At its most basic instantiation, the display controller of the hardware takes the frame represented in memory and outputs it to an interface connected to the display. The memory associated with the display is known as the frame buffer. In embedded systems the frame buffer is usually allocated from system memory. The display controller copies the contents from the memory every frame *(per second)* and outputs to the display across

one of the many physical interface standards. Below Fig. 5.5 shows this transformation of memory data to the display. A pixel can be represented in memory in a number of ways; the most common is Red-Green-Blue-Alpha (RGBA), where a 32-bit memory word represents the pixel. The 32-bit value is comprised of four separate 8-bit elements, red, green, and blue obviously represent the three pixel colors, and alpha signifies the amount of opacity of that pixel. The display controller reads the memory address of the frame buffer and generates the appropriate interface signals to encode the pixel color directed to the display.

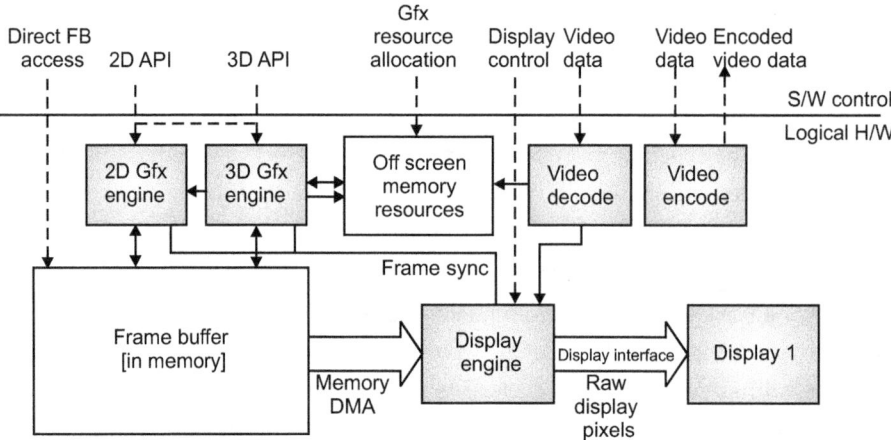

Fig. 5.5

Graphics Overview

- The contents of the frame buffer can be generated using a number of different hardware capabilities. In some cases the software simply writes to the frame buffer directly. There are also 2D and 3D graphics acceleration functions that take a command sequence and update the frame buffer based on these high-order commands. The 2D/3D engines rely on-off screen resources (stored in memory) to construct/update the image in the frame buffer. In addition, there is a video decode engine, where the decoded video output can be directed to the display engine, frame buffer, or an off-screen memory region to be included as part of a 3D command sequence. All these capabilities are used when creating sophisticated multimedia human–machine interfaces. The display engine needs to provide indications of the frame start, so the software and hardware accelerator updates can occur to the frame buffer when the system is not accessing data via DMA from the frame buffer. If the frame buffer is updated during the DMA sequence, tearing artifacts may appear on the screen.

Screen Display

There are two key techniques for rendering image and HMI data from multiple application data onto the screen.

- The first technique uses hardware planes to merge different image/frame sources into a single output display. Each plane consists of an individual frame buffer. The display controller blends each of the planes into a single output image. The mixing of the plane data is controlled by the display controller and the content of the per pixel alpha fields.
- The second technique uses software that relies on graphics processor resources to compose multiple display elements into a sophisticated screen rendering. Earlier embedded SOC devices primarily used hardware-supported layers, but now embedded low-power Graphics Processing Units (GPUs) are being exploited to support the merging of multiple content streams to the output display.

Display Engine

- The display system takes a number of input frame buffer sources and merges the frames into a single composite output frame image. The output image can then be sent to the display interfaces for transmission to the display (for example, the LCD screen). Each individual input frame source is known as a *display plane*.
- There are a variety of planes (such as display, overlay, sprite, and cursor). A *plane* consists of a rectangular image that has characteristics such as source, size, position, method, and pixel format. These planes get attached to source surfaces, which are rectangular areas in memory with a similar set of characteristics. They are also associated with a particular destination pipe. A pipe consists of a blender that combines a set of planes and an independent timing generator. These timing generators provide distinct timing information for each of the display pipes. The E6xx Series SOCs have two independent display pipes that can generate two independent display streams. The individual pipes do not have to have the same timing, resolution, or refresh rate. There is also an option to clone the content between pipes so the same output goes to the two displays at the same or different resolutions. Below Fig. 5.6 shows the relationship between the pipes and displays. When a pipe is cloned, there is a reduction in memory bandwidth (versus two non-cloned displays), and the displays may have different timing (as the pipe generates the appropriate timing for the attached display).

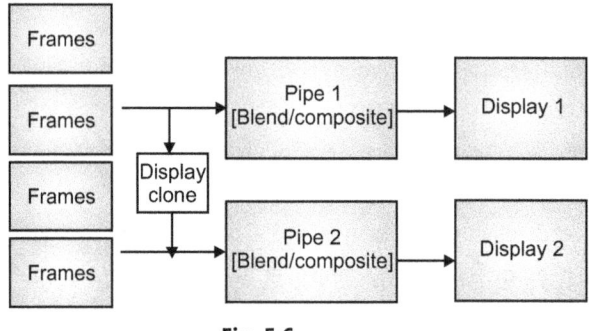

Fig. 5.6

Application Frameworks

Application frameworks for embedded systems are evolving rapidly. Two popular frameworks are: Android and Qt.

Android

- Android is an open-source software platform for mobile devices. As we will see, it is based upon a modified version of the Linux kernel. In 2008, Google released the full source code of the platform under an Apache open-source license. Google does maintain Android as a copyrighted term and only licenses use of the Android copyright for devices that have adhered to a Google-managed certification process. Similarly, certain critical Android applications provided by Google are closed-source and only available for license to certified manufacturers, perhaps most notably the Android Market, which hosts the vast majority of the Android App ecosystem.

Android has been designed with a number of features and characteristics that make it a compelling embedded software application framework. These features include the following :

- **A Modern Software Architecture :** The Android architecture enables the construction of applications in an object-oriented style with novel methods for achieving code reuse and component-level concurrency.

- **A Familiar Development Language On An Optimized Runtime System :** Android applications are written in Java and adhere to Java interface definitions, but the underlying runtime system is not based on the Java virtual machine or Java bytecodes. Android applications are compiled for execution on the Dalvik virtual machine, which is optimized for battery-constrained and connected mobile devices.

- **A Familiar Development Environment :** Android's best supported development tool chain is built upon Eclipse and includes a handset emulator and other development tools.

- **Substantial Reliance On Other Open-Source Technologies :** As mentioned previously, a modified version of the Linux kernel forms the foundation of the Android platform. The integrated web browser is based on WebKit, the same engine used in the Chrome and Safari browsers.
- **Integrated Library Support :** A library layer is provided to insulate application developers from many of the hardware- or vendor-specific details of interacting with units that support 2D/3D graphics, audio/image/video formats, telephony, wireless network links, and a rich variety of mobile peripherals, including cameras and GPS receivers.

Qt : Qt (commonly pronounced "Q T" but officially pronounced "cute") is a cross-platform development framework for GUI-based applications. Qt, like Android, is an object-oriented development environment, but based on C++ rather than Java.

Qt Modules : Qt is an object-oriented, event-driven framework. To developers familiar with GUI-based applications, the architectural concepts are for the most part recognizable. Its applications make use of library modules organized around specific types of functionality, such as the following :

- **QtCore :** The QtCore module contains the core framework classes. These implement the event loop and the interobject communications mechanisms described below. The core classes also provide much of Qt's support for platform independence, including threads, shared memory, and Unicode support.
- **QtGui :** The QtGui module includes the GUI classes, including widgets and canvases. Aggregate layouts, such as grids, lists, and trees that make use of multiple panes, are included and are organized around the familiar model-view-controller (MVC) design pattern.
- **QtMultimedia :** This module provides platform-independent access to media display and capture.
- **QtNetwork :** The QtNetwork module includes classes for TCP/IP networking, including high-level protocols such as HTTP and IP services such as DNS.
- **QtOpenGL :** Platform-independent OpenGL 3D graphics rendering is provided via classes in the QtOpenGL modules.
- **QtSql :** The QtSql module contains classes that provides access to relational databases. It also includes an implementation of SQLite.
- **QtWebKit :** The QtWebKit module provides a web browser layout engine based on the WebKit open-source project.

QUESTIONS

1. Explain in detail different development tools.
2. Write a short note on GNU debugger.
3. Explain the working of data display debugger.
4. Write a short note on cbrowser/cscope.
5. What are the different types of tracing and profiling tools used for embedded OS?
6. Write a short note on strace.
7. Explain in detail strace variations.
8. Write a short note on ltrace.
9. Write a short note on ps.
10. Write a short note on top command line.
11. Write a note on mtrace.
12. Explain challenges to kernel debugging.
13. Explain in detail kernel debugging techniques.
14. Write a short note on : Target Debugging, Remote Debugging, gdbserver.
15. Explain in detail debugging with shared library.
16. Write a note on Embedded Graphics and Multimedia Tools and its Applications.

UNIT VI

EMBEDDED ANDROID

6.1 PORTING LINUX

6.1.1 Why Port Linux Anyway?

Linux is Very Portable
- Supports 23 architectures in the upstream "mainline" kernel tree of Linus Torvalds.
- Kernel is mostly written in C, with some assembly (most architectures only need a dozen such files).
- Split between high-level generic functions and low-level functions to abstract architectural differences.

Linux is Competitive
- The number of Linux kernel developers contributing to the official kernel has tripled since 2005.
- Feature growth continues with an average of 10K new lines of source code added every day.
- In the hour you spend here 5.45 patches will on an average be added to the upstream Linux kernel.

Linux is Cost Effective
- A large amount of code to build upon.
- Large (growing) community of developers.

6.1.2 Background Pre-Requisites

Hardware
- Development board or simulator.

Software
- Toolchain(GCC, binutils etc.).
- Some kind of IDE
  - Likely to be Eclipse based, e.g. all the vendors.
- Experience
  - Kernel development experience.
  - Hardware reference documentation.
  - Books and resources.

Early Board Work
- Test the board actually works.
- Test the debugger actually works.

6.1.3 Bootloader Bringup

Many Open Source friendly projects use U-Boot, supports ARM, AVR32, Blackfin, Microblaze, MIPS, NIOS, PowerPC, SH, and more.
- Typically stored in on-board NOR or NAND.
  - Relocates itself into RAM, loads a kernel (and root filesystem in an initramfs).

U-Boot Design Principles
- "Keep it small"
  - A build of U-Boot with network support (if applicable) should fit in 256KiB.
- "Keep it simple"
  - U-Boot should only do what is necessary to boot.
- "Keep it fast"
  - Get things running and then get out of the way.
- "Keep it portable"
  - U-Boot is (like Linux) mostly written in C, with some assembly for unavoidable reset/CPU init/RAM setup/C stack environment setup.

U-Boot is highly configurable
- Many if (CONFIG_) conditionals.

Implementation split between "board" and "cpu"
- Platform stuff under "board", arch under "cpu".

6.1.4 Porting the Linux Kernel

- The Linux kernel supports a lot of different CPU architectures.
- Each of them is maintained by a different group of contributors.
- The organization of the source code and the methods to port the Linux kernel to a new board are therefore very architecture dependent For example, PowerPC and ARM are very different.
- PowerPC relies on device trees to describe hardware details.
- ARM relies on source code only.

6.1.5 Architecture, CPU and Machine

In the source tree, each architecture has its own directory arch/arm for the ARM architecture. This directory contains generic ARM code.
- boot, common, configs, kernel, lib, mm, nwfpe, vfp, oprofile, tools.

And many directories for different CPU families.
- mach-*, directories : mach-pxa for PXA CPUs, mach-imx for Freescale iMX CPUs, etc. Each of these directories contain support for the CPU, support for several boards using this CPU Some CPU types share some code, in an entity called a platform.
- plat-omap contains common code from mach-omap1 and mach-omap2.

6.2 LINUX AND REAL TIME

Linux is increasingly being used in systems where real-time performance is required.
Examples include multimedia applications and robot, industrial, and automotive controllers.

6.2.1 Real-Time System

1. Real-time computing is an important emerging discipline in CS and CE.
2. Control of lab experiments, robotics, process control, telecommunication etc.
3. It is a type of computing where correctness of the computation depends not only on the logical results but also on the time at which the results are produced.
4. **Hard Real-Time Systems :** Must meet deadline. Example : Space shuttle rendezvous with other space station.
5. **Soft Real-Time Systems :** Deadlines are there but not mandatory. Results are discarded if the deadline is not met.
6. **Hard Real-Time Systems :** Required to complete a critical task within a guaranteed amount of time.
7. **Soft Real-Time Computing :** Requires that critical processes receive priority over less fortunate ones.

Characteristics of Real-Time (RT) Systems
- Determinism.
- Responsiveness.
- User control.
- Reliability.
- Fail-soft operation.

Deterministic Response
- External event and timings dictate the request of service.
- OS's response depends on the speed at which it can respond to interrupts and on whether the system has sufficient capacity to handle requests.
- Determinism is concerned with how long the OS delays before acknowledging an interrupt.
- In non-RT this delay may be in the order of 10's and 100's of millisecs, whereas in an RT it may have an upper-bound of few microsec to 1 millisec.

Responsiveness
- Responsiveness is the time for servicing the interrupt once it has been acknowledged.
- Comprises time to transfer control, (and context switch) and execute the ISR.
- Time to handle nested interrupts, the interrupts that should be serviced when executing this ISR. Higher priority Interrupts.
- Response time = F(responsiveness, determinism).

User Control
- User has a much broader control in RT-OS than in regular OS.
- Priority.
- Hard or soft deadlines.
- Deadlines.
- Memory Management : paging or swapping.
- Name the processes to be resident in memory.
- Scheduling policies.

6.2.2 Real Time Linux

Objectives
- The key RTLinux design objective is that the system should be transparent, modular, and extensible.
- Transparency means that there are no unopenable black boxes and the cost of any operation should be determinable.
- Modularity means that it is possible to omit functionality and the expense of that functionality if it is not needed.
- The base RTLinux system supports high speed interrupt handling and no more. And extensibility means that programmers should be able to add modules and tailor the system to their requirements.
- It has simple priority scheduler that can be easily replaced by schedulers more suited to the needs of some specific application.
- When developing RTLinux, it was designed to maximize the advantage we get from having Linux and its powerful capabilities available.

Core Components
- RTLinux is structured as a small core component and a set of optional components.
- The core component permits installation of very low latency interrupt handlers that cannot be delayed or preempted by Linux itself and some low level synchronization and interrupt control routines.
- This core component has been extended to support SMP and at the same time it has been simplified by removing some functionality that can be provided outside the core.

Functionality
- The majority of RTLinux functionality is in a collection of loadable kernel modules that provide optional services and levels of abstraction.
- These modules include : rtl sched a priority scheduler that supports both a "lite POSIX" interface described below and the original V1 RTLinux API. rtl time which controls the processor clocks and exports an abstract interface for connecting handlers to clocks. rtl posixio supports POSIX style read/write/open interface to device drivers.
1. rtl fifo connects RT tasks and interrupt handlers to Linux processes through a device layer so that Linux processes can read/write to RT components.
2. semaphore is a contributed package by Jerry Epplin which gives RT tasks blocking semaphores.
3. POSIX mutex support is planned to be available in the next minor version update of RTLinux.
4. mbuff is a contributed package written by Tomasz Motylewski for providing shared memory between RT components and Linux processes.

6.2.3 Linux Scheduling
- UNIX and Linux were both designed for fairness in their process scheduling. That is, the scheduler tries its best to allocate available resources across all processes that need the CPU and guarantee each process that it can make progress.
- This very design objective is counter to the requirement for a real-time process.
- A real-time process must be given absolute priority to run when it becomes ready to run.
- Real time means having predictable and repeatable latency.

6.2.4 Latency
- Real-time processes are often associated with a physical event, such as an interrupt arriving from a peripheral device. Fig. 6.1 illustrates the latency components in a Linux system. Latency measurement begins upon receipt of the interrupt we want to process.

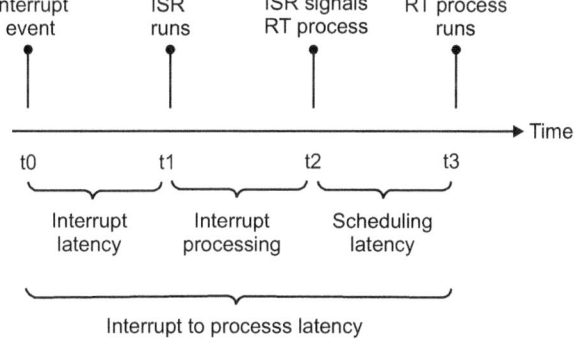

Fig. 6.1 : Latency components

- This is indicated by time t0 in Fig. 6.1. Sometime later, the interrupt occurs, and control is passed to the Interrupt Service Routine (ISR), as indicated by time t1. This interrupt latency is almost entirely dictated by the maximum interrupt off time 1 the time spent in a thread of execution that has hardware interrupts disabled.
- It is considered good design practice to minimize the processing done in the actual ISR. Indeed, this execution context is limited in capability (for example, an ISR cannot call a blocking function, one that might sleep). Therefore, it is desirable to simply service the hardware device and leave the data processing to a Linux bottom half, also called softirqs.
- When the ISR/bottom half has finished its processing, the usual case is to wake up a user space process that is waiting for the data. This is indicated by time t2 in Fig. 6.1. Some time later, the scheduler selects the real-time process to run, and the process is given the CPU.
- This is indicated by time t3 in Fig. 6.1. Scheduling latency is affected primarily by the number of processes waiting for the CPU and the priorities among them.
- Setting the Real Time attribute on a process (SCHED_FIFO or SCHED_RR) gives it higher priority over normal Linux processes and allows it to be the next process selected to run, assuming that it is the highest-priority real-time process waiting for the CPU.
- The highest-priority real-time process that is ready to run (not blocked on I/O) will always run.

6.2.5 Kernel Preemption

- In the early Linux days of Linux 1.x, kernel preemption did not exist. This meant that when a user space process requested kernel services, no other task could be scheduled to run until that process blocked (went to sleep) waiting on something (usually I/O) or until the kernel request completed.
- Making the kernel preemptable meant that while one process was running in the kernel, another process could preempt the first and be allowed to run even though the first process had not completed its in-kernel processing. Fig. 6.2 illustrates this sequence of events.
- In the Fig. 6.2, Process A has entered the kernel via a system call. Perhaps it was a call to write() to a device such as the console or a file.
- While executing in the kernel on behalf of Process A, Process B with higher priority is woken up by an interrupt. The kernel preempts Process A and assigns the CPU to Process B, even though Process A had neither blocked nor completed its kernel processing.

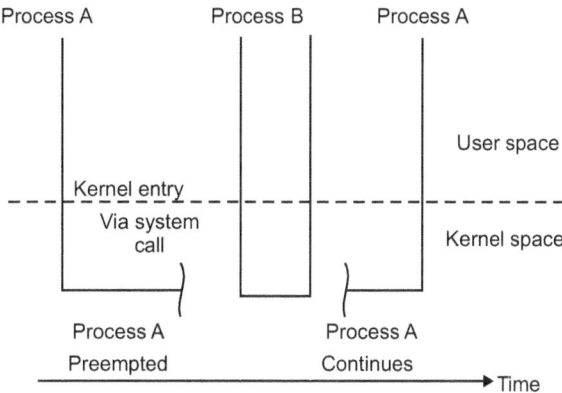

Fig. 6.2 : Kernel preemption

Linux Scheduling

The main purpose of the project Scheduling in Linux is adding a scheduling policy to the Linux Kernel 2.4. It also aims at providing a clear yet concrete overview of the scheduling process in Linux.

Introduction

1. The Linux scheduler is a priority based scheduler that schedules tasks based upon their static and dynamic priorities. When these priorities are combined they form a task's goodness.

2. Each time the Linux scheduler runs, every task on the run queue is examined and its goodness value is computed. The task with the highest goodness is chosen to run next.

3. When there are CPU bound tasks running in the system, the Linux scheduler may not be called for intervals of up to 40 seconds.

4. This means that the currently running task has the CPU to itself for periods of up to 40 seconds (how long depends upon the task's priority and whether it blocks or not).

5. This is good for throughput because there are few computationally uneccessary context switches. However it can kill interactivity because Linux only reschedules when a task blocks or when the task's dynamic priority (counter) reaches zero.

6. Linux scheduler has been gone through some big improvements since kernel version 2.4. There were a lot of complaints about the interactivity of the scheduler in kernel 2.4. During this version, the scheduler was implemented with one running queue for all available processors.

7. At every scheduling, this queue was locked and every task on this queue got its timeslice update. This implementation caused poor performance in all aspects. The scheduler algorithm and supporting code went through a large rewrite early in the 2.5 kernel development series.

8. The new scheduler was arisen to achieve O(1) run-time regardless number of runnable tasks in the system. To achieve this, each processor has its own running queue. This helps a lot in reducing lock contention.
9. The priority array was introduced which used active array and expired array to keep track running tasks in the system. The O(1) running time is primarily drawn from this new data structure. The scheduler puts all expired processes into expired array.
10. When there is no active process available in active array, it swaps active array with expired array, which makes active array becomes expired array and expired array becomes active array.
11. There were some twists made into this scheduler to optimize further by putting expired task back to active array instead of expired array in some cases.

Kernel 2.4 Major Features

- **An O(n) Scheduler :** Goes through the entire " global runqueue" to determine the next task to be run. This is an O(n) algorithm where 'n' is the number of processes. The time taken was proportional to the number of active processes in the system.

- **A Global Runqueue :** All CPUs had to wait for other CPUs to finish execution. A Global runqueue for all processors in a Symmetric Multiprocessing System (SMP). This meant a task could be scheduled on any processor which can be good for load balancing but bad for memory caches. For example, suppose a task executed on CPU-1, and its data was in that processor's cache. If the task got rescheduled to CPU-2, its data would need to be invalidated in CPU-1 and brought into CPU-2. This lead to large performance hits during heavy workload.

Kernel 2.4 Scheduler Policies

- **SCHED_FIFO :** A First-In, First-Out real-time process. When the scheduler assigns the CPU to the process, it leaves the process descriptor in its current position in the runqueue list. If no other higher-priority real-time process is runnable, the process will continue to use the CPU as long as it wishes, even if other real-time processes having the same priority are runnable.

- **SCHED_RR :** A Round Robin real-time process. When the scheduler assigns the CPU to the process, it puts the process descriptor at the end of the runqueue list. This policy ensures a fair assignment of CPU time to all SCHED_RR real-time processes that have the same priority.

- **SCHED_OTHER :** A conventional, time-shared process. The policy field also encodes a SCHED_YIELD binary flag. This flag is set when the process invokes the sched_yield( ) system call (a way of voluntarily relinquishing the processor without the need to start an I/O operation or go to sleep. The scheduler puts the process descriptor at the bottom of the runqueue list.

Kernel 2.6 - Major Features

- The 2.6 scheduler was designed and implemented by Ingo Molnar. His motivation in working on the new scheduler was to create a completely O(1) scheduler for wakeup, context-switch, and timer interrupt overhead.

- One of the issues that triggered the need for a new scheduler was the use of Java virtual machines (JVMs). The Java programming model uses many threads of execution, which results in lots of overhead for scheduling in an O(n) scheduler.

- Each CPU has a runqueue made up of 140 priority lists that are serviced in FIFO order. Tasks that are scheduled to execute are added to the end of their respective runqueue's priority list.

- Each task has a time slice that determines how much time it is permitted to execute.

- The first 100 priority lists of the runqueue are reserved for real-time tasks, and the last 40 are used for user tasks (MAX_RT_PRIO=100 and MAX_PRIO=140).

- In addition to the CPU's runqueue, which is called the active runqueue, there's also an expired runqueue.

- When a task on the active runqueue uses all of its time slice, it is moved to the expired runqueue. During the move, its time slice is recalculated (and so is its priority).

- If no tasks exist on the active runqueue for a given priority, the pointers for the active and expired runqueues are swapped, thus making the expired priority list the active one.

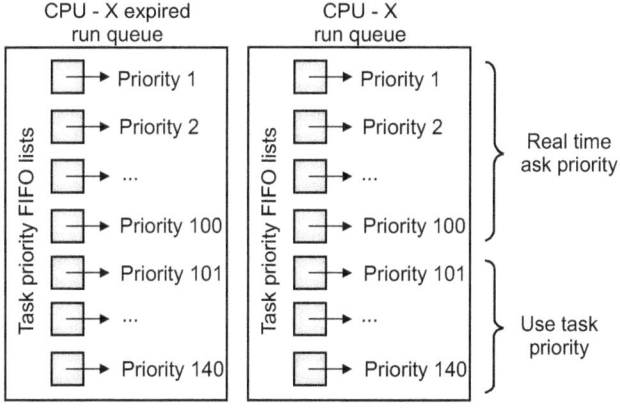

Fig. 6.3

Overview (typical Kernel 2.6 Scheduler)

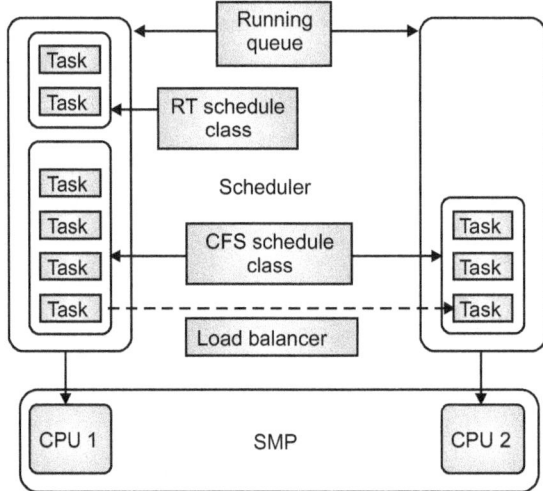

Fig. 6.4

Linux Scheduler Contains

- **A Running Queue :** A running queue (rq) is created for each processor (CPU). It is defined in kernel/sched.c as struct_runqueue. Each rq contains a list of runnable processes on a given processor. The struct_runqueue is defined in sched.c notsched.h to abstract the internal data structure of the scheduler.

- **Schedule Class :** It is an extensible hierarchy of scheduler modules. These modules encapsulate scheduling policy details and are called from the scheduler core without the core code assuming too much about them. Scheduling classes are implemented through the sched_class structure, which contains hooks to functions that must be called whenever an interesting event occurs. Tasks refer to their schedule policy through struct task_struct and sched_class.

- **Completely Fair Schedule Class :** Schedules tasks following Completely Fair Scheduler (CFS) algorithm. Tasks which have policy set to SCHED_NORMAL (SCHED_OTHER), SCHED_BATCH, SCHED_IDLE are scheduled by this schedule class. The implementation of this class is in kernel /sched_fair.c.

- **RT Schedule Class :** schedules tasks following real-time mechanism defined in POSIX standard. Tasks which have policy set to SCHED_FIFO, SCHED_RR are scheduled using this schedule class. The implementation of this class is kernel/sched_rt.c.

- **Load Balancer :** In SMP environment, each CPU has its own rq. These queues might be unbalanced from time to time. A running queue with empty task pushes its associated CPU to idle, which does not take full advantage of symmetric multiprocessor systems.

Load balancer is to address this issue. It is called every time the system requires scheduling tasks. If running queues are unbalanced, load balancer will try to pull idle tasks from busiest processors to idle processor.

- **Interactivity :** Interactivity is an important goal for the Linux scheduler, especially given the growing effort to optimize Linux for desktop environments. Interactivity often flies in the face of efficiency, but it is very important none the less.
- **SMP Kernel :** Symmetric Multi processing (SMP) is a multiprocessing architecture in which multiple CPUs, usually residing on one board, share the same memory and other resources. The SMP challenge is more complex than the uniprocessor challenge because there is an additional element of concurrency to protect against. In the uniprocessor model, only a single task can execute in the kernel at a time. Protection from concurrency involves only protection from interrupt or exception processing. In the SMP model, multiple threads of execution in the kernel are possible in addition to the threat from interrupt and exception processing.

6.3 EMBEDDED ANDROID

- Embedded Android is required for anyone who wants to seriously work the Android internals and bring up Android on new platforms.
- It helps in navigating the extensive AOSP(Android Open Source Project) codebase, and understanding the overall architecture and design of the system.
- It is a useful when porting Android to new hardware or integrating new features at a low level.

Android Boot Process

Understanding of the boot process of the target platform is the starting point for the optimizing the boot time. Generally on any platform, following components are loaded and executed step by step

- Boot loader.
- U-boot (optional).
- Kernel.
- Android.

The Android process has the following sequence :

- Init.
- Zygote.
- System Server.
- Service Manager.
- Other Daemons and processes.

- Applications.

The following Fig. 6.5 depicts the boot process.

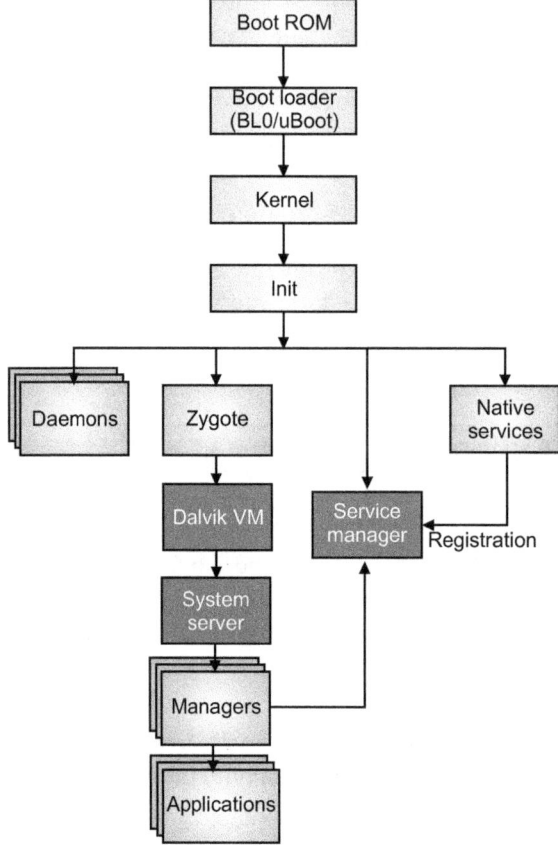

Fig. 6.5

Boot Loader

- Upon power up, the processor boots from a ROM area typically located internally. This code determines the boot media and loads the boot loader from the media. The boot loader can be used to initialize the DRAM and load another level of loader or directly the Linux kernel. It is generally dependent on the processor architecture and implementation.

U-Boot

- U-Boot is used as a first or second level boot loader. It reads the Linux and ramdisk images from boot media and validates them. While it may not be mandatory to use u-boot, it offers some flexibility like passing arguments to the kernel (easily used to enter the recovery mode), fast boot modes, as a backup option to reprogram the OS etc.

Kernel
- Linux kernel is the heart of the Android responsible for the process creation, inter process communication, device drivers, file system management etc. Android applies a custom patch on the main stream kernel to support certain features like Wake locks etc needed for operation of the Android.
- The kernel can be either loaded as uncompressed image or as a compressed image. Up on loading, it mounts the root file system (typically passed as kernel command line arguments) and starts the first application in user space.

Android
- Android typically operates wholly on the user space. The android applications are executed over a Virtual Machine called the Dalvik. The following section explains the internals in detail.

init and init.rc
- The first user space application executed on booting the kernel is the init executable located in the root folder. The process parses a start up script called the "init.rc" script. This is written in a language designed for android used to start all the necessary processes, daemons and services for a proper operation of android. It offers various types of execution timings such as early-init, on-boot, on-post-fs etc. A detailed explanation of the scripting model is available on Android documentation site.

Demons and Services
- The init process creates various daemons and processes like rild, vold, mediaserver, adb, etc each responsible for its own functionality. Descriptions of these processes are not in the scope of this post. Rather we will discuss more about "Zygote" process.

Service Manager
- The service manager process manages all the services running in the system. Every service created registers itself with this process and this information is used for future references by other processes/applications.

Zygote
- Zygote is one of the first init process created on boot. The term "zygote" is based the biological "initial cell formed that divides to produce offsprings". Similarly "zygote in android" initializes the Dalivik VM and forks to create multiple instances to support each android process. It facilitates using a shared code across the VM instances resulting in a low memory foot print and short load time, ideal for an embedded system.
- Zygote apart from installing a listener on the server socket, also preloads classes and resources to be used later in the Android applications. Once done, the system server is started.

Android System Services (SystemServer)

- SystemServer process starts all services available in the Android. Some of them are described below :

Service	Description
Activity Manager	Manages activities life cycle and new services.
Package Manager	Manages application package handling (install, uninstall, upgrade, permissions).
Window Manager	Manages all the window manipulations (like input events, orientation).
AppWidget Service	Handles Android widgets.
Backup Manager	Manages backup scheduling and transfer.
Status Bar	Shows software/hardware status. It works with other managers like Notification, Network Status, Battery Status.
Power Manager	Handles power management while Android's different modes (lock mode, sleep mode, Adjust brightness).
Network Management Service	Deals with network related activities.
Notification Manager	Manages all notifications (Toasts).
Location Manager	Manages location providers.
Entropy Mixer	Handles (load & save periodically) kernel randomness.
Display Manager	Manages display properties.
Telephony Registry	Provides telephony information.
Scheduling Policy	Manages the process scheduling.
Account Manager	Handles the users account credential of different online services.
Content Manager	Handles all the data's on a device.
Battery Service	Manages battery level and charging states.
Alarm Manager	Used to schedule the user applications to be run at future.

Input Manager	Handles input devices and key layouts.
Device Policy	Enforces security policies for the device.
Clipboard Service	Provides Clipboard based copy/past operations.
NetworkStats Service	Monitors Network connection Status.
Network Policy Service	Enforces network security policies.
Wi-Fi P2pService	Handles WiFi peer to peer connection.
Ethernet Service	Manages Ethernet connectivity.
Wi-Fi Service	Manage WiFi connectivity.
Connectivity Service	Monitors and handles network connection state changes.
Network Service Discovery Service	Used to find local network devices to share app data.

Once all the services are started and are executing, the Android broadcasts a "ACTION_BOOT_COMPLETED" message implying end of the boot process.

Android Home Screen

The Android Package Manager on start up, parses each package (".apk" file) available in the "/system/app" and "/system/vendor/app" and validates its AndroidManifest.xml. The application that is configured as the "Home" in its manifest is launched there by showing the android UI. Typically the Launcher application is launched as it is the default home application.

6.4 EMBEDDED ANDROID APPLICATIONS

1. Calculator.
2. Twitter Search App.
3. Slide Show App.

6.4.1. Calculator

- The following steps are a shortened version of what's on the Android developer website; you can check the website for more details.

- Prepare your development computer : You may need to install JDK version 5 or 6, and Eclipse (version 3.4 or 3.5, but not 3.6) if you don't already have these installed.
- Download and install the SDK starter package and extract its contents to a folder, then add the folder location to your PATH variable (especially if using Windows).
- Install the ADT (Android Development Tools) plugin in Eclipse : Via Help –> Install New Software –> Add, set up the remote update site *https:// dlssl. google. com / android / eclipse/*. If you have problems with this URL, replace https with http. Install the ADT plugin (see Fig. 6.6), restart Eclipse, and set the 'Android' preferences in Eclipse to point to the location where you've extracted the SDK.

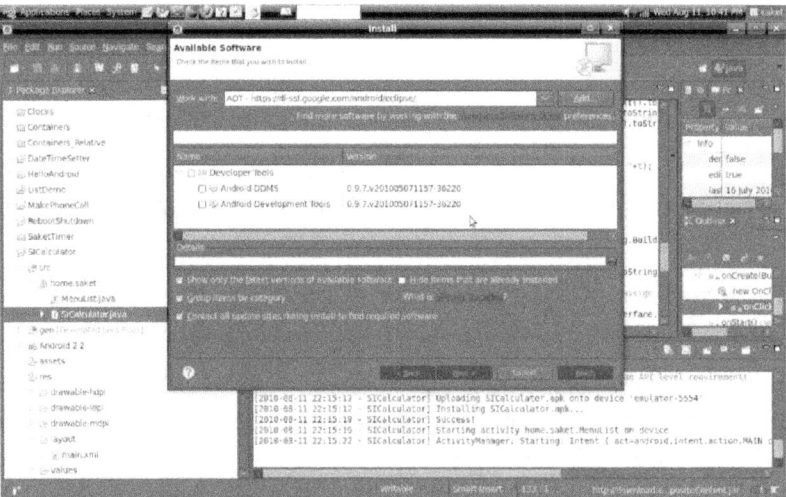

Fig. 6.6

Add Android platforms and other components to your SDK : Use the Android SDK and AVD (Android Virtual Device) Manager included in the SDK starter package, which is represented by the Eclipse toolbar button shown in Fig. 6.6. With it, you can add one or more Android platforms that you intend to develop (e.g., Android 2.0 or Android 2.2) and other components to your SDK. You can also install the documentation for the version of Android you are downloading. To launch the Android SDK and AVD Manager, you can also execute the Android tool in the SDK's /tools folder.

Creating a New Android Project

Once you've set up the environment, you can create a sample Android Project in Eclipse; the new Android project dialogue is shown in Fig. 6.7.

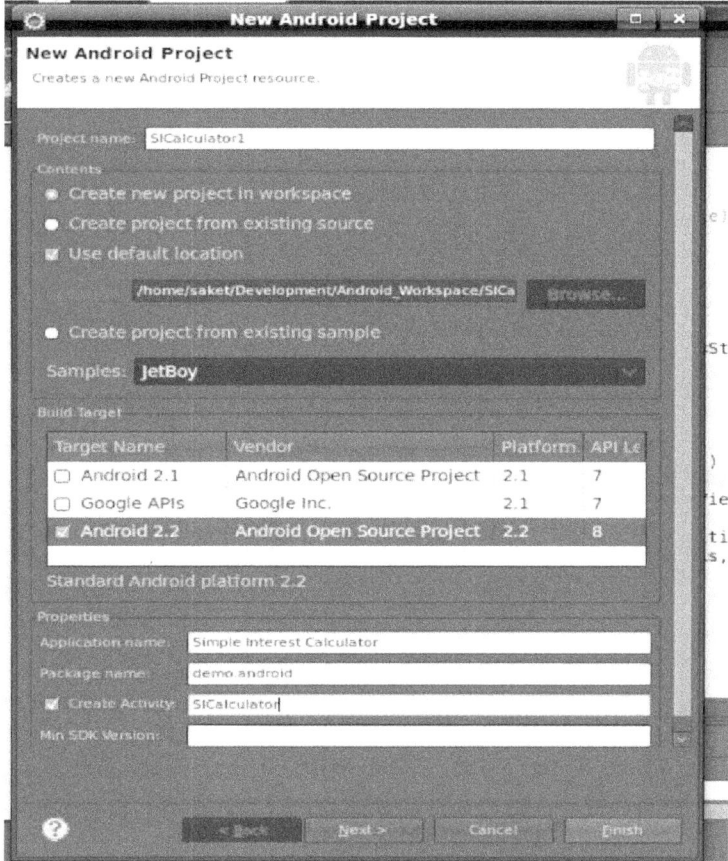

Fig. 6.7

Some important fields in this dialogue :
- Build Target lets you choose one of the Android SDK versions you have installed with the SDK and AVD Manager.
- Application name is the title that is shown when you run your application.
- Package name must be at least two levels deep (for example, "home.saket").
- The Activity name specifies the name of your class (that is going to be created), which will extend the Activity class from the Android library. We will cover the Activity class in some other tutorial.

Android Project Folder Structure

When the new Android project is created on disk, it has a folder structure as shown in Fig. 6.8. This helps you organize your application resources in a logical manner :

Fig. 6.8 : Project folder structure

- **src :** Holds all the Java classes that you create.
- **res :** Short for Resource, it holds all your images, layout files, and string class = "Apple-converted-space" value XML.
- **drawable :** Contains three folders for storing images with different sizes based on the resolution of mobile phone screens.
- **layout :** Consists of a single XML file initially defining the layout configurations.
- **values :** Holds an XML file named strings.xml which maps values of IDs to string values. Discussed later in the tutorial.
- **AndroidManifest.xml :** This is the main configuration file for the whole of Android application. It defines the way your application will be launched, the number of activities present in your application, the permissions that your application has, etc.
- **default.properties :** This file is generally used for localisation purposes.

User Interface

Let's begin with *res/layout/main.xml*, which configures the layout of the application. The layout terms/tags that we use are very similar to Java Swing components :

- **LinearLayout :** A layout that arranges its children in a single row or column. The orientation attribute specifies whether the layout is horizontal or vertical (a row or a column).
- **Button :** Specifies a push-button.
- **EditText :** Corresponds to an editable text box where the user can enter data.
- **TextView :** Corresponds to a Label field.

You can either use the UI layout tool provided by ADT, or hand-edit the XML. I prefer the latter because I have more control over the UI, and the ADT tool is a bit jerky as of now, needing a lot of improvement.

Using the tags listed above, I created the layout of the demo application in *main.xml*.

Now, let's examine how we build the layout. As the first step, I used LinearLayout to set the layout on the screen :

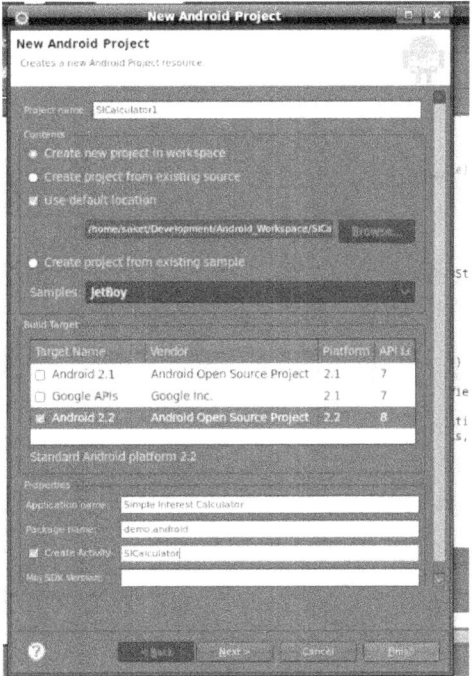

Fig. 6.9

```xml
<LinearLayout android:id="@+id/LinearLayout01"
    android:layout_width="fill_parent"
    android:layout_height="fill_parent"
    android:orientation="vertical"
    android:background="@drawable/simpleinterest1"
    xmlns:android="http://schemas.android.com/apk/res/android">
```

- **android-id :** A unique ID for the component, which can be used to refer to it in application code.
- **android-layout_width and android-layout_height :** Gives the instruction on how the layout should occupy the screen. The fill_parent value fills the screen completely, while wrap_content varies size as per the size of contained content.
- **android-orientation :** Orientation of the layout. When horizontal, components are added side by side; when vertical, components are added one below the other.
- **android : background :** Indicates a background image a resource in the drawable folder. In this case, it is the file *res/drawable-hdpi/simpleinterest1.jpg*, which you can obtain from the GitHub repository.

The next step is to add a TextView specifying the title, the result of which is shown in Fig. 6.10.

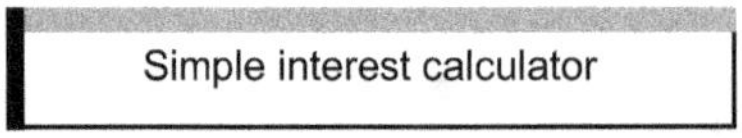

Simple interest calculator

Fig. 6.10

We then add another LinearLayout nested inside the parent LinearLayout, with horizontal orientation, so that we can have a label and a text-box beside each other, as shown in Fig. 6.11

```xml
<LinearLayout android:id="@+id/LinearLayout02"
    android:layout_width="fill_parent"
    android:layout_height="wrap_content"
    android:orientation="horizontal"
    android:layout_marginTop="20dp"
    android:layout_marginLeft="25dp"
    >
        <TextView android:text="@string/principal"
        android:layout_width="wrap_content"
        android:layout_height="wrap_content"
        android:id="@+id/TextPrincipal"
        android:textSize="20dp"
```

```
        >
    </TextView>

    <EditText android:id="@+id/pAmount"
        android:layout_width="wrap_content"
        android:layout_height="wrap_content"
        android:width="100dp"
        android:height="15dp"
        android:layout_marginLeft="95dp"
        android:inputType="numberDecimal"
        >
    </EditText>
</LinearLayout>
```

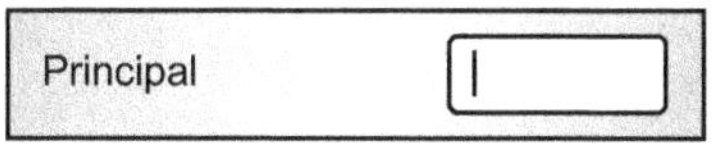

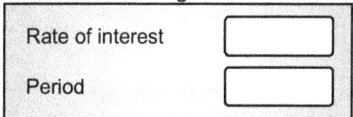

Fig. 6.11 : Component 1

Note : 100 dp is 100 density points. These units abstract away screen-size issues; they translate to differing numbers of pixels based on differing screen resolutions on different devices. That is, 100 dp is different for a 7.6 cm (3 inch) screen and for a 10.2 cm (4 inch) screen, making your UI specification independent of physical screen sizes.

Our fourth step is to repeat the previous step, modifying IDs and labels for the other two components, the result of which is shown in Fig. 6.12.

Fig. 6.12 : Component 2

Now that we have done with the UI, let's move on to the functionality of our application to calculate simple interest based on the given input, and display it to the user.

The Java Code

I have created just one Java class here; as an application grows more complex, you can have multiple Java classes performing operations.

As promised earlier, let's look at the Activity class. An Activity, in Android terms, is nothing but a screen window. We extend our class with Activity because we need to display a screen window with the application UI. When you want to perform different actions, or have multiple screens in your application, you need to have separate Java classes extending the Activity class, one for each of the screen windows. When you create a new Android project, these three lines of code will be automatically generated for you :

```java
public void onCreate(Bundle savedInstanceState) {
super.onCreate(savedInstanceState);
setContentView(R.layout.main);
```

The *onCreate()* method is invoked when your application starts. It calls the super-class' *onCreate()* method to set the initial parameters of the screen window. setContentView(R.layout.main) initialises the screen layout with the UI described in *main.xml*.

Next, your Java code has to obtain references to the UI elements, to retrieve user inputs. For this, use a method named *findViewById()*, passing the unique ID that we assigned to each UI component in *main.xml*.

```java
principal = (EditText)findViewById(R.id.pAmount);
rate = (EditText)findViewById(R.id.rate);
period = (EditText)findViewById(R.id.period);
messageBox = (Button)findViewById(R.id.box);
```

The basic steps taken are :

Obtain a reference to the Calculate button so you can assign an *OnClickListener()* to the button. This catches the click event of the button, and makes the user override the *onClick()* method of the listener.

```java
messageBox.setOnClickListener(new OnClickListener() {
   public void onClick(View v) {
}
```

Perform basic validations for NULL values, on the contents of the *EditText* elements.

Use the Double wrapper class to convert the string values to their actual Double values.

If any error occurs, display aToast message a pop-up message telling the user about the error.

If all the validations are passed, then calculate the simple interest and display it in an alert dialogue box. The syntax used to show the *AlertDialog* is as follows :

```java
// prepare the alert box
AlertDialog.Builder alertbox = new AlertDialog.Builder(v.getContext());
System.out.println("Alert builder");
// set the message to display
alertbox.setMessage("Simple Interest = "+si.toString());
// add a neutral button to the alert box and assign a click listener
alertbox.setNeutralButton("Ok", new DialogInterface.OnClickListener() {
   // click listener on the alert box
   public void onClick(DialogInterface arg0, int arg1) {
      // the button was clicked
```

```
    Toast.makeText(getApplicationContext(), "Thank You !!!!",
Toast.LENGTH_LONG).show();
   }
});
// show it
alertbox.show();
```

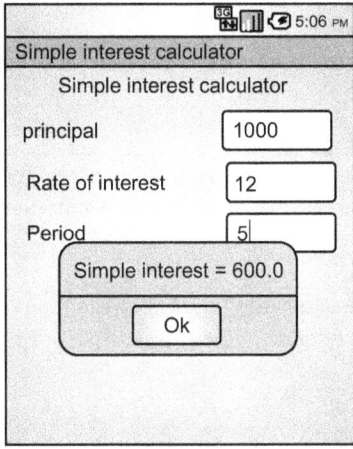

Fig. 6.13

6.4.2 Twitter Search App

- An Embedded Tweet brings the best content created on Twitter into your article or website. An Embedded Tweet may include unique photos or a video created for display on Twitter or interactive link previews to highlight additional content. Author attribution, hashtags, mentions, and other key components of the Twitter experience helps your site's audience connect with the global conversation happening on Twitter.

- An Embedded Tweet combines HTML preview content with Twitter-hosted JavaScript to display a fully-rendered Tweet experience. Publishers may copy-and-paste Embedded Tweet markup generated on a Tweet detail page, pass a URL to a supporting CMS, or add a Tweet to the page using a JavaScript factory function.

Twitter Kit for Android

The Android SDK is a collection of individual feature modules, called Kits. The SDK provides the following Kits :

- **TwitterCore**

Enable users to log in with Twitter via Single Sign-On. Make authenticated requests to the Twitter API to load Tweets, users, search results, and other Twitter content.

- **TweetUi**

Embed media-forward or compact Tweet views into your views and list views to show users information that is relevant to your app. Turn on sharing for Tweets discovered via your app.

- **TweetComposer**

Let users compose new Tweets as part of your app or share content discovered via your app. This Kit provides a lightweight mechanism for creating intents to interact with the installed Twitter app or a browser.

- **Digits**

Allow users to create an account or sign into your app using nothing but their phone number.

6.4.3 Slide Show App

Building an iOS photo slideshow application from scratch. You will put some XML code and photos on the server, build the iOS application, add an image view, get the XML, and do the slideshow animation.

Building the Back End

The back end of the example slideshow application is really just an XML file that you can drop on your server. Listing 6-1 shows the example XML, with some sample images.

LISTING 6-1 : photos.xml

```
<photos>
<photo url="http://localhost/photos/CRW_0675.jpg" />
<photo url="http://localhost/photos/CRW_1488.jpg" />
<photo url="http://localhost/photos/CRW_3273.jpg" />
<photo url="http://localhost/photos/CRW_3296.jpg" />
<photo url="http://localhost/photos/CRW_3303.jpg" />
<photo url="http://localhost/photos/CRW_3359.jpg" />
<photo url="http://localhost/photos/CRW_3445.jpg" />
<photo url="http://localhost/photos/CRW_3752.jpg" />
<photo url="http://localhost/photos/CRW_3754.jpg" />
<photo url="http://localhost/photos/CRW_4525.jpg" />
<photo url="http://localhost/photos/CRW_4547.jpg" />
<photo url="http://localhost/photos/CRW_4700.jpg" />
<photo url="http://localhost/photos/CRW_4860.jpg" />
</photos>
```

The XML is remarkably simple. The <photos> tag contains multiple <photo> tags. Each <photo>tag has the URL of the image you want to display. The URL needs to be fully qualified and absolute; the client application will load the URL directly not through any type of browser that handles relative URLs.

To complete the back end, modify the XML to include references to your photos and upload that XML to a known location on your server. If everything goes as planned, you should be able to browse to the XML using Safari (or whatever browser you choose) and see something like Fig. 6.14.

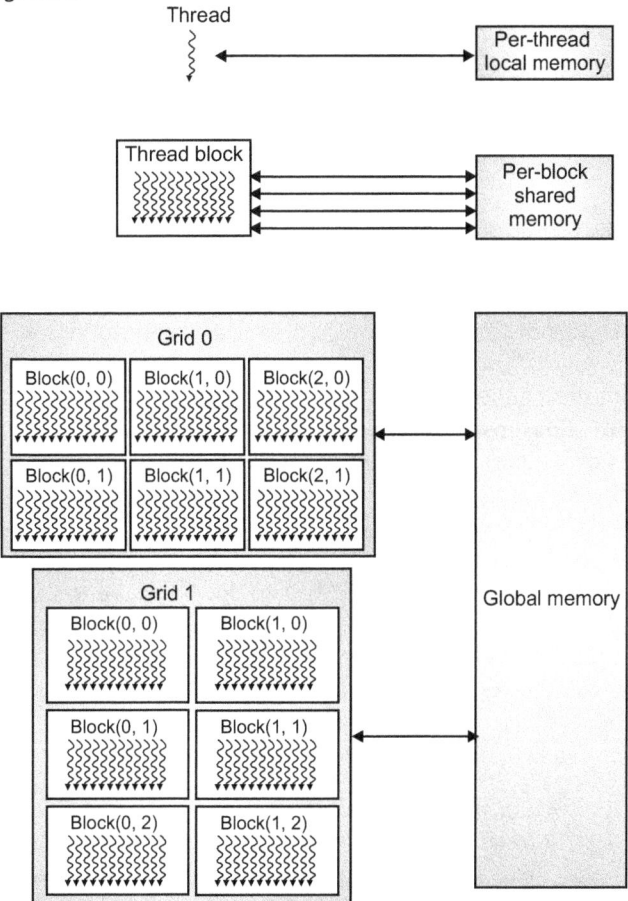

Fig. 6.14 : XML on the server

Fig. 6.14 shows the XML from Listing 6-1 formatted as text. The result will be different from browser to browser, as this is just simple XML (and there is no standard among browsers).

To test that the URLs are correct :

- Select one of the URLs.
- Copy and paste it into the browser URL area.
- Press the **Return** key.

You should see something similar to Fig. 6.15.

Fig. 6.15 : One of the photos on the server

A photo, located on the server, is referenced by one of the URLs in the XML. If you do not see the XML, or do not see the photos, then you need to check your web server configuration and your URLs. If you can't see a photo in the browser, then your new iOS application can not see it either.

Building the Client Slideshow Application

After the server is configured and the photos are uploaded, you can start to build the iOS application. The first step is to install the Apple Developer Tools (see Resources for a link). If you are :

- Pre-Lion, you need to download the developer tools from the Apple Developer site.
- Running Lion, you can use the Mac App Store to download the tools.

After you install the developer tools, run the XCode environment, which is Apple's IDE for both iOS and Mac OS X development. From the XCode environment, select the menu option for a **NewProject**. You should see the first page of the application wizard that you wll use to build iOS or MacOS X applications, as in Fig. 6.16.

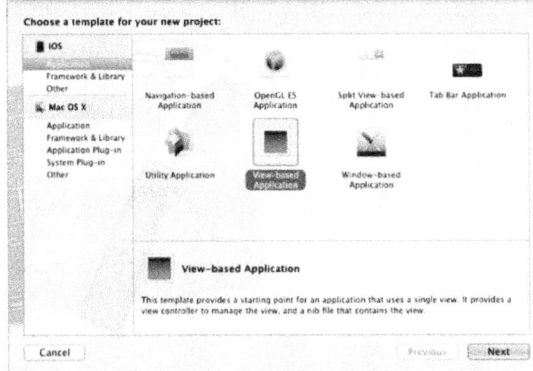

Fig. 6.16 : Application wizard

You can choose from several different application templates. For this example, select **View-basedApplication** and click **Next**. You should see the final page of the wizard, as in Fig. 6.17.

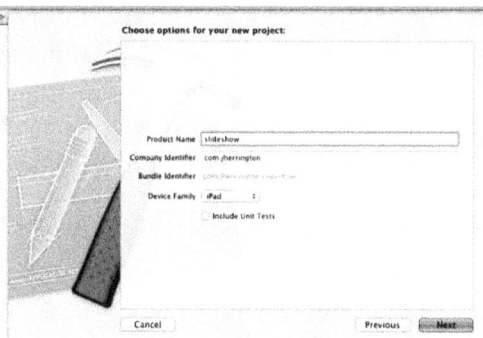

Fig. 6.17 : Project options

On the second page of the wizard, name your application and select the default device family(iPad or iPhone). The Product Name of the example application is slideshow. The value in the Company Identifier field indicates the application is in the com.jherrington namespace. (Ofcourse, you can choose whatever name and company identifier you like.) Choose **iPad** for theDevice Family and click **Next**.

The project is created. At this point it is always best to select the big **Play** button at the upper left of the interface to run your application for the first time. This step compiles everything and brings up the iPad emulator.

Adding the Image View

The next step is to add the image view for displaying the images. The iOS framework comes with a rich set of built-in controls that you can use to build your application. For the example, you'll use the UIImage View control. With UIImage View you can display images that are compiled into the application, stored locally on the device, or, as in the example, downloaded from a website.

To add the UIImage View, open the slide show Controller View. XIB file, which is the user interface definition file for the slides how Controller View. With the XIB open, go to the object palette and select **Image View**, as in Fig. 6.18.

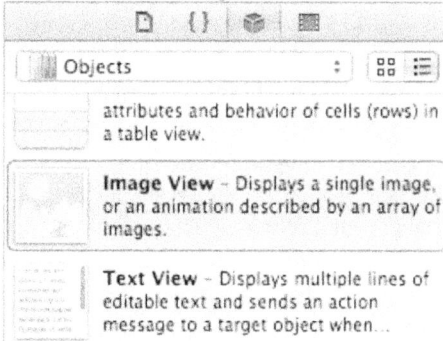

Fig. 6.18 : Add a UIImageView object to the view controller XIB

With the Image View selected, drag and drop it onto the slideshowControllerView. Usually the IDEauto-scales the control to fit the available space. If it does not, simply drag the control to adjust its size until it fills the entire display area.

After the control is on the view, set some of the parameters to get the optimal look and feel for the application. Fig. 6.19 shows the settings on the attributes screen for the Image View control.

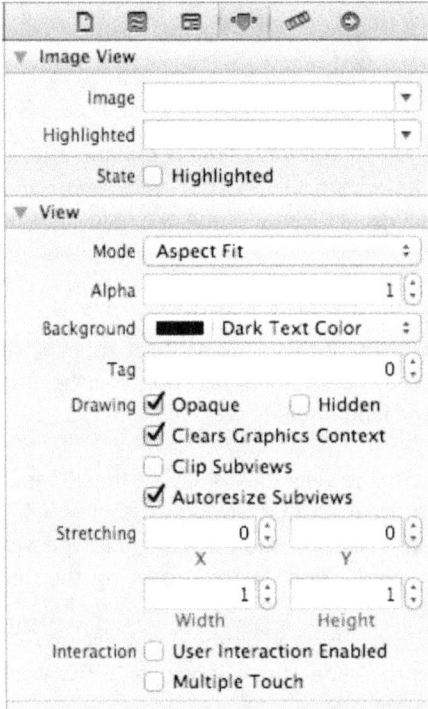

Fig. 6.19 : Configure the UIImageView

The two modifications you need to make are to the Mode and the Background. Set the Mode to **Aspect Fit** so the image is scaled but still preserves the aspect ratio of the original. If you do not use Aspect Fit, your images will stretch and scale to match the display area of the image view and that can end up looking fairly funky.

Because the image might not always fit the available area, you also need to set the Background attribute to **Dark Text Colour** or use the colour picker to select a deep black. By default, this value is white. Most photos do not look good when bracketed in a brilliant white.

Save the XIB file and move over to the SlideshowViewController.h file. Make the small modification in Listing 6-2.

LISTING 6-2 : SlideshowViewController.h

```objc
#import <UIKit/UIKit.h>

@interface slideshowViewController : UIViewController {
 IBOutlet UIImageView *imgView;
}
@end
```

You need to add an Outlet to the *slideshowViewController* that allows the control defined in the XIB to connect to the view controller class.

After the outlet is added, return to the XIB file, select the *UIImageView*, and use the connections inspector to hook the *UIImageView* object to the *imgView* variable in the *slideshowViewControllerclass*.

After that connection is made, then make the code modifications to the slideshow view controller class itself to load an image. Listing 6-3 shows the complete first version of the class.

LISTING 6-3 : SlideshowViewController.m

```objc
#import "slideshowViewController.h"
@implementation slideshowViewController
- (void)didReceiveMemoryWarning
{
   [super didReceiveMemoryWarning];
}
#pragma mark - View lifecycle
- (void)viewDidLoad
{
   [super viewDidLoad];
   NSURL *imageURL=[NSURL URLWithString:@"http://localhost/photos/CRW_0675.jpg"];
   NSData *imageData = [NSData dataWithContentsOfURL:imageURL];
   UIImage *image = [UIImage imageWithData:imageData];
   [imgView setImage:image];
}
- (void)viewDidUnload
{
   [super viewDidUnload];
}
```

```
- (BOOL)shouldAutorotateToInterfaceOrientation:
  (UIInterfaceOrientation)interfaceOrientation
{
   return YES;
}
@end
```

The serious work in the slide show View Controller class is done in the view Did Load method, which now :

- Loads the data from a URL.
- Turns that into an image.
- Uses the setImage method on the image view to display the image.

At this point, you should run the application to test whether an image comes up. You should see something similar to Fig. 6.20, which shows an image displayed in the iPad emulator.

Fig. 6.20 : First image from the server

If you don't see the image, the problem is likely with the *setImage* method call to *imgView*. Verify that the *UIImageView* object is properly connected to the *imgView* variable. If the application fails before that, you might not have the correct URL, or something is not correct on the server.

Parsing the XML

Now that you have a way to display the images on an iPad, the next step is to load the XML to get a list of all of the images to display. The iOS framework has a built-in XML parser, so you simply need to create the parser object and listen for the callbacks for the various tags.

Extend the class itself with the *NSXMLParserDelegate* interface, which tells the iOS framework that this class is capable of receiving callbacks from the XML parser. You also need to add an array called photos that holds the list of URLs that are extracted from the XML. Listing 6-4 shows the updates.

LISTING 6-4 : SlideshowViewController.h with Photos

```
#import <UIKit/UIKit.h>

@interface slideshowViewController : UIViewController<NSXMLParserDelegate> {
  IBOutlet UIImageView *imgView;
  NSMutableArray *photos;
}

@end
```

As you write more iOS applications, you will find that you use more and more delegates to connect to various APIs. There are data callbacks for tables, UI elements, GPS callbacks, and more. You can even create your own custom interfaces for your own libraries.

To use the XML parser, extend the view controller class, as in Listing 6-5.

LISTING 6-5 : SlideshowViewController.m with Photos

```
- (void)viewDidLoad
{
  [super viewDidLoad];

  photos = [[NSMutableArray alloc] init];

  NSXMLParser *photoParser = [[[NSXMLParser alloc]
    initWithContentsOfURL:
    [NSURL URLWithString:@"http://localhost/photos/index.xml"]] autorelease];
  [photoParser setDelegate:self];
  [photoParser parse];

  NSURL *imageURL = [NSURL URLWithString:[photos objectAtIndex:0]];
  NSData *imageData = [NSData dataWithContentsOfURL:imageURL];
  UIImage *image = [UIImage imageWithData:imageData];
  [imgView setImage:image];
}
- (void)parser:(NSXMLParser *)parser didStartElement:(NSString *)elementName
  namespaceURI:(NSString *)namespaceURI qualifiedName:(NSString *)qName
  attributes:(NSDictionary *)attributeDict {
  if ( [elementName isEqualToString:@"photo"]) {
    [photos addObject:[attributeDict objectForKey:@"url"]];
  }
}
```

The class now creates a parser in the *viewDidLoad* method and has it request and parse the XML from the server. It also sets the delegate for the parser back to itself so that it gets callbacks.

In the example, you want to listen for the *didStartElement* callback that is triggered whenever a tag is encountered. The *didStartElement* function then looks at the tag name to see if it is a photo tag. If it is, *didStartElement* adds the value of the url attribute to the photos array.

After the array of photos is completed, the *viewDidLoad* method continues and sets the image to the first image in the array.

Run the application to test your progress. You should see the first image specified in the XML appear in the emulator. If you do not see the first image, you might have an issue with the XML on the server. Set a breakpoint in the *didStartElement* method to see if it is getting called. If it is not, then you are not getting any valid XML back from your sever.

Animating the Slideshow

The final step is to use the array of photos to animate a slideshow. You will need two things :
- A timer.
- A variable to hold your current location in the slideshow.

Add both of these items to the class definition, as in Listing 6.

LISTING 6-6 : SlideshowViewController.h Completed

```
#import <UIKit/UIKit.h>

@interface slideshowViewController : UIViewController<NSXMLParserDelegate> {
    IBOutlet UIImageView *imgView;
    NSMutableArray *photos;
    NSTimer *timer;
    int currentImage;
}

@end
```

The timer is an object that will fire off events at an interval that you specify. The current Image is simply an index into the photos array that you will use to iterate through all of the images.

Listing 6-7 shows the final version of the slideshow application code.

Listing 6-7 : Slide show View Controller.m Completed

```
#import "slideshowViewController.h"

@implementation slideshowViewController

- (void)didReceiveMemoryWarning
{
    [super didReceiveMemoryWarning];
```

}

#pragma mark - View lifecycle

- (void)viewDidLoad
{
    [super viewDidLoad];

    photos = [[NSMutableArray alloc] init];

    NSXMLParser *photoParser = [[[NSXMLParser alloc]
        initWithContentsOfURL:[NSURL URLWithString:
        @"http://localhost/photos/index.xml"]] autorelease];
    [photoParser setDelegate:self];
    [photoParser parse];

    currentImage = 0;

    NSURL *imageURL = [NSURL URLWithString:[photos objectAtIndex:0]];
    NSData *imageData = [NSData dataWithContentsOfURL:imageURL];
    [imgView setImage:[UIImage imageWithData:imageData]];

    timer = [NSTimer scheduledTimerWithTimeInterval: 5.0
                            target: self
                            selector: @selector(handleTimer:)
                            userInfo: nil
                            repeats: YES];
}

- (void) handleTimer: (NSTimer *) timer {
    currentImage++;
    if (currentImage >= photos.count)
        currentImage = 0;

    NSURL *imageURL = [NSURL URLWithString:[photos objectAtIndex:currentImage]];
    NSData *imageData = [NSData dataWithContentsOfURL:imageURL];
    [imgView setImage:[UIImage imageWithData:imageData]];
}

- (void)parser:(NSXMLParser *)parser didStartElement:(NSString *)elementName
```
```

```
namespaceURI:(NSString *)namespaceURI qualifiedName:(NSString *)qName
attributes:(NSDictionary *)attributeDict {
  if ( [elementName isEqualToString:@"photo"]) {
    [photos addObject:[attributeDict objectForKey:@"url"]];
  }
}

- (void)viewDidUnload
{
  [super viewDidUnload];
}
- (BOOL)shouldAutorotateToInterfaceOrientation:
   (UIInterfaceOrientation)interfaceOrientation
{
  return YES;
}
@end
```

The two new elements in Listing 6-7 are the creation of the timer in the viewDidLoad method and the addition of the handle Timer method, which is called when the timer fires. The handleTimer method simply increments the current Image, then rolls the index around if it hits the end of the array. It also uses the standard image fetching logic to get the image at the given index and display it.

Timers have two modes : They can fire once, or they can fire continuously. In the viewDidLoad method, the example specifies YES for repeats so that the handleTimer method is called over and over for the lifetime of the application.

QUESTIONS

1. Write a short note on porting linux?
2. What do you mean by Embedded Linux?
3. What do you mean by Real time operating system?
4. What do you mean by Real time Linux?
5. Explain the terms latency and kernel preemption?
6. Write a short note on Embedded Android?
7. Explain Android boot process in detail?
8. Write a short note on any embedded Android application?
9. Write short note on (i) Calculator. (ii) Twitter Search App. (iii) slide show App.
10. Explain twitter Search app. in detail.
11. Explain slide show App in detail.

MODEL QUESTION PAPERS FOR IN SEMESTER ASSESSMENT (PHASE - I)
[30 Marks]

MODEL QUESTION PAPER – I — 30 Marks

1. Write a short note on priority inversion? [6 M]
2. Numerical on following algorithms? [4 M]
   (a) FCFS
   (b) SJF
   (c) RR
   (d) Priority
3. Is Embedded system and real time systems are same? [3 M]
4. List down and explain the important features of ARM. [3 M]
5. Explain 3 stage and 5 stage pipelining in ARM. [4 M]
6. Explain in detail LSB? [6 M]
7. Write short note on OSDL? [4 M]

MODEL QUESTION PAPER – II — 30 Marks

1. What is Real Time Task? [4 M]
2. Explain in detail the Concept of Real time operating Systems and their necessity? [6 M]
3. How to differentiate between soft, hard and firm real-time tasks? [4 M]
4. Explain the ARM register set. [4 M]
5. Explain the following shifting ARM instructions with example. [6 M]
   LSL, LSR, ASR, ROR, RRX
6. Explain with neat diagram kernel image components? [6 M]

MODEL QUESTION PAPER – III — 30 Marks

1. Explain in detail Real Time Systems? [4 M]
2. Explain load and store instruction set in ARM with example. [6 M]
3. Explain multiple register load and store instruction set in ARM with example. [6 M]

4. Discuss the important features of BeagleBone Black. What makes it so popular among embedded developers? [4 M]
5. Write short note on Tool Chain? [4 M]
6. Write short note on [6 M]
   (a) The Dot-Config
   (b) Makefile Targets
   (c) U-Boot
   (d) Cross-Development Environment
   (e) Busy box
   (f) Subsystem Initialization

MODEL QUESTION PAPER – IV   30 Marks

1. What are the different types of real time tasks? [6 M]
2. Explain following instruction set in ARM: [4 M]
   Compare instructions, Branch Instructions
3. Explain following aspects related to ARM : [6 M]
   Data Bus Width, Computational Capability, Power Consumption, Multiple register Instructions, DSP Enhancements, Jazzle DBX
4. Write a code for comparing two numbers stored in register R1 and R2. If the numbers are equal move it in R9 register, if not equal the bigger number should be placed r0 register. [6 M]
5. Explain in detail Anatomy of an Embedded System? [4 M]
6. Explain in detail Process Virtual Memory? [4 M]

www.ingramcontent.com/pod-product-compliance
Lightning Source LLC
Chambersburg PA
CBHW080422230426
43662CB00015B/2185